THE HUMANIST FRAME

To
Leonard and Dorothy Elmhirst
Pioneers of Humanist Planning

EDITED BY
JULIAN HUXLEY

THE
HUMANIST
FRAME

HARPER & BROTHERS   PUBLISHERS   NEW YORK

PREFACE

This book is an attempt to present Humanism as a comprehensive system of ideas. It is no sudden venture, but the natural outcome of a long process of gestation and development, begun more than half a century ago in an attempt to reconcile or integrate various aspects of my life— my biological training, my twin loves of nature and poetry, my wrestlings with the problems of morality and belief, and continued in the effort to extend the concept of evolution over the widest possible range of phenomena.

The idea of evolution had kindled my imagination while I was still at school. As an undergraduate I became a firm Darwinian. As a young teacher, the first public lecture I gave was on the evolutionary relativism of the senses, the second on the critical point or discontinuity between biological and human evolution. In the twenties I became concerned with the idea of progress, as an evolutionary movement in a certain definable direction; and with religion as a general human function, not necessarily involving a belief in God or in revelation.

In the thirties, thanks to visits to East Africa, the USSR and the TVA, I became interested in human ecology and overall planning, and worked with PEP (Political and Economic Planning) on various projects, including the place of the arts in national life, and (later) the world population problem. During the war I joined a private group whose discussion of post-war aims had some influence on current thinking; and as Romanes Lecturer at Oxford, attempted to explore the relations of ethics and evolution.

After the war, my unexpected appointment as Secretary-General of the Preparatory Commission for Unesco brought me into collision with the divergent ideologies at work in the international world. Believing that the Organization would work more efficiently on the basis of an agreed set of general ideas and principles, I tried to outline such a basis in a pamphlet entitled 'A Philosophy for Unesco': but it speedily became apparent that no single system of ideas could be acceptable to any United Nations Agency in the world's state of ideological chaos.

My subsequent period as Director-General made me realize what a vast quantity of knowledge was lying about unused, for lack of any such 'philosophy', and indeed of any agreed system of concepts and ideas to order the disorderly facts and put them to useful work; and after leaving Unesco I got together a group of friends and colleagues in very various fields to wrestle with the problem. It had no formal title —we referred to it as the Idea-Systems Group—and it never published any findings. But its two years of discussion vitally influenced my own ideas, and I am sure those of other members (several of whom have contributed to the present volume). It led us to the realization that the knowledge-explosion of the last hundred years was providing man with a new revelation, a new vision of his destiny. It stimulated me to write a number of articles on 'ideological' subjects, culminating in an attempt to construct a unified framework of ideas which I called Evolutionary Humanism.

The implications of this integrated idea-system seemed fairly satisfying. It related every kind of human activity to the yardstick of desirable evolutionary direction. It related individual and community within the frame of the continuing psychosocial process. It reconciled 'mind' and 'matter' in a dual-aspect monism, and put all phenomena, cosmological and biological, material and human, short-term and long-term, into relation with the embracing process of evolution. It could bridge the gap between Sir Charles Snow's 'two cultures' and heal the split between the two sides in the ideological cold war. It forced one to reject Absolutes and to think in terms of patterns of inter-relation. In its light man's higher activities, of science, art and religion, appeared not as independent entities but as interlocking functions of our evolving species. It showed that all general concepts, such as *justice* or *phlogiston*, *atom* or *soul*, are best regarded as mechanisms for ordering and handling our experience —as hypotheses which must be checked against experience, and either adjusted and elaborated (as with *justice* and *atom*) or rejected (as with *phlogiston*) or transcended (as with *soul*). It could provide an all-inclusive aim for the human species, in the shape of greater fulfilment through increased realization of possibilities. It assigned man to his proper place in nature, and showed him his true destiny. It was not a rigid set of dogmas, resistant or impervious to change: it was an open system, capable of indefinite further development. Above all it could give reassurance to all those searching for some firm ground of belief and moral direction in the violence and disorder of contemporary existence.

So it seemed to me: but how to get it across to others? How to persuade people that it was both coherent and comprehensive, and relevant in every aspect of life? I decided that I must enlist the help of fellow humanists in various fields of human endeavour. Several of those whom I approached demurred on the grounds that they did not sincerely feel that they could call themselves Humanists. I feel happy in having persuaded them that, like Monsieur Jourdain in the matter of prose, they had been Humanists all their lives without knowing it. And I am grateful to all my twenty-five distinguished contributors for their valuable contribution to the clearer definition of an effective Humanism.

The gist of the book can be summed up in a few sentences. There have been two critical points in the past of evolution, points at which the process transcended itself by passing from an old state to a fresh one with quite new properties. The first was marked by the passage from the inorganic phase to the biological, the second by that from the biological to the psychosocial. Now we are on the threshold of a third. As the bubbles in a cauldron on the boil mark the onset of the critical passage of water from the liquid to the gaseous state, so the ebullition of humanist ideas in the cauldron of present-day thought marks the onset of the passage from the psychosocial to the consciously purposive phase of evolution.

Today, in twentieth-century man, the evolutionary process is at last becoming conscious of itself and is beginning to study itself with a view to directing its future course. Human knowledge worked over by human imagination is seen as the basis of human understanding and belief, and the ultimate guide to human progress. The distillation of raw knowledge according to Humanist recipes can produce ideas and principles which illuminate the human condition in general and have the widest range of particular application.

A prerequisite for the safe passage of this critical threshold, and for the efficient working of the evolutionary process in its new self-conscious state, will be the emergence of a new comprehensive pattern or system of ideas, beliefs and guiding principles which are of general validity for the entire human community. I hope that this book will help in indicating the outline of that pattern and in laying foundations on which that system can later be erected.

JULIAN HUXLEY,
London, March 1961

CONTENTS

JULIAN HUXLEY

THE HUMANIST FRAME

SIR JULIAN HUXLEY, F.R.S.

Born 1887. Educated: Eton (King's Scholar); Balliol College, Oxford (Brackenbury Scholar). Fellow of New College and Senior Demonstrator in Zoology, Oxford, 1919–25. Professor of Zoology, King's College, London, 1925–27.

Publications: *The Stream of Life*, 1926; *Science of Life* (co-author), 1929; *Bird Watching and Bird Behaviour*, 1930; *Problems of Relative Growth*, 1932; *At the Zoo*, 1936; *Evolution: The Modern Synthesis*, 1942; *Evolution in Action*, 1952; *Biological Aspects of Cancer*, 1956, etc.

THE HUMANIST FRAME

Man is embarked on the psychosocial stage of evolution. Major advance in that stage of the evolutionary process involves radical change in the dominant idea-systems.* It is marked by the passage from an old to a new general organization of thought and belief; and the new pattern of thinking and attitude is necessitated by the increase of knowledge, demanding to be organized in new and more comprehensive ways, and by the failure of older ideas which attempted to organize beliefs round a core of ignorance.

General idea-systems are always concerned, consciously or unconsciously, with beliefs about human destiny, and always influence men's general attitude to life and approach to practical affairs. People brought up in different idea-systems find it difficult to understand each other's approaches and attitudes. Modern industrial man finds it hard to understand tribal peoples, whose idea-systems are organized round the concept of magic power; and equally difficult to understand medieval Western man, whose idea-system was centred round the concept of a central earth, created and ruled by an omnipotent, omniscient and omnibenevolent supernatural Being.†

The present uneasy age of disillusion after two Great Wars has witnessed a widespread breakdown of traditional beliefs, but also a growing realization that a purely materialistic outlook cannot provide an adequate basis for human life. It has also witnessed a fantastic growth of knowledge—about the material universe, about life and mind, about human nature and human societies, about art and history and religion; but large chunks of this new knowledge are lying around unused, not

---

* If a technical term is needed, I suggest *noösystem*, following Teilhard de Chardin's use (in *The Phenomenon of Man*, London, Collins, 1959) of the word *noösphere* to denote the realm of mind and its products which man has created and which he inhabits. Meanwhile I shall stick to the non-technical term *idea-system*; with the proviso that it includes beliefs, attitudes and symbols as well as intellectual concepts and ideas.

† A salutary exercise for an inhabitant of the mid-twentieth century is to try to give sympathetic consideration to the arguments about angels in St Thomas Aquinas's *Summa Theologiae*, or to attempt to understand the ideological basis of many of the practices described in Frazer's *Golden Bough*.

worked up or integrated into fruitful concepts and principles, not brought into relevance to human life and its problems.

Meanwhile an increasing number of people are coming to feel that man must rely only on himself in coping with the business of living and the problem of destiny, but feel increasingly sceptical about the possibility of his achieving this at all adequately.

If the situation is not to lead to chaos, despair or escapism, man must reunify his life within the framework of a satisfactory idea-system. To achieve this, he needs to survey the resources available to him, both in the outer world and within himself, to define his aims and chart his position, and to plan the outline of his future course. He needs to use his best efforts of knowledge and imagination to build a system of thought and belief which will provide both a supporting framework for his present existence, an ultimate or ideal goal for his future development as a species, and a guide and directive for practical action and planning.

This new idea-system, whose birth we of the mid-twentieth century are witnessing, I shall simply call *Humanism*, because it can only be based on our understanding of man and his relations with the rest of his environment. It must be focused on man as an organism, though one with unique properties. It must be organized round the facts and ideas of evolution, taking account of the discovery that man is part of a comprehensive evolutionary process, and cannot avoid playing a decisive role in it.

Such a Humanism is necessarily unitary instead of dualistic, affirming the unity of mind and body; universal instead of particularist, affirming the continuity of man with the rest of life, and of life with the rest of the universe; naturalistic instead of supernaturalist, affirming the unity of the spiritual and the material; and global instead of divisive, affirming the unity of all mankind. *Nihil humanum a me alienum puto* is the Humanist's motto. Humanism thinks in terms of directional process instead of in those of static mechanism, in terms of quality and diversity as well as quantity and unity. It will have nothing to do with Absolutes, including absolute truth, absolute morality, absolute perfection and absolute authority, but insists that we can find standards to which our actions and our aims can properly be related. It affirms that knowledge and understanding can be increased, that conduct and social organization can be improved, and that more desirable directions for individual and social development can be found. As the overriding aim of evolving man, it is driven to reject power, or mere numbers of people, or efficiency, or material exploitation, and to envisage greater fulfilment and fuller achievement as his true goal.

Most important of all, it brings together the scattered and largely unutilized resources of our knowledge, and orders them to provide a new vision of human destiny, illuminating its every aspect, from the broad and enduring sweep of cosmic process to present-day polities, from the planetary web of world ecology to the individual lives entangled in it, from the dim roots of man's past to the dawning possibilities of his far future.

This new vision is inevitably an evolutionary one. At the University of Chicago's Centennial Celebration of Darwin's launching of the theory of Evolution, I was honoured by being asked to give the Commemoration Address. To give some idea of this new vision, I cannot do better than quote from it:

*   *   *   *   *

This centennial celebration is one of the first occasions on which it has been frankly faced that all aspects of reality are subject to evolution, from atoms and stars to fish and flowers, from fish and flowers to human societies and values—indeed that all reality is a single process of evolution. And ours is the first period in which we have acquired sufficient knowledge to begin to see the outline of this vast process as a whole.

Our evolutionary vision now includes the discovery that biological advance exists, and that it takes place in a series of steps or grades, each grade occupied by a successful group of animals or plants, each group sprung from a pre-existing one and characterized by a new and improved pattern of organization.

Improved organization gives biological advantage. Accordingly the new type becomes a successful or *dominant* group. It spreads and multiplies and differentiates into a multiplicity of branches. This new biological success is usually achieved at the biological expense of the older dominant group from which it sprang, or whose place it has usurped. Thus the rise of the placental mammals was correlated with the decline of the terrestrial reptiles, and the birds replaced the pterosaurs as dominant in the air.

Occasionally, however, when the breakthrough to a new type of organization is also a breakthrough into a wholly new environment, the new type may not come into competition with the old, and both may continue to co-exist in full flourishment. Thus the evolution of land vertebrates in no way interfered with the continued success of the sea's dominant group, the teleost bony fish.

The successive patterns of successful organization are stable patterns: they exemplify continuity, and tend to persist over long periods. Reptiles have remained reptiles for a quarter of a billion years: tortoises, snakes, lizards and crocodiles are all still recognizably reptilian, all variations of one organizational theme.

It is difficult for life to transcend this stability and achieve a new successful organization. That is why breakthroughs to new dominant types are so rare—and also so important. The reptilian type radiated out into well over a dozen important groups or orders: but all of them remained within the reptilian framework except two, which broke through to the new and wonderfully successful patterns of bird and mammal.

In the early stages, a new group, however successful it will eventually become, is few and feeble and shows no signs of the success it may eventually achieve. Its breakthrough is not an instantaneous matter, but has to be implemented by a series of improvements which eventually become welded into the new stabilized organization.

With mammals there was first hair, then milk, then partial and later full temperature regulation, then brief and finally prolonged internal development, with evolution of a placenta. Mammals of a small and insignificant sort had existed and evolved for a hundred million years or so before they achieved the full breakthrough to their explosive dominance in the Cenozoic.

Something very similar occurred during our own breakthrough from mammalian to psychosocial organization. Our prehuman ape ancestors were never particularly successful or abundant. For their transformation into man a series of steps were needed. Descent from the trees; erect posture; some enlargement of brain; more carnivorous habits; the use and then the making of tools; further enlargement of brain; the discovery of fire; true speech and language; elaboration of tools and rituals. These steps took the better part of half a million years; it was not until less than a hundred thousand years ago that man could begin to deserve the title of dominant type, and not till less than 10,000 years ago that he became fully dominant.

After man's emergence as truly man, this same sort of thing continued to happen, but with an important difference. Man's evolution is not biological but psychosocial: it operates by the mechanism of cultural tradition, which involves the cumulative self-reproduction and self-variation of mental activities and their products. Accordingly, major steps in the human phase of evolution are achieved by breakthroughs to new dominant patterns of mental organization, of knowledge, ideas and beliefs—ideological instead of physiological or biological organization.*

There is thus a succession of successful idea-systems instead of a succession of successful bodily organizations. Each new successful idea-

* See J. S. Huxley, *Evolution in Action*, London, Chatto & Windus, 1953, and *New Bottles for New Wine*, London, Chatto & Windus; New York, Harper & Bros., 1957.

system spreads and dominates some important sector of the world, until it is superseded by a rival system, or itself gives birth to its successor by a breakthrough to a new organized system of thought and belief. We need only think of the magic pattern of tribal thought, the god-centred medieval pattern organized round the concept of divine authority and revelation, and the rise in the last three centuries of the science-centred pattern, organized round the concept of human progress, but progress somehow under the control of supernatural authority. In 1859 Darwin opened the door to a new pattern of ideological organization—the evolution-centred organization of thought and belief.

Through the telescope of our scientific imagination we can discern the existence of this new and improved ideological organization, albeit in embryonic form; but many of its details are not yet clear, and we can also see that the upward steps needed to reach its full development are many and hard to take.

Let me change the metaphor. To all save those who deliberately shut or averted their eyes, or were not allowed by their pastors or masters to look, it was at once clear that the fact and concept of evolution was bound to act as the central germ or living template of a new dominant thought-organization. And in the century since *The Origin of Species* there have been many attempts to understand the implications of evolution in many fields, from the affairs of the stellar universe to the affairs of men, and a number of preliminary and largely premature efforts to integrate the facts of evolution and our knowledge of its processes into the overall organization of our general thought.

All dominant thought-organizations are concerned with the ultimate as well as with the immediate problems of existence: or, I should rather say, with the most ultimate problems that the thought of the time is capable of envisaging or even formulating. They are all concerned with giving some interpretation of man, of the world which he is to live in, and of his place and role in that world—in other words some comprehensible picture of human destiny and significance.

The broad outlines of the new evolutionary picture of ultimates are beginning to be clearly visible. Man's destiny is to be the sole agent for the future evolution of this planet. He is the highest dominant type to be produced by over two and a half billion years of the slow biological improvement effected by the blind opportunistic workings of natural selection; if he does not destroy himself, he has at least an equal stretch of evolutionary time before him to exercise his agency.

During the later part of biological evolution, mind—our word for the mental activities and properties of organisms—emerged with greater clarity and intensity, and came to play a more important role in the individual lives of animals. Eventually it broke through to become the foundation and the main source of further evolution, though the essential character of evolution now became cultural instead of genetic or biological. It was to this breakthrough, brought about by the automatic mechanism of natural selection and not by any conscious effort on his own part, that man owes his dominant evolutionary position.

Man therefore is of immense significance. He has been ousted from his self-imagined centrality in the universe to an infinitesimal location in a peripheral position in one of a million of galaxies. Nor, it would appear, is he likely to be unique as a sentient being. On the other hand, the evolution of mind or sentiency is an extremely rare event in the vast meaninglessness of the insentient universe, and man's particular brand of sentiency may well be unique. But in any case he is highly significant. He is a reminder of the existence, here and there, in the quantitative vastness of cosmic matter and its energy-equivalents, of a trend towards mind, with its accompaniment of quality and richness of existence; and, what is more, a proof of the importance of mind and quality in the all-embracing evolutionary process.

It is only through possessing a mind that he has become the dominant portion of this planet and the agent responsible for its future evolution; and it will only be by the right use of that mind that he will be able to exercise that responsibility rightly. He could all too readily be a failure in the job; he will only succeed if he faces it consciously and if he uses all his mental resources—knowledge and reason, imagination and sensitivity, capacities for wonder and love, for comprehension and compassion, for spiritual aspiration and moral effort.

And he must face it unaided by outside help. In the evolutionary pattern of thought there is no longer either need or room for the supernatural. The earth was not created: it evolved. So did all the animals and plants that inhabit it, including our human selves, mind and soul as well as brain and body. So did religion. Religions are organs of psychosocial man concerned with human destiny and with experiences of sacredness and transcendence. In their evolution, some (but by no means all) have given birth to the concept of gods as supernatural beings endowed with mental and spiritual properties and capable of intervening in the affairs of nature, including man. These theistic religions are organizations of human thought in its interaction with the puzzling, complex world with which it has to contend—the outer world of nature and the inner world of man's own nature. In this, they resemble other early organizations of human thought confronted with nature, like the doctrine of the Four Elements,

earth, air, fire and water, or the Eastern concept of rebirth and reincar-
nation. Like these, they are destined to disappear in competition with
other, truer, and more embracing thought-organizations which are
handling the same range of raw or processed experience.

Evolutionary man can no longer take refuge from his loneliness by
creeping for shelter into the arms of a divinized father-figure whom he has
himself created, nor escape from the responsibility of making decisions by
sheltering under the umbrella of Divine Authority, nor absolve himself
from the hard task of meeting his present problems and planning his
future by relying on the will of an omniscient but unfortunately inscrutable
Providence. On the other hand, his loneliness is only apparent. He is not
alone as a type. Thanks to the astronomers, he now knows that he is one
among the many organisms that bear witness to the trend towards
sentience, mind and richness of being, operating so widely but so sparsely
in the cosmos. More immediately important, thanks to Darwin, he now
knows that he is not an isolated phenomenon, cut off from the rest of
nature by his uniqueness. Not only is he made of the same matter and
operated by the same energy as all the rest of the cosmos, but for all his
distinctiveness, he is linked by genetic continuity with all the other living
inhabitants of his planet. Animals, plants, and micro-organisms, they
are all his cousins or remoter kin, all parts of one single branching and
evolving flow of metabolizing protoplasm.

Nor is he individually alone in his thinking. He exists and has his being
in the intangible sea of thought which Teilhard de Chardin has christened
the noösphere, in the same sort of way that fish exist and have their being
in the material sea of water which the geographers include in the term
hydrosphere. Floating in this noösphere there are, for his taking, the
daring speculations and aspiring ideals of man long dead, the organized
knowledge of science, the hoary wisdom of the ancients, the creative
imaginings of all the world's poets and artists. And in his own nature
there are, waiting to be called upon, an array of potential helpers—all the
possibilities of wonder and knowledge, of delight and reverence, of
creative belief and moral purpose, of passionate effort and embracing love.

Turning the eye of an evolutionary biologist on the situation, I would
compare the present stage of evolving man to the geological moment,
some three hundred million years ago, when our amphibian ancestors were
just establishing themselves out of the world of water. They had created a
bridgehead into a wholly new environment. No longer buoyed up by
water, they had to learn how to support their own weight; debarred from
swimming with their muscular tail, they had to learn to crawl with clumsy
limbs. The newly discovered realm of air gave them direct access to the

oxygen they needed to breathe, but it also threatened their moist bodies
with desiccation. And though they managed to make do on land during
their adult existence, they found themselves still compulsorily fishy during
the early stages of their lives.

On the other hand, they had emerged into completely new freedom. As
fish, they had been confined below a bounding surface. Now the air above
them expanded out into the infinity of space. Now they were free of the
banquet of small creatures prepared by the previous hundred million
years of life's terrestrial evolution. The earth's land surface provided a
greater variety of opportunity than did its waters, and also a much greater
range of challenge to evolving life. Could the early Stegocephalians have
been gifted with imagination, they might have seen before them the
possibility of walking, running, perhaps even flying over the earth; the
probability of their descendants escaping from bondage to winter cold by
regulating their temperature, escaping from bondage to the waters by
constructing private ponds for their early development; the inevitability
of an upsurge of their dim minds to new levels of clarity and performance.
But meanwhile they would see themselves tied to an ambiguous existence,
neither one thing nor the other, on the narrow moist margin between
water and air. They could have seen the promised land afar off, though
but dimly through their bleary newtish eyes. But they would also have
seen that, to reach it, they would have to achieve many difficult and
arduous transformations of their being and way of life.

So with ourselves. We have only recently emerged from the biological
to the psychosocial area of evolution, from the earthy biosphere into the
freedom of the noösphere. Do not let us forget how recently: we have
been truly men for perhaps a tenth of a million years—one tick of
evolution's clock: even as proto-men, we have existed for under one
million years—less than a two-thousandth fraction of evolutionary time.
No longer supported and steered by a framework of instincts, we try to
use our conscious thoughts and purposes as organs of psychosocial
locomotion and direction through the tangles of our existence; but so far
with only moderate success, and with the production of much evil and
horror as well as of some beauty and glory of achievement. We too have
colonized only an ambiguous margin between an old bounded environment and the new territories of freedom. Our feet still drag in the
biological mud, even when we lift our heads into the conscious air. But
unlike those remote ancestors of ours, we can truly see something of the
promised land beyond. We can do so with the aid of our new instrument
of vision—our rational, knowledge-based imagination. Like the earliest
pre-Galilean telescopes, it is still a very primitive instrument, and gives a

feeble and often distorted view. But, like the early telescopes, it is capable
of immense improvement, and could reveal many secrets of our noöspheric
home and destiny.

Meanwhile no mental telescope is needed to see the immediate
evolutionary landscape, and the frightening problems which inhabit it.
All that is required—but that is plenty—is for us to cease being intellectual
and moral ostriches, and take our heads out of the sand of wilful blindness.
If we do so, we shall soon see that the alarming problems are two-faced,
and are also stimulating challenges.

What are those challenging monsters in our evolutionary path? I would
list them as follows. The threat of super-scientific war, nuclear, chemical,
and biological; the threat of over-population; the rise and appeal of
Communist ideology, especially in the under-privileged sectors of the
world's people; the failure to bring China, with nearly a quarter of the
world's population, into the world organization of the United Nations;
the over-exploitation of natural resources; the erosion of the world's
cultural variety; our general preoccupation with means rather than ends,
with technology and quantity rather than creativity and quality; and the
Revolution of Expectation, caused by the widening gap between the
haves and the have-nots, between the rich and the poor nations. This day
of Darwinian celebration is Thanksgiving Day in America. But millions
of people now living have little cause to give thanks for anything. When
I was in India last spring, a Hindu man was arrested for the murder of his
small son. He explained that his life was so miserable that he had killed
the boy as a sacrifice to the goddess Kali, in the hope that she would help
him in return. That is an extreme case, but let us remember that two
thirds of the world's people are under-privileged—under-fed, under-
healthy, under-educated—and that many millions of them live in squalor
and suffering. They have little to be thankful for save hope that they will
be helped to escape from this misery. If we in the West do not give them
aid, they will look to other systems for help—or even turn from hope to
destructive despair.

We attempt to deal with these problems piecemeal, often half-heartedly;
sometimes, as with population, we refuse to recognize it officially as a
World Problem (just as we refuse to recognize Communist China as a
World Power). In reality, they are not separate monsters to be dealt with
by a series of separate ventures, however heroic or saintly. They are all
symptoms of a new evolutionary situation; and this can only be successfully met in the light and with the aid of a new organization of thought
and belief, a new dominant pattern of ideas relevant to the new situation.

It is hard to break through the firm framework of an accepted belief-system, and build new and complex successors, but it is necessary. It is necessary to organize our *ad hoc* ideas and scattered values into a unitive pattern, transcending conflicts and divisions in its unitary web. Only by such a reconciliation of opposites and disparates can our belief-system release us from inner conflicts: only so can we gain that peaceful assurance which will help unlock our energies for development in strenuous practical action.

Our new pattern of thinking will be evolution-centred. It will give us assurance by reminding us of our long evolutionary rise; how this was also, strangely and wonderfully, the rise of mind; and how that rise culminated in the eruption of mind as the dominant factor in evolution and led to our own spectacular but precarious evolutionary success. It will give us hope by pointing to the aeons of evolutionary time that lie ahead of our species if it does not destroy itself or nullify its own opportunities; by recalling how the increase of man's understanding and the improved organization of knowledge has in fact enabled him to make a whole series of advances, such as control of infectious disease or efficiency of tele-communication, and to transcend a whole set of apparently unbridgeable oppositions, like the conflict between Islam and Christendom, or that between the seven kingdoms of the Heptarchy; and by reminding us of the vast stores of human effectiveness—of intelligence, imagination, co-operative goodwill—which still remain untapped.

Our new organization of thought—belief-system, framework of values, ideology, call it what you will—must grow and be developed in the light of our new evolutionary vision. So, in the first place, it must of course itself be evolutionary: that is to say, it must help us to think in terms of an overriding process of change, development, and possible improvement, to have our eyes on the future rather than on the past, to find support in the growing, spreading, upreaching body of our knowledge, instead of in the rigid frame of fixed dogma or ancient authority. Equally, of course, the evolutionary outlook must be scientific, not in the sense that it rejects or neglects other human activities, but in believing in the value of the scientific method for eliciting knowledge from ignorance and truth from error, and in basing itself on the firm ground of scientifically established knowledge. Unlike most theologies, it accepts the inevitability and indeed the desirability of change, and advances by welcoming new discovery even when it conflicts with old ways of thinking.

The only way in which the present split between religion and science could be mended would be through the acceptance by science of the fact and value of religion as an organ of evolving man, and the acceptance by religion that religions must evolve if they are not to become extinct, or at best turn into outdated living fossils struggling to survive in a new and alien environment.

Next, the evolutionary outlook must be global. Man is strong and successful in so far as he operates in inter-thinking groups, which are able to pool their knowledge and beliefs. To have any success in fulfilling his destiny as the controller or agent of future evolution on earth, he must become one single inter-thinking group, with one general framework of ideas: otherwise his mental energies will be dissipated in ideological conflict. Science gives us a foretaste of what could be. It is already global, with scientists of every nation contributing to its advance: and because it is global, it is advancing fast. In every field we must aim to transcend nationalism: and the first step towards this is to think globally—how could this or that task be achieved by international co-operation rather than by separate action?

But our thinking must also be concerned with the individual. The well-developed well-patterned individual human being is, in a strictly scientific sense, the highest phenomenon of which we have any knowledge; and the variety of individual personalities is the world's highest richness.

In the light of the evolutionary vision the individual need not feel just a meaningless cog in the social machine, nor merely the helpless prey and sport of vast impersonal forces. He can do something to develop his own personality, to discover his own talents and possibilities, to interact personally and fruitfully with other individuals, to discover something of his own significance. If so, in his own person he is realizing an important quantum of evolutionary possibility; he is contributing his own personal quality to the fulfilment of human destiny; and he has assurance of his own significance in the vaster and more enduring whole of which he is a part.

I spoke of quality. This must be the dominant concept of our belief-system—quality and richness as against quantity and uniformity. Though our new idea-pattern must be unitary, it need not and should not be cramping, or impose a drab or boring cultural uniformity. An organized system, whether of thought, expression, social life or anything else, has some degree both of unity and richness. Cultural variety, both in the world as a whole and within its separate countries, is the spice of life: yet it is being threatened and indeed eroded away by mass-production, mass-communications, mass-conformity, and all the other forces making for uniformization—an ugly word for an ugly thing! We have to work hard to preserve and foster it.

One sphere where individual variety could and should be encouraged is education. In many school systems, under the pretext of so-called democratic equality, variety of gifts and capacity is now actually being discouraged. As a result the duller children become frustrated by being rushed too fast, the brighter become frustrated by being held back and bored. Our new idea-system must jettison the democratic myth of equality. Human beings are not born equal in gifts or potentialities, and human progress stems largely from the very fact of their inequality. 'Free but unequal' should be our motto, and diversity of excellence, not conformist normalcy or mere adjustment, should be the aim of education.

Population is people in the mass; and it is in regard to population that the most drastic reversal or reorientation of our thinking has become necessary. The unprecedented population-explosion of the last half-century has strikingly exemplified the Marxist principle of the passage of quantity into quality. Mere increase in quantity of people is increasingly affecting the quality of their lives and their future, and affecting it almost wholly for the worse.

Population-increase is already destroying or eroding many of the world's resources, both those for material subsistence and those—equally essential but often neglected—for human enjoyment and fulfilment. Early in man's history the injunction to increase and multiply was right. Today it is wrong, and to obey it will be disastrous. The Western World, and the United States in particular, has to achieve the difficult task of reversing the direction of its thought about population. It has to begin thinking that our aim should be not increase but decrease—certainly and quickly, decrease in the rate of population-growth; and in the long run equally certainly, decrease in the absolute number of people in the world, including our own countries. The spectacle of explosive population-increase is prompting us to ask the simple but basic question, *what are people for?* And we see that the answer has to do with their quality as human beings, and the quality of their lives and achievements.

We must make the same reversal of ideas about our economic system. At the moment (and again I take the United States as most representative) our Western economic system (which is steadily invading new regions) is based on expanding production for profit; and production for profit is based on expanding consumption. As one writer has put it, the American economy depends on persuading more people to believe that they want to consume more products. This is leading to gross over-exploitation of resources that ought to be conserved, to excessive advertising, to the dissipation of talent and energy into unproductive channels, and to a diversion of the economy as a whole away from its true functions. (See the references to Galbraith, Krutch and Vance Packard in Dr Marris's chapter.)

But, like the population-explosion, this consumption-explosion cannot continue much longer: it is an inherently self-defeating process. Sooner rather than later we shall be forced to get away from a system based on artificially increasing the number of human wants, and set about constructing one aimed at the qualitative satisfaction of real human needs, spiritual and mental as well as material and physiological. This means abandoning the pernicious habit of evaluating every human project solely in terms of its utility—by which the evaluators mean solely its material utility, and especially its utility in making a profit for somebody. Once we truly believe (and true belief, however necessary, is rarely easy), once we truly believe that man's destiny is to make possible greater fulfilment for more human beings and fuller achievement by human societies, utility in the customary sense becomes subordinate. Quantity of material production is, of course, necessary as the basis for the satisfaction of elementary human needs—but only up to a certain degree. More than a certain number of calories or cocktails or TV sets or washing machines per person, is not merely unnecessary but bad. Quantity of material production can only be a means to a further end, not an end in itself.

The important ends of man's life include the creation and enjoyment of beauty, both natural and man-made; increased comprehension and a more assured sense of significance; the preservation of all sources of pure wonder and delight, like fine scenery, wild animals in freedom, or unspoiled nature; the attainment of inner peace and harmony; the feeling of active participation in embracing and enduring projects, including the cosmic project of evolution. It is through such things that individuals attain greater fulfilment. As for nations and societies, they are remembered not for their wealth or comforts or technologies, but for their great buildings and works of art, their achievements in science or law or political philosophy, their success in liberating human life from the shackles of fear and ignorance.

Although it is to his mind that man owes both his present dominant position in evolution, and any advances he may have made during his tenure of that position, he is still strangely ignorant and even superstitious about it.* The exploration of the mind has barely begun. It must be one of the main tasks of the coming era, just as was the exploration of the world's surface a few centuries ago. Psychological exploration will doubtless

---

* The pseudo-scientific behaviourist superstition consists in denying it any effective existence beyond that of a pale ghost, and in dismissing it and its products as outside the range of scientific investigation. The philosophical idealist superstition, on the contrary, denies the effective existence of anything else.

reveal as many surprises as did geographical exploration, and will make available to our descendants all kinds of new possibilities of full and richer living.

Finally, the evolutionary vision is enabling us to discern, however incompletely, the lineaments of the new religion that we can be sure will arise to serve the needs of the coming era. Just as stomachs are bodily organs concerned with digestion, and involving the biochemical activity of special juices, so are religions psychosocial organs concerned with the problems of human destiny, and involving the emotion of sacredness and the sense of right and wrong. Religion of some sort is probably necessary. But it is not necessarily a good thing. It was not a good thing when the Hindu I read about last spring killed his son as a religious sacrifice. It is not a good thing that religious pressure has made it illegal to teach evolution in Tennessee, because it conflicts with Fundamentalist beliefs. It is not a good thing that in Connecticut and Massachusetts women should be subject to grievous suffering because Roman Catholic pressure refuses to allow even doctors to give information on birth-control even to non-Catholics. It was not a good thing for Christians to persecute and even burn heretics; it is not a good thing when Communism, in its dogmatic-religious aspect, persecutes and even executes deviationists.

The emergent religion of the near future could be a good thing. It will believe in knowledge. It will be able to take advantage of the vast amount of new knowledge produced by the knowledge-explosion of the last few centuries in constructing what we may call its theology—the framework of facts and ideas which provide it with intellectual support: it should be able, with our increased knowledge of mind, to define man's sense of right and wrong more clearly so as to provide a better moral support, and to focus the feeling of sacredness on fitter objects. Instead of worshipping supernatural rulers, it will sanctify the higher manifestations of human nature, in art and love, in intellectual comprehension and aspiring adoration, and will emphasize the fuller realization of life's possibilities as a sacred trust.

Thus the evolutionary vision, first opened up for us by Charles Darwin a century back, illuminates our existence in a simple but almost over-whelming way. It exemplifies the truth that truth is great and will prevail, and the greater truth that truth will set us free. Evolutionary truth frees us from subservient fear of the unknown and supernatural, and exhorts us to face this new freedom with courage tempered with wisdom, and hope tempered with knowledge. It shows us our destiny and our duty. It shows us mind enthroned above matter, quantity subordinate to quality. It gives our anxious minds support by revealing the incredible possibilities that have already been realized in evolution's past; and, by pointing to the hidden treasure of fresh possibilities that still remain to be realized, it gives us a potent incentive for fulfilling our evolutionary role in the long future of our planet.

*   *   *   *

In the remaining chapters of this volume, twenty-five distinguished contributors have set forth their special subject as it appears in a Humanist framework of ideas.* But before leaving the reader to enjoy their treatment of particular problems, of economy and ethics, music and sociology, education and brain physiology, I must attempt to prepare the ground, however inadequately, by outlining what I conceive to be the Humanist view of the three great activities of man in which he transcends the material business of making a living—art, science and religion.

I use these terms broadly—art to cover all organized expression of experience in significant and aesthetically effective form, science in the continental sense of all organized knowledge and learning, and religion as including all systems of belief and morality primarily concerned with the problem of destiny.

The three types of activity overlap and interlock; but they are essentially distinct, for they perform different psychosocial functions.

Art is almost exclusively a human characteristic. Almost, but not quite. Male bowerbirds show marked aesthetic preferences (for different colours and different kinds of objects for their bowers), and some individuals even paint the lower part of their bowers with pigments; while chimpanzees (and apparently elephants) provided with the requisite materials will enjoy producing paintings which show an elementary sense of design. But such instances are rare among animals; while in man, art in some form is a universal phenomenon, playing an important role in all types of human society and at all levels of human development.

I leave to the philosophers and aestheticians the job of defining Art: as a Humanist I am concerned with the concrete question of the function of art, or, still more concretely, with what the various arts do in various human societies. First of all we must give ourselves the semantic reminder that there is no such *thing* as art. Art is not an entity, any more than life is an entity. It is a word, a general term conveniently but often loosely used to cover a certain rather wide-ranging type of human activity and its products. It is impossible to delimit either the type

* On reading this in proof, I realize, too late, that the book should have included a chapter on the psychosocial function of Humour and Satire.

or its range with precision. Here I shall use *art* to cover the effective organization of experience into integrated forms which are emotionally significant and aesthetically satisfying. This includes some of the practice and some of the products of activities like painting and sculpture, literature and drama, dance and ritual celebration, music and architecture. But, of course, in the spectrum of all these activities art slips over into non-art. Literature grades into straightforward information and into propaganda, visual art into decoration on the one hand and advertisement on the other, drama into mere entertainment, ritual into meaningless formalism, dance into pastime, architecture into utilitarian and sometimes extremely unaesthetic building. And, also of course, every art has its own spectrum, from bad to good: it is impossible to have good art without some bad and much indifferent art.

The essential distinctness of art, I would say, is that it provides a qualitative enrichment of life, by creating a diversity of new experience. For one thing, art can tap emotional resources of human personality which might otherwise remain unutilized, either individually or socially—'dark levels of feeling, both conscious and unconscious, which are a kind of driving power and a determinant of happiness'. It is 'a process of extending ourselves, through our sensibilities and our imagination, to something we have not reached before. It is a process of discovery about ourselves and about life.'* Art helps us to assimilate the experience provided by our senses and emotions. It is an essential part of our psycho-metabolic system. 'Even as we feed our bodies, so do we need to feed and sustain the imagination': and art can potently help in this. Imagine a world without any art: life in it would be intolerable.

But although art is in general a process of differentiation and proliferates variety, it is in particular always a process of integration and synthesis; any work of art, however humble, brings together a number of separate (and sometimes apparently disparate) elements and moulds them into an organic unity.

Art can exert the most profound effects on the minds of men. To many people poetry or painting or music have conveyed an overwhelming sense of revelation. I like to recall that Bertrand Russell as a Cambridge under-graduate was so much overcome by his first hearing of Blake's *Tiger, tiger, burning bright* which a friend recited as they were walking up a college staircase, that he had to lean against the wall for physical support. At the play, as Aristotle said, we can be 'purged by pity and fear' or gripped by powerful and liberating collective emotion, and many people

---

* The admirable phrases within inverted commas are from a private document from which I have been permitted to quote.

have found that first visit to the theatre was also their induction into a new and compelling mode of experience. We are not quite the same after we have read Tolstoy's *War and Peace*. And Beethoven's posthumous quartets can transport us to another world, make us free of another realm of being.

That is the point. Art opens the doors of that other world in which matter and quantity are transcended by mind and quality. Art is sometimes contemptuously dismissed as escapism. But we all need escape. Apart from our modern need to escape from the dullness of routine and from the over-mechanized life of cities, there is the universal and permanent need to escape from the cage of the practical and actual present in which we have of necessity to spend so much of our lives, and above all from the prison of our single and limited selves. The question is, where and how shall we escape? We can escape downwards, through drink or drugs or dissipation: but that is not the best way. Or sideways, through sport or pastime or entertainment: that is within wide limits desirable and indeed necessary. Or we may escape upwards, into a new world (think of Blake's title, *The Mental Traveller*) comprising new countries of life and new levels of being, where we make contact with something more enduring, more satisfying and in a certain true sense higher than is to be found in the world of material needs and everyday routine.

Man by his very nature has the possibility and indeed the necessity of living his life in two worlds at different levels of meaning—the world of matter and mechanical operations, and that of mind and psychological operations—the level of material needs and that of mental satisfactions. And the mental world is in the strict sense of the word transcendent. In it, we manage to escape from the material world and its quantitative exigencies by transcending it in some higher synthesis in which qualitative elements of our being are organized into effective forms. In the light of evolutionary Humanism, man is seen as struggling, consciously or unconsciously, to create more areas of this matter-transcending world of mental operation, and pressing painfully on towards fuller emergence into its satisfying realms.

Operationally, a work of art exerts its effects by conveying multiple meaning in a single synthesis. The meaning is often best conveyed by suggestion rather than by attempts at rigid and accurate affirmation, as Gombritch so well demonstrates in *Art and Illusion*. The suggestion may work on the basis of long-forgotten and even unconsciously assimilated early experience, or on remembered association, or by way of potent symbol or of effective design. The multiplicity of meaning may be conveyed by single elements in the work—think of the multivalency of words or phrases in great poetry like Blake's *Tiger* or Coleridge's *Kubla Khan*, or Traherne's 'the corn was orient and immortal wheat', the multivalency of an individual character in a play, like Shakespeare's *Hamlet*, the bringing together of single elements with separate meanings into a multisignificant whole pattern, as in a great pictorial composition like Raphael's *School of Athens*, or a great musical composition like Bach's B Minor Mass, or a great novel like Tolstoy's *War and Peace*.

The artist can utilize intellectual ideas and moral concepts among the raw materials which he organizes, thus transmuting reason and morality into art and giving a further dimension to his work. In painting, we need only think of the conceptual background of Michelangelo's *Creation of Adam*, of the combination of the concepts of maternity and divinity in pictures of the Madonna and Child, and indeed of all effective use of accepted iconography and symbolism. Greek tragedy flowered out of the ground of current ideas and beliefs, and Dante's *Divina Commedia* owes its compelling greatness to the strong and beautifully organized intellectual framework on which it is supported.

Inferior artists will be incapable of organizing these non-aesthetic elements into an aesthetic unity, and their work will not rise above the didactic or the propagandist, the moralistic or the merely representational. But the good artist can fuse them into a richer whole in the creative crucible of his imagination.*

The cruciform plan of Christian churches, for all its symbolic and ideological significance, has no particular aesthetic merit. But the great cathedral and abbey builders of the Middle Ages utilized it to produce results of intense architectural value, which the world would otherwise never have enjoyed, by organizing glorious patterns of enclosed space in the meeting of transept, nave and choir. Symbols and ideas are not art, but they can support it, can enrich it, and can enlarge its scope. By posing a problem, they can be a stimulating challenge to the artist, whether architect or painter, in the same way as can problems of material or space or site.

The idea that art is in some way equatable with beauty, or is confined to the creation of beauty, is still widespread, though its fallacy has often been demonstrated. What art creates is significance—emotionally and aesthetically effective significance. Beauty is among its significant products, so

* Books like Kenneth Clark's *Looking at Pictures*, London, Murray, 1960, and E. S. Gombritch's *Art and Illusion*, London, 1960, help us in understanding the artist's creative ability.

that art will increase the store of beauty in the world: but beauty is not its sole or even its main product, and there are many other fields in which beauty can be conserved or created for human fulfilment.

Looked at in the long perspective, both art and science can be said to be progressive, though in different ways. While art increases the qualitative richness and the emotional range of human experience and insight, science increases the volume and the depth of knowledge, its operative efficiency and its better organization, and enlarges the area and the grasp of human understanding.

Art results in the creation of individual works, each qualitatively different from the rest, and embodying a particular organization of experience. A particular work of art may be timeless, in the sense that men can continue to enjoy it in spite of lapse of time and change of circumstance. Science is mainly cumulative and co-operative; the scientist makes his contribution to a growing and enlarging whole, whose unity is more important and more overriding than the unitary quality of the individual contributions which are incorporated into it. But art is not cumulative or co-operative in this way. It is, in evolutionary terms, a cladogenetic or branching process, promoting differentiation and diversity. In its historical development, art plays somewhat the same role as does adaptive radiation and diversification in biological evolution. Both lead to a fuller utilization of the potential resources and opportunities of the environment—in the case of adaptive radiation, of the material resources and opportunities available for organic metabolism in the physical environment; in the case of art, of the emotional aesthetic resources and possibilities available for psycho-metabolism in the total environment, both physical and cultural. This is art's main evolutionary aspect. But it is progressive or directional in other ways. It is summatively progressive. In his chapter, Stephen Spender discusses the striking fact, first emphasized by Malraux, that today, for the first time in history, the whole sum of past art is available for present enjoyment. It is technically progressive: painters, for instance, either build on past techniques or react against them and search for a new one. And it is essentially progressive, in that with the lapse of time men not only learn to turn new aspects of experience into art (as Renaissance painters did with space and perspective, or as contemporary artists are doing with abstract or action painting), but discover how to organize a greater number of different components, of thought and emotion as well as of technique, into a single work which shall be a significant whole; in other words, how to create higher patterns of aesthetic organization. A symphony is in a certain real sense a higher achievement than a song or a military march, Giotto's Arena Chapel in Padua than a single drawing or than Lascaux, Dante's *Divina Commedia* than a sonnet, Tolstoy's *War and Peace* than a Maupassant short story or even Don Quixote.

Of course, within each type or grade of organization there is every possible range from good to bad, just as there is every possible range from successful to unsuccessful species and lineages within one grade of biological organization like the mammals or the reptiles. But this does not invalidate the fact that some grades of aesthetic organization are truly 'higher' than others, just as mammalian organization is in a strictly scientific sense higher than reptilian. In both cases it is clear that real advance is involved.

It is also clear that in some periods, like the Victorian era, official or generally acceptable art tends to become mediocre or insignificant. This in turn generates minor rebellions or reactions, which may remain without much effective issue, like Pre-Raphaelitism in England, or may burst through the traditional crust to initiate a new and fruitful stream of development, like Impressionism in France.

The rebels usually strengthen their psychological position by forming more or less definite labelled groups—the Pre-Raphaelites, the Barbizon School, the Post-Impressionists, the Cubists, the Surrealists. But a leading role will always be played by individual creative artists of genius and determination—Giotto, Michelangelo, Rembrandt; Constable, Turner, Manet; in our own days, Picasso, Klee, Henry Moore.

There can be little dispute that many developments of the arts in Western countries since 1945 reflect or express the nihilism of the post-war period, the fragmentation of its life between frustration and hope, its intellectual chaos and moral disillusionment. (The rise of existentialism was a symptom of the same pathological malaise.) The very different course of events in Communist countries is also an example of the influence of ideas and beliefs and attitudes on art, in this case the influence of a dogmatic ideology, operating by authoritarian methods and sometimes even downright persecution. In both camps the spread of Humanist ideas would tend to heal the split between creative art and its social environment.

Within its major and embracing function, art has a number of applications. Art can play an important educational role both *in* education and *as* education. Most young children, including especially those who are neither mechanically nor intellectually minded, can enjoy themselves, and (what is more important) find themselves more fully through some form of what is rather pompously called 'creative expression', particularly perhaps in paint or clay. It can help them to develop their little personalities in a more emotionally integrated way, and can introduce them both to an enlarged experience of the world and to the discovery of new inner possibilities in themselves. With the self-consciousness of adolescence, it is all too easy to cramp their freedom and conventionalize their expression: but with proper methods the arts can continue to play an important role throughout the years of education.

Although 'creative expression' sounds pompous when applied to young children, it is in fact perfectly correct. All art, even the scribblings and daubings of little boys and girls, not merely provides an outlet for self-expression, but is in some sort a creation, a personal integration imposed by the imagination on some fraction of the fleeting flux of experience. As such, it can act both as a liberating and as an integrative force in the developing human creature.

This combined liberation and integration, one may assume, is the chief function of most art practised as a hobby or a relaxation by adults. It may be egotistically slanted towards self-expression to provide a heightened sense of personal significance; but it seems often to be based simply on the felt need to express some powerful subjective experience in the objective form of a poem or a painting. To achieve this (as anyone knows who has been impelled to write poetry in his youth) demands a special creative effort, but the mere process of achievement, however inadequate, also affords a special satisfaction.

Art may also be therapeutically slanted. The practice of some art can keep certain psychological types from becoming neurotic, and can often assist recovery from a neurotic breakdown.

But though the Humanist is interested in these various ways in which what we may call amateur art may help individual development and promote individual fulfilment, his major concern must be with professional art and its psychosocial functions. How and to what extent does art reflect or express a period or a people; how and to what extent does it promote cultural richness and achievement—in a word, what part does it play in man's evolution?

It is clear that within a given region the arts evolve. Consciously or unconsciously, each new period, each new generation, demands change. Sometimes the change consists primarily in the fuller development or even the exaggeration of an existing style or tradition; sometimes it is a reaction against it, with the emergence of radically new approaches, attitudes, and techniques; sometimes a combination of the two. Gombritch gives plenty of examples in his fascinating book,* and Stephen Spender's chapter in the

* E. J. Gombritch, *Art and Illusion*, London 1960. See also Kenneth Clark, *The Nude in Art*, for a penetrating study of the changing treatment of a particular subject-matter.

present volume is an interesting study of the relation of the individual artist to his social and ideological environment.

But this is only one element in the problem. I would say that the most general answer runs somewhat like this. The individual artist has two main functions—that of creator and that of interpreter. As interpreter, he translates complex and emotion-tinged experience into directly communicable forms and so is able to express what otherwise would remain unexpressible. He bears witness to the variety of the world and its significance, to its wonder and beauty, but also to its horror and nastiness. His witness may be by way of affirmation or by way of protest. But his function, even when he is not conscious of it, is to interpret the world to man, and man to himself. As creator, on the other hand, he provides experiences of stimulus and enjoyment, sometimes enlargements of experience itself (think of Turner or Stravinsky, or, most obviously, of Shakespeare). Art as a collective social activity has the same two main functions. I should say that it *can* have; for in some societies it is neglected or distorted, or even, as in ancient Sparta, rejected. Nor must we forget that architecture is an art, or, to spell the matter out, that art plays an essential role in architecture, layout and planning. Architecture in this extended sense can perform its own particular function in expressing human ideas and aspirations. Good architecture can enrich human life, especially urban life, while bad architecture can impoverish it, as is all too obvious in the many ugly towns and drab city fringes and subtopian sprawls of our age. To the Humanist, the importance of architecture's social function is obvious: the problem is to persuade officials and taxpayers to recognize its importance in practice.

We must also remember that art spills over into design. Art is as essential for the design of pots and pans and pillar-boxes, of pencils, porcelain and posters, as it is for the quality of paintings or sculptures. Indeed some pots are better works of art than many paintings. And though design has a humbler role than the fine arts, its social function is just as indispensable.

In the fulfilment society envisaged by Humanism, art would be assigned a large role—to beautify the public sector, to bear witness to the richness of existence, to affirm values in concrete effective form, to provide achievements of which human societies can be proud and through which mankind can find itself more adequately. But before anything of the sort can be realized, the psychosocial possibilities of art and the best methods for realizing them in practice will need to be intensively studied.

So we come to man's second main higher activity—science. We must beware of the misuse of words like *science* and *scientific*, especially by those who want to cash in on the prestige of science to advance their own views or interests. Thus theology once arrogated to itself the title of Queen of the Sciences, and still claims rather plaintively to be a science—a claim which it could only justify by adopting scientific method. The most obvious modern example is that of the Marxists. Marx himself asserted that he had discovered the iron scientific laws that inevitably rule the development of society, and many people still accept Communism as a political creed because they have been told that it is 'scientific'. In actual fact Marxism is no more a science than theology—largely because it is itself a kind of theology, in the sense that it consists of a body of doctrines whose truth is guaranteed by dogmatic authority instead of being constantly tested against fact, and relies on a narrow and arrogant scholastic logic instead of on the patient humility of free enquiry.

Science, like art, is a loose and general term for a broad range of human activities and their products. Though its growing core is firm and clear, it is thus inevitably fluffy at the edges, and grades imperceptibly into non-science, as art does into non-art. It is perhaps best thought of as a process —the process of discovering, establishing, and organizing knowledge. To do this effectively, it must rely on scientific method, as stressed by Dr Bronowski in his chapter.*

Looked at in the long perspective, science is seen as the continuation by new methods of the trend towards fuller and better-organized awareness which runs through the whole of animal evolution, from before the dawn of anything that could be called mind or memory, up to mammals and men. This trend was fostered by natural selection because it was biologically useful. Fuller and better-organized awareness enables its possessors to cope better and more fully with the changes and chances of their lives and their environment. In particular, it is a time-binder, enabling them to utilize past experience to guide future action.

Science has two interrelated psychosocial functions: it increases both comprehension and control. It enlarges man's understanding of the world, both the strange world of external nature and the equally strange world of his own internal nature; and it increases his capacity to control or guide various aspects and processes of that world.

As a result, everything in psychosocial evolution which can properly be

* See also, e.g., J. Bronowski and B. Mazlish, *The Western Intellectual Tradition*, London, Hutchinson's; New York, Harper, 1960, and C. G. Gillispie, *The Edge of Objectivity*, Princeton, 1960.

called advance, or progress, or improvement, is due directly or indirectly
to the increase or improvement of knowledge.*

Science, as Dr Bronowski stresses, is not merely a discovery of pre-
existent fact: it is also, and more importantly, a creation of something new.
It is just as creative as art, though in a different way. Scientific laws are
not something existing from eternity in their own right or in the mind of
God, waiting to be discovered by man: they did not exist before men of
science formulated them. The same is true of scientific concepts, like *atom*,
or *electric potential*, or *evolution*.

Scientific laws and concepts alike are organized creations of the human
mind, by means of which the disorderly raw material of natural phenomena
presented to crude experience is worked into orderly and manageable
forms. A scientific concept is an intellectually effective integration of
experience just as a painting is an aesthetically effective one.

Thus science is not only concerned with discovering facts: it is still
more concerned with establishing relations between phenomena. Scientific
comprehension was increased by relating the supposedly opposed qualities
of heat and cold in the common concept of a scale of temperature; by
bringing a number of apparently unrelated physical activities in relation
with each other through the principle of the conservation of energy; by
employing the concept of metabolism to perform the same service for a
number of biological activities. A good scientific theory brings together a
swarm of separate phenomena and their attendant concepts in a single
unified pattern of relatedness. Modern evolution theory, for instance, has
spun a comprehensive web of relations between the phenomena of
cytology, genetics, adaptation, palaeontology, reproduction, embryology,
behaviour, selection, systematics, and biochemistry.

Science is also concerned with understanding the systems of relatedness
to be found in nature. This means the study of organization on every
level—the level of atoms, of molecules, of individual organisms, of
societies, of ecological communities. That being so, science cannot be
only a matter of analysis, as is often erroneously supposed. It must start
from the organizations to be found on any level. After studying them
descriptively, comparatively and functionally, it can then try to analyse
them into lower-level elements, and finally attempt a theoretical re-
synthesis. It is no good trying to start from a lower level. Nobody could
have built up the triumphant principles of modern genetics merely from a

* The increase of knowledge is, of course, also responsible for much that is an obstacle to
advance or even the reverse of it (a fact partly symbolized in the legend of the Fall). But
this in no way impairs the validity of the fact that knowledge is the necessary basis for
improvement.

knowledge of biochemistry: genetic theory had to start with phenomena on the biological level, like mitosis and mendelian segregation, taking the facts of biological organization for granted. Only much later was it possible to analyse and understand genetic phenomena in biochemical terms, as we can now begin to do, thanks to Watson and Crick's brilliant theory of the self-replication of certain kinds of nucleic acid molecules.

We must beware of reductionism. It is hardly ever true that something is 'nothing but' something else. Because we are descended from anthropoid primates, it does not follow that we are nothing but developed apes: because we are made of matter, it does not follow that we have nothing but material properties. An organization is always more than the mere sum of its elements, and must be studied as a unitary whole as well as analysed into its component parts.

Science is a self-correcting and self-enlarging system. It aims to unify experience. It creates patches of organized knowledge in the vast expanse of human ignorance. The patches of knowledge grow, and may fuse to form more comprehensive patterns. The trend is clearly towards an eventual single organization of conceptual thought, holding all aspects of experience in its web of relations, uniting all the separate patches of knowledge into one living and growing body of organized understanding. But meanwhile great gaps of ignorance still separate some of the partial systems, some of which are still isolated islands scientifically cut off from their neighbours, while some areas of experience are still recalcitrant to the method of science and remain outside its system.

The immediate need is for the scientific study of values. Philosophers and theologians sometimes assert that this is impossible, claiming that values lie outside the range of science. The Humanist cannot accept this: after all, values are phenomena, and therefore capable of being investigated by the methods of science. They are phenomena which only appear on the psychological level, and accordingly science must first approach them on this level. It must ask appropriate questions about them: In what psychological circumstances do values come into being? Out of what raw materials are they constructed by man's psychometabolic activity? What functions do they perform in psychosocial evolution? How do they change and evolve? And just as science had to devise special methods for dealing adequately with multicausal phenomena, especially where they are not amenable to experiment, so, as time goes on, it will have to devise special methods for dealing effectively with phenomena with a strong subjective component. But a successful beginning has already been made.

The study of values is a part of the one really major problem now before science—the problem of relating mind and mental activities to the rest of the phenomenal universe in a single scientific picture. Here too there is much hard work ahead; but here too, as Sir Russell Brain shows in his chapter in this book, a considerable measure of success has already been achieved, partly through the evolutionary study of animal behaviour, partly through the developmental study of human behaviour, partly through a joint physiological and psychological attack on human mental activity.

The irresistible trend towards the creation of one comprehensive scientific picture of the world of man's experience emerges even more clearly when we look at science historically. Since the dawn of the scientific revolution some three hundred and fifty years ago, science has steadily invaded new fields. First of all, mechanics, astronomy, physics; then chemistry and natural history; next followed geology and physiology and embryology, and then experimental and evolutionary biology; next was the turn of ethnology, then psychology, then sociology. Science then proceeded to establish a footing in new territories like economics, archaeology, and social anthropology, and established connections between various separate disciplines with the aid of bridging sciences like biochemistry, social psychology, epigenetics, and astrophysics. We are now witnessing the invasion of the field of psychosocial phenomena by science.

The only field still remaining outside the range of the scientific system is that of so-called paranormal phenomena like telepathy and ESP. If and when they are brought within its scope, some pretty radical alterations will presumably become necessary in its theoretical framework.

Meanwhile, however, science has attained a new and very real unity and firmness of organization and is giving us a scientifically-based picture of human destiny and human possibilities. For the first time in history, science can become the ally of religion instead of its rival or its enemy, for it can provide a 'scientific' theology, a scientifically-ordered framework of belief, to whatever new religion emerges from the present ideological disorder.

This is imperative, since theology in this broad sense is a statement of beliefs and of their intellectual or rational justification: it dictates the general approach and character of a religion, as well as determining many of its particular features. Thus a theological system is to a religion what a framework of hypotheses and theories is to a science.

All theistic religions are based on the God hypothesis (or, to use Ralph Turner's more inclusive term, the daimonic hypothesis)—the belief that there exist supernatural beings of a personal or super-personal nature, capable of influencing natural events, including events in human minds. This is a dualistic theory, for it implies the existence of a basic and essential cleavage between natural and supernatural realms of being.

Early theologies are all polytheistic. Christian theology calls itself monotheistic, but permits itself a partial polytheism in the doctrine of the Trinity, while the position ascribed to the Virgin, the Angels and the Saints in Catholicism and to a lesser degree in other sects, gives full rein to polydaimonism. Christian theology bases itself on revelation and on belief in the historical reality of supernatural events such as the incarnation and resurrection of Jesus as the Son of God. It also maintains the reality of miracles.

A theological system incorporating such beliefs has a number of consequences which Humanists find undesirable. The belief in supernatural beings capable of affecting human destiny leads to petitionary rather than aspirational prayer, and to all kinds of propitiatory practices, from the use of incense to the bequeathing of rich gifts, from asceticism to penitential sacrifice. Belief in a supernatural after-life leads to concentration on attaining salvation in the other world and to a lack of concern for life in this world and its possible improvement. Belief in the fall of man and the necessity of redemption through an incarnate divine Saviour has led to the cruel (and untrue) doctrines of Original Sin and Damnation for unbelievers, as well as to a belief in the guilt and inherent inferiority of the female sex. Belief in the value of orthodox Christian beliefs and practices as the sole or main means of achieving salvation leads to the rejection or playing down of other ideas as to what constitutes 'salvation', and of other methods of transcending selfhood. Belief in the Bible as the inspired word of God, and in the Church and its representatives as the sole source of correct doctrine, leads to a regrettable dogmatism and to the rejection or playing down of secular knowledge and scientific method.

Belief in a supernatural Ruler, endowed with absolute wisdom and the capacity of issuing absolute moral edicts, coupled with an ignorance of the workings of the unconscious as revealed by modern psychology, permits would-be dictators, fanatical moralists and other power-hungry men to believe that their subjective feelings of internal certainty are 'really' the voice of an objective and external God and to claim divine guidance and sanction as a convenient disguise for their ambitions, and enables them with a good conscience to project their own guilt and resentful inferiority on to their enemies, and to canalize their repressed sadism on to their victims. How unfortunate for mankind that the Lord is reported by Holy Writ as having said 'Vengeance is mine!'

Belief in the efficacy of ritual practices for ensuring salvation or other kinds of religious advancement has a deadening effect on the religious and moral life. Belief in supernaturalism and the miraculous and magical elements which go with it always leads to gross superstition, and usually to its financial exploitation. Think of the cult of relics, the complete repudiation of any scientific approach shown by the promulgation of doctrines like the bodily assumption of the Virgin Mary, by the proclamation of the miracle of Fatima, or by highly profitable pilgrimages to sites of 'miraculous' cures like Lourdes.

Such theistically-based beliefs in various combinations can lead to a materialistic degradation of religion, sometimes silly, sometimes serious and sometimes horrible, as seen in the prayer-wheels of Tibetan Buddhism, the scandal of indulgences which started off the Reformation, or the human sacrifices of the Aztecs and the Carthaginians.

Above all, belief in an omnipotent, omniscient and omnibenevolent God leads to a frustrating dilemma at the very heart of our approach to reality. For many thinking people, it is incompatible with our knowledge of nature and history and with the facts of evil, suffering, and human misery. Even when, as in some modernist versions of Christian theology, the idea of a personal God is watered down and transmogrified into some abstract principle or supposed Absolute behind phenomena, and the Deity is removed farther and farther from any possibility of active interference in natural or human events, the dilemma remains. The human mind and spirit is not interested in such a Pickwickian God, and refuses to be fobbed off by assertions as to our inherent incapacity to understand Him. The theologian's assertion of divine incomprehensibility does not satisfy man in his modern world any more than Humpty Dumpty's remark, 'Impenetrability, that's what I say,' satisfied Alice in her Wonderland.

To sum up, any belief in supernatural creators, rulers, or influencers of natural or human process introduces an irreparable split into the universe, and prevents us from grasping its real unity. Any belief in Absolutes, whether the absolute validity of moral commandments, of authority of revelation, of inner certitude, or of divine inspiration, erects a formidable barrier against progress and the possibility of improvement, moral, rational, or religious. And the all-too-frequent combination of the two constitutes a grave brake on human advance, and, by obfuscating all the major problems of existence, prevents the attainment of a full and comprehensive vision of human destiny.

All this merely spells out the consequences of the fact that theistic religions, with their inescapable basis of divine revelations and dogmatic theologies, are today not merely incompatible with human progress and the advance of human knowledge but are obstacles to the emergence of new types of religion which could be compatible with our knowledge and capable of promoting our future progress.

Although destructive criticism of established religious systems, such as that of orthodox Christianity by militant Rationalism around the turn of the nineteenth century, may be necessary at certain periods, the time for negative activities is now past. It was not for nothing that Goethe made the Devil proclaim himself as *der Geist der stets verneint*.

What the world now needs is not merely a rationalist denial of the old but a religious affirmation of something new. However, it is harder to affirm, at least to affirm anything of lasting value, than to deny. It is harder for the same reason that, as the world has experienced on a gigantic scale, it is easier to destroy than to construct, easier to smash a cathedral, a city or a statue than to create one.

Construction needs a positive plan of some sort to work to and cooperative effort for its execution, and this demands intelligence, imagination, goodwill, and above all vision.

One of the main things needed by the world today is a new single religious system to replace the multiplicity of conflicting and incompatible religious systems that are now competing for the spirit of man. Our new vision of the universe and man's role in it is beginning to indicate the lines of its construction.

All religions, as I pointed out earlier, are psychosocial organs of evolving man: their function is to help him to cope with the problems of his destiny. They themselves evolve. But they always involve the emotion of sacred mystery experienced by men confronted with what Otto calls the numinous, the *mysterium tremendum*; the sense of right and wrong; and feelings of guilt, shame, or sin. They are always concerned in some way or another with the relation between the individual and the community, and with the possibility of his escaping from the prisoning immediacies of space, time, and selfhood by relating himself to some broader frame of reference, or in some self-transcending experience of union or communion with a larger reality.

They always possess what we may broadly call an ideology, a morality, and a ritual—an intellectual framework of beliefs, myths, and theological principles, an ethical framework of moral codes and injunctions, and an expressive framework of actions expressing or enhancing religious emotion.

As I have set forth at greater length in my *Religion Without Revolution*,* the raw materials out of which religions are formed consist of actual religious experiences, numinous or holy, mystical or transcendent. But

* *Religion Without Revolution*, London, Parrish, 1957.

the particular form which they take is primarily the result of their ideological framework of belief: I have given various examples of how the
morality and the ritual expressions of a religion are determined by its
beliefs to a much greater extent than its beliefs are determined by its
morality or ritual.

Let us look at some of the major ideas which our new vision will
contribute or dictate to the new belief-system. In the first place we have
a totally different view of the mysterious. With the advance of scientific
knowledge, many phenomena which once appeared wholly mysterious
can now be described or explained in rationally intelligible or naturalistic
terms. This applies not only to physical phenomena like rainbows and
eclipses, pestilences and earthquakes, but also to biological phenomena
like reproduction and sex, heredity and evolution, and to psychological
phenomena such as obsession and possession, insanity and inspiration.

The clear light of science, we are often told, has abolished mystery,
leaving only logic and reason. This is quite untrue. Science has removed
the obscuring veil of mystery from many phenomena, much to the
benefit of the human race: but it confronts us with a basic and universal
mystery—the mystery of existence in general, and of the existence of mind
in particular. Why does the world exist? Why is the world-stuff what it
is? Why does it have mental or subjective aspects as well as material or
objective ones? We do not know. All we can do is to admit the facts.

This means that, as Margaret Fuller said, we accept the universe. In
spite of Carlyle's comment, 'Gad, she'd better', this is not easy: there is
great resistance to such acceptance. Initially, the universe reveals itself
as too vast and varied to be accepted as a unitary whole by our small
human minds; many of its components are apparently incommensurable
with human thought and feeling, and in many of its aspects it appears
alien and even hostile to human aspiration and endeavour. But we must
learn to accept it, and to accept its and our existence as the one basic
mystery.

Accordingly, any new emergent religion must have a background of
reverence and awe in its belief-system, and must seek to keep alive man's
sense of wonder, strangeness and challenge in all his particular dealings
with the general problem of existence.

But though all we can do about the universe in its total existence is to
discover it as an irreducible mystery, to be humanly assimilated only by
wonder and free acceptance, yet the details of its phenomenal working
and the relations of its operative parts can be profitably clarified by human
intellectual and imaginative effort. And this applies to religion as well as
to science or to art. In all of them the ecological approach is essential.

Religion can be usefully regarded as applied spiritual ecology. The relations with which a religion must attempt to deal are the relations of mankind with the rest of external nature, the relation of man's individualized self with the rest of his internal nature, and the relation of individual men and women with other men and women and with their communities.

All these can be much clarified by our new humanist vision. In its light the universe is seen as a unitary and evolutionary process. Man is part and a product of the process, but a very peculiar part, capable of affecting its further course on earth and perhaps elsewhere. But he is only able to affect the process constructively by understanding its workings.

The rightness of relation he must aim at has two aspects. One is a relation of right position in an integrated and harmonious pattern; the other (and this is the major novelty introduced by the new vision) is a relation of right direction with the whole process. Man's religious aim must therefore be to achieve not a static but a dynamic spiritual equilibrium. And his emergent religion must therefore learn how to be an open and self-correcting system, like that of his science.

All religions provide for some ceremonial sanctification of life, especially of events like birth, marriage and death, and those marking the transition from one stage of life to another, like initiation or the taking of a degree: his new emergent religion must continue to do this, though it must translate the ceremonials into terms that are relevant to the new vision and the new circumstances of his life.

This reformulation of traditional religious concepts and beliefs and ceremonies, their translation into a new terminology and a new framework of ideas, is a major task for Humanism.

Man makes his concepts. He constructs them out of the raw material of his experience, immediate and accumulated, with the aid of his psychological machinery of reason and imagination.

This is true not only of religious concepts but of scientific concepts like the atom or natural selection today, or the four elements or the inheritance of acquired characters in earlier times.

But whereas science is constantly and willingly improving its terminology and reformulating its concepts, even scrapping them and constructing quite new ones, religion on the whole resists any such transformation.

Religious concepts like God, incarnation, the soul, salvation, original sin, grace, atonement, all have a basis in man's experiences of phenomenal reality. It is necessary now to analyse that basis of reality into its component parts, and then to reassemble these elements, together with any new factors that have come to light, into concepts which correspond more closely to reality and are more relevant to present circumstances.

Thus, if I may over-simplify the matter, *God* appears to be a semantic symbol denoting what Matthew Arnold called 'the power not ourselves', or rather the various powers felt to be greater than our narrow selves, whether the forces of external nature or the forces imminent in our own nature, all bound together in the concept of a personal or super-personal sacred being in some way capable of affecting or guiding or interfering in the course of events. The forces are real enough: what we have done is, quite illegitimately, to project the god concept into them. And in so doing we have distorted their true significance, and effectively altered the course of history.*

Once this is realized, it should be possible to reformulate such ideas as Divine Law, obedience to God's will, or union with the mind of God, in an evolutionary terminology consonant with existing scientific knowledge.

Again, Christian ethics (to which the world owes a great debt) is based on the doctrine of Original Sin resulting from the Fall of Man. This attempts to give an intelligible interpretation of such general and wellnigh universal phenomena as our sense of guilt, our search for atonement, our authoritarian consciences, our rigorous sense of right and wrong, our consequent persecution of those who deviate from what we feel is the right path.

As Professor Waddington points out in his chapter, and reinforces with a wealth of supporting argument in his recent admirable book, *The Ethical Animal*,† psychology and evolutionary biology between them are now indicating a rational and coherent explanation for these facts.

Psychosocial life is based on the transmission of accumulated experience in the form of tradition. And this, Waddington makes clear, cannot be effective unless the human infant is genetically equipped as an 'authority-acceptor': he is constructed so as to accept what he is told by his parents as authoritative, in the same sort of way as baby birds are equipped with an imprinting mechanism which makes them accept any moving object within certain limits of size as a parent.

This 'proto-ethical mechanism' involves the internalization of external authority in the baby's primitive conscience, a process accompanied by all-or-nothing repression of impulses of hate for the authority who is also the loved parent. As a result, a quality of absoluteness becomes

* For a valuable discussion of the semantic, symbolic and functional aspects of religion, see Raymond Firth's Huxley Memorial Lecture for 1959 (*J. Roy. Anthrop. Inst.*, **89**, 129).

† *The Ethical Animal*, London: Allen & Unwin, 1960.

attached to the baby's sense of rightness and wrongness, together with an ambivalent attitude to authority in general: his morality is burdened with a load of guilt, and his feelings towards authority become impregnated with ambivalence.

All this happens before he is old enough to verify his ideas by experience. During his later development he will modify and rectify the content and authoritarianism of what he has accepted, but will generally retain a great deal of both. The aim of the Humanist must be, not to destroy the inner authority of conscience, but to help the growing individual to escape from the shackles of an imposed authority-system into the supporting arms of one freely and consciously built up. And this will involve a thorough reformulation of the ethical aspects of religion.

Reformulation—even reappraisal—is perhaps most necessary in regard to man's inner life and what, for want of a better terminology, is called spiritual development.

Religious experiences such as those of communion with some higher reality, or inspiration from outside the personality, or a sense of transcendent power or glory, or sudden conversion, or apparently supernormal beauty or ineffable sacredness, or the healing power of prayer or repentant adoration, or, above all, the deep sense of inner peace and assurance in spite of disorder and suffering, can no longer be interpreted in the traditional terms of communication with a personal God or with a supernatural realm of being. But neither can they be denied or explained away by over-zealous rationalism as merely illusory products. They are the outcome of human minds in their strange commerce with outer reality and in the still stranger and often unconscious internal struggle between their components. But they are none the less real* and they can be of great importance to the individual who experiences them: but further, as the Churches well know, they need to be examined and disciplined.

Religious experiences often are or appear to be ineffable in the literal sense of the word, which makes their discussion very difficult. But their significance is a matter both high and deep (as I am in all humility aware); and they certainly need re-examination and reappraisal if their great potential value is to be realized.

Further, experiential religion should enlist the aid of psychological science in a radical study of man's actual and potential spiritual resources. Such a study would, of course, have to start from the presuppositions

* Besides William James's famous book, there are many valuable descriptions and studies of the varieties of religious experience, a number of which I have cited and discussed in my *Religion Without Revelation*.

that 'man' is a new type of organism consisting of individual mind-bodies interacting with a superindividual and continuing system of ideas and beliefs, whose destiny is to actualize more and more of his possibilities for greater fulfilment during further evolution; and that 'religion' is an organ of man primarily concerned with what is felt and believed to be sacred in that destiny.

But our new vision illuminates our existence and our destiny in a new way, and necessitates a new approach to their problems. In its light we see at once that the reappraisal of religious experience must be a part of something much larger—a thorough investigation of man's inner world, a great project of 'Mind Exploration' which could and should rival and surpass 'Space Exploration' in interest and importance. This would open up a new realm of being for colonization and fruitful occupation by man, a realm of mental realities, built on but transcending the realm of material realities, a world of satisfactions transcending physical satisfactions, in some way felt as more absolute and more perfect. Ordinary men and women obtain occasional glimpses of it through falling in love, or through overwhelming experiences of ecstasy, beauty or awe. And we have the reports of the occasional mental explorers, poets, thinkers, scientists and mystics who have penetrated into its interior. Think of St Teresa, or of Blake as the Mental Traveller, or of Wordsworth anticipating Freud by revealing in us the 'high instincts before which our mortal nature Doth tremble like a guilty thief surprised'.

No concerted effort has yet been made towards its exploration or adequate mapping. There is as yet no proper terminology for its discussion. In describing its workings and results, ordinary language falls back on terms like *rapture* and *inspiration*, *magical* and *heavenly*, *bewitching* and *divine*, while the first attempts at scientific terminology, like *repression* and *sublimation*, *id* and *superego*, deal only with its fringes.

From the specifically religious point of view, the desirable direction of evolution might be defined as the divinization of existence—but for this to have operative significance, we must frame a new definition of 'the divine', free from all connotations of external supernatural beings.

Religion today is imprisoned in a theistic frame of ideas, compelled to operate in the unrealities of a dualistic world. In the unitary Humanist frame it acquires a new look and a new freedom. With the aid of our new vision, it has the opportunity of escaping from the theistic impasse, and of playing its proper role in the real world of unitary existence.

This brings me back to where I started—to our new and revolutionary vision of reality. Like all true visions it is prophetic; by enabling us to understand the present condition of life in terms of its extraordinary past, it helps us not only to envisage an equally extraordinary future, but to inject planned purpose into its course.

In its light, fulfilment and enrichment of life are seen as the overriding aims of existence, to be achieved by the realization of life's inherent possibilities. Thus the development of man's vast potential of realizable possibility provides the prime motive for collective action—the only motive on which all men or nations could agree, the only basis for transcending conflicting ideologies. It makes it possible to heal the splits between religion and science and art by enlisting man's religious and scientific and artistic capacities in a new common enterprise. It prescribes an agenda for the world's discussions of that enterprise and suggests the practical methods to be employed in running it.

It indicates the urgent need for survey and research in all fields of human development. This includes the promotion of what I may call a psychosocial technology, including the production of ideological machine-tools like concepts and beliefs for the better processing of experience.

We also need to develop a new ecology, an ecology of the human evolutionary enterprise. This means thinking out a new pattern of our relations with each other and with the rest of our environment, including the mental environment which we both create and inhabit.

Psychosocial ecology must aim at a right balance between different values, between continuity and change, and between the evolutionary process for whose guidance we have responsibility and the resources with which we have to operate. Those resources are of two kinds— material and quantitative, for maintenance and utility; and psychological and qualitative, for enjoyment and fulfilment—such things as food, and energy, mines and industrial plants on the one hand; solitude, landscape beauty, marine and mountain adventure, the wonder and interest of wild life on the other. Planned human ecology must balance and where possible reconcile the two kinds of resource.

What is the place of the individual in all this? At first sight the individual human being appears as a little, temporary, and insignificant creature, of no account in the vast enterprise of mankind as a whole. But in Evolutionary Humanism, unlike some other ideologies, the human individual has high significance. Quite apart from the practical function which he performs in society and its collective enterprises, he can help in fulfilling human destiny by the fuller realization of his own personal possibilities. A strong and rich personality is the individual's unique and wonderful contribution to the psychosocial process.

*   *   *   *

Santayana has come close to the central idea of Evolutionary Humanism in sane and splendid words. 'There is only one world, the natural world, and only one truth about it; but this world has a spiritual life in it, which looks not to another world but to the beauty and perfection that this world suggests, approaches and misses.'

If we aspire to realize this potential beauty and perfection more fully, we shall have to utilize all the resources available—not only those of the external world, but those internal resources of our own nature— wonder and intelligence, creative freedom and love, imagination and belief. The central belief of Evolutionary Humanism is that existence can be improved, that vast untapped possibilities can be increasingly realized, that greater fulfilment can replace frustration. This belief is now firmly grounded in knowledge: it could become in turn the firm ground for action.

But it is time to bring this Introduction to a summary conclusion. Increase of knowledge leads to new idea-systems—new organizations of thought, feeling and beliefs. Idea-systems in this sense provide the supporting framework of human societies and cultures and in large measure determine their policies and course. During human history (psychosocial evolution), the adoption of each new type of idea-system has initiated a new type of society, a new step in psychosocial evolution.

At the moment, the increase of knowledge is driving us towards the radically new type of idea-system which I have called Evolutionary Humanism. The position is critical, because the guidance of this new type of idea-system is needed to prevent psychosocial evolution from becoming self-defeating or even self-destroying.

The immediate effort needed is an intellectual and imaginative one—to understand this new revelation made to us by the growth of knowledge. Humanism is seminal. We must learn what it means, then disseminate Humanist ideas, and finally inject them whenever possible into practical affairs as a guiding framework for policy and action.

RUSSELL BRAIN

BODY, BRAIN, MIND
AND SOUL

SIR RUSSELL BRAIN, BT.

Born 1895. Educated: Mill Hill School; New College, Oxford, and the London Hospital. President of the Royal College of Physicians since 1950.

Publications: *Man, Society and Religion*, 1944; *Recent Advances in Neurology*, 6th ed. 1944; *Diseases of the Nervous System*, 5th ed. 1955, etc.

BODY, BRAIN, MIND
AND SOUL

―――――――

Historical Introduction

Primitive man understands little of the things which surround him, and is largely at the mercy of unknown forces. He interprets these as good or malignant spirits or gods with wills like his own. The more he comes to understand the workings of nature, the less he needs to postulate animistic activities to account for them, but that is not true of primitive man only. Samuel Butler[1] wrote: 'God makes the grass grow because we do not understand how the air and earth and water near a piece of grass are seized by the grass and converted into more grass; but God does not mow the grass and make hay of it. As soon as we understand a thing we remove it from the sphere of God's action.' Similarly, when the cause of epidemics was unknown, they were often regarded as God's will, and a punishment for sin. But as soon as a disease was discovered to be due to a germ, and spread by bad hygiene, the Deity was no longer held responsible for it.

With one part of his mind the dualist thinker accepts evolutionary theory, which implies the gradual development of mind and a naturalistic interpretation of consciousness and values: with another part he derives his soul and values from a supernatural source. Those who seek for ethical sanctions in the evolutionary process are sometimes told that this comprises no criterion of value, but those who derive their values from divine revelation do not escape this difficulty. Different revelations, or even different deductions from the same revelation, lead to conflicting ethical judgments on diet, marriage, divorce, birth-control, racial discrimination, war and the atom bomb, and in the last resort those who claim that one revelation is 'higher' than another tend to justify their view by appealing to the revelation itself.

Initially common sense seems to support dualism. For primitive man the difference between a living man and his dead body is explained by the departure of the soul from the body. Plato[2] regarded soul and body as independent entities, the soul surviving the body. Aristotle's[3] doctrine is obscure, and difficult to express in modern terms. In so far as he considered the soul to be the form of the body, it is capable of a monistic interpretation, but he seems also to have accepted mind as a non-material principle in the soul, though whether he regarded this as personal is doubtful. Jewish teaching on the subject was monistic, for, though it recognized a 'breath-soul', this was little more than a vital principle, and was not conceived as surviving in isolation from the body. Christianity took over this monistic idea from Judaism, but added the idea of personal immortality. It was still monistic, however, for it pictured the resurrection of the body in some form as essential to the after-life of the soul, the eternal destiny of which was to be decided by the individual's conduct, or even merely by his beliefs, during life. It also adopted the current Jewish belief (very general in primitive thought) in good and evil spirits, the latter being held capable of invading the body of a human being and causing disease, especially mental disorder. Christianity has perpetuated this belief to the present day, when even in England some Christians still believe in demoniacal possession, and services of exorcism are conducted by clergy with the object of relieving the mentally disordered.

Christianity received from Platonism a stimulus to a belief in the dichotomy of body and soul. Augustine emphasized the immateriality of the soul. The doctrines of the Manichaeans, a sect to which he originally belonged, associated matter with evil, and were not without influence on Christianity. One effect of separating an immaterial soul from a material body was to find in the body a source of sin—'the sinful lusts of the flesh', though in Pauline thought 'spirit' and 'flesh' were names for good and bad principles, and not equated with soul and body. Aquinas,[4] under the influence of Aristotle, regarded the soul as the form of the body, created by God at the same time, present in every part, nevertheless surviving it. What we should now call the mind was in his view related partly to the body and partly to the soul. He distinguished between a lower, sensuous, and a higher, rational grade of consciousness. Believing that it was impossible to reduce the higher reasoning powers, free-will, and self-consciousness to organic processes, he held that the intellect was dependent upon the senses for its material data, but independent of the body in respect of thought and volition: this was the proof of its spirituality. Soul is immortal, but body, in a changed form, is ultimately to be reunited with it.

Thus Christian thought on the body-mind relationship, as Robinson[5] points out, is fundamentally monistic, and 'involves the rejection of dualism'. Nevertheless under the influence of Platonism, a disguised Manichaeanism, Puritanism, or the Cartesian philosophy, it has always been liable to lapse into dualism, and identify the personality with the soul viewed in isolation from the body.

Eastern thought on the subject differs so much from Western that it can hardly be expressed in the same terms.[6] To the Chinese and to some Indian schools of thought it appeared obvious that the individual was a microcosm or mirror of the universe, and subject therefore to the same laws which were invoked to explain the universe. No relationship between the mind and the brain was known to either, though it was accepted in the West at least as early as Hippocrates, but in India the heart was thought to be the seat of some psychological functions. The Chinese did not believe in a mind or soul which survived the body: in India there were several different conceptions, and both Hindu and Buddhist beliefs included the idea that the psychical faculties survived the body, the individual soul being a particle of a world soul. The doctrine of the transmigration of the soul envisages its re-embodiment in a succession of lives, its fate being determined by the individual's behaviour. The aim is to escape from this by attaining Nirvana, which means deliverance, and which has been regarded by some as a purely negative, by others as a positive state.

The modern form of the problem of the brain-mind relationship dates from Descartes,[7] who sought to express scientifically beliefs hitherto held in varying and often vaguer ways by philosophers and theologians. Descartes, arguing from the observation that many human movements and other activities were automatic, concluded that animals were pure automata, devoid of mind or consciousness. Man alone possessed a mind guiding the automatisms of his body, and distinguished from it by being unextended and indivisible instead of extended and divisible. This doctrine had many consequences. The most obvious question it raised was how body and mind could act upon one another, and so far nobody has succeeded in answering this question to the general satisfaction. An attempt was made to escape from the difficulty by the theory of psycho-physical parallelism, which conceived body and mind not as interacting but running parallel with one another in a pre-established harmony. In practice this usually led to treating them as though they were two aspects of the same thing, and increasing knowledge of physics and physiology soon showed that it provided no more than a verbal solution. For as it came to be believed that bodily events, including the functions of the nervous system, could, theoretically at least, be explained in purely mechanical terms, this reinforced Descartes' view of animals as automata, but added to the difficulty of seeing how mind and brain could interact. Moreover, if mental activities were to be regarded as parallel with mechanically-determined cerebral ones, it would seem that they too must be determined.

The problem was further complicated by the discovery of evolution. If man's body, which included his brain, was to be explained as having developed from the simpler bodies of lower animals, was the same true of his mind also? If not, the evolution of man from his subhuman ancestors could not have been a continuous process: he must be qualitatively different from the animals, and some additional factor—mind or soul— must have been introduced into evolution at some point by some super-natural agency. The same question arises in the development of the individual, and Christian theology teaches that the soul is created by God at the moment of conception.

It should be clear by now that questions involving the use of the terms body, mind, and soul, are beset by confusions originating in the past. Scientists, philosophers, and theologians have differed as to what con-stitutes body and mind, and as to the distinction between mind and soul. Other ill-defined terms, such as reason and spirit, have made the confusion worse. Mind has sometimes been regarded as superior to soul, and for many centuries a multiplicity of souls was postulated to preside over different bodily functions. Spirit, now identified for the most part with soul, was in the past used as a name for various supposed physiological entities. Reason, again, has been subdivided into higher and lower, and frequently treated as a function distinguishing man from the animals.

Psychology, rather surprisingly perhaps, contributed to this process of hypostatization. Mind was divided into conscious and unconscious, and the latter subdivided again. Freud created a variety of semi-autonomous mental entities, such as the id, ego, superego and censor, conceived as often in conflict with one another.

Among present-day philosophers there is no agreement as to the proper use of the words mind and mental, but much of the confusion, which appears to be semantic in origin, might have been avoided if people had been content to speak in terms of human subjective experiences and behaviour rather than of hypothetical entities.

It would take too long to trace all the consequences of this confusion, even those which have sprung from the theological distinction between body and soul. Some have already been mentioned, and a few more should perhaps be borne in mind. For centuries the Christian Church taught that it was justifiable to inflict the most horrible tortures on the body with the object of saving the soul, and medicine in the past under the influence of the daemonic hypothesis has advocated the infliction of all sorts of distresses upon the bodies of the insane, in order to drive out the evil spirits which were supposed to be causing the illness. Today, theological doctrines on the subject still have many practical implications; for example, the Catholic teaching that it is wrong to sacrifice an unborn child to save the life of its mother. A not insignificant by-product of the doctrine that animals are unfeeling automata, or that man alone has an immortal soul, has been the toleration of cruelty to animals in some countries where this belief obtains.

Brain and Mind

I shall use the term 'mind' to describe our subjective experiences, such as thinking, knowing, feeling and willing. We infer the existence of mind in other people, and most animal psychologists infer mental activities in animals, from their behaviour. The evidence for the unconscious mind is that mental activities, which if they were conscious we should describe as feeling and willing, can influence a man's actions without his knowledge.

Ignorance of the functions of the brain has until recently favoured the dualist view, because, while some kind of dependence of the mind upon the brain was obvious from such common experiences as unconsciousness produced by a blow on the head, until comparatively recently we have lacked any detailed correlation between cerebral and mental functions. Some account of this new knowledge will now be given.

A very large amount of experimental work has been carried out upon animals with the object of ascertaining how their behaviour can be correlated with the activity of their nervous systems. Comparative anatomy has contributed to this by showing how during evolution increasing complexity of behaviour is paralleled by the development of particular parts of the brain. Experimental lesions have demonstrated the dependence of learning, perceptual discrimination and memory upon particular brain areas. Genetics is elucidating the inheritance of behaviour traits, including those involving qualitatively different sensory experiences; and evolutionary theory, as will be shown later, has thrown light upon the role of mental activity in social and cultural evolution. And—a point of particular importance when we come to consider man —it has been shown that in animals the most anterior part of the brain, part of the cortex of the frontal lobe, is concerned with the ability to bring past experience to the solution of present problems.[8]

Turning now to man, we may begin with the familiar observation that the failure of the brain to develop limits the development of the mind and leads to mental deficiency and, conversely, a general deterioration of brain function produced by disease in adult life is paralleled by a progressive deterioration in mental function. These general correlations, however, are perhaps less important than the specific effects of localized brain damage upon mind.

In this connection, behaviour disorders are of particular general interest, because it is often held that a sense of social and moral responsibility is a distinctively human characteristic. Attention was first directed to this aspect of brain damage by the disease known as encephalitis lethargica, which appeared in epidemic form during the decade following 1916. It was then noted that some children who had been attacked by this infection, and as a result suffered from destruction of the basal parts of the brain, became delinquent. They were often aggressive, committed criminal offences, and proved quite unamenable to ordinary social and legal sanctions. Temporary outbursts of aggressive and sometimes violent behaviour are known to occur in patients with other lesions, particularly in the temporal and less often in the frontal lobes, and in some cases surgical removal of the lesion leads to cessation of the outbursts of violence.

Studies of frontal lobe function in man[9] have shown that, as already hinted in the case of animals, this part of the brain is particularly concerned in the integration of personality. After sufficiently extensive damage here, the patient, though his general level of intelligence may be in no way impaired, lacks forethought and social consideration. The operation of prefrontal leucotomy is designed to reduce incapacitating pathological emotional tensions. After the older, more extensive, operations it was often observed that there was a loss of initiative and sense of social responsibility. The value of this operation springs from the close relationship between the frontal lobes and those basal parts of the brain which are active when we experience emotions. Something has been learned about the physiological basis of emotion and its control, and it is interesting that a powerful emotion, such as intense fear, may be experienced without any other cause than a localized discharge of nerve impulses which forms part of an epileptic attack.[10]

Memory plays such a vital part in maintaining the personality, that some dualist philosophers have maintained with Bergson that it is a function of an independent mind, being merely brought into play, as it were, by the activity of the brain. If, however, we study the effects of damage to the brain upon memory, we find that there is no simple or single function which can be so described, and that the availability of past experiences is not a general function but a series of specific ones related to particular activities. These various kinds of memory depend upon the integrity of different parts of the brain. Thus permanent damage to quite a small area of the brain (the hippocampal region) has been shown to abolish permanently the ability to recall recent experiences.[11] Patients with such damage will have no recollection of what happened to them only an hour or two previously. Nevertheless, they may have no difficulty in recalling the distant past, and their mental life may be in all other respects unimpaired: they continue to recognize people and things, and to retain their previous skills. More diffuse types of brain damage, however, may abolish the memories of the remote as well as the immediate past, and, not surprisingly, such loss of virtually all memory is associated with a severe disintegration of the personality. On the other hand, there may be a highly selective loss of a particular kind of memory. Thus a patient whose vision is unimpaired may lose the kind of memory which enables him to recognize objects, or even people, by sight, yet he may still recognize objects by touch or people by their voices. He may be able accurately to describe a familiar route near his home, as if he were looking at it on a map, and yet unable to find his way on that route owing to failure to recognize the various landmarks. Another patient may be able to recognize landmarks, but have lost the 'topographical' memory for routes. The electrical stimulation of the brain carried out in the course of surgical operations on conscious patients under local anaesthesia has established that it may be possible to evoke a particular memory again and again by stimulating the same area, usually in the temporal lobe.[12]

Neurologists are familiar with the fact that a patient suffering from a brain lesion may not only lose a particular kind of awareness, but be unaware that it has been lost. Striking instances of this occur in connection with the perception of the body itself.[13] For example, a patient may be unaware that one of his arms belongs to him, and deny that it does so, saying that it belongs to the patient in the next bed, or that it is some foreign body. He may lose the awareness of one half of the body in this way, and neglect to wash it, or to put the clothes on it when he dresses. Something similar occurs in a certain variety of aphasia, in which the patient talks complete nonsense, but is unaware that he is doing so, in contrast to patients with other forms of aphasia, who realize that they are making mistakes in speech, and do their best to correct them.

The foregoing are all examples of disorders of mental functions produced by damage to the brain. The type of disorder is inexplicable in terms of mental organization unless that is another aspect of the anatomical and physiological organization of the brain. None of the instances cited supports the view that mental functions exist independently of the brain. For example, there is nothing to point to a mental storage of memories separate from their physical basis; and none of the disorders of mental function described provides any evidence of an independent mind able to compensate for difficulties created by the disorganization of the brain. On the contrary, it is striking that in the cases of disordered awareness of the body, and unawareness of aphasia, what is left of the patient's mind continues as if unaware that anything is wrong. As two writers on the subject recently put it, 'it is as if the part of mind related to the particular function in question did not exist'.[14] This is in contrast to Lashley's observations on rats that learned reactions could survive the removal of any part of the brain.

Apart from the effects of localized brain lesions which we have just been considering, the more serious forms of mental illness demonstrate, perhaps even more pointedly and poignantly, the relation between brain and mind. Though there is still much to be learned, there is an increasing belief that the cause of both cyclothymia and schizophrenia is likely to be a bio-chemical disorder of brain function, in some cases genetically determined. But from the monistic standpoint there is nothing surprising in the fact that such illnesses may be precipitated by psychological stress. Moreover, there exist many degrees of variation between the normal and the grossly abnormal, and it is a paradox of psychology that such pathological variations seem often to have contributed to the creative insights of great artists and thinkers. What is significant for our present purpose, however, is the evidence that the whole personality can be changed, temporarily or permanently, by what appear to be changes in brain physiology. The remarkable temporary effects upon perception and feeling of the hallucinogenic drugs, mescaline and lysergic acid, and the therapeutic value of the 'tranquillizers', are further evidence of the importance of the physical basis of mind; even though as yet they do no more than hint at possible causes of mental illness.

At this point it is natural to ask how far neurophysiology has progressed towards an understanding of the physiological basis in cellular function of the highest mental functions, such as conceptual thought, and memory. In this field there is still a very long way to go. Let me quote a frank statement recently made by a neurophysiologist.[15] Speaking of the dualist position adopted by Sherrington and Eccles, he says: 'This position is not acceptable to all physiologists. It appears to some of them, including myself, a position into which one may be forced by exclusion of alter-natives, but we are far from having the evidence to exclude such alternatives. We hesitate, though, when it comes to formulating more tenable proposals in familiar terms. One way of expressing our faith— and it is just that—is to say that there remain to be discovered new and emergent levels of physiological relations between neurons in masses, which will explain the gaps in our understanding of the phenomena of behaviour, and that mind is simply a name for some of these relations or their consequences.' This faith is shared by many leading physiologists and psychologists. What emerges from the facts we already know is that knowledge of brain physiology both in man and animals has an ever-increasing contribution to make to our understanding of the highest mental functions—thought, memory, feeling and social responsibility.

The Psychological Interpretation of Mind

So far we have been considering disturbances of mental function which have to be explained in terms of disordered brain function. Now let us turn to the explanation of disorders of the mind in psychological terms. The patient's present mental symptoms may be traced back to, and understood in terms of, his previous mental experiences, which constituted his reactions to what happened to him in the past. Psychoanalysis is of course the outstanding example of a system of psychopathology which seeks to explain psychological symptoms in this way, with particular reference to the experiences of infancy and the early years of life, but there are other schools which put forward similar claims, with different interpretations. Freud's doctrines are still being criticized and modified, but it seems likely that at least two of his ideas are of great and permanent importance—his concept of unconscious mental activity, and his stress upon the determining force of infantile experiences on subsequent psychological development, which has important ethical implications. Work such as Bowlby's,[16] which correlates the psychological development of man and animals, seems likely to be illuminating. Psychopathology has also contributed the fruitful concept of mental dissociation, characteristic of hysteria, whereby elements in the mental life are cut off from the rest of the personality. This reaches its extreme form in multiple personality, in which several alternating personalities, with mutually exclusive memories, co-exist in the same 'individual', if we may use a term which seems paradoxical in the circumstances!

The Evolution of Mind

The monistic view implies that mind is present from the beginning, inherent in the stuff of which the world is made. Seen from one aspect this is matter, from the other, mind, but each at first is extremely simple in organization. One of the most striking developments in recent evolutionary thought has been the increasing recognition of the part played by mind, or behaviour, in the evolutionary process, for behaviour may influence the survival value of genetic changes as well as sometimes modifying the environment itself. Some salient features in the evolution of mind have been reviewed in de Chardin's recent book, *The Phenomenon of Man*.[17] The two cardinal characteristics of the correlative development of matter and mind are that increasing complexity of material organizational units is paralleled by increasing complexity of mind, and that this developing process is not throughout uniform and gradual, but after a period of gradual progress reaches a point at which a sudden disturbance of equilibrium occurs, which permits the emergence of new qualities and activities. One such was the transition from 'non-living' to 'living' matter: a much later one with which we are more particularly concerned, was that which characterized the development of man from his hominid ancestors, namely the development of conceptual thought and the addition of self-consciousness to consciousness. The anatomical, physiological and psychological factors which contributed to bring this about were, no doubt, complex, but it is probable that the two outstanding ones were the closely-linked development of social life and the acquisition of speech. There is abundant evidence that animals possess the capacity both for learning, and up to a point abstracting certain features from a perceptual situation. They also communicate with one another. In man, however, all these capacities are, as it were, raised to a higher power. Speech alone makes the leap of symbolic representation whereby it becomes possible not merely to excite reactions or feelings in others, but to convey ideas in a most economical fashion, and this process in itself becomes a tool in the service of conceptual thought. From this arises a new 'layer' of evolution, which de Chardin in his pregnant phrase calls the noösphere, and which now extends over the whole earth.

The noösphere has been evolving and is continuing to evolve with an accelerating acceleration in ways which have no counterpart in the pre-human phases of life. Before the development of speech the mind of the individual exercised no influence on later generations, except in so far as its simple patterns of behaviour might be copied by its offspring, or other members of its social group. Speech at once made it possible for the experiences of the individual to be handed on in the social group in the form of verbal tradition, and this important transcendence by mind of the life of the individual was enormously enhanced by the development first of writing, and then of printing. By these cumulative achievements social cultures became established, moulding the lives of the individuals composing societies, interacting in various ways with one another, and exhibiting their own phases of growth and decay. And within the memory of many now living, the noösphere has undergone further developments which future historians may regard as initiating a new state of culture for mankind, namely the transmission of ideas and pictures by the radio. This, coupled with the air transport of people, is rapidly breaking down the geographical isolation which in the past has done much to maintain the cultural differences between human societies.

Conclusion

Thus we are now, for the first time, beginning to acquire a comprehensive view of mind. We see it inherent in the evolutionary process, growing from elementary beginnings into a subordinate, and finally the dominant factor in evolutionary advance. We see the great transition from individual to psychosocial evolution, the latter the matrix for the development not only of conceptual thought and the techniques that it has produced, but also of 'spiritual' values, ethics, and artistic creativeness. We are beginning to achieve a scientific understanding of the factors which influence the development of the individual mind, and its relationship to society, and we may hope in time to attain to something better than the haphazard and empirical approach which now determines so many questions of vital importance to both the individual and society. It has not been possible in this short essay to discuss the philosophy and implications of the views put forward, but at least it should be emphasized that monism is not materialistic. On the contrary, we have direct knowledge of mind; while our knowledge of physical events is always mediated through mind, and described in the symbolic terms employed by science. As Lashley[18] says, 'psychology is to-day a more fundamental science than neurophysiology. By this I mean that the latter offers few principles from which we may predict or define the normal organisation of behavior, whereas the study of psychological processes furnishes a mass of factual material to which the laws of nervous action in behavior must conform.' Furthermore, while the brain is an object extended in space we are all familiar with mental activities, for example thoughts and feelings, which are not thus extended. This is Descartes' problem again, but the solution would seem to lie, not in postulating some relationship between an unextended mind and an extended body, but in finding a new unitary field geometry to describe the spatio-temporal events in living organisms. The possibility that we may here be touching the fringe of regions of knowledge of which we have little apprehension is suggested by telepathy, extra-sensory perception, and mystical experiences, all of which many reject because they appear to conflict with our existing scientific concepts of the universe, but which nevertheless demand open-minded investigation.

Moreover, man is not merely intelligent and self-conscious: he has been since prehistoric times an artist. In the vast range and variety of the arts he uses creative imagery to express his insights and enjoyments. No doubt. a psychological and even a physiological account of artistic activity could be given, but in such analyses 'we murder to dissect', and the experience itself escapes us, for it can be known only by being experienced, and is its own validation. Science provides very real emotional satisfactions, but it cannot, and does not seek to, replace the modes of awareness which appeal directly to human feelings.

Man has always created images also of the universe as a whole—images to satisfy his need, not only to comprehend it intellectually, but to respond to it emotionally. No such image has hitherto gained universal acceptance, or enabled us to solve the major problems of human culture. Humanism can contribute the vision of life as one, and an understanding of man's nature both as body and mind in the light of the development of the race and the individual, and of all that science can teach. But Jung's psychology, decried by the psycho-analytical school, has at least shown in a wider context the place of imagery in the expression of the dark non-rational side of human nature, and in the relation between the attitudes of the conscious and the unconscious mind to life and the universe. The emotional needs which are embodied in such images must also find expression, understanding and satisfaction in the religion of the future.

REFERENCES

(1) The Notebooks of Samuel Butler, 1915, p. 324.
(2) Plato. *The Phaedo* and *The Republic*, Book 4.
(3) Aristotle. *De Anima*.
(4) Aquinas, Thomas. *The Summa Contra Gentiles*. Vol. 2, London, 1923.
(5) Robinson, H. Wheeler, in J. Hasting's *Encyclopaedia of Religion and Ethics*. New York: Scribner.
(6) Keith, Ilza. 'Non-western Concepts of Psychic Function' in *The History and Philosophy of the Brain and its Functions*. Springfield, Ill.: Thomas, 1959.
(7) Descartes' *Philosophical Writings*, selected and translated by Norman Kemp-Smith. New York: St Martin's Press, 1953.
(8) Pribram, Karl, in *Behavior and Evolution*, edited by Anne Roe and George Gaylord Simpson, Yale University Press, 1958, p. 140.
(9) *The Frontal Lobes*. Research Publications Association for Research in Nervous and Mental Disease, 1948, Vol. 27.
(10) Williams, Denis. 'The Structure of the Emotions Reflected in Epileptic Experiences.' *Brain*, 1956, pp. 79, 29.
(11) Scoville, W. B., and Milner, B. 'Loss of Recent Memory After Bilateral Hippocampal Lesions.' *Journal of Neurology, Neurosurgery and Psychiatry*, 1957, pp. 20, 11; also Walker, A. E. 'Recent Memory Impairment in Unilateral Temporal Lobe Lesions.' *Archives of Neurology and Psychiatry*, 1957, pp. 78, 543.
(12) Penfield, Wilder, and Jasper, Herbert. *Epilepsy and the Functional Anatomy of the Human Brain*. Boston: Little, 1954.

(13) Critchley, Macdonald. *The Parietal Lobes*. New York: Williams & Wilkins, 1953.

(14) Denny-Brown, D., and Chambers, R. A., in *The Brain and Human Behavior*. London: Research Publications Association for Research in Nervous and Mental Disease, Vol. 36, 1958, p. 110.

(15) Bullock, T. H., in *Behavior and Evolution*, edited by Anne Roe and George Gaylord Simpson. Yale University Press, 1958, p. 166.

(16) Bowlby, John. 'The Nature of the Child's Tie to Its Mother.' *International Journal of Psychoanalysis*, 1958, Part 1, p. 39.

(17) Teilhard de Chardin, Pierre. *The Phenomenon of Man*. New York: Harper, 1959.

(18) Lashley, K. *The Neuropsychology of Lashley*. New York: McGraw-Hill, 1960.

GENERAL READING

Cerebral Mechanisms in Behavior; the Hixon Symposium, edited by Lloyd A. Jeffress. New York: Wiley, 1951.

Brain and Consciousness; by Hartwig Kuhlenbeck. Basle and New York, 1957.

The Brain and Human Behavior; Research Publications Association for Research in Nervous and Mental Disease, Vol. 36, 1958.

Brain Mechanisms and Consciousness; a symposium edited by J. F. Delafresnaye. Oxford, 1954.

Brain, Memory, Learning; W. Ritchie Russell, New York: Oxford University Press, 1959.

Behavior and Evolution; edited by Anne Roe and George Gaylord Simpson. Yale University Press, 1958.

The Physical Foundation of Biology; Walter M. Elsasser. New York: Pergamon; Los Angeles, 1958.

Biological and Biochemical Bases of Behavior; Symposium on Interdisciplinary Research, University of Wisconsin, 1955, edited by Harry F. Harlow and Clinton N. Woolsey. Madison: University of Wisconsin Press, 1958.

'Physiological Mechanisms in Animal Behaviour'; Symposia of the Society for Experimental Biology, No. 4, New York: Academic Press, 1950.

'Intelligence, Brain Function and the Theory of Mind'; D. O. Hebb. *Brain*, 1959, pp. 82, 260.

C. H. WADDINGTON

THE HUMAN ANIMAL

C. H. WADDINGTON, C.B.E., M.A.,
SC.D., F.R.S.

Born 1905. Educated: Clifton College;
Sidney Sussex College, Cambridge.
Buchanan Professor of Animal Genetics,
Edinburgh University since 1947.

Publications: *Introduction to Modern
Genetics*, 1939; *Principles of Embryology*,
1956; *The Strategy of the Genes*, 1957; *The
Ethical Animal*, 1960, etc., and many articles
in scientific journals.

THE HUMAN ANIMAL

The biologist who looks from his professional standpoint at the human race sees man, of course, first as an animal: *Homo sapiens*, one of the species belonging to the family of primates, who are a subclass of the mammals and a branch of the great vertebrate stock. Even that bald identification carries with it many implications and it is as well to begin by enquiring just what they are.

From the earliest beginnings of scientific enquiry until quite recently, biology has been in two minds as to how to envisage the essential nature of animals and plants. One tendency has been to see them as nothing but rather elaborate machines. Descartes can be taken as an early and fairly extreme exponent of this view. The other tendency has been to suggest that, quite apart from any question of a specifically human soul in the theological sense, all animals and plants contain in their essence some non-material or vital principle. Even many of those who provided straight-forward causal or mechanical explanations of some particular activities of living things have frequently argued that, over and above such detailed processes, or, if you like, behind them, there must be some essential, living, non-material agency. This was the view, for instance, of Harvey who, with his discovery of the circulation of the blood, actually did considerably more than Descartes himself to reveal some of the mechanical processes on which animal life depends. The logical opposition between these two views grew deeper as knowledge of material mechanisms became more clear-cut and more precisely formulated. It reached its height perhaps in the latter years of the nineteenth century, at a time when the physical scientists were profoundly convinced that matter consists of billiard-ball atoms and that is all there is to it. By this time the practical successes of physical theory were so great, and had won for it such a dominating position in scientific thought, that the few remaining vitalists, such as Driesch, had almost the position of isolated eccentrics.

Within a decade or two, around the turn of the century, the whole picture changed radically, and the long-standing 'vitalist-mechanist controversy' effectively vanished from the scene of biological thought. It disappeared because it was borne in on both sides that they had been over-simplifying matters. On the one hand, the physical scientists discovered that it is inadequate to reduce matter to a collection of impenetrable and unchanging billiard-ball-like atoms. They found themselves instead forced to think in terms of subatomic particles, wave-mechanics, relativity and the interconvertibility of energy and matter, and even at a loss to support the principle of causal determinacy. No force was left in the statement that living things were nothing but matter, since it had transpired that matter itself was still a most incompletely comprehended mystery.

At the same time, thinkers about biology realized that when simple units become structurally arranged into complicated systems, these systems can exhibit new properties which can be understood by hindsight but not necessarily by foresight.[1] That is to say, certain properties of the units may never be exemplified except in the conditions created by the assemblage of the units into organized structural complexes. The crucial point is that one cannot expect, from examining the behaviour of the units in isolation, to deduce all the activities which may be shown by a suitably structured arrangement of them; any more than by looking at a few pieces of wire, glass, plastics, nuts and bolts, etc., we could deduce that when suitably arranged as an electronic computer they could beat us at chess.

It became obvious, in fact, that the explicative power of architecture or organization—what has sometimes been rather grandiloquently referred to as emergent evolution—is so enormous that any temptation to invoke a vitalistic principle over and above this, almost totally vanishes. We can safely say that living things are complex arrangements of 'matter', but since we have scarcely any clue to what matter is, and the main information we have about complex arrangement is that it is almost incredibly efficient at producing unexpected results, this statement can do little more than allay uncalled-for philosophical qualms, and in point of fact adds next to nothing to our understanding of the situation.

Biologists were then able to devote themselves with an open mind to the study of their proper subject-matter, the living world. One aspect of their endeavour has been to try to discover what should be taken as the basic units out of which living things are built. Putting it very briefly, the conclusion that has emerged so far is that the most characteristic processes of life depend on the activities of protein molecules operating as organic catalysts or enzymes which speed up certain reactions to rates much faster than they would otherwise show; but that the specific character of these enzymes is determined at a more fundamental level by the hereditary factors, or genes (in whose composition nucleic acids are probably more important than proteins), which an animal or plant inherits from its parents.

These studies on the basic mechanisms of living processes do not offer much illumination on the problems of how human life should be conducted. More suggestive insights arise in connection with the other major aspect of biological study, that is, the investigation of the ways in which the ultimate units are combined together. The most important point is an extremely general one, namely that all biological organization, whether of cells, individual organisms or populations, is involved in temporal change. Life is through and through a dynamic process. Any mode of thought which attempts to attribute to man or any other organism any form of unchanging essence, or any character that is conceived as *being* rather than *becoming*, flies in the face of our whole understanding of biology.

The flux of becoming which is so characteristic of all living things is perhaps most clearly and inescapably expressed in the phenomena of embryonic development. We can watch a fertilized egg begin its life as a small almost featureless lump of living material, and gradually develop into an adult of considerable obvious structural complexity. In many cases, for instance in birds, it carries out this performance inside an eggshell which effectively insulates it from outside influences, except of such a crude and general kind as a reasonable temperature. It is clear that the fertilized egg must already contain within it substances whose reactions with one another suffice to ensure the production of the various different organs and tissues out of which the adult is built.

One of the best analogies for the type of process that must be going on is the homely one of cheesemaking. A mass of milk-curds infected, perhaps by chance or by careful design, with appropriate strains of bacteria will, if left quite to itself in a cellar, pass in a stately manner through a series of changes by which it becomes metamorphosed into a Stilton in all its glory of ripeness. In a developing egg, the situation has many similarities with this, but is much more complex. In the first place, one and the same mixture can develop as it were into a Cheddar, a Camembert, a Brie, etc., as well as into a Stilton. The egg, composed of the cytoplasm together with a collection of hereditary genes, can develop into a liver as well as lungs, nerves as well as muscles, and in fact into a large range of sharply distinct types of cells and organs. It does not follow only a single pathway of change, but has a number of alternative possible pathways open to it, one part of the egg taking one path and another a different one. Again, it is a fact of observation that these pathways of change are rather resistant to modification. A part of an egg may develop into muscle or it may develop into nerve, but it is difficult to persuade it to develop into something intermediate between the two. Once it has started developing, for instance into muscle, it shows a strong tendency to produce a normal muscle even in the face of interferences that might be expected to divert it from its normal course and produce an abnormal end-result. The paths of change are, as I have said elsewhere, *canalized*. They are not like roads across Salisbury Plain, where it would be relatively easy to drive between them over the grass. They are more like Devonshire lanes; once you are in one, it is very difficult to get out again and you have to go on to where the lane ends.[2]

These pathways of change, along which the various parts of the egg proceed as it develops, are inherent in the constituents of the egg at the time when it begins its development after fertilization. The specification of the direction the paths take, and the nature of the end-result to which they lead, is in the main carried out by the hereditary genes which the egg has received from the two parents. If one of these genes is changed, some of the paths will be altered and an abnormal end-result obtained. There is no simple English word which can be used for this concept of a pathway which is followed by a system, and whose characteristics are defined by the nature of the system which enters on it. I have suggested that we might call them 'creodes', from the Greek words χρή, necessity, and ὁδός, a path.

A system is exhibiting creodic behaviour when it is changing along the course whose direction is defined by the system's own essential nature. It is not being creodic in so far as it is diverted from this path by the accidents which it encounters on its way. One could, of course, discuss how far the development of individual human personality, or the socio-economic development of particular societies, are or are not creodic in nature. Such questions are interesting but I do not think that our biological knowledge is necessarily very enlightening in connection with them.

It is more to the point here to turn to consider the other major type of temporal change with which biology is concerned. That is, of course, the process of evolution. The whole realm of living things as we know them today has been brought into being by evolution; and this, of course, includes man. The notion of evolution is by now not solely a theory about certain processes which may go on in the living world, but is one of the essential dimensions within which biological thought must take place. We cannot think of living things in modern biological terms without at the same time employing the concept of their evolution.

From the very beginnings of biological thought, for instance in the works of Aristotle, it has been clear to mankind that living things can be arranged in some sort of natural order; an order which in late medieval times was referred to as the Great Ladder of Being.[3] This stretched from the lowliest creatures, such as slugs and worms, through a series of intermediates to the lion, the lord of beasts, then to man, and then above him to the circles of angels and archangels. As this classification implies, untutored man has never hesitated to consider some of the classes of living things as lower and others as higher. Selfconscious and sophisticated thinkers may sometimes be heard to enquire by what right man classifies the living kingdom into a hierarchy in which—is it by chance?—he turns out to be at the top. Nearly all biologists, however, essentially agree with Aristotle in this matter, perhaps mainly for reasons rather similar to those by which Doctor Johnson refuted Berkeley; they would be willing to consider the claims of a worm to a higher status than man when the worm comes up and presents them. The overwhelmingly general view of biology, indeed, is that there not only is a natural order but that this is an evolutionary order, the higher stages having appeared on the earth's surface later than, and by derivation from, the earlier.

This type of evolutionary progression from lower to higher is technically known as *anagenesis*.[4] It has been discussed by many recent authors and in particular by Julian Huxley, who has emphasized the fact that it is by no means the only type of result that evolution brings about. As he points out, evolution may bring into being a type of creature which succeeds in surviving with comparatively little change through long periods of geological time, a process for which he uses the word *stasigenesis*. Again, another typical result of evolution in the non-human world is the breaking-up of a group of organisms by branching into a large number of species which differ in detail while still resembling one another in the broad outline of their type of organization—a process for which Rensch has coined another technical word, *cladogenesis*.[4] But these two kinds of evolutionary result are embroideries on a main theme; which is the succession, throughout the history of life on the earth, of a series of dominant types of organization, each a clear-cut advance on what went before—the unicellular organization succeeded by the multicellular, the primitive multicellular types, such as sponges, succeeded by more complex types such as sea-anemones and worms, those again by insects and fish, the fish by amphibia, reptiles, birds and mammals.

How, in terms of these concepts, do we see the situation of man? His appearance on the world scene is clearly not a case of mere stasigenesis, since he has changed from his non-human ancestors. Again, his mastery of conceptual thought and social communication mark off his biological organization as something radically different from that of his nearest biological relatives, the higher apes: he therefore cannot be considered the product of mere cladogenesis, but must be considered to have resulted from anagenesis, a real progressive change and not a mere modification in detail.

If one inspects the anagenetic changes which have gone on in the sub-human animal world, it is not too difficult to discern some of their general characteristics. For instance, one of the most important of them has been an increasing independence of the external environment, exemplified, for instance, in the evolution of creatures that can live on dry land or even in the air, as well as in the sea, and of animals which can maintain a constant body-temperature. Again, there has been an evolution of more precise and sensitive sense-organs, and a concentration of the nervous systems into a single central and ever further-evolving brain, leading to improved capacities of knowledge and feeling and awareness in general, and to the emergence of mind as an increasingly important factor in evolution. Both these trends can be considered as aspects of the evolution of an increasing capacity to make use of, or exploit, the openings for life offered by the earth's surface. Both also would lead to what, considered from the point of view of the individual, must be considered as an increased richness of experience. It is immediately obvious that the evolution of man is a further step in the same direction. No creature has been able to become so independent as he of the accidents of its environment; no creature has such faculties for experiencing not merely the elementary processes of the world, but the relations between them. The capacities with which man's evolution has endowed him are an immensely extended carrying-forward of the main progressive lines of pre-human evolution into radically new realms.

The most important respect in which the appearance of the human race extends the lines of advance of the sub-human world are in connection not with the results brought about by evolution, but with its very mechanism. Evolution depends, of course, on the passing from one generation to the next of something which will determine the character which that following generation will develop. In the sub-human world this transmission of what we may call, in a general sense, 'information' is carried out by the passing on of hereditary units or genes contained in the germ-cells. Evolutionary change involves the gradual modification of the store of genetically transmitted information. A few animals can pass on a meagre amount of information to their offspring by other methods: for instance, in mammals some virus-like agents which have effects very like hereditary factors may pass through the milk; in some birds, by the adults serving as models whose song is imitated by the youngsters, and so on. Man, alone among animals, has developed this extra-genetic mode of transmission to a state where it rivals and indeed exceeds the genetic mode in importance. Man acquired the ability to fly not by any noteworthy change in the store of genes available to the species, but by the transmission of information through the cumulative mechanism of social teaching and learning. He has developed a sociogenetic or psychosocial* mechanism of evolution which overlies, and often overrides, the biological mechanism depending solely on genes. Man is not merely an animal which reasons and talks, and has therefore developed a rational mentality which other animals lack. His faculty for conceptual thinking and communication has provided him with what amounts to a completely new mechanism for the most fundamental biological process of all, that of evolution.[5]

It is becoming common to say now that man must take charge in the future of his own evolution, but many who say this seem to be implying no more than that man must try to control the store of genes which are available and which will be available in later populations. In point of fact, the type of evolution of which man should take control is one which he has as it were invented for himself. His biological evolution—that is, the changes in the genes in future populations—will presumably continue, but these changes seem likely to be of relatively minor importance, at least in the near future, although they might eventually become a limiting factor.[6] For the alterations in which mankind is at present primarily interested—the types of change, let us say, which distinguish the societies which produced Newton, Shakespeare, Buddha, Confucius and Jesus Christ from scattered bands of neolithic hunters—the crucial evolutionary mechanism is one which depends on the sociogenetic transmission of information by teaching and learning.

If we can, in this way, see mankind as at present the most advanced phase in a process of progressive or anagenetic evolution in which the whole living kingdom is involved, it would seem to follow, clearly enough to convince most of those sympathetic to Humanist thought, that it is man's duty, not only to mankind but to the living world as a whole, to use his special faculties of reason and social organization to ensure that his own future evolution carries forward the same general trend.[6] This is, I think, the accepted Humanist position, as it is put forward for instance by Julian Huxley, Needham, and others, and accepted by bolder minds even among those who adhere to traditional religions, such as Canon Raven and Pierre Teilhard de Chardin.[6] I certainly do not dissent from the

---

* 'Psychosocial' is Huxley's word. To my mind, it suffers from some redundancy, since the social can hardly avoid being psychological. I prefer to use 'sociogenetic', which emphasizes the importance of the mechanism as a means of transmitting information from one generation to the next, which is the crucial point.

conclusions which such thinkers have drawn as to man's duty at the present time, but I feel that our actual understanding of the biological world and of man's nature allows us to carry the argument forward by two not unimportant steps. These arguments, which I shall now advance, are by no means yet generally accepted.

In the first place, we may ask whether the process of anagenesis which can be seen in the animal kingdom, and the farthest step in this direction which has been taken by the appearance of the human race, are mere contingent happenings, which have actually transpired but for which no underlying causes can be envisaged. I do not think so. I think one can see reasons why processes of an anagenetic kind must be among the types of change which evolution will bring about. The biological mechanism of evolution is, as we have said, founded on the genetic transmission of information from parent to offspring through the formation of gametes and their union to form fertilized eggs. This process, however, constitutes only the essential transmission by which the generations are connected. Several other components are necessary to make up the total machinery by which evolutionary change occurs. The best-known of these components is, of course, natural selection, which by favouring the reproduction of certain individuals more than that of others brings about alterations in the store of genes as they pass from generation to generation. But natural selection and heredity do not work alone. As I have argued in more detail elsewhere,[5] we have to take account also of the capacity of animals to select, out of the range open to them, the particular environment.in which they will pass their life, and thus to have an influence on the type of natural selective pressure to which they will be subjected. For instance, a rabbit or a blackbird, released among fields, will take refuge in the hedges or banks, while a hare or a lark will choose to live in the open grassland. And again, we should not forget the type of responsiveness which comes to characterize the various developmental pathways which the egg can follow, which has an influence on the effects which will be produced by any new hereditary modification that may occur. Thus, the complete evolutionary mechanism, or evolutionary system as I have called it, comprises at least four major sub-systems—the genetic system, the natural selective system, the exploitive system, and the developmental or epigenetic system.

Darlington[7] added a new dimension to evolutionary thought by pointing out that the genetic system would itself be subject to natural-selective pressures, and might itself evolve in such a way as to make it more efficient in passing on hereditary information in a form in which it is easily utilizable for the furtherance of evolutionary advance. For instance, the fully developed system of sexual reproduction found in the great majority of organisms, which is based on two sexes whose gametes unite to produce the offspring, is a very efficient mechanism for evolution, since it provides a way of recombining hereditary factors into a large number of new combinations, some of which may prove useful; but it itself is a considerable evolutionary achievement, since the most primitive living things, such as bacteria, do not possess it, though some of them have less advanced, so-called *parasexual* mechanisms which make some degree of recombination possible.[8] Now this same argument can be applied to the other sub-systems, and indeed to the evolutionary system as a whole. If we start with a world of living things capable of evolving, then not only will they do so, but the very pressures that bring about evolution will also tend to bring about an improvement in the mechanism by which evolution is mediated. Put in such abstract terms, this may sound a formidably complex notion, but actually it is easy to find quite everyday analogies for it. At the beginning of the Industrial Revolution, for instance, there were many factories capable of producing manufactured products; and the forces of competition between the factories, which we may for the purposes of this analogy compare to natural selection, not only brought about an evolution of the factory products (which correspond to the animals) into more elaborate and better fabricated articles, but equally brought to pass improvements in the organization of the factories themselves, that is to say, in the mechanisms by which the articles are produced. Again, to take another example, if a group of beginners take up the practice of playing card games with one another, they would not only become more skilful at playing the game they first start on, but are likely to pass on to playing subtler and more complicated games. Thus, this, as it were, two-tier evolution—an evolution of the end-product itself and also an evolution of the mechanism by which the end-product comes into being—is quite a normal sort of happening.

If we regard the biological evolutionary process from this point of view, we can see reasons why evolutionary changes, of the general character of those which are actually found, should have been expected to occur. One of the major components on which evolution depends is what we have called the exploitive system—the system by which animals choose and make use of the various possibilities for living which the world offers them. One of the evolutionary pressures which is bound to arise is, therefore, a tendency for an improvement in efficiency of the exploitive system. This is most clearly expressed in the evolution of the sense-organs and nervous system, and is, as we have seen, one of the major components of anagenetic evolution as we can trace it from the lowliest flatworms and jellyfish up to the higher vertebrates. Again, there will be evolutionary pressures acting to improve the genetic system. The enormous improvement—in rapidity of action, subtlety of recombination and regrouping of items, and so on—which has been brought about by the human sociogenetic system, as compared to the biological genic system, can therefore be seen as one example of a general category of change which evolution must have tended to produce.

We can in this way at least begin to envisage the course of evolution as we find it, not as something completely accidental but as exemplifications of general trends or types of change which we should expect. We shall perhaps never be able to assign precise reasons why that particular change which actually occurred was the one that did so out of all those possible. It is only in the broadest outline, when we are considering its general direction and categories of effects rather than particular effects, that we can see evolution as a creodic process whose course follows from the characteristics of the system itself; but even an understanding in very broad outline is preferable to the state of complete incomprehension which can do no better than accept what it finds in the living world as mere 'happening to be so'.

Although we can see that there would be an evolutionary pressure towards the production of an improved system of transmitting information, and that if one were to appear which was in any way more effective than the biological genetic system, it would bring with it great evolutionary advantages, we still could not have foreseen that this step would have been taken by means of the very remarkable and peculiar mechanism which seems to characterize the human species. Even the remarkable work which is now being carried out on the behaviour of sub-human animals, in which the psychosocial stage has not yet been attained, gives us little hint of what to expect.[9] Just how remarkable the human system is has only recently been brought home to us, largely as the result of the work of the psychoanalysts.

It is clear on first principles that any system of social transmission of information can only operate if in some way the potential recipients can be brought into a condition when they are ready to accept the content of the messages which are directed at them. In man, it appears that the moulding of the newborn infant into an effective recipient of social communications involves a most surprising process of projection and re-introjection of certain of his own impulses, together with the building up of internal representatives of parental authority, and a whole peculiar mechanism which is described in terms of such concepts as the super-ego, the ego-ideal and so on. At first sight, the story the psychoanalysts tell may seem extremely unlikely, but it seems to me they have now produced enough evidence to render it rather plausible, at least in broad outline; and on reflection one realizes that unless one is prepared to make the question-begging assumption that man is simply born socially receptive, some sort of process or other would have to be imagined by which he is brought into this condition.

Now, the second point I wish to urge, in extension of the normal Humanist argument, is that man's ethical feelings are essentially involved with, and in fact are actually a part of, the mental mechanism by which he is developed into a being capable of receiving and accepting socially-transmitted information. Unless some sort of authority-bearing system is developed in the mind of the growing individual, social transmission would break down because nobody would believe what they were told. One part of this authority-bearing system develops into what we call our ethical beliefs, to which indeed we usually attach an almost overwhelming authoritativeness. Another aspect of the system seems to be, unfortunately, a tendency to develop feelings of inferiority, guilt and anxiety—a situation in which one may, perhaps, glimpse, from the scientific angle of approach, the human predicament which is enshrined in the myth of the Fall of Man.*

Obviously more than mere acceptance of authority is involved in a fully developed system for the social transmission of information. One can, and in later life one must, compare what one is told with objective reality, and reject what proves false. Education is to some degree concerned with such corrective verification. But all this is really a second-order process. There must first be a reliable system of transmission, which corresponds to biological heredity, before there can be a process of verification, which we might compare to natural selection. Again, it is certainly true that man's innate genetic constitution provides him with potentialities, which are presumably absent or very weak in other animals, for developing his social transmission mechanism. One of the most impressive pieces of evidence for this genetic predisposition is provided by the life of Helen Keller, who although blind and deaf from early infancy, nevertheless came to grasp the fact that 'things have names', and thus showed that she had the basic faculty for apprehending language.[10] But it is only with the development, normally in the first few months of life, of these innate capacities to the point where the child accepts transmitted information that man's second evolutionary system begins to function.

If this argument is accepted, the connection between evolution and man's ethical nature is much closer and more intimate than even most

* These arguments are more fully developed in a recent book, *The Ethical Animal*.

Humanists have previously recognized. It is not merely the case that we can see ourselves as part of an all-embracing process of evolution and therefore can recognize a duty to further the general evolutionary tendencies. According to the argument advanced above, man is characterized by the emergence of a new evolutionary mechanism based on sociogenetic transmission, and in this transmission the development of something akin to ethical belief is an absolutely essential item in the mechanism. The orthodox Humanist argument is that it would be a recognizably good thing if we took steps to see that our ethical beliefs effectively controlled the further course of evolution. What I am arguing is that our ethical beliefs *must* influence the course of human evolution, since that is based on a mechanism of which those beliefs are an essential part. The question that is really at issue is not whether evolution shall be guided by ethical beliefs, but what kind of ethical beliefs shall guide it.

What the situation of man calls for, in fact, is the formulation of some criterion by which one could judge as between the various ethical beliefs to be found in different individual men and women or different human societies. It is not sufficient that Humanists should demand that future human evolution should be guided by ethical principles, since inevitably some sort of ethical principles—quite possibly, as the psychoanalysts have taught us, unconscious or only partially conscious ones—will in fact play an essential role in bringing it about. What we should be aiming at is that the ethical principles themselves should be subject to assessment according to some more inclusive criterion. The real contribution of the study of human biology and human evolution will come when it is used to help in the formulation of this supra-ethical criterion.

If the essential reason why mankind develops ethical beliefs at all is because this is necessary as an essential cog in the machine of social transmission by which human evolution is brought about, then it follows that we can judge between different ethical systems by considering how far they fulfil their function in furthering human evolutionary progress. I am not for a moment suggesting that we shall find it easy to reach a clear, let alone an agreed, answer, but we shall at least know what we are trying to do, and this, though by no means easy, is well worth doing—for instance, when one is weighing against one another the values of individualism and collective organization, of nationalism and internationalism, of increase in population numbers and increases in standard of living, and so on through the list of the major moral and social quandaries of today.

The basic Humanist position, derived from considering man's place in the biological world, is that in approaching such problems we have to consider them in relation to what we know of the actual *course* of progressive evolution in the sub-human, and in particular of the human world. The arguments I have put forward in the last few paragraphs, although they go beyond the orthodox Humanist case, only serve to reinforce its conclusions. Evolution is the very essence of living. Life could, indeed, be defined as the state of a system which is capable of evolving, and the essential characteristic of man—if you like to put it so, the 'soul'—which distinguishes him from the animals, is that he evolved by a mechanism that belongs to him alone, and which he alone can modify and improve.

BIBLIOGRAPHY

The best general references for modern views on the mechanism of biological evolution are:

Dobzhansky, T. *The Biological Basis of Human Freedom.* Columbia University Press, 1956.
Huxley, J. S. *Evolution: the Modern Synthesis.* New York: Harper & Brothers, 1942. *Evolution in Action.* New York: Harper & Brothers, 1953.
Simpson, G. G. *The Meaning of Evolution.* Yale University Press, 1949.
Waddington, C. H. *The Strategy of the Genes.* New York: Macmillan, 1957.

For the ethical implications of evolution, see Simpson and Dobzhansky's books above and:

Huxley, J. S. *Touchstone for Ethics.* New York: Harper & Brothers, 1947.
Teilhard de Chardin, Pierre. *The Phenomenon of Man.* New York: Harper & Brothers, 1959.
Waddington, C. H., and others. *Science and Ethics.* London: Allen & Unwin, 1942.
Waddington, C. H. *The Ethical Animal.* London: Allen & Unwin, 1960.

REFERENCES

(1) Needham, J. *Order and Life.* Yale University Press, 1936.
(2) Waddington, C. H. *Principles of Embryology.* New York: Macmillan, 1956.
(3) The expression of this idea in English poetry is discussed by E. M. W. Tillyard, *The Elizabethan World Picture.* New York: Macmillan, 1944.
(4) Rensch, B. *Evolution above the Species Level.* New York: Columbia, 1960. Translation and partial revision of *Neuere Probleme der Abstammungslehre*, 2nd ed. Stuttgart, Enke Verlag, 1947. For end-directed or teleonomic (adaptive) evolution, see C. S. Pittendrigh, 'Adaptation, Selection and Behavior', in *Behavior and Evolution*, ed. A. Roe and G. G. Simpson, Yale University Press, 1958.
(5) Waddington, C. H. 'Evolutionary Systems—Animal and Human', *Nature*, 183, 1634-1638; J. S. Huxley, 'Evolution, Cultural and Biological', *Yearbk. of Anthropol.*, ed. Morris, 1955; B. Rensch, *Homo Sapiens. Vom Tier zum Halbgott*, Göttingen, 1959.
(6) Muller, H. J. 'The Guidance of Human Evolution'. *Evolution After Darwin*,

Vol. 2. *Evolution of Man*, Chicago University Press, 1960; Teilhard de Chardin, Pierre. *The Phenomenon of Man*. New York: Harper & Brothers, 1959.

(7) Darlington, C. D. *The Evolution of Genetic Systems*. New York: Macmillan, 1939.

(8) Pontecorvo, G. *Trends in Genetic Analysis*. Columbia University Press, 1959.

(9) See the forthcoming book *Animal Behaviour*, ed. W. H. Thorpe, Cambridge University Press.

(10) Discussed in S. Langer, *Philosophy in a New Key*. Harvard University Press, 1942, Chap. 3.

J. BRONOWSKI

SCIENCE IS HUMAN

J. BRONOWSKI, M.A., PH.D.

Born 1908. Educated: Central Foundation
School; Jesus College, Cambridge. Director-
General of Process Development Depart-
ment of the National Coal Board since 1959.

Publications: *The Poet's Defence*, 1939; The
Common Sense of Science, 1951; *Science and
Human Values*, 1958, etc.

SCIENCE IS HUMAN

―――――

It is a paradox that the words 'human' and 'scientific' carry for us an undertone of opposition. We think of the humanities and the sciences as rivals for the minds of men, and we often picture the professional scientist as lacking, not merely in humane education, but in humane feelings. When we say tartly of a judgment that it is 'scientific', we usually imply that it ignores the human context in which it ought to be set.

This usage is odd because it flies in the face of history: it belies the beginning of modern civilization. Humanism entered the world that we know, and began to shape it, at the Renaissance in the fifteenth century.[1] It is true that the Renaissance is usually remembered for its achievements in the humanities: in literature, in art, and in architecture. But only elderly scholars still teach that these achievements, and these alone, make the Renaissance. Every young scholar now knows that the Renaissance had a second face; it was also the beginning of what historians have just learned to call the Scientific Revolution.[2]

In an exact sense, Renaissance Humanism was two movements in one: a movement of recovery of ancient knowledge, and a movement of discovery of new knowledge. The first of these movements was the classical Renaissance, which idolized the Latin poets and the Greek view of life; it was natural that the ancient knowledge that this movement recovered was mainly in the arts. But there was also very soon a more popular Renaissance which was inspired by the ancient models to look with fresh eyes directly at nature herself; and it was natural that much of the new knowledge that this movement discovered was in the sciences.[3] A characteristic classicist figure was of course Erasmus, who learned Greek at the age of thirty-four, and spent his life in trying to reconcile Christian morality with the Greek love of life. A characteristic popular figure was Leonardo da Vinci, who never learned Greek, and deliberately walked out of the rich Platonic culture of Florence. And the popular interest moved naturally from the exact and original drawings of men by Leonardo to the illustrated textbook of human anatomy by Andreas

Vesalius, which was one of the two pioneer works of the Scientific Revolution to be published in 1543.[4]

Thus there were two faces of the Renaissance, one of which we now call the humanist movement, and the other what we should now call a scientific movement. The two faces sneered at one another then as they have done ever since. Leonardo was contemptuous of more learned painters who did not go directly to nature, and boasted of himself, by contrast, that 'he who has access to the fountain does not need to go to the water-pot'.[5] On the other hand, the popular men seemed uncouth and overbearing to their classical rivals, and about 1540 Gyraldus (Giraldi), a representative and erudite humanist scholar, was already looking back with regret to 'the golden age, when no such thing as science existed on the earth'.[6]

2

If the two faces of the Renaissance were so soon at loggerheads, how had they ever come to start from one point? What had been the common impulse to recovery and discovery, that could link the humanist dream and the Scientific Revolution?

The answer, of course, is that both movements equally were in revolt against the dogmatism of the Middle Ages. Europe had been dominated for centuries by religious prohibition, which was visible in the absolutism of the Popes and in the asceticism of the monasteries. Man is a poor and sinful creature, the Middle Ages had said; the only goodness in the world comes from God; and this divine goodness must be imposed on man by absolute edicts. The Renaissance was in blunt opposition to these forbidding doctrines, and to the authoritarian structure of the Church which imposed them. Men can be good, it said; they can find the springs of right action in their own natures; and they have to find these springs for themselves. The Renaissance was inspired by the sense that man is and must be the source of his own strength.

This renewed sense of human self-confidence drove both the classical and the popular Renaissance. It is really a mistake to call the first of these the humanist movement, and the second the scientific movement, as if humanism had inspired only one of the two. The classical movement was a recovery of the unfettered knowledge of Greece, some of which was in fact scientific knowledge: the recovery of Greek mathematics in particular gave an important tool to the Scientific Revolution. The popular movement was an urge to independent discovery, in art as well as in science. Both movements asserted a common Humanism: that man has a right to take pride in his achievements, and that he must himself find whatever knowledge he claims.

Thus the Scientific Revolution, whether expressed in the anatomy of Vesalius or in the astronomy of Copernicus (whose book on the movement of the planets was also published in 1543), was always part of the Humanist Revolution. It was part of the Humanist aspiration to look at nature simply and directly through man's own eyes. And equally the Scientific Revolution was part of the Humanist revolt against accepting any doctrine on an authority which could not be challenged.

3

These two marks of Humanism, its self-confidence and its anti-authoritarianism, are visible in all the further developments of science since then. We may see them, for example, in the personalities of the men who have led the advances of science in every age. The first group of scientists to meet regularly, about 1610 in Rome, called itself, characteristically, the Academy of the Lynx-Eyed, and was started by an unorthodox young nobleman: Galileo was a member by invitation. The next important body, the Royal Society, was started by two groups of men who met fairly regularly during the troubles of Charles I and Cromwell, from about 1635. They were men whose sympathies, in politics and in religion, were mostly against the King. The ground of their opposition was essentially a protestant ground: that the only source of authority, in politics and in religion, is the consent of free men.[7]

The leadership in science of men with a reforming and protesting outlook, in the widest sense, has continued. For example, Isaac Newton was, strictly speaking, a heretic: he denied the doctrine of the Trinity, which was indeed a main stumbling-block to scientists in the seventeenth century. There continued to be many other scientists with unitarian views in the next century too, of whom Joseph Priestley (who was a unitarian preacher as well as a scientist) was perhaps the greatest. As English university education in the eighteenth century fell farther and farther behind new scientific and liberal thought, so these modern topics became more important in the private colleges run by dissenters. Most of the original scientific minds of the century were dissenters: sometimes they were tactful dissenters like Benjamin Franklin, but more often they were Quakers who accepted no kind of authority, like Benjamin Huntsman, the inventor of cast steel, and John Dalton, founder of the atomic theory and discoverer of colour-blindness.

In the nineteenth century also the leaders of science in England and in America came most often from nonconformist groups. Some of them took their rejection of Church authority so far that they were fundamentalists; Faraday and Philip Gosse were among these. To this day, it is striking that throughout the world the proportion of scientists who come from Roman Catholic families is small. And in our century, of course, the men who have made scientific history have come more and more from liberal and unorthodox backgrounds. The characteristic figure who comes into our minds when we think of a representative of science in our age is Albert Einstein—a great Humanist, both by upbringing and by temperament.

4

The scientist's sense of human confidence, and his rejection of dogmatic authority, were wonderfully expressed by Galileo before the Inquisition humbled him. When the Grand Duchess of Tuscany asked in 1613 how the movement of the planets round the sun proposed by Copernicus could be reconciled with the Bible, he answered in a long letter which hinges on one central assertion.[8] 'The Bible is not chained in every expression to conditions as strict as those which govern all physical effects,' wrote Galileo, 'nor is God any less excellently revealed in nature's actions than in the sacred statements of the Bible.'

Galileo is saying that nature is at bottom the most profound source of knowledge; and what he says implies that he conceives science not as a mere accumulation of observations and discoveries, but as a world picture. For when Galileo speaks of the revelation of God in nature, he cannot have in mind a chaos of isolated facts; he is thinking of a design, or at least an order, which the facts reveal to those who seek rightly. In the same way, Copernicus's general theory of 1543, and the elegant laws which Kepler then found in 1609 and 1619, were not intended merely to provide better timetables for the planets.[9] Copernicus and Kepler were both urged on by the belief that their analysis of the heavenly movements was more profound, more coherent, and more satisfying than that of their predecessors. To both of them, and they say this explicitly, nature became more beautiful when they understood her laws.

It will be well to make this point strongly: and to do so, I suggest that the reader (whether scientist or layman) asks himself what have been the outstanding advances in science since then. Each reader will have his own list, but there are some advances which every list ought to include.[10] Among these are Newton's theory of gravitation; the work of Linnaeus and others in systematically classifying plants and animals; the orderly arrangement of the chemical compounds by Lavoisier, and of the elements by Mendeleeff; Pasteur's overthrow of the vitalistic doctrine of spontaneous generation; Darwin's theory of evolution by natural selection, and Mendel's particulate theory of heredity which provided the genetical basis for it; Freud's elucidation of the relation of conscious to unconscious modes of thinking; the work of J. J. Thomson and Rutherford on the structure of the atom; the establishment by Planck of the discontinuity of energy, and by Einstein of the relativity of physical laws; and the most original idea in biology in our century, the elucidation by Watson and Crick of the pattern of atoms which enables life to reproduce itself.[11]

Every item in this list has practical consequences which have reshaped, or will reshape, the life of ordinary people everywhere. Yet every one of these theories is, or was in its day, a revolution of the mind: a change in the total picture of the world which civilized people carried in their heads. Each of these systems is a vision of nature, deriving its power, not from isolated new facts or inventions, but from a fundamental revision of men's ideas of the inner organization of nature. In this sense, each of these theories is not merely a discovery, but is truly a new creation.

5

What is it that science as we understand it has been looking for? It has looked for the secrets of nature, her hidden sources of understanding and of power. And here the difference between science since the Renaissance, and science before it, is very plain. Astrology, alchemy, and the other sciences of the Middle Ages believed that the power hidden in nature would be commanded by those who discovered a magic that would contradict her laws—would make the sun stand still, would turn base metal into gold, or would make men live for ever. A medieval formula was meant to be a spell to stop nature in her tracks, and to force her to give to the magician some power, some philosopher's stone, which is essentially unnatural. Humanism and the Scientific Revolution together overthrew this fantasy, and in its place put the modern conception: that the power of nature is at the command of those who use her laws, not of those who flout them. We see that nature is indeed a great store of power which, however, can be reached only in one way: by understanding the laws of nature. In spreading this view, science has of course cut the tap-root of all superstitions: the belief that the laws of nature can be supernaturally violated by divine miracles.

The mechanism of modern civilization needs to be served by practical science, and there is on the face of it no reason why it should foster theoretical science for this purpose. The practical attempts of the alchemists to make gold, for example, were quite divorced from their theoretical belief in the physics of Aristotle and Aquinas. If then theoretical physics has become the pampered darling of the Foundations in the last twenty years, it is because we have a conviction about nature which the Middle Ages did not have. This is the conviction that nature can be commanded only by those who understand her design.

This conviction expresses two basic beliefs together. One is the belief that nature is a coherent unity, and is never the plaything of supernatural forces. The Middle Ages thought that nature was kept going from instant to instant by a renewed miracle, and they could therefore suppose that the miracle might as easily be changed. Today only the addicts of the comic strip think of science in this way, as the casual miracle-mongering of (the word is characteristic) a Superman.

The other basic belief of science is that nature is accessible to the human mind. We have to hold that nature is rational, in the sense that she can be grasped by human reason. She follows consistent laws, and these laws can be discovered and understood by the human mind.

6

The essence of the scientific method is to extract laws from nature: that is, to organize our experience in such a way that it displays recognizable patterns. We analyse the experience, but we have to construct from our analysis a larger order which is necessarily a synthesis. We do not find order in nature, we put it there; or better, we put a substratum or framework of order as a basis under those natural appearances which form our experience. Copernicus did not see the earth go round the sun with his bodily eye, Newton did not see the moon fall a foot towards the earth in every ten miles of her travel, Darwin did not witness the descent of man, and Planck did not see energy arriving in a hail of quanta. Each of these pioneers elucidated a pattern of behaviour which underlies the appearances and makes them intelligible. The very words tell their story: what can be seen is only the appearances—the pattern must be inferred.

The order which science finds in nature is *derived* from our experience; it makes our experience comprehensible, but it cannot itself be directly experienced. Therefore we can have no assurance that the order we find at any one time is final. It is idle to seek in advance a guarantee that the

laws of nature that we have discovered will also cover all events which
will be experienced in the future. This simply cannot be demanded or
supposed. We base our arrangement of nature on our past experience, and
it must therefore be a partial arrangement. If the future were to conform
entirely to this partial glimpse, we should all be machines acting out a play
that we understood perfectly and yet could not change.

No, what science does is to make models of nature, which act out only
the consequences of the limited and partial mechanisms which we have
put into them. And we judge what we call the truth of the mechanism by
the closeness with which it continues to reproduce the events of our
experience. This is the inductive method, by which we first look for laws,
and then judge them to be confirmed if their consequences go on fitting
the observed facts.

7

The observed facts therefore come to preoccupy the day-to-day work of
scientists. Of course it seems odd that scientists, who want to make a model
of how the world *works*, spend most of their time in observing how the
world *is*. And as a result, most non-scientists think of science simply as a
procedure to accumulate new facts.[12] The excitement of science as a
world view, the parade of major theories which I have given, seem remote
from what the men with test-tubes do—and are indeed remote from what
the newspapers report them to have done.

The reason for this modern dichotomy of theory and fact, of ends and
means, is now apparent. Things were not always so. Aquinas could present
Aristotle's view of the world with an authority which could not be
challenged. He was not showing a model; he was stating a theory as a
fact, on divine authority, and he then needed to do no more than to point
to its general, rough accord with nature. But when Humanism challenged
divine authority, it opened an awkward question: on what ground is one
model of nature to be preferred to a rival model? And if the answer is to be
that one model is nearer the truth than another, we must have a test of
truth which is not authoritarian. If there is no absolute truth for a scientific
theory, if the models we construct can be supported but never completely
proved, then support must come from the consonance of the theory with
that which is beyond dispute—with the facts as they are. Facts have
become important because they form the only accessible support for a
theory. Even so, the correct prediction of facts is not an ultimate test for
the truth of a theory. Theories which have turned out to be only approximate, and which we no longer hold, have predicted a new fact correctly

before now, as Newton's system predicted the unknown planet Neptune.[13] No ultimate test for the truth of a theory exists. But at least, a prediction of new facts which proves to be false is a conclusive test for the falsity of the theory!

8

The subtle relation between theory and fact has been a stumbling-block to the humane understanding of science by non-scientists. Because this relation imposes on scientists the constant and continuing responsibility to test their world-picture by the facts, they have become preoccupied with the need, almost a moral need, to have the facts exactly right. As a result, scientists have often seemed to others, and even to themselves, to be little more than compilers of an accurate card-index. Nevertheless, the book of nature is not a card-index, and what science is looking for is still, always, the way the book is put together—the order into which the facts on the index cards fit.[14]

For example, if the book of nature did no more than list the facts in alphabetical order, we should then have to explain to ourselves what an alphabet is. And although any given alphabet, printed on a given piece of paper, is simply a thing, there is certainly no such abstract entity as 'an alphabet' in existence ready-made outside ourselves. 'Alphabet' is a human creation, a concept of order; and it illustrates that we cannot express any order or arrangement that we seek in nature without creating some general concept for it.

Each of the great scientific concepts of the last centuries was created to express a new order in nature. Newton did not observe the force of gravitation; he postulated it as a concept which would organize under a single idea all the movements of falling bodies and of the planets. Indeed, Newton did not observe any forces. He formulated the concept of force as part of his laws of motion, and it was an abstract concept (which Relativity has now discarded)—even though it was derived by analogy from the physical sense of effort which human beings feel when they push or pull something.

All scientific concepts have been created in this way, to act as kingpins and centres of organization for our thought, on which the mechanisms which we picture to lie behind the observed appearances revolve. For example, we can judge the importance of the theories which I listed earlier by noting the new concepts which they created. If we turn back to the list, we find that these new concepts include mass, energy, families or natural groupings of plants and animals, chemical combination and the chemical

elements, evolution, natural selection, particulate heredity, the unconscious, the fundamental particles, quanta, space-time, molecular structure,
and the profound concept of chance as a form of natural law.

9

Behind these particular concepts stands the concept at the base of all
science, the concept of law. Of course the concept of law derives from
legal ideas, and they were adequate to explain it in science so long as men
believed in a divine law-giver. That is, the word 'law' in science made
legal sense so long as it was supposed that there was an authority which
imposed these laws on nature, and which was free at any time to impose
other laws. But from the seventeenth century, scientists were no longer
willing to accept God as an arbitrary, and therefore essentially lawless,
imposer of laws. Instead, the Puritan scientists formed the strange picture
of God as a servant of the laws of nature, which took their force from Him
and yet which bound Him. For example, Newton held that the planets run
like a simple clockwork ever since God started them. Yet Newton also
held, with his characteristic oddity, that God has still to attend to this
clockwork from time to time when outside accidents disturb it. Thus God
became a watchman who saw to it that the laws of nature were not
disobeyed. In effect, it became the business of God to see that there should
be no miracles.

A remarkable result of this new view of law in science was that it
changed the view of law in society also. Hobbes, Locke, and the eighteenth-
century philosophers in France struggled towards a new theory of the
State, in which the State was seen as an organization not for imposing
social laws but for discovering them. Thus the idea of natural law became
a social doctrine by way of its scientific influence, which Locke in particular acknowledged; and the revolutions of 1689 in England and of 1789 in
France took their justification, and much of their inspiration, from a
concept imported from science.

10

The history of science is often presented as a dry catalogue of inventions
and theories. Now we see in these examples that it is an exhilarating branch
of human history, because it is the history of the most fertile ideas which
have subtly changed human society since the Renaissance.

Consider as a last example the concept of Relativity. It began in 1905 as a formal explanation of some contradictions implied in the findings of nineteenth-century physics. As a concept, Relativity shows that the observer enters in an essential way into the events that he observes, and that there is therefore an inescapable connection between scientific laws and those who formulate them. This concept has since spread far beyond science, and has become the most disruptive but also the most formative of the general ideas which have entered social thinking in this century.

We are now about to witness the discovery of concepts as subtle as those of physics in new fields: immediately in the field of biology, then in psychology, and soon in the whole field of social studies. Of course social science already has much practical influence to its credit, and has liberalized the public mind on issues which once carried a fierce double charge of prejudice and emotion—issues such as flogging, capital punishment, homosexuality and sex-relations in general. But hitherto, the new ideas in social science have been at bottom simple and direct; they have not aspired to the subtlety or to the revolutionary impact of the concepts of physics from Newton onwards, or even of biology in the nineteenth century. The history of science as I have given it, however, shows that the most influential ideas in the long perspective of social change are by no means those that are obviously practical. It is ideas as subterranean as those of Hobbes on natural law and Mach on Relativity, of Pasteur on the material basis of life and Darwin on natural selection which, fifty years after they entered the intellectual life of society by the narrow door of science, are suddenly seen to have transformed it. So there are now beginning to appear, in the borderlands between biology and psychology, ideas which will have equally profound effects in social science. I have in mind, for example, the discoveries of recent years of the influence of drugs on perception and behaviour, which have opened a new field of understanding on the relation of body-chemistry to personality, and more generally of matter to mind. Here I think there is a starting-point for new ideas which will transform our understanding of social conduct and its organization.

II

One central idea which has come to us from biology has already demonstrated, a hundred years after its formulation, its gathering social force. This is the idea of evolution, in whose light history appears not as a random but as a directed process. It happens that Darwin's promulgation of evolution in *The Origin of Species* in 1859 touched off the most profound crisis in religious belief since Wesley's Revival, and perhaps since the Reformation. This is a just mark of the importance of the concept of evolution, because in fact the vision of history as a process is incompatible with the static vision of religious dogma. All the great religions have resisted change, in medieval Europe, in the Far East, in the Mohammedan countries of the Mediterranean, because change appears purposeless, and ultimately is unthinkable, in a world which God has already ordered to His design. In such a world, evolution is pointless as well as heretical. The apologists for religion in the last century protested against the thought that men are descended from an ape stock; but truly their protest sprang more deeply from a sense of outrage at the thought that man has changed at all, and is still changing. Bishop Wilberforce at Oxford in 1860 no doubt disliked T. H. Huxley for casting doubt on his ancestry, but perhaps at bottom what he could not stomach was that Huxley implied that there would one day be different and even better human beings than Bishop Wilberforce.

Since then we have grown familiar with the evolution of species and the evolution of societies, and we are beginning to see the importance of the evolution of ideas themselves—for example, of the evolution of scientific concepts. Some of the concepts that I have listed owe their importance precisely to the changes that they have undergone progressively in order to fit new scientific facts and new ways of holding them together. For example, space and time, mass and energy, molecular structure and reproduction, are concepts that have evolved by becoming linked and related one to another.

Science grows as these links grow; the relation of all things within the human vision is its lesson. This was conceived by the Renaissance, and has been the Humanist message ever since. In the last hundred years, it has grown in strength because we have seen a new order among the relations of matter, life, and mind. The new order is given by evolution, which is a movement from the less complex to the more complex in which, however, the more complex is also more highly integrated. In this sense, the evolution of nature and of society is a continuing exploration of possibilities which have always existed as potentialities. The capacity for greater complexity and higher integration has always been there, and we now see that we are tracing the realization of more and more of that latent capacity. The Humanist dream of the Renaissance has become the urge to find, by the process of understanding which is science, the steps in the fulfilment of the possibilities which lie in nature and in men. We are struggling to break down the dualism of the last four centuries, and to make, from knowledge so long fragmented, a new unitary vision of the full potential of man.

REFERENCES

(1) Burckhardt, Jacob. *The Civilization of the Renaissance in Italy*, ed. L. Gold-scheider. New York: Oxford University Press, 1945.

(2) Butterfield, H. *The Origins of Modern Science*. New York: Macmillan, 1951.

(3) Bronowski, J., and Mazlish, Bruce. *The Western Intellectual Tradition*. New York: Harper & Brothers, 1960. This book discusses several of the personages referred to there, and in particular Erasmus and Leonardo da Vinci.

(4) Hall, A. R. *The Scientific Revolution*. New York: Longmans, 1954.

(5) MacCurdy, Edward. *The Notebooks of Leonardo da Vinci*. New York: Braziller, 1954.

(6) Burckhardt, *op. cit.*, Part III, 'The Revival of Antiquity'.

(7) Bronowski and Mazlish, *op. cit.*, Chapter 10, 'The Royal Society'.

(8) Discoveries and Opinions of Galileo, ed. Stillman Drake. New York: Doubleday, 1957.

(9) Koestler, Arthur. *The Sleepwalkers*. New York: Macmillan, 1959.

(10) Bronowski, J. *The Common Sense of Science*. Harvard University Press, 1953.

(11) 'The Structure of the Hereditary Material', by F. H. Crick, in *The Physics and Chemistry of Life*, New York: Simon & Schuster, 1955.

(12) Polanyi, Michael. *Personal Knowledge*. University of Chicago Press, 1958.

(13) Bronowski, *op. cit.*, Chapter V, 'The Nineteenth Century and the Idea of Causes'.

(14) I have discussed these matters in a book, *Science and Human Values*, New York: Messner, 1958, which deals at length with the subject of this essay.

FRANCIS WILLIAMS

THE DEMOCRATIC CHALLENGE

FRANCIS WILLIAMS, C.B.E.

Born 1903. Educated: Queen Elizabeth
Grammar School, Middleton. Author,
journalist and T.V. commentator. Editor of
the *Daily Herald*, 1936–40. Adviser on
Public Relations to the Prime Minister,
1945–47. A Governor of the B.B.C.,
1951–52.

Publications: *War by Revolution*, 1940;
Press, Parliament and People, 1946; *The
Triple Challenge: The Future of Socialist
Britain*, 1948; *Ernest Bevin: Portrait of a
Great Englishman*, 1952; *History of the
W.T.A.*, 1960, etc.

THE DEMOCRATIC CHALLENGE

The most significant political fact we have to deal with in the second half of the twentieth century is the universal acceptance of the idea of democracy. With equal vehemence and possibly equal sincerity Capitalist West and Communist East proclaim themselves the only true democracies; no new state struggling to independence anywhere in the world but proclaims its adherence to the same political philosophy even if the first intention of those on the way to power is to imprison or cut the throats of their opponents and impose a strict censorship on the Press in its name. Democracy is the myth word of our age.

No doubt part of the popularity of the phraseology of democracy derives from the material skill of the democracies and their success in war: the more democratic side, that is the side giving most weight to the popular will, has been victorious in practically every major war for the past 250 years (the Franco-Prussian War is the only possible exception if that can be regarded as a major war). Yet even when this is taken into account, the triumph of the idea of democracy, as what politics is fundamentally about, is astonishing in both the speed and breadth of its advance. Central governments have been in existence for at least 5,000 years, democratic ones for less than a twentieth of that time. Indeed as a system of practical politics for societies larger than a city state, democracy is only about forty years older than the steam engine and the very thought of it was for long repugnant to some of the most benevolent of political philosophers; to Burke for instance, when he described it as a system that would place the highest powers of the state in the hands 'of churchwardens and constables and other such officers, guided by the prudence of litigious attorneys and Jew brokers and set in motion by shameless women of the lowest condition, by keepers of hotels, taverns and brothels, by pert apprentices, by clerks, shop-boys, hairdressers, fiddlers and dancers on the stage,' or to Madison when he fought against it in the Philadelphia Convention of 1787.

Yet the idea of democracy has swept the world as no other has ever done: it has become the yeast which is today the activating agent in every major social eruption in Africa and Asia as well as in America and Europe.

This is a much more significant political fact than the clash between Communism and Capitalism or between either and Democratic Socialism, for although the struggle between them is real enough, yet each in fact represents one aspect of the same movement of ideas and all have in common the need to justify themselves in terms of the rule of the people. This identity of purpose, although not of method, was instinctively recognized during the war. It made an alliance between the Western Allies and Soviet Russia against Nazi Germany not only expedient but natural and satisfying to most ordinary people because it seemed a genuine expression of unity in a war against counter-democratic principles. Communism in Western eyes is a distortion of democracy, but Nazism was its complete negation, founded on principles wholly antithetical to it: the last stand of an anti-evolutionary force in politics, much of whose gibberish would have appeared respectable enough in many earlier societies. With its defeat the triumph of the democratic idea became complete.

This, as I said earlier, is the most significant political fact of the second half of the twentieth century. It could be the most hopeful also. But it is not automatically so. On the contrary it is also the most ominous, for there are no wars so bitter as those between rival creeds of the same religion and there is nothing in human history to suggest the existence of a natural law to prevent believers in democracy killing each other in its name. The history of Christianity is sodden with blood, torture and warfare, and as things stand at present there seems no good reason, other than our increased, and now total, capacity to destroy ourselves, why the universal acclaim for democracy should not usher in a period of conflict between rival democratic sects as exhausting and inhuman as the Wars of Religion. Moreover, our vastly increased talent for mass murder makes it unlikely should this happen that there will on this occasion be anyone left alive to benefit from the greater toleration which the exhaustion produced by such conflicts has previously left. We have to find other ways to make it possible for rival democrats to live with each other, as rival Christians have now settled down to doing after trying to kill each other for so long.

This is the primary political function of Humanism, which alone is fitted for it.

The central problem of democracy is that since it is a system of 'rule by the people', or at the very least one in which 'the people' are persuaded that they are theoretically the rulers, and will be so in practice when one or two necessary adjustments from the old order have been made, it releases such forces of individual and national initiative, inventiveness and hope, that when tried on a world scale it is in danger of becoming self-destructive, unless means can be found to harness it to a philosophy of life which makes co-operation and toleration seem both natural and inevitable. Change is inherent in democracy, which is why it was opposed by high-principled reasoners in the eighteenth century who believed that any change was likely to be for the worse, as well as by those who were against it for the more practical reason that they thought change might take away from them what their forefathers had stolen. It is thus ultimately inimical to all systems of authority, whether Christian or Muslim, Capitalist or Communist, which believe themselves to be possessed of absolute and final truths, and this conflict between democracy and authoritarianism remains even if the authoritarian systems themselves contain, as all these do, important democratic elements.

Since the Middle Ages the history of Christianity as a social and political force has been the history of a struggle between the slowly developing idea of democracy and the religious doctrine of Christianity, with the latter almost continuously on the retreat. Medieval Christianity could encompass the whole edifice of feudal society, it could endorse serfdom and stamp its moral seal upon unchangeable class privilege and class exploitation—concepts which appear to us today as not only undemocratic but also unchristian—because feudal society was a closed society in which the primacy of the religious law was accepted as a principle by all, although not of course honoured in practice by most. In that society the authority of the Christian Commonwealth might be avoided, it could not be fundamentally challenged. It was supreme in all branches of human activity, political, economic, social, because all activities were seen as part of a single system directed to a single end and that end a Christian one. It was therefore proper that the Church, as the agent of the Christian Commonwealth on earth, should lay down rules for the payment of labour, for the establishment of a just price, for the control of profit and for the curbing of usury (much of which we should call investment), and that these rules should be founded on an assumption universally accepted, the assumption that the real business of life is salvation, that all economic appetites or worldly ambitions are subordinate to this, and that man's life on earth is no more than a preparation for the hereafter.

The secular authority of the Christian religion has at no other time been so all-embracing and so supreme, its power as a political force so great. But this was because the social order possessed no elements of democracy and as soon as such elements began to appear, even if only at first as a crude reflection of the change to a more open society brought by the opportunities offered to the vigorous and ambitious by the mercantile revolution, the social and political authority of Christianity began to contract.

It has gone on contracting ever since, constantly subject to the pulls of two opposing themes: the one the affirmation of Christianity's basic unconcern with the material world or the social order, its interest only in salvation; the other the attempt to retain some footing in the world of political and economic decision, even at the cost of adapting Christianity's own teaching to the requirements of this world and the temporal power of those of status within it. For Luther the first theme was the important one, for although he reaffirmed the moral imperatives of the Medieval Church and asserted in still more rigid terms the primacy of its laws relating to commerce, he also affirmed that these laws had little or nothing to do with salvation; this depended solely upon inner grace, for the soul 'is justified by faith alone and not by any works'. But for Calvin, a product of the advanced economic and commercial society of Geneva whose most influential adherents were to be found in the great urban commercial communities like Amsterdam, London and Antwerp, it was not only natural to accept the world of the businessman and the moneylender, the entrepreneur and middleman, with their need for an open society, but also to re-establish the authority of the Christian religion by suiting its political and social role to the requirements of an expanding economy, to discover in fact that the very qualities required for commercial success—thrift and diligence and seriousness of mind—were those most likely to bring salvation.

It is this conception of the social role of Christianity, coarsened and vulgarized by prosperity, that strikes one so strongly in the Victorian Age when it was actually possible for Christians to persuade themselves that to be poor was to be immoral, and to feel so confident that material success was evidence of God's approval that in their assurance of supernatural grace they could find it perfectly Christian to send girls of seven, as the Shaftesbury Commission of 1842 on the Employment of Children and Young Persons reported, 'chained, belted, harnessed like dogs in a go-cart, saturated with wet and more than half naked', to haul coal underground in the dark—so long as they were children of the poor.

Whether Roman Catholic, Anglican or Nonconformist, the vast body of Church authority (although not, let it be said, all its members) has almost always been ready, as it then was, to compromise the social message of Jesus of Nazareth out of existence so long as its supernatural authority was left untouched. Such political and social authority as Christianity has from time to time exercised has not been due to consistency of political or even ethical purpose, for there has been none, but to the awe it has been able to induce as the alleged agent of a supernatural power and the presumed custodian of the Keys of Heaven. Since Darwin and Huxley took for an ever-growing number of people even this power away from it, Christianity has ceased to exercise more than a fringe influence on the political policies of Christendom, although one capable of considerable negative or delaying effect.

Indeed, whatever its merits or demerits as a personal faith for those who need the assurance of revelation and the promise of immortality as a support to ethics, Christianity is wholly unsuited to the task of providing an effective political dynamic for society in process of change and development. This was implicitly recognized by the writers of the most resounding democratic statement in history, the American Declaration of Independence, when they set out to enunciate the principles that should govern a free and expanding society, clear of the old tyrannies. Although fully convinced, most of them, that they were Christians, they were compelled by their democratic beliefs to produce a most unchristian document, for Christianity, to which material existence is no more than a prelude to a future life in Heaven or Hell, which believes not in liberty but in authority, and which is concerned not with happiness but with sin and salvation, has no true point of contact with a political vision founded on a belief in man's right to life, liberty and the pursuit of happiness.

It is true of course that the Christian faith—especially as expressed by Jesus—contains important elements of democracy and that these were of value in helping democracy to establish itself in Christian countries earlier than in those of other religions. The Christian belief in the value of the individual, that we are members one of another, and that all are equal in the sight of God, are manifestly very relevant to the development of political democracy. But although relevant they are incomplete. The Christian emphasis on the supernatural, on this life as a preparation for the next, and on the doctrine of absolute truth, runs counter to what is deepest and most fundamental in democratic philosophy, which is the conception of continuing debate.

The attempt to reconcile in the political field the Christian idea of revealed and final truth, of absolute good and absolute evil, with the idea of a society based on belief in the dignity of human personality and on confidence in human reason and scientific inquiry (which is itself the quintessence of the continuing dialogue on which the democratic method depends) is damaging to both. It makes the Churches casuistical and places Christianity in a social position which detracts from the purity of its appeal to those who psychologically require the support of revelation in ordering their personal lives. And it demands from democracy genuflections to unreason which erode its ethos.

Unlike autocracies, which can impose their own idea-systems and social regulations from above, democracies must generate their own dynamic from below. Because government by the people cannot work unless the people themselves participate in developing their own light to live by and are conscious of a purpose of their own choosing, the pretence that Western democracy rests upon the social and political acceptance of a supernatural explanation of human history which only a minority any longer takes seriously, has left a kind of nihilism at the heart of modern civilisation which has permitted its increasing domination by two great materialist heresies: the heresy of twentieth-century Capitalism and the heresy of twentieth-century Communism.

The common fallacy in which both these heresies are rooted, and which is no less fallacious for having, as all powerful fallacies do, some elements of truth in it, is that of economic man: the belief that because material advance is necessary to survival it is the only necessity. Both share the same profoundly sceptical and pessimistic view of human nature. This finds in Capitalist terms expression in the belief that the *only* human instinct upon which a society can absolutely depend is the acquisitive instinct, and, in Communist ones the conviction that, as Engels argued, economic motives are so all-compelling that the economic stage of society *alone* determines its form, its political pattern and its cultural development.

Now, of course, the acquisitive instinct is important, and of course the economic stage reached by a society exercises a strong influence on its total pattern.

But the insistence by Capitalist societies that the acquisitive instinct is all-pervading and all-important, their emphasis on purely materialist standards of achievement, their naïve belief that everything will be fine so long as it keeps on getting bigger, and their exaggeration of competitive success as a proof of character, so that men are forced to go through life hag-ridden by the fear that they may fail in the one test of manhood accepted by their fellows, has made them the prey of a profound neurosis, confining human personality within a framework so rigid and mutilating that it distorts the real values of civilization and much that is warm and generous in human fellowship. There is nothing so pitiable as the man who has no values other than grossly material ones. The strains and conflicts imposed by the acceptance of materialist competitive success as the primary test of manhood afflicts all Western societies. The point of no return to which this salesman's philosophy brings those who give themselves wholly to the Capitalist dream has perhaps been reached more quickly for more people in American society than elsewhere. But this is only because American society is the product of Western Capitalism at its most successful. British and European societies make their way no less compulsively to the well-appointed penitentiary of the economic man.

Nor does the heresy of Communism offer any way out of the impasse. Indeed it has produced results even more crippling to the ideals of human brotherhood which originally inspired it, by riveting the seal of permanent and final truth on to an economic theory most of whose assumptions have been proved wrong by the march of events. Communism was not authoritarian in principle. Nor was it anti-democratic in theory. On the contrary it advocated a more complete democracy. Its creed is not that political equality is a bad thing but that it is meaningless without economic equality. Nor, as some of its less instructed critics imagine, does it advocate class war as good and desirable in itself. Its thesis is the simpler one that because men act solely according to their economic interests the class war is inevitable at one stage of social development. This the Communist believes for the same reason that the Christian believes that man is born sinful and can only be redeemed by salvation, because the founder of his religion said so; and no subsequent experience of how societies develop can be allowed to deny what is accepted as absolutely true. Moreover, since the actual proletariat has in most cases been unable to understand Marx, and unwilling to read him, and has refused to follow the pattern of behaviour declared inevitable by Marxian analysis, it has become necessary for the dictatorship of the proletariat, which was to be the prelude to a truly classless society, to be itself preceded by a dictatorship of the Communist Party in the interests of an idealized proletariat whose 'real will' the Communist, by reason of the Marxist discipline, understands better than it does itself. Thus the thesis that economic forces absolutely determine human behaviour narrows from a belief in a period of pro-letarian dictatorship during the weeding out of bourgeoisie elements which stand in the way of a classless society, to the necessity for a dictatorship of the proletariat by a disciplined Communist Party which alone understands its 'real will', and from that, as in all armies operating through a chain of command, to the centralized authority of one man or small group of men at the top: what was democratic in theory becomes anti-democratic in practice.

This pattern, so contrary to the ideal principles of Communism, was given more durable life than it might otherwise have had by the fact that what Lenin called 'the great, mighty, all-powerful *regisseur*', war, brought revolution to Russia before it had passed through the economic stages regarded by Marx as the essential precursor of a dictatorship of the proletariat. The February Revolution was a revolution that did not know what it wanted: a revolution in search of a leader. The October Revolution was Lenin's, not Communism's: a revolution that had found its leader. But although this historical accident has confirmed the pattern of one-man dictatorship in Russia, such a dictatorship follows naturally from the interior logic of the Marxist analysis with its insistence that the pre-eminence of economic motives, and the resistance of the possessing groups to change, makes the peaceful development of society to higher forms impossible. It follows no less naturally from this thesis that in modern conditions it is impossible for the class struggle to be other than inter-national in its implications.

Thus despite their common belief in democracy, which is real enough in both cases (for it is as absurd for the believer in democratic Capitalism to deny the genuine elements of democracy in Communist philosophy, and even in much Communist practice at the lower levels of debate, as for the Communist to deny that the Capitalist belief in the primacy of the acquisitive instinct has proved compatible in practice with a greal deal of political democracy), twentieth-century Capitalism and twentieth-century Communism confront each other on the world stage with the same implacability as the two main branches of Christianity, Catholicism and Protestantism, formerly did on the European, or as Christianity and Islam did earlier.

However, the schisms within democracy have this advantage when set against those between Christians: neither Capitalism nor Communism as yet actually claims supernatural origin. Marx, though prophetic, is not God. There are thus some grounds for hoping that Communism may outlive its terrorist and totalitarian phase more quickly than Christianity did. Like Charlemagne, Communists have done what they can to make their creed universal by killing off those who do not accept it. They have paralleled, and with the greater scientific learning at their command improved on, the techniques of the Inquisition, had their own versions of the massacre of St Bartholemew, and suppressed heresy in Hungary with a ferocity unequalled since the 'wars of religion'. But they have had the power to do so for only just over forty years and there are already some signs that they are less pleased with murder than they were. It may be unpleasant if one is a fallen Minister to be sent as an Ambassador to a remote and inconvenient territory or to find oneself posted to a subordinate job in a Collective, but it is preferable to being killed, and less final. The industrial empire of the MVD (ex-NKVD, ex-GPU, ex-Cheka), with its network of prison camps containing anywhere between three and four million prisoners, has been liquidated in Russia and most of the prisoners released. The formerly unlimited powers of arbitrary arrest and imprisonment without trial have been ended, and there is now a good deal of evidence that not only is the ordinary Soviet citizen much better fed and clothed than he was but that he feels a good deal freer than he did. We cannot build too much on this; but forty years is not long in the history of religions and it is something that the authoritarian materialist religion of Communism should give some evidence of turning away from violence so much more quickly than the supernatural religions did.

Although the two great democratic heresies of our time continue to confront each other in frozen gestures of hatred it is, moreover, increasingly plain as time passes that they have much more in common than they like to admit, even if it is only that they travel to the same dead end. In the social organizations developed by both there is to be found the same sense of imprisonment within a pattern that has steadily less mercy on the nonconformist and that increasing'y dictates what is socially acceptable to wear, to eat, to read, to say, and to think. Nor in the one instance of the so-called Free World is this moulding of the individual to a conventionally acceptable type from which it is un-American, or un-middle-class-English-suburban, to diverge, less significant, or less frightening, because it is not at the dictation of one man or one political party but of a way of life and a consumer economy. The Corporation Man is in some ways very like the Communist Man—at least in the middle and lower levels of economic organization—and a managerial society that takes to itself the right to check up on a man's wife, his hobbies and his friends before deciding on his suitability for promotion is leaving itself with alarmingly few stones to throw at the Communist Party for its assumption of total authority over the personal lives of those it enrolls. Twentieth-century Communism and twentieth-century Capitalism are, in fact, breeding-grounds of some very similar vices and virtues.

Soviet Communism has had to compress its industrial revolution into a much shorter space of time than Capitalism did. In the process it has demanded sacrifices from its working population which seem appalling by current Western standards. They would not have disturbed most industrial employers or mine-owners in Britain in the nineteenth century, practically all of whom took it for granted that those who worked the machines or cut the coal should live in poverty and squalor and die young, since the advance of industrialist Capitalism and the greatness of Britain required it of them. Less hampered by belief in the acquisitive instinct, and so less conditioned to underpay its public servants because they do not make profits or to treat the field of public effort as a slum area because it is not business, Marxist Communism has outstripped Christian Capitalism in the manufacture of nuclear missiles and the ability to hit the moon. It is still behind in the provision of consumer goods, but even here it is beginning to catch up, accepting as it does so, very much the same conception of the good life here on earth.

Economically and socially these politically divergent and ideologically hostile philosophies converge more and more—a prospect that of itself offers no particular pleasure to sensible civilized men and women who regard washing machines, television sets and super-markets as conveniences of living but not its goals. Yet each remains doctrinally convinced that the other is morally wicked and incapable of radical change. So long as they do so, meetings of the United Nations are no more likely to bring us nearer to world unity than are meetings between representatives of the Church of England and the Church of Rome to bring Christian unity.

These frozen postures might not matter so much were they not struck from the top of armouries of land- and sea-based missiles capable of delivering megaton nuclear warheads at fifteen times the speed of sound on targets 1,800 miles distant, to which may shortly be added operational ICBM's with ranges up to 6,200 miles (the USSR indeed probably already has some), although naturally in such circumstances neither side wants war. We thus find ourselves in a position where what began as an argument about two economic interpretations of history, both based on inadequate evidence, has become a confrontation of absolutes in which almost every fact takes on an entirely different meaning according to which side is looking at it and we are all in danger of being blown to pieces, not out of criminal intent but because one side may miscalculate the motive behind some quite simple and innocent move of the other. It is a highly precarious stance from which to run a world.

Meanwhile the uncommitted nations of Africa, Asia and the Middle East who want neither Communism nor Capitalism (and assuredly have no particular interest in Christianity, having their own religions to guide themselves by or shake themselves free from), but who do, it would seem, want democracy, find themselves incapable of doing almost anything constructive without offending one or other of the two major groups in the world, neither of which can bring itself to believe that those who do not accept them wholly are not thereby their enemies—a common religious fallacy. At the same time problems central to the future of humanity, as for example the balance between birth-rates and food-resources, or the fact that the United States with less than 10 per cent of the world's population is now using up nearly two-thirds of the world's mineral production, or the relationship of man to his physical environment, the whole ecology of man and nature—are pushed to the periphery of politics, being lucky indeed to find a foothold even there.

We run our world with a degree of specialized intelligence that brings us new marvels of scientific, inventive, and industrial achievement almost every day, but with a degree of general intelligence so abject as to defy belief had it not become a commonplace of our lives—so commonplace, in fact, that I run the risk of being accused of the extremest political naïveté even for mentioning it and thereby showing ignorance of the 'natural law' requiring nations to behave like lunatics.

Having got ourselves into such a dangerous absolutist position, is there any way in which we can escape from it without mass murder and suicide?

The short answer is that there is none unless we are prepared to stop thinking politically as Capitalists, or Communists, Christians, Muslims, Hindus or Buddhists, and think as Humanists. The world's democratic dialogue can only be conducted in a global humanist frame. A world in which men have both hydrogen bombs and closed minds is altogether too dangerous.

The Humanist does not, of course, deny that real conflicts of national interest exist and are likely to go on existing, that the passion for clothing religious, political and economic beliefs in ideological vestments runs so deep that it is not likely to be easily eradicated, and that these ideological differences are not only genuine but of great significance to the future of the human condition. Nor on the personal level does he doubt (at any rate this one does not) the reality of mystical experience for some people or that such mystical experience has value for them.

But politics is a matter of social organization. Its business is that of finding means by which men can live together. It is concerned with the possibilities and limitations of human action.

Where the democratic idea takes hold in politics, as it has now done in some form or another over most of the world, these possibilities and limitations have to be made understandable to ordinary citizens. This is so even where many of the forms of political democracy that the West (rightly in my view) considers essential do not exist. Although people may be persuaded by propaganda, or by fear, that only one party, or even only one group of men within one party is fit to govern, nevertheless if the appeal is to their participation in a social purpose (which is democracy) and not simply to their obedience (which is autocracy), they have to be brought to accept not only that it is possible and desirable for their governments to do certain things, but that it may not be possible for them to do others which seem equally desirable, or desirable to do some which seem equally possible: government is a matter of priorities, of compromise not dogma. Democratic power can only operate within a framework of consent. But although this framework of consent is the first essential it is by no means the last. Something more than consent is required if democracy is to be more than negatively successful—there must be a common belief in the value and importance of what is being done and a common sense that all have in some measure the opportunity of contributing to it.

This is difficult enough in a national society. It becomes even more so in the international one, within which the ambitions, fears, and favoured dogmas of national democratic groups clash. To operate successfully in a world context democracy must be related to a view of the world and man's place in it that is capable of judging national and ideological differences in historical perspective and of generating, within them, a sense of participation in the human story, sufficiently strong and sufficiently universal to act as a solvent to national and ideological hostility. The history of political advance is the history of ever-widening loyalties. The loyalties we now require have to be wide enough to embrace the continuing human race as a whole, even though they still contain within themselves smaller and earlier loyalties which have their own validity in their own context.

Humanism offers the possibility of such a loyalty. It sees man in his true stature as the highest product and only agent of the evolutionary process, called upon by his destiny constantly to explore and extend the frontiers of knowledge so that he may better understand his own nature and the environment in which he lives. It provides a frame within which conflicts of world political systems fall into place, not as a struggle of absolutes, of all or nothing, decisive and final, but as stages in a continuous process of change in which each new development brings new needs and calls for new adjustments. In such a frame the differences between political and social organizations, as well as what is common to them, can be seen as part of a natural chain of action and reaction in the evolutionary movement towards a more unified system of political ideas and beliefs, of which the almost universal reaching out towards the democratic idea is already one sign. They present a case for enquiry and understanding, for an examination of what may be fruitful and creative in each as well as what is likely to prove no more than a false start along a blind alley. They present no case for absolute judgment and implacable hostility.

It is not, of course, possible to promise that by the light of Humanism we shall progress unhampered to greater political understanding. Men although rational are not wholly or always so. Nor would anyone aware of the power of emotion and imagination and of the still uncharted reaches of human experience wish that they should be. We cannot be sure that they will follow reason in their political arrangements even when the path of reason is clear and unimpeded. But at least Humanism builds no deliberate barriers to human understanding and sets no booby-traps of its own along the political road. Nor does it ask that those who travel shall be blindfolded. It makes instead the revolutionary proposal that we should advance with our eyes open and our minds ready to learn from experience, and should take with us an honest knowledge of our past to enrich our future. It does not offer a sure guarantee against political disaster: nothing can do that. But at least it offers us the means to arm ourselves against the worst follies of ignorance and intolerance, and a route to the mountains. We cannot expect more.

MORRIS GINSBERG

A HUMANIST VIEW OF PROGRESS

MORRIS GINSBERG

Born 1889. Educated: University College, London. Fellow and Lecturer in Philosophy, University College. Professor of Sociology in the London School of Economics. President of the Aristotelian Society, 1942–43. Joint editor *British Journal of Sociology*.

Publications: *The Idea of Progress: a Revaluation*, 1953; *Reason and Experience in Ethics* (Auguste Comte lecture, 1956); *Essays in Sociology and Social Philosophy*.

A HUMANIST VIEW OF PROGRESS

I propose in this essay to restate the case for the belief in progress and the part played by the growth of rationality in the shaping of progress.

As formulated in the eighteenth century the theory of progress contained three tenets.[1] Firstly, the belief in human perfectibility, in the power of reason not only to utilize the forces of nature in the service of human needs, but also to bring about improvements in human relations and the behaviour of men. Secondly, the belief in the unity of mankind. This rested on the assumption that the powers of the mind were in essentials the same in all men, and that there was a moral obligation to reduce inequalities and break down the barriers that separate them. Thirdly, the belief that in the history of man there was in fact a movement towards these ends and that progress consisted in this movement.

Let us consider what is living and what dead in these beliefs. It seems to me that the essential point in the theory of progress remains true, namely, that in the course of historical development man is slowly rationalized and that man is moralized in proportion as he becomes more rational.

As to the first of the three tenets, no one doubts that there has been intellectual progress, in the sense that there has been an advance in our knowledge of nature and therewith in our power of reacting upon it. This does not mean that men are born more intelligent than in former ages. There is no evidence of any general change in inborn faculty. What has grown is the body of knowledge and its better organization. This is a social product, the result of co-operative effort, mutual stimulus and cumulative experience. Furthermore, there is not only development but progress. There may be doubt about the ultimate validity of the conceptions employed by the natural sciences at any one stage in their growth. But, apart from a few inveterate sceptics, there is general agreement that the successive transformations which they have undergone represent genuine advances of insight into the working of things.[2] Leaving aside the ethical implications of the growth of knowledge (and it is at once obvious that neither in the individual nor in society does knowledge necessarily connote wisdom or justice), there are epistemological standards in the light of which progress can be estimated. Advance in knowledge is estimated, I take it, not by reference to final or absolute truth, nor even by agreement with first principles taken as beyond doubt, but by the degree of consistency and mutual support attained by the explanations offered and by the range or inclusiveness of the experiences covered. Finality is not expected, but we look for increased coherence, a widening of experience, a better balance between the conceptual and experiential modes of enquiry, a growth in the capacity of self-criticism and reconstruction—in short, increasing range and systematization of thought and experience. What reason claims is not that it can reach ultimate truth here and now, but that it is the method of growth in understanding. From this point of view the notion of development is to be conceived as lying at the basis of validity itself. The system of knowledge is in process of correlated growth, changes in any one part inducing or being accompanied by changes in others, so that the whole undergoes transformation, while maintaining its identity through modification. The wider and more coherent the system, the stronger are its claims to represent reality. Judged in this way there has undoubtedly been progress in knowledge.

In moving from intellectual to moral progress the early theories were at their weakest. They took it for granted that 'enlightenment' would bring virtue and happiness with it. It is strange that it was not realized that the simple identification of virtue with knowledge and vice with ignorance had already been shown to be untenable by the post-Socratic philosophers of ancient Greece and again and again by religious thinkers. It does not follow that we have to accept a doctrine of original sin, or that the immense contribution of the growth of knowledge to the development of morality is seriously in doubt. It is true that modern psychology and psycho-pathology have laid great stress on the irrational elements in human nature. But they are far from denying the power of reason. On the contrary, both the theory and the practice of psychoanalysis rest on the assumption that the instinctive and repressed tendencies can be brought under rational control.[3] There are, of course, other strong anti-intellectual trends in modern views of human life. But oddly enough, these rest on a quaint survival of faculty psychology, which leads to an unduly narrow view of reason and to an over-simplification of the relations between thought, feeling and impulse. These are in fact always interwoven, though in varying degrees: there are feelings and desires which are only possible at a certain level of cognition and there are thoughts which are only possible at certain levels of emotional intensity.

On the side of knowledge the role of reason is to organize experience by the methods of analysis and synthesis. In essentials reason is the effort towards greater unity and systematic connection. This effort is rooted in tendencies lying deeper than consciousness, though it is only when it reaches the conscious level that it becomes subject to logical tests. The role of reason in action is similar. But in this case the elements to be linked or connected include not only sensory experiences but impulses and emotions and apprehensions of values. The synthesis involves the formation of character and the growth of conscience.[4] In these developments cognitive and affective factors are interwoven at all stages. The fully developed conscience is a highly complex configuration of beliefs or judgments and sentiments. The judgments assert that certain acts or classes of acts are right or wrong, good or bad. Around these judgments there cluster emotional dispositions and conative tendencies, such as respect, loyalty and sympathy, resentment and anger, shame, remorse, fear of punishment or of the loss of love, the desire for approval. The emotional components and the rational level of the judgments vary greatly in different individuals and in the same individual, not only at different times, but in the different clusters or patterns of the dispositions which make up the whole of the conscience. In other words, there are great differences in the degree of clarity with which the rules of action and the grounds for them are grasped by different individuals. Similarly the emotional sanctions may be very different for different rules, so that a person may be highly 'conscientious' in some spheres of conduct and not in others, while emotion and judgment may not correspond in strength and may even vary inversely. The possibilities of failure are thus many and various. Impulses may be dissociated from the organized part of the personality and so escape control. The emotional and cognitive dispositions may be dissevered, and a state of apathy may result, in which thought loses the power of inducing or controlling action. Under the sway of strong emotions reason itself may be used to defeat reason. There are endless possibilities of sophistication and rationalization, of self-deception, conscious and unconscious. On this view reason is not the slave of the impulses and feelings, nor independent of them. We may conceive of it as that in our personality which strives for integration, deeper than conscious thought, but the more effective the more it uses thought, working within and through the basic impulses and interests and deriving its energy from them. Its power is great, greater perhaps, as Bertrand Russell once said,[5] 'than any other human power'. But equally great are the chances of failure and defeat.

In turning to the larger field of the historical development of morality, it is again clear that the part played by reason was over-stated in the early theories of progress and that they rested on too simple and optimistic a view of the influence exerted by moral factors on changes in the social structure. Thus, for example, a prime source of social change is discontent, especially discontent sharpened by a sense or feeling of injustice. But the strength of the feeling may be out of all proportion to the clarity of the thought. People may have a strong feeling of resentment against injustice, though they might find it very hard to say what they mean by justice. Ideas or beliefs may serve to canalize or sharpen discontent and occasionally they may initiate the discontent, but often they emerge in the course of the movements generated by the feelings and impulses and may drag behind. In whatever ways they originate, the general acceptance of ideas depends on social conditions. They may remain dormant for long periods and then burst upon the world with resounding effect.

Moral ideas appear to influence society mainly through religion and law, and in both spheres rational factors play a great but complex role and are liable to be overborne by factors making for unreason. The ethical ideas embodied in the great religions have, as Whitehead has said,[6] been at once 'gadflies irritating and beacons luring, the victims among whom they dwell'. Religious teachers have again and again pointed to a way of life far in advance of the morality of their day. On the other hand, religious conservatism has often stood in the way of moral innovation, and in descending from the world of grace to the world of nature, churches have made compromises which are far from compatible with the teaching of their founders. Thus they have found no difficulty in turning the God of love into the God of battles, and they have sought to persuade men to endure present injustice by bidding them find consolation 'in the final proportions of eternal justice'. Their comparative failure in practice is not due entirely, or even mainly, to the hard-heartedness of men, but to their inherent limitations, their tendency to a morbid exaggeration of the ascetic elements in morality, their inability to apply the principles of personal morality to the problems of social organization. This seems to be true in varying degree of Christianity, Buddhism and Hinduism. In so far as there has been an improvement in the morality of the modern world it owed probably more to the impact of rational inquiry and its tendency to moralize religion rather than to any developments within religion as such. In any case, the moral strength of the religions does not seem to be directly related to the logical rigour of their theologies. Thus, as Hobhouse has pointed out,[7] the moral influence of Christianity was never so great as in the nineteenth century, which was the time of the most serious intellectual attack on its foundations.

The impact of moral ideas on the evolution of law has not been systematically explored by students of comparative jurisprudence. There are clearly enormous variations in the relations between the various forms of social control. In the early stages law, morals and religion are not clearly differentiated, and changes are slow and unconscious. This unconscious growth persists even in higher phases, in response to the pressure of new needs or of changes in the balance of social forces, but conscious efforts at generalization and systematization gain in importance.[8] The extension of the area of communal organization brings the ruling authorities into contact with different, possibly conflicting, customs, which have to be adapted, modified or even replaced to meet the larger common requirements. This is the stage of the declaration and codification of the law. In the self-governing communities of what has been called the civic phase the transition is made from declaration to legislation. In this phase the relations between morals and law are very complex and variable. There are periods in which stress is laid on precision and formality. There is a tendency for law to harden and to become indifferent to moral elements. On the theoretical side, the view then tends to prevail that law as such is non-moral. On the other hand, periods of this character alternate with others in which the rigidity of the law is broken down, through contact with other legal systems or with moral ideas, or again under the pressure of social changes. At such periods, though not exclusively in them, the law comes to be subjected to criticism in the light of more or less systematic conceptions of social well-being. In our own times jurists in democratic countries are often inclined to dismiss moral theories, such as those of natural law or natural justice, as irrelevant. But while they may be right in protesting against vague generalizations, the history of legislation in democratic countries does show the growing influence—often promoted by a small number of individuals or voluntary associations—of conceptions of well-being: witness the reform of the criminal law, the regulation of industrial relations, or the changes in the legal status of women.

The important point is that in democratic societies not only is law in increasingly closer contact with the moral sense of the community, but that efforts are made to define the limits of law, that is to distinguish spheres of action which both require and permit of the sanctions of the law, and spheres, notably in the area of self-development and self-expression, which are best left to individual choice and initiative. On the other hand, in modern authoritarian regimes public opinion is given little opportunity of systematic expression, is starved of independent information, and is pauperized by being subjected to perpetual and highly organized emotional propaganda. At the same time the claim is made that the distinction between law and morals has been overcome—in other words, that the law has been completely moralized. From the point of view of the democratic societies this is not a step forward but backward. In attempting to regulate every detail of life juridically, the distinction between inward and outward sanctions is blurred, and this, by diminishing the area of individual choice, cannot but be inimical to the full growth of the moral consciousness.

From this brief survey it emerges that the influence of moral factors, whether direct or through religion and law, is highly variable, and is only one and by no means the most powerful of the forces shaping the life of societies. Intellectual, religious and ethical development each follow their own course in varying degrees of independence from the rest. The social structure, in turn, is affected by structural strains resulting from countless interactions, moral, non-moral, and immoral. In the higher phases, however, the various developments increasingly interpenetrate and their mutual implications come to be better understood. There is no certainty that the ethical elements will triumph: what may be reasonably hoped for is that as moral ideas gain in rational coherence with the growth of our knowledge of human nature and its possibilities, they will also gain in their power to instigate and sustain social action.

The assumption underlying the belief in perfectibility was that human nature did not consist of radically discrepant elements, that there was nothing contradictory or self-defeating in the effort to direct and control the further course of social evolution. I can see nothing in the facts adduced by later studies to invalidate this assumption. The conception that control is possible is relatively new and in need of further clarification. But what has so far been attained in some societies in equalizing rights and removing the barriers that divide men, in reconciling order with freedom, in bringing together the principles of personality with the principles of social responsibility, justifies the conclusion that we are beginning to discover the conditions of correlated growth and that steadier progress will become possible as our knowledge grows. All this, of course, is subject to the overhanging doubt that the necessary work may not be done in time to prevent the disruptive forces at present threatening the world, in part themselves due to the growth of knowledge, from accomplishing their work of destruction.

I turn now to the second element in the theories of progress, namely, the unity of mankind, including the belief that progress is something shareable by all mankind.

In dealing with this problem the early theories were undoubtedly Europe-centred. They tended to identify the progress of mankind with the progress of the European peoples, or even with the peoples they took to be the European *élite*. Nowadays this would be condemned as cultural imperialism, and stress is frequently laid on the plurality and distinctiveness of cultures or civilizations. This is undoubtedly a healthy reaction. But it does not follow that the theory that progress is something in which all peoples can share, each in its own way, is thereby shaken. On the contrary, it is now clearer than ever that if there is to be progress, it must be the concern of all mankind. The problems confronting the peoples of the world are problems in which all are involved and in the solution of which all must play their part. Today, I suppose, mankind may be considered as divisible into five or six major groups: (1) East Asia (China and Japan); (2) India and Indonesia; (3) Islam; (4) Russia and its satellites; (5) the Western World; (6) the emergent African peoples. It is plain that none of these either does or can develop independently of the rest. Economically, it is realized, further development can only be achieved within a world economy. Politically, peace is now more clearly indivisible than when Litvinov first uttered this famous maxim. The pace of unification, in the sense of growing contacts and interdependence, is clearly increasing before our eyes. Is there a growth of unity also in the deeper sense of unity of aim or purpose? There are many who think that real unity can only come from unity of religious beliefs. But though the development of existing religions shows a certain convergence, and though they may in future learn more from each other than they have in the past, I can see no reason for believing that any one of them, however modified by contact with the others, is likely to provide a basis acceptable to all for the spiritual unification of mankind. What is to be hoped for is rather that each religion will contribute in its own way to the enrichment of spiritual experience and that this will result in mutual tolerance and respect, and in the general acceptance of a broadly based Humanist ethic.

Whatever the evolution of religion may have in store, it is clear that a process is now going on in large areas of the world, familiar enough in the history of Christianity, namely, the secularization of law and politics and the laicization of culture. Thus India has deliberately adopted the policy of creating a secular welfare state. The Turks have formally committed themselves to building up a secular state not tied to religious faith. It seems likely that Pakistan and Indonesia will follow a similar line.[9] In European history secularization and the separation, not always complete, of spiritual and temporal powers are plausibly regarded as among the main sources of the dynamism and fermentation of Western societies, and as contributing not only to political liberty, but also to the emancipation of mind and spirit and the liberation of rational effort. The values involved were largely those of the Humanist tradition—order, justice, reason. It remains to be seen to what extent they will affect the secularization now going on in the non-Western world and in what ways it will come to terms with the prevailing religious traditions.

In the Communist portions of the world an opposed process seems to be going on. They have reverted to the fusion of spiritual and temporal power by subjecting art and science to political control. Furthermore, Communism seems to have many of the qualities of an exclusive religion, and by seeking to penetrate all areas of life, it tends to legalize morality and to give it the characteristics formerly possessed by the jural morality of medieval casuistry or the all-pervading discipline of the age of Puritanism.

A deeper doubt is raised by the question whether, as is frequently alleged, the Communists are divided from the rest of the world by irreducible differences in moral outlook. This calls for careful scrutiny.[10] As far as theory is concerned it would not be difficult to show that Marxist views of the ends of life or of the principles of social justice do not differ markedly from those of Humanist rationalism. Nominally, both aim at a form of life in which 'the free development of each is the condition of the free development of all' (Marx). Both aim at 'increasing the power of man over nature and the abolition of the power of man over man' (Trotsky). The difference, in so far as it has an ethical basis and is not due to different views of the forces at work in social change, lies elsewhere. It lies in the acceptance of a dual morality; a universal morality, 'a really human morality' as Engels calls it, which can only be operative when class antagonisms have been overcome, and an 'interim' morality, applicable to the period of revolutionary struggle, a morality of war and of war à outrance. The distinction between the two moralities has its analogies with that found in the world religions, between the morality of perfection and the morality of ordinary life, the world of grace and the world of nature, the morality of the open society and that of the closed society. This distinction has led to social indifferentism and worse. Yet in Western societies the two moralities have in various ways inter-penetrated and the tension between them has been an important factor in moral progress. It is arguable that in Communist society the fissure is deeper and a danger to future liberalization and humanization. On the other hand, the hope is not excluded that the spirit of free enquiry and free expression will reassert itself and bring about a revival of the moral elements which gave Socialism its dynamic quality in its early stages.

An important aspect of the unification of mankind is the unification of law. There are, I believe, now only eight or ten legal systems in the world and most of them are hybrids. More than half the population of the world is under the influence of the Common law or the systems derived from Roman law. It is true that within each region local differences remain. But as against this it is to be noted that a conscious movement to facilitate unification has been in existence for some time and that it has achieved a fair measure of success in the Commonwealth countries, the United States, and the Scandinavian peoples.[11] In the Islamic states the impact of Western law was, as was to be expected, first felt in the field of commercial and civil relations, but recently it has begun to affect even the family, for so long under the influence of religious law.

The Soviet legal system differs profoundly from other legal systems. It has altered the legal structure of ownership and contract, including the contract of marriage. Yet it seems that in the forty years of its existence no new concepts or legal relationships have emerged, and that on the whole, the machinery of justice operates in forms and procedures comparable to those of other countries.[12]

To these developments must be added the growth of international law and of numerous institutions serving international economic and social functions. Yet the nations remain deeply divided and nationalist movements create ever new nations. We are still a very long way from an inclusive world order. The immediate hope seems to be rather in regional or functional groupings among kindred states. These groupings may eventually overcome their fears and suspicions and arrive at a *modus vivendi* enabling them to avoid the now patent dangers of mutual destruction made possible by the development of science and technology.

Despite the doubts suggested by these considerations, the growth of legality is impressive evidence of progress in the rational ordering of human relations. In estimating future possibilities we should take into consideration not only the failures but also the successes. The systematization and rationalization of the Common Law of England took about a thousand years and is far from being fully achieved: the rationalization of world law may well not take so long.

The general conclusions which emerge from the comparative study of civilization may now be briefly indicated.

(1) The history of morals establishes the reality of moral progress along certain lines. This has consisted in the clarification of ideals, in the growth of insight into human needs and purposes and the conditions of their satisfaction, and in the extension of the range of sympathy and imaginative identification. The process can be followed in the gradual elimination of the magical elements in morality, in the distinctions drawn

between ritual and moral rules, in the recurrent criticisms of existing institutions in the light of ethical ideals, and in the demands that religion itself must satisfy ethical requirements. The development is not unilinear and is subject to reversals and retrogression. It goes on in numerous distinct centres, each with its own tradition. Comparative study shows that amid a good deal of diversity, they have much in common, and I believe there are principles of appraisal in the light of which their own development and their contributions to the general development of morality can be evaluated. I have elsewhere tried to show that there are five criteria which may be thus used:

(a) *Differentiation* of morals from custom, law and religion involving the emergence of a distinctively moral attitude, i.e. the recognition of values and obligations as self-sustained and independent of external sanctions; (b) Growing *universalization* of the range of persons to whom moral rules are held to apply and increasing impartiality in applying them. This trend involves not only a firmer grasp of principles, but a widening of the range of sympathy and altruistic sentiments; (c) Widening *comprehensiveness* of the range of needs and values of which morality takes account, greater sensitivity in dealing with them and openness to new values; (d) Increasing *coherence* in systematizing moral judgments and disentangling underlying assumptions; (e) Expansion of the scope of *self-criticism* and self-direction, as shown more particularly in the extent to which impartial investigation of relevant facts and scrutiny of the ends which are pursued, or might be pursued, are allowed to shape public policy.[13]

It is easy to see that advance in one direction does not necessarily carry with it advance in others. Thus a system may be internally coherent, but narrow and exclusive; or it may be comprehensive in seeking to penetrate large areas of life, but rely on coercion or other external sanctions, and thus fail to satisfy the criterion of differentiation as defined above. It would seem that formally the notion of self-direction and of a social responsibility to shape policy so as to provide the conditions of well-being for all is now very commonly accepted, though, of course, societies differ widely in their capacity for self-criticism and in the methods adopted. There are similarly wide variations in respect of systematization, universalization, and the view taken of the relations between law, morals and religion. But the general trends are traceable in all modern societies, though of course it would be very difficult to balance gains and losses or estimate overall advance.

(2) Moral development is multilinear not only in the sense that it goes on in different centres, each with its own tradition, but also that within

each centre there are various lines of growth, traceable to different sources. Thus, for example, the ideals of a community may be due mainly to its religion, whilst the law and the working moral code may have different roots, and the three may stand to each other in varying relations of juxtaposition, conflict or synthesis. Both law and religion may influence, and be influenced by, changes in moral outlook, but only at certain periods and in certain spheres of life. So again development in ethico-religious outlook may lag behind development in science and learning, and the clarification of moral ideas may not be immediately reflected in institutional change or actual conduct. In other words, there is no direct connection, step by step, between moral development and the development of knowledge, religion, or the structure of society. In the later phases, however, the various movements tend to converge and, as the connection comes to be better understood, conscious efforts towards their harmonization become possible. There may well be critical points in these developments beyond which progress may be more continuous and assured.

(3) Knowledge has increasingly to cope with problems which its own development brings about. Thus, for example, it has made possible an enormous increase in the scale and efficiency of social organization. But in doing so it brought with it more terrible forms of war and an increasing fear of war, and great inequalities of possessions and power. It is clearer than ever that knowledge can be used for evil as for good purposes and that the situation is the more serious when to the power over nature is added the power over the minds of men. The unequal distribution of knowledge and understanding within populations and the fact that the peoples of the world differ widely in their rate of advance are obviously of great importance for the general progress of mankind. In the ancient world civilizations were mere islands in a sea of barbarism, liable to submersion or re-barbarization. Today, inequalities in political and economic power are still causes of wars. Even the efforts to mitigate inequalities may generate new inequalities: for the organization needed in the course of the struggle tends to perpetuate the power acquired during the struggle and in this way may give rise to new and even greater inequalities. Similarly, nationalism may in one of its phases be an instrument of self-respect and freedom, and in another, of domination and oppression. In short, the elements involved in development are ill-balanced, and advance in one direction is often effected at the cost of loss in another.

If this were all, progress would be impossible. The case for progress rests on the fact that in the course of historical development some degree of progress has definitely been achieved, that various possibilities of synthesis have been opened out, and on the hope that with the advance of social knowledge and moral insight, the causes making for discrepancies or one-sidedness in development may be discovered and brought increasingly under control. This is not just a pious wish. We know from experience that liberty and order are not incompatible, that societies which encourage spontaneity, tolerance of differences, openness to new values, are not necessarily weaker and indeed may well have greater chances of survival than those based on rigid organization, fanaticism and the suppression of individual variety.

There is no reason for thinking that there is any permanent disharmony between social justice and social efficiency. We can now see that conflicts within and between nations are far more likely to be resolved by rational discussion and an appeal to underlying common interests than by force or the threat of force. We can see that the risks which knowledge brings with it must be met not by suppression but by the search for yet further knowledge. There is no scientific or other warrant for the jeremiads about the long-term evil effects of improvements in hygiene and medicine on the quality and quantity of the population. For social evils social remedies must and can be found. The choice lies with ourselves.

(4) I conclude that the early theories of progress were substantially right in regarding progress as a movement towards 'reason and justice'. Of the quest for justice we can say confidently that it persistently shows an upward trend. And it is a rational quest, for it is the nature of reason to exclude arbitrariness and to make for unity and integration. Justice, as Aristotle tells us, is 'a kind of equality'. We can now see that progress has consisted in the effort to determine what kind, and to define the relations between freedom and equality. These ideas have now spread all over the world and are everywhere contributing to the emancipation of peoples.

Despite the sceptics I believe that the ideas of equality and liberty, if properly redefined, are of value also in dealing with the relations between states. The problem both in the case of individuals and of states is not only to curb arbitrary power but also to use the common resources in accordance with the principles of distributive justice. No doubt what has so far been achieved in this direction is very small in comparison with what, given the will, could even now be attempted. Yet there are the beginnings of an international conscience, and serious efforts have been made to define the principles by which this conscience might be guided. Witness the lively discussions of the value and limitations of national sovereignty, the increasing recognition of a duty on the part of the 'advanced' states to

come to the aid of the less advanced or 'underdeveloped', the movements
to define basic human rights.

The belief in progress is the belief that the quest for justice will continue
and that the partial successes so far attained point the way to further
successes. There is no law of necessary or automatic progress. Men will
not be moralized despite themselves, and knowledge alone will not
suffice to moralize them. What is asserted is that morality is rooted in the
rational nature of man and that historically there is a growing correlation
between the development of knowledge and moral and social development.

However, the correlation is incomplete and the future remains
uncertain. Some of the reasons which might account for this failure in
correlation have already been indicated, but may now be somewhat more
fully set out. Firstly, though knowledge as a whole undergoes development in the sense of correlated growth, the sciences dealing with the
different spheres of reality tend to have a life of their own and to differ in
their rates of advance. Without following Comte in details, we can see
that the sciences reach the 'positive' stage, that is the stage in which
theoretical construction and empirical verification are duly balanced and
correct each other, at different points of time. We must agree further that
earlier modes of thought may and often do persist in the later phases.
Thus the tendency to personify abstractions and to mistake words for
facts and myths for reality still dominates not only the popular mind, but
also the mind of many scientists, especially when dealing with matters
outside their chosen field. Witness the havoc wrought by the reification of
an abstraction like 'Capitalism' or the confusion of thought and the
passions engendered by the personification of collective entities, for
example, nations.

Secondly, as we have seen, the function of reason is to organize thought
and experience. But experience is not all of a piece. Moral, religious and
aesthetic experiences contain elements which are not easily integrated with
the sensory and cognitive experiences utilized by the natural sciences.
Hence the complexity of the relations between science, art, religion and
morals. On the one hand the growth of science has affected religion
profoundly, in the sense that events and experiences which once had a
religious explanation are in later phases left to the sciences to interpret. On
the other hand, philosophy has been greatly influenced by religious belief,
in so far at any rate as much of its work has been devoted to elucidating the
concept of God. Though ideally the reorganization for which reason is
searching will have to take into account the contributions of science,

religion and metaphysics, in fact these have often gone their own way and have certainly not always been in sympathy. Similar remarks apply to the relations between religion and morals. No doubt, men's conception of the ordering of human life must be affected by the conception they form of the ordering of the universe, of which human life is a part. In fact the relations between the beliefs defining the two orders have varied greatly. Religion is slowly moralized and progress in religion has often depended on fresh ethical insight. The problem of evil, including moral evil, has haunted all the religions of the world: yet neither religion nor philosophy is identical with morals and, in practice, religion and goodness often fall apart.

Thirdly, social institutions may be conceived as arising out of efforts to adjust human relations to the needs of life. These efforts in their early phases are, so to say, trial-and-error experiments whose results are embodied and hardened in habits and customs. In later phases man begins to pose the problem of human relations consciously, and slowly the notion of common purposes and common responsibilities arises and widens in scope and clarity. Deliberate attempts are then made to remedy faults in existing institutions and to resist changes making for deterioration. Even then, however, social changes are still largely unconscious or the unintended results of conscious actions. Nevertheless ideas and beliefs play an increasingly important part, though they may be ineffectual if unable to make a strong emotional appeal.

The efficacy of ideas is often denied on the ground that it is not they but the emotions that supply the driving energy. But this is an odd and unconvincing argument. The fact remains that if emotions can engender beliefs, beliefs can arouse emotions that otherwise might be dormant and that if the beliefs are changed so are the emotions. Moral ideas, in particular, are often proclaimed by tough realists of our day to be mere rationalizations of selfish interests. But here again the fact that rationalization is found necessary shows that ideas are not without power. In any event the predominant influence of self-interest is a dogma long ago refuted by philosophical analysis and by the teaching of modern biology and psychology. Support for it is often sought in the writings of Freud and Pareto. It is true that Freud commits himself to the view that the striving for justice is rooted in the desire that no one shall fare better than ourselves, and that Pareto interprets the demand for equality as a hidden desire for another kind of inequality. But neither supports his case by an examination of the motives which inspired the great humanitarians or comes any way near suggesting a method of analysing those of the thousands of individuals who have sacrificed their lives in the struggle against arbitrary power. I see no reason for taking these facile generalizations about the motives of altruistic action seriously.

This is not to claim supremacy for the moral factor in social life. It is only one among the many factors shaping social change, and its task is made difficult not only by inherent weaknesses arising out of the vagueness and one-sidedness of moral ideals, but by the fact that political and economic institutions have a momentum of their own indifferent to moral considerations and involving differentiations and divisions gravely hindering moral advance.

Finally, in dealing with the development of mankind as a whole, we have to take into account differences of level and rate of advance. Technological achievements are now readily diffusible and even the theoretical equipment involved can now be acquired more quickly than used to be thought. To transmit institutions, whether social or political, is a much more difficult matter, since they cannot be made to work efficiently without widespread changes in mentality and character. In general, it is clear that the peoples of the world are now rapidly coming to resemble each other more closely in matters of technique and the material basis of life. It has to be noted further that in recent times the Western ideas of freedom, self-determination and the rational use of natural forces to meet human needs have spread all over the world. This has meant a release of energies; but as usual has brought with it collisions, the danger of collisions, violence and the justification of violence. The immediate task for a Humanist ethic is to rid the world of the now palpable irrationality of war. Once freed from the fear of war, the peoples of the world will be free to develop each in its own way, but in relation to the whole human community, and to deal with the problems that knowledge can deal with, the conquest of disease and poverty and the removal of the barriers that divide men. They will then realize that they have a common positive aim—the unfolding and fulfilment of human faculty. Both sociological analysis and historical survey show that this aim can only be achieved by an organization covering the whole world and by methods which call forth the willing response of all its members. In this conclusion ethics and sociology are at one. The task before them is now to clarify further the conception of a self-directing humanity, to work out its practical implications, and to give it the vivid and imaginative expression which would convert it into a guiding force.

REFERENCES

(1) Bury, J. B. *The Idea of Progress*. New York: Macmillan, 1920.
(2) Singer, Charles. *Short History of Science*. New York: Oxford University Press, 1941.

(3) Flugel, J. C. *Man, Morals and Society*. London: Duckworth, 1955.

(4) Huxley, T. H. and J. S. *Touchstone for Ethics*. New York: Harper & Brothers, 1947, and C. H. Waddington's chapter in this book.

(5) Russell, Bertrand. *Principles of Social Reconstruction*. London: Allen & Unwin, 1920.

(6) Whitehead, A. N. *Adventures of Ideas*. New York: Macmillan, 1933.

(7) Hobhouse, L. T. *Comparative Ethics*. Encycl. Brit. 14th ed. On the whole subject of social development see also: *Morals in Evolution*. New York: Macmillan, 1951, 7th ed., and *Social Development*. New York: Holt, 1924.

(8) Friedmann, W. *Legal Theory*. London: Stevens, 1944.

(9) Smith, W. C. *Islam in Modern History*. Princeton University Press, 1957.

(10) Ginsberg, M. *On the Diversity of Morals*. New York: Macmillan, 1957.

(11) Gutteridge, H. C. *Comparative Law*. New York: Macmillan, 1946.

(12) Friedmann, W. *Law in a Changing Society*. Berkeley: University of California Press, 1959; Hazard, J. N. *Law and Social Change in the U. S. S. R.* London: Stevens, 1953; Guins, G. C. *Soviet Law and Soviet Society*. London: Batsford, 1954.

(13) Ginsberg, M. *Reason and Experience in Ethics*. Oxford University Press, 1956.

H. J. BLACKHAM

THE HUMAN PROGRAMME

H. J. BLACKHAM

Born 1903. Educated: Birmingham University. Secretary of the Ethical Union since 1945, and of the International and Humanist Ethical Union since its foundation in 1952.

Publications: *Six Existentialist Thinkers*, 1952; *The Human Tradition*, 1953; *Political Discipline in a Free Society*, 1961: editor of *Living as a Humanist*, 1949; J. B. Bury's *A History of Freedom of Thought*, 1952; *The Plain View: A Journal of Humanist Thought*.

THE HUMAN PROGRAMME

The Way Things Are

Before deciding how to live, one wants to know how things are; at any rate, this is a question that comes first logically. It is not a question that is simply answered by taking thought; a fully reliable answer is the delayed outcome of persistently trying to find out, and learning thereby how to find out. Meanwhile, life goes on, generations come and go, and make do with traditional assumptions, the body of established knowledge, and some current speculations.

In the European tradition, for some dozen centuries after the fall of Rome, thought was dominated by Christian theology, an amalgam of Platonic and Aristotelian ways of thinking with Judaistic concepts and Christian claims. Three component ideas in this product are relevant to Humanist thinking. (1) The universe is purposive throughout; purpose is built into the structure of everything. (2) Men are free to conform to or defy this purpose, but not to alter it; and they doom themselves to futility and nullity, or worse, by failing to conform. (3) The temporal order of nature is in some sense inferior and illusory, secondary to an eternal order that is ultimate reality.

The relevance to Humanist thinking of these three ideas of the way things are is that Humanists hold their contraries to be true: (i) they believe that the order discovered in nature is not properly teleological; (ii) that men are free to introduce valid purposes of their own, and to multiply the possibilities of purpose by exploring the uses of things; (iii) that there is no reason for thinking that the temporal order of nature is not, first and last, the condition of all human experience and achievement. How are these affirmations and the consequent rejection of the traditional ideas justified? The answer is, first, that tradition can be matched with tradition, and, secondly, that the Humanist affirmations stand or fall with reliance on the rational methods of learning from experience.

On the first point, although Christian theology, taking up the main strand of Greek philosophical thought, was dominant in the European tradition for so many centuries, there was an alternative and contrary tradition derived from the Greeks. This began to come into its own in the seventeenth century when its renascence assisted the nascent scientific movement by helping the pioneers of science to find their way.[1] This alternative tradition was based on the materialism of Democritus, the most learned man of his time and the great rival of Plato, a philosophy made popular by the Epicureans who rivalled the Stoics for nearly six centuries as guides to thinking and living in the Roman world. Democritus, 'the greatest investigator of nature in antiquity', was free from the pre-occupation with purpose of Socrates, the greatest investigator of human opinion in antiquity.[2] He posited self-subsistent, self-moving atoms, whose union and separation by mechanical necessity was the ground for the explanation of all phenomena. This natural causal model for thinking, in place of the human purposive model, was the neglected clue to learning from nature.

Two major developments in European thought have served to confirm and extend the type of explanation explored by this eclipsed line of Greek thinking: (i) 'reason' has ceased to be thought of as an inborn faculty of the mind, and is identified with the use of certain techniques for formulating and resolving questions in a reliable and progressive way; (ii) the theory of biological evolution has shown how to make sense of the idea of an order in nature which is not teleological but *teleonomic*, to use Professor Pittendrigh's necessary distinction.[3]

On the second point, if the evidence does not support the traditional assumptions, and is nowadays not even invoked in support of them, they can be maintained only on psychological or other non-logical grounds, which is to suppose that there are other means than scientific enquiry of finding out what the facts are, and that these other means are superior means, although their dominance belongs to an early phase of human thinking and they have proved incapable of achieving progressive knowledge.[4] To fall back on such a supposition to justify the traditional assumptions is to turn human experience topsy-turvy. In effect, it is to deny the possibility of learning from experience, because it is a rejection of the method by which men have learned how to do so.

The Global Frame

If Humanists are fully justified, then, in holding that there is no evidence of a divine purpose, revealed in history or at work in nature, to which one ought to try to conform, how does this view of the way things are affect the way of living? When God is dead, are all things permissible? Having rejected the traditional theistic, not to say Christian, basis and framework (which gives a destined perfection as the highest reality and the goal of striving), are Humanists thrown into the chaos of ethical relativism or must they logically lapse into the ethical solipsism of some existentialist philosophies?[5] No, not merely because they know that they are human only because they are social (and society requires rules as thinking requires rules), but also because, as Humanists, they stand upon the continent of history; their ethical thinking has historical concreteness and historical direction towards definite achievements if no goal of history.

What does this mean? Mainly two things: (i) the ethical thinking of Humanists is empirically at grips with the great social alternatives of better and worse possibilities which history poses in every age and to every generation; (ii) whether or not there is a constant called 'human nature', there is a variable called 'human behaviour', and Humanists have learned from history that human behaviour is a response to social conditions; they have seen that institutions, situations, education, devices, and techniques have made it better or worse.

These statements of course raise severe questions. How does one distinguish between 'better' and 'worse' possibilities? If human behaviour is socially determined, what becomes of personal responsibility? If one sets about controlling and 'improving' human behaviour, why not employ the most efficient totalitarian methods, up to and including 'brain-washing'? Before going on to develop the argument in a way that will meet such questions, I must indicate where the Humanist stands in relation to the position of the Marxist, who also claims that his ethical thinking is historical.[6]

That human thought and behaviour are socially conditioned is a fact. If one decides to have nothing to do with this fact, out of a scrupulous regard for individual dignity and personal responsibility, there is that much less chance of providing the necessary conditions of individual dignity and personal responsibility. It works both ways: free institutions are as deliberate an attempt at social conditioning as totalitarian methods. Free institutions are necessary, though not sufficient, conditions for maximizing spontaneity and diversity in a society. The human person, as the maker of value by his creative activities, and as the marker of standards by his enjoyments and his critical activities, is given the greatest practicable scope, stimulus, and protection in a developed political democracy. Thus, other things being equal, just because Humanists cherish human values, including of course the human personality which is their source, seat, and seal, they want and uphold a society based on agreed rules and agreed rules for changing the rules.

Other things *are* more or less equal in modern industrial societies, in the sense that economic plenty is widely available, and therefore the Marxist argument of the mid-nineteenth century that plenty could never be made available to all so long as the economic machine (and the political and military machines) remained effectively in the hands of a few owners, has lost its power to force the issue.

The eighteenth-century Humanists supposed that the accumulation of capital, the expansion of trade and industry, and the development of the arts and sciences would, with the spread of enlightenment and emancipation, benefit mankind universally.[7] They were right in principle, except in so far as they did not reckon seriously enough with the exclusiveness of possessing classes and nation-states. The distinction of Marx is that he saw this exclusiveness as a total obstruction that could not and would not be tolerated. Although the exclusiveness of classes and nations has been greatly relaxed since the Second World War, and is everywhere under challenge, it is now clear that it is only by enlightened, deliberate, and sustained policies and plans that the benefits of civilization can be made universal. They will not become universal in the eighteenth-century manner by a natural expansion and diffusion. There is of course an element of natural expansion and diffusion, today reinforced by the impatient demands of underdeveloped peoples for these benefits, inadequately met by responsive efforts on the part of the most advanced industrial nations. If the haphazard and hazardous working of these three elements could be superseded by a world development project, initiated jointly by the advanced industrial powers, both Communist states and political democracies, the dangerous and widening gap between rich and poor peoples could be reduced, and the hopeless and helpless masses made capable of participating by their own efforts in the growing wealth of the world.[8] This is the 'better possibility' of our time, to set against the worse possibilities of rivalry in exploiting the needs and demands of the underdeveloped peoples, local resistance to them, or inadequate response. If one completes the outline of better and worse possibilities by bringing in the danger of total war, of mounting populations, of dwindling resources, one is not likely to start an *ethical* argument. The whole ethical landscape is dominated by what is plainly good or bad, right or wrong, to most thinking people not plainly prejudiced.

The idea of a world development project is not utopian, because the need, the incentives, and the means are present. The moral unity and responsibility of mankind are the results of advances in knowledge and technology. Ethical thinking today gets its universality not merely from abstract principles but mainly from the pressure of a universal concrete situation which constrains mankind to decide its own fate.

The Distribution of Moral Responsibility

To speak of the responsibility of mankind is vast and vague. Who is responsible to whom for what? The men and women of the generations adult today are responsible to their children and to posterity for taking the necessary steps to create a universal human civilization, a human providence. This is of course a moral responsibility; it cannot be enforced. What makes it a moral responsibility is a situation which demands it (and in default threatens the worse possibilities of the age) and the availability of the technological and institutional means for doing it. This still leaves vast and vague what the responsibilities are and who is to shoulder them.

Three overriding problems about which all thinking people are worried define the responsibility more closely: the prevention of war, the control of population, the conservation of resources. These are problems that can be resolved only on a global scale, and the beginnings of a definite, if not definitive, solution of them would be the foundation of a universal civilization and a human providence. On the other hand, everybody who has thought about it knows that failure to deal with them adequately will bring general disaster. The clear recognition of this situation constitutes the awakening of mankind to its collective responsibility and necessary solidarity, the condition of a universal ethics.

How is this general responsibility of mankind for human fate at the present time divided? Thought of as responsibility for decisions, policies, and programmes in connection with the three major problems just mentioned, the responsibility falls inevitably most heavily on those, persons and powers, who are in a position to make effective decisions, form policies, and initiate and sustain programmes. The great problem of organizing world security and preventing war, for example, is mainly the joint responsibility of those who control the policy of NATO and of the USSR. It takes two to make a bargain, and without agreement the arms race cannot be halted and the first step taken in the reverse direction of controlled general disarmament and the institution of a World Security Authority.[9] Three related points are relevant to this stubborn difficulty, and they are of the first importance.

(1) Human thought and behaviour are largely socially determined. This has nowhere been seen more conspicuously than in the case of war. Nations of course have been aggressive, and have sought and gained aggrandizement. They have done so partly because otherwise they were liable to become victims. Even a purely defensive policy was bound to prove provocative. In this situation of inescapable rivalry, war is a further step in politics which sooner or later will have to be taken. That is to say, war is a product not simply of human iniquity but necessarily of the

situation of international anarchy. Neither peace-loving peoples nor diplomatic skill can permanently keep the sovereign nation-state out of war. The situation calls for an institutional solution. Better behaviour will follow because it will have been made possible, as well as because the old patterns of behaviour will have become inexcusable and would be universally censured.

(2) An institutional solution requires the agreement in the first place of the main parties, the nuclear powers. How can those on one side make the other side agree? The side which, whilst continuing to make itself efficient in defence, ceases to rely on its own armed power as a solution of the security problem, and therefore genuinely seeks controlled general disarmament and an institutional solution as necessary to its defence, is likely to succeed if it persists. At least it is true that to negotiate disarmament for advantage, whilst continuing to rely for security on armed power and diplomatic skill, is fatal to success in disarmament—and ultimately to security—and is ethically indefensible now that the destructive power of weapons has nullified the political justifications of war.

(3) Although the responsibility rests finally on those who have the power to act decisively, their responsibility is brought home to them by those to whom they are accountable, those whose interests are affected by their decisions. In democratic states this accountability is formally organized, and democratic peoples therefore have a heavy share of responsibility; but all peoples in some measure, and by whatever means are available to them, are responsible for the responsibility of their leaders. Only the pressure of expectation and demand make moral responsibility, as distinct from political accountability, more than a matter of conscience; and there is a responsibility for making this expectation and demand lively and exigent, a responsibility for responsibility. In turn, only in so far as it is organized is this responsibility for responsibility more than a matter of conscience. In this many agencies play their parts, but it is obvious that they have greatest scope in a society which enjoys free institutions. Again, the political democracies bear a heavy share of this secondary responsibility. To seek the costly security of graduated defence by deterrence *in order to be able to exchange it* for the security of agreed and tested international control (the professed policy of NATO) is so extraordinarily difficult a policy that an exceptionally alert and informed public opinion is needed to insist that neither form of security shall be sacrificed to an illusion of the other.

In sum, the general responsibility of mankind for these global matters cannot be neatly divided. It is shared and shaded, and levies specific demands on everybody. As moral demands, these are demands of an enlightened conscience, and that requires organized enlightenment and organized pressures. The history of all social achievement exemplifies this, and history calls now to those who have ears to hear.

Progress Within the Affluent Society

The big world problems of organizing security, controlling population, conserving resources, developing backward regions, intrude into national affairs and private lives, and demand a concerted world project with due priorities and an institutional organization of power and responsibility for dealing with them. Otherwise they continue to threaten the foundations of human existence. If and when peace and plenty are assured, social problems will not vanish, however. Better and worse possibilities are evident within affluent societies today. Human prospects are to be judged very largely by what happens on this front.

The worse possibilities of social organization in our time have been horribly delineated in *Nineteen Eighty Four* and *Brave New World*. With the prospect of affluence in the USSR, it is *Brave New World* that raises questions for modern highly organized mass industrial societies. Its author has recently pointed out that his fable has been documented by the sociologists since it was first written.[10] Human problems can be solved on these inhuman terms. What better possibilities are there, and what social conditions do they require?

The vision of human progress which the eighteenth-century Humanists had was comprehensive and not fundamentally mistaken. They relied on four main agencies. (1) Progressive knowledge by scientific enquiry was the key that opened every door. Bacon had written the great manifesto of human advance in the treatise (*Novum Organum*, 1620) which pleaded for empirical enquiry as the source of human confidence, freedom, and power. The practical arts were linked with the sciences, because they promoted the sciences and were in turn promoted by them. (2) The organization of mass-production by the accumulation and investment of capital and the division of labour was seen to be the means of progressive wealth. (3) If anarchy was the worst of social evils, tyrannical government was hardly less bad and worse than natural calamities, but the remedy was in the hands of the governed, who could adopt devices by which capable and trustworthy rulers were selected and kept under control. If the social rules were agreed rules they would be upheld by all and could be equally enforced on each, and there were rules by which rules could be agreed, and changed to keep them agreed. (4) Education was a primary public interest, not only because it furnished the trained ability which promoted the arts and sciences and industrial enterprise and supplied the public service, but also because it made men self-dependent and responsible. Therefore it should be available to all, and not merely to the mentally gifted.

All these fundamentals of human progress were argued out in the eighteenth century. Not one of them can be seriously challenged in the light of experience since that time. Of course, under each head the formula of that day was far too simple for the needs and problems of ours, but the general orientation and commitments remain the same. We are still governed by the ideals set by the tasks under each of these heads, and there can be no serious question of turning away from them in any other direction. One ought to discuss present problems and trends under each of them. I have space to say something only about education.

Every culture propagates itself by means of its pattern of child-rearing and education. Except in advanced cultures, this is not based on child study, but on immemorial customs. Even modern sophisticated societies reproduce themselves largely in their own image through the family and through the schools, but child study has had a say as well as social exigencies in most modern educational policy and practice, and in some places has gone so far as to transform the content of the curriculum and the methods of teaching. At any rate, where child study is allowed a continuous influence upon educational policy and practice, in a society of free institutions, there are the optimum social conditions of human development.

The earliest years are of proved importance for character and personality, in determining whether the child will be able to accept and deal with reality, within and without, or will helplessly impose upon it his own fantasies.[11] For instance, every child is normally and necessarily checked and corrected. In being frustrated by correction the child is made to feel hostile and aggressive against the adult who checks him, and he projects this hatred and aggressiveness on to the adult, that is, he cannot help feeling that the adult hates him and wants to hurt him. At the same time, the adult is, or may be, the one on whom he is utterly dependent, the source of all good. Thus a conflict is set up within the child which may become an unbearable tension, resulting in a total repression of the hostility and aggressiveness and a total submission to adult authority. Thereafter, the child is either impaired in his vitality by the repressed conflict, or he projects the repressed guilt on to some object in the world which he treats as wholly evil and pursues with hatred. He tends to see and to seek in the world what is wholly good which he can worship and with which he can be identified and what is wholly bad which he is justified in pursuing with hate and harm and on which he can project his buried guilty self. Here is the authoritarian (who is also the submissive) personality in the making, e.g. the Hitler who deifies the Aryan-Nordic-Teuton and projects his guilt upon the Jew and imposes these fantasies on his countrymen when the frustrations of their social situation have made them responsive.[12]

On the other hand, if the child is enabled to come to terms with his conflict, his ambivalent feelings of love and hate, because he is assured in the act of correction that he is also loved, he learns to tolerate his own guilt and that of others, that is to say, to meet reality, within and without, with sane discrimination.[13]

If the child's vitality and sanity are well founded in this way, he can be enabled to become self-dependent, that is to say, to acquire required competence and to accomplish recognized achievements within the range of his own abilities and aptitudes. With his interests thus initiated and given scope and encouragement, he can be socialized, that is to say, learn to recognize and accept and respect the 'other' and to participate and play his part in a co-operative world, as one among many. At adolescence, he can be shown how to make up his mind, how to solve his problems, how to overcome his failures, by being put into possession of appropriate techniques. In such ways he can be made capable of a life of his own. Meanwhile, through the subjects of the curriculum and the activities of the school he has been introduced to the great themes of human living, so that in the manifold interests brought within his experience he finds congenial soil in which to strike root and thrive.

Whatever on these lines is done to good purpose in the home and the school is after all to no purpose if society at large faces the school-leaver with the Big-Brotherly features of Ad-mass and Organization-Man.[14] If he is drafted and routed and required to conform to prescribed procedures and practices, if his wife has to keep up with the Joneses, if he has to buy what the advertisers want, and if the entertainment which is laid on for all hours of the day fills in the time which should be his own, then there is no point in preparing him for a life of his own; he might as well be left to the 'other-directed' pattern of life which the structure of contemporary society tends to impose upon him.[15] This is the kind of dilemma which, it is widely supposed, vitiates the hope of progress within the affluent society.

The dilemma is probably false, but the problem is certainly real. Of course our mass-industrial societies are shaped into general patterns of conformity one way or another by massive social and commercial influences. It is the price that is paid for the productive power of highly populated and highly organized societies. These powerful influences, however, although they may destroy individual initiative and taste, do not necessarily do so. If people in the formative phases of their lives are made capable of living lives of their own, they will normally want to do so. Much that is made available by commercial means or by social policy is excellently to their purpose and can be selectively used. It is by means of standardization that standards have been raised; and if one may judge by the amazing vagaries of individual style in young men's dress in Britain, standardization of products does not entail uniformity in use and enjoyment.

The standard of living is rising in the affluent society not only in terms of income and expenditure but also in real terms: physical and mental health, personal relations, taste, and achievement. How can one say this when it is about this that so many people have depressing doubts and fears supported by the evidence of adolescent discontent and delinquency in all the affluent societies? For some things, of course, there are figures, health for example, but general assurance can be drawn from argument on these lines: there are many social services and other agencies besides the schools which are engaged in raising the standard of living in these real terms; the workers in these services will not utterly fail, and their skill and their techniques will improve with experience and practice, and some of this improvement will be funded in training and transmitted, just as the beneficiaries of these services, as parents, as husbands and wives, as employers (benefiting from industrial management studies and institutes) will transmit benefits through their own improved standards. If the rise of real standards is not cumulative in this way (as knowledge and wealth are progressive), this will be the first case in which effort based on study and improved by experience is not rewarded. We live and move and have our being in a material organized world which is dependable and improvable because it is material and organized. This is the foundation of the Humanist's faith in man. The affluent society is one that can afford to invest in society continuously knowledge, capital, and service. These valuable commodities are not being laid out to no purpose, and they will be increasingly laid out to better purpose, like successful investments in industry. The faith in man that has confidence in this kind of argument is a faith inspired by history. It is not daunted by two world wars, by Nazi enormities, by the crime-rate, nor by the extent of juvenile delinquency, not because these are not serious and shocking matters, but because they have causes that can be understood and because reasonable human behaviour also has causes and can be achieved.

Secular Faith

It is reasonable, then, to think that it is not beyond the wit of man to bring about situations and conditions everywhere in which it will be reasonable for men to behave reasonably. Irrational behaviour is not a wanton manifestation of an original evil; it is understandable, and its drives and goals are the common drives and goals of men. If the social situation between nations and within nations can be made conducive to reasonable and reliable behaviour, so also can the situation within the human person and within the family, the root sources of tension and of destructive passions. Deliberate decisions and policies and programmes will be necessary at all levels, and most urgently at the international level; but the need for them is evident and the means are at hand.

The high Baconian confidence of the eighteenth-century Humanists has flagged; it can be renewed at the source, for Bacon rallied his contemporaries to the standard of method, a method at that time undeveloped and imperfectly understood. We are in a better position to see what method can do, applied by man to himself for his own orderly fulfilment in freedom and responsibility. Faith in progress on the road to a universal high civilization can be restored if it can be shown to be a reasonable faith.[16] Is this secular faith in conflict with the older faiths of traditional religion, particularly the Christian faith? Yes, if it belongs to the Christian faith to 'sit loose to civilization'. That is the test. The Humanist is reconciled to reality and makes his home there, and has a horror of the black-and-white fantasy of heaven and hell. Of course reality is tolerable only in so far as it is being transcended. But that is the human vocation.

The Decalogue, the Sermon on the Mount, the ethics of the Stoics or of Kant, the ethics of Aristotle, and not less the ethics of the Epicureans and of the Utilitarians, have all had an immense formative influence in the moral tradition of Western peoples, and no doubt they will continue to do so and will not be simply superseded. All the same, a new Humanist ethic is needed, to create in the climate of modern ideals and in the context of new possibilities an ethos of personal excellence and public spirit worthy of the human vocation, the ethos of an enlightened universal civilization.

Such an ethic is not likely to be couched in the language either of abstract principle or of moral codes. On the private side, it is likely to be evocative rather than repressive, exemplary rather than prohibitive. On the public side, it is likely to be more definite, pointing to particular practical imperatives which govern the preventive and constructive work peremptorily required on behalf of mankind.

Justice and morality between equals may be left to take care of themselves. The moral responsibility that tends to fail and requires to be reinforced is a responsibility of the strong for the weak, or a responsibility that arises from new knowledge, or a responsibility for the future and the unborn, or a responsibility due to relevant considerations not usually taken into account. In such cases, Humanists have been conspicuously forward in reinforcing moral responsibility; they have ever been an *avant-garde* in morals, because of their concern for human welfare and their eagerness for the advancement of knowledge and the use and enjoyment of its fruits.

To reinforce moral responsibility where it is weak does not mean to lay down the law in enlightened codes of ethics to govern the great departments of human activity—an international code, an economic code, an educational code. Such codes have been drafted. Their rudiments have even been subscribed by the nations in the Universal Declaration of Human Rights of 1948. They have their uses. They ought not to give the satisfaction of duty done. To get an informed and exigent public opinion to operate as an effective sanction on all who bear any share of any given moral responsibility is an altogether bigger and longer affair, an always unfinished campaign on many fronts of thought and action. This practical reinforcement of moral responsibility where it is weak is the unending matter of daily excursions and encounters in the public arena and within the precincts of private and professional gardens. Humanists, by their acceptance of human responsibility for establishing the conditions of human fulfilment, are committed to exceptional efforts to raise the standard of behaviour in this way. Theirs is the dedication of an order. They ought to be in modest anonymity the unacknowledged legislators of the world. They are a cadre of activists who insistently and persistently make high expectations the measure of man.

REFERENCES

(1) Hall, A. R. *The Scientific Revolution* 1500–1800. New York: Longmans, 1954.

(2) Windelband, W. *History of Ancient Philosophy*. New York: Dover Publications, 1957.

(3) Pittendrigh, C. S. 'Adaptation, Selection and Behavior' in *Behavior and Evolution*, ed. A. Roe and G. G. Simpson. Yale University Press, 1958.

(4) Broad, C. D. 'The Present Relations of Science and Religion' in *Philosophy*, Vol. XIV, No. 54, April 1939.

(5) For an understanding of what is true and what is false in ethical relativism, see M. Ginsburg, 'On the Diversity of Morals' in the volume with that title. New York: Macmillan, 1957, and A. MacBeath, *Experiments in Living*. New York: St Martin's Press, 1952.

(6) Blackham, H. J. *The Human Tradition*. New York: Beacon Press, 1954.

(7) Condorcet, A.–N. de. *The Progress of the Human Mind*, 1795. Tr. June Barraclough, ed. Stuart Hampshire. New York: Noonday Press, 1955.

(8) Myrdal, Gunnar. *Rich Lands and Poor*, World Perspectives Series. New York: Harper & Brothers, 1957.

(9) Noel–Baker, Philip. *The Arms Race*. New York: Oceana Publications, 1958.

(10) Huxley, Aldous. *Brave New World Revisited*. New York: Harper & Brothers, 1959.

(11) Cp. E. H. Erikson's essay in this volume.

(12) Adorno, T. W. (ed.) *et al. The Authoritarian Personality*. New York: Harper & Brothers, 1958; and J. C. Flugel, *Man, Morals and Society*. London: Duckworth, 1955, especially Chapter IX.

(13) In his Romanes Lecture, Section III, printed in *Touchstone for Ethics* (New York: Harper & Brothers, 1947), Sir Julian Huxley stresses the *ethical superiority* of this internal ethical realism—it is the primary ethical standard—and therefore the ethical importance of educational disciplines which enable the child to achieve it.

(14) Whyte, William H. *The Organization Man*. New York: Simon & Schuster, 1956.

(15) Potter, D. M. *People of Plenty*. University of Chicago Press, 1954.

(16) Frankel, Charles. *The Case for Modern Man*. New York: Harper & Brothers, 1956. For the grounds of a reasonable faith, see my *Political Discipline in a Free Society*. London: Allen & Unwin, 1961.

Representative treatment of ethical theory from a humanist point of view can be found in the following:

Dewey, John. *Human Nature and Conduct*. New York: Henry Holt & Co., 1922.
Fromm, Erich. *Man for Himself*. New York: Rinehart & Company, 1947.
Nowell–Smith, P. H. *Ethics*. New York: Philosophical Library, 1958.
Hourani, George F. *Ethical Value*. University of Michigan Press, 1956.
Osborn, R. *Humanism and Moral Theory*. London: Allen & Unwin, 1959.
Waddington, C. H., *The Ethical Animal*. London: Allen & Unwin, 1960.

E. H. ERIKSON

THE ROOTS OF VIRTUE

E. H. ERIKSON

Born 1902. Educated: Germany; studied art in Italy, psychoanalysis in Vienna. At present Professor of Human Development at Harvard University. Senior Staff, Austen Riggs Center.

Publications: Books as listed in references; papers and monographs on children's play and child-training among American Indians. Papers on clinical subjects.

THE ROOTS OF VIRTUE

―――――――

1. *Ego and Virtue*

In this essay I intend to investigate the genetic roots and the evolutionary rationale of certain basic human qualities which I will call virtues. We have learned to be cautious in the use of this powerful little word ever since Freud introduced us to the study of 'the much furrowed ground from which our virtues proudly spring'. Yet the very development of psychoanalytic thought, and its recent preoccupation with 'ego-strength', suggest that human virtue be reconsidered—not, of course, in the now more widespread sense of moral nobility and rectitude, but in that older, simpler sense of an 'inherent strength', an 'active quality'. 'By virtue of' what qualities, then, can man claim to be, or to be able to become, humanly strong?

What we call virtue, we value; and in approaching the origin of value we face a dilemma which Darwinian biology and Freudian psychology seem to share. Together they have focused on what is popularly considered man's 'lower nature': the descent and evolution of the genus man from a pre-human state of *animality*; the emergence of civilized man from degrees of *savagery* and *barbarism*; and the evolution of individual man from the stages of *infantility*. They have shown the relation of rational man's everyday irrationalities to *insanity*, and revealed political man's propensity for mob *anarchy*. Each of these insights was at first met with derision and disbelief; but they soon assumed the form of modern myths. Popular thought (and that includes specialists in non-biological fields) generalized Darwin's theory as a 'tooth-and-claw' struggle for survival, in which the crown of creation would go to what T. H. Huxley called the 'gladiatorial' type of man. Similarly, popular thought (and that includes scientists not familiar with the advancements of psychoanalysis) crudely over-simplifies Freud's theory of inner conflict. It clings to the earliest formulation of this conflict and conceives of it as an inner tooth-and-claw struggle between ravenous instincts (the impersonal 'Id') and cruel conscience (the moralistic 'Super-Ego'). Thus the moral alternatives seemingly implicit in Darwin's and Freud's discoveries were over-dramatized—as if mankind were taking revenge on these fearless men by forcing them into the role of tragic high priests in the cult of 'facing man's lower nature', a 'nature' often owned up to so eagerly that it soon excuses everything. This double myth of an inner and outer struggle to the death has thus made it difficult for both biology and psychoanalysis to come to grips with the question of man's moral strength—except, perhaps, by drawing the obvious and yet already stereotyped conclusion that man's future, if it were dependent on his overweening conscience and his absolutist morality alone, could predictably end in species-wide suicide in the name of the highest principles.[1]

Julian Huxley summed the matter up at the end of his Romanes Lecture:

'The peculiar difficulties which surround our individual moral adjustment are seen to be largely due to our evolutionary history. Like our prolonged helplessness in infancy, our tendency to hernia and sinusitis, our troubles in learning to walk upright, they are a consequence of our having developed from a simian ancestry. Once we realize that the primitive super-ego is merely a makeshift developmental mechanism, no more intended to be the permanent central support of our morality than is our embryonic notochord intended to be the permanent central support of our bodily frame, we shall not take its dictates so seriously (have they not often been interpreted as the authentic Voice of God?), and shall regard its supersession by some more rational and less cruel mechanism as the central ethical problem confronting every human individual'.[2]

This passage expresses a view to which, in fact, psychoanalysis is dedicated both as a clinical technique and a system of thought. Every step in treatment and every act of clarification is directed toward the 'supersession by some more rational and less cruel mechanisms'. And it is not difficult for a psychoanalyst to subscribe to Huxley's 'Humanist Frame', if for no other reason than that, to the scientist and scholar, it seems the best of all possible Utopias:

'While to the evolutionist ethics can no longer be regarded as having any absolute value, yet their relativity is neither chaotic nor meaningless: ethics are relative to a process which is both meaningful and of indefinitely long duration—that of evolutionary progress'.[2]

The fact is that the rapprochement between evolutionary biology and psychoanalytic psychology is one well prepared for by an aspect of Freud's thought which has not provoked the imagination of other scientists as his instinct theory has done: I refer to his Ego-Psychology.

Almost from the beginning of psychoanalysis, Freud worked continuously on an area of enquiry concerning the 'coherent organization of mental processes'[3] which, in all conflict and danger, guarantees to the human person a measure of individuality, mature sexuality, intelligence, and integrity.*

Before indicating what the ego is, it is necessary to state what it is not; for the term has been much abused. Popularly, the term 'ego' implies an inflated sense of one's own importance, a precarious sense subject to sudden deflation by the pricks of fate—and of gossip. As a brief designation of modern man's vulnerable sense of a self-made self, this usage has become so popular that even highly informed individuals prefer it to, or use it alongside, the psychoanalytic meaning of ego as designating an inner-psychic regulator which organizes inner experience and guards such organization *both* against the untimely impact of *drives* and the undue pressure of an overweening *conscience*. Actually, ego is an age-old term which in scholastics stood for the *unity* of body and soul, and in philosophy in general for the *permanency* of conscious experience. Psychoanalysis, of course, has not concerned itself with matters of soul and has assigned to consciousness a limited role in mental life by demonstrating that man's thoughts and acts are co-determined by unconscious motives which, upon analysis, prove him to be both worse and better than he thinks he is. But this also means that his motives as well as his feelings, thoughts and acts, often 'hang together' much better than he could (or should) be conscious of. The ego in psychoanalysis, then, is analogous to what it was in philosophy in earlier usage: a selective, integrating, coherent and persistent agency central to personality formation. First studied clinically in its impaired states, the ego has also been revealed as a control regulator of remarkable endurance and power. It is the inner 'organ' which makes it possible for man to bind together the two great evolutionary developments, his *inner life* and his *social planning*.

But where, in animal nature, is the precursor of the human ego? Man has always tended to project what he calls his own 'animal nature' on

* The study of the ego has been pursued most significantly by Anna Freud[4] and Heinz Hartmann, who was the first to point to the central role of the ego in all human adaptation. See his comprehensive monograph 'Ego-Psychology and the Problem of Adaptation',[5] in which he approached such previously neglected problems as 'the regulation by the will'. David Rapaport has in recent years worked on the systematization of the theory of the ego,[6, 7] and has enriched it with an investigation of the problems of activity and passivity.[8] My own studies in the relation of ego-psychology, society, and history[7, 9, 10] prompt this attempt to speculate on the psychosocial implications of human evolution.

animals, comparing, for example, his ravenousness with the eating style of dogs, or his rage with that of provoked tigers. Yet man has also been inclined to use animals as images of ideals, calling himself as courageous as a lion, or as meek as a lamb. For an analogy to what we call ego, however, we must contemplate a certain chaste restraint and selective discipline[11] in the life of even the 'wildest' animals: a built-in regulator which prevents (or 'inhibits') carnivorous excess, inappropriate sexuality, useless rage, and damaging panic, permitting rest and play along with the readiness to attack when hungry, or intruded upon. Similarly, different species of animals share environments with a minimum of mutual interference or distraction, each minding its own section of the environment unless, and until, vital interests prove to intersect. Thus, the state of the adapted animal is defined by what we might call *ecological integrity*; a combination of mutual regulation and reciprocal avoidance which safeguards adaptation within the characteristic environment and with other species sharing it. Man, who has evolved into a creature always in the process of readjusting to historical change in his man-made world, obviously over-reacts (in suffering, for example, from affect-incontinence as Konrad Lorenz has said): for him, to live up, on his level, to the animal's adaptive integrity, would call for a mutual regulation of inner motivation and technical-social invention which he seems to approach only during certain glorious but unpredictable periods. To take his place more consciously in the succession of generations within his psychosocial universe, he must learn to know and to use what we here call the Ego.

I will call 'virtues', then, the specifically human qualities of strength which are implicit in man's psychosocial evolution, and I will relate them to that process, by which *ego strength* is both developed and imparted, from generation to generation.

2. *A Schedule of Virtues*

The paradox of human life is man's collective power to create his own environment, although each individual is born with a naked vulnerability extending into a prolonged infantile dependence. The weakness of the newborn, however, is truly relative. While far removed from any measure of mastery over the physical world, newborn man is endowed with an appearance and with responses which appeal to the tending adults' tenderness and make them wish to attend his needs; which arouse concern in those who are concerned with his well-being; and which, in making adults care, stimulate their active care-taking. I employ the repetition of the words tending, concern, and caring, not for a poetic effect, but in order to underscore the fundamental fact, that in life in general and in human life in particular, the vulnerability of being newly born and the meekness of innocent needfulness have a power all of their own. Defenceless as babies are, there are mothers at their command, families to protect the mothers, societies to support the structure of families, and traditions to give a cultural continuity to systems of tending and training. All of this, however, the human infant does need in order to evolve humanly: for his environment must provide that *outer wholeness and continuity* which, like a second womb, permits the child to develop his separate capacities in distinct steps, and to unify them only in a series of psychosocial crises.

In recent years, psychiatry has concerned itself with the mother-child relationship, and has, at times, burdened it with the whole responsibility for man's sanity and maturation. This concentration on earliest development seemed to find powerful support in the young science of ethology, which analyses the innate mechanisms by which mother animal and young animal release in each other the behaviour necessary for the survival of the young—and thus the species.[12] However, a true ethological comparison must juxtapose the first period in animal life (such as the nest-occupancy of certain birds) with man's whole pre-adult life, including adolescence. For man's psychosocial survival is safeguarded only by virtues which develop in the interplay of successive and overlapping generations, living together in organized settings. Here, living together means more than incidental proximity: it means that the individual's life-stages are 'interliving', cogwheeling with the stages of others which move him along as he moves them. I have, therefore, in recent years, attempted to delineate the whole life-cycle as an integrated psychosocial phenomenon, instead of following what (in analogy to teleology) may be called the 'originological' approach, that is, the attempt to derive the meaning of development primarily from a reconstruction of the infant's beginnings.[13]

When it finally comes to naming the basic virtues, with which human beings steer themselves and others along the path of life, one is at first tempted to make up new words out of Latin roots. Latin always suggests expertness and explicitness, while everyday words have countless connotations: to optimists they make virtues sound like gay and easy accomplishments, and to pessimists, like idealistic pretences. Yet when we approach phenomena closer to the ego, the everyday words of living languages, ripened in the usage of generations, will serve best as a means of discourse.

I will, therefore, speak of *Hope*, *Will*, *Purpose*, and *Skill*, as the rudiments of virtue developed in childhood; of *Fidelity* as an adolescent virtue; and of *Love*, *Care*, and *Wisdom* as the central virtues of adulthood. In all their seeming discontinuity, these qualities depend on each other:

C. Evolving Social Attitudes →

	1	2	3	4	5	6	7	8	B. Expanding Interpersonal Reciprocity ↑
Philosophical	WISDOM								Generations demanding Integrated Heritage
Productive		CARE							Progeny and Production Challenging Competency
Interpersonal			LOVE						Mates and Partners in Search of Shared Identity
Ideological				FIDELITY					Confirming Adults Affirming Peers
Technical					SKILL				Instructive Adults Co-operative Peers
Moral						PURPOSE			Exemplary Basic Family
Judicious							WILL		Judicious Parental Persons
Reverent								HOPE	Trustworthy Maternal Environment
Lifestages →	Senescence	Adulthood	Young Adulthood	School Age		Play Age		Infancy	

A. Lifestages (physiological, psychosexual, cognitive, psychosocial)

A SCHEDULE OF BASIC VIRTUES

will cannot be trained until hope is secure, nor love become reciprocal until fidelity has proven reliable. Also, each virtue and its place in the schedule of all virtues is vitally interrelated to other segments of human development, such as the stages of psychosexuality,[14, 9, 15] the psycho-social crises,[7, 16] and the steps of cognitive maturation.[17, 18] These schedules I must take for granted, as I restrict myself to a parallel time-table of the evolving virtues.

The Chart is an *epigenetic diagram*: it indicates that each virtue, in some form, exists from the beginning of life, but that each has its *stage of ascendancy* (diagonal) when its rudiments must develop from the interplay of the advancing lifestages (A) with an expanding social interaction (B), or remain retarded and stunted. Thus the virtues, step by step, become the inner strength of the human life-cycle which has evolved as a safeguard of the continuity of psychosocial evolution. Col. C, finally, indicates those social attitudes which re-evolve in each individual and his generation giving renewed support to the institutions and traditions of society, which in turn are to safeguard the process of virtue-formation in all successive generations.

3. *Hope*

If we ascribe to the healthy infant the rudiments of Hope, it would, indeed, be hard to specify the criteria for this state, and harder to measure it: yet he who has seen a hopeless child, knows what is *not* there. Hope is both the earliest and the most indispensable virtue inherent in the state of being alive.[19] Others have called this deepest quality *confidence*, and I have referred to *trust* as the earliest positive psychosocial attitude: but if life is to be sustained, hope must remain, even where confidence is wounded, trust impaired. Clinicians know that an adult who has lost all hope, regresses into as lifeless a state as a living organism can sustain. But there is something in the anatomy even of mature Hope which suggests that it is the most childlike of all ego-qualities, and the most dependent for its verification on the charity of fate; wherefore religious sentiment induces adults to restore their hopefulness in periodic petitionary prayer, assuming a measure of childlikeness toward unseen, omnipotent powers.

Nothing in *human* life, however, is secured in its origin unless it is verified in the intimate meeting of partners in favourable social settings. Thus the rudiments of hope rely on the new being's first encounter with *trustworthy maternal persons* who respond to his reach for *intake* and *contact* with appropriate provision, and prevent experiences of the kind which all too regularly bring too little too late.

Hope thus rests its case on a combination of experiences in the individual's 'prehistoric' era, the time before speech and verbal memory. Both psychoanalysis and genetic psychology consider central in that period of growth the secure apperception of an 'object': by which the psychologists mean the ability to perceive the *enduring quality* of the *thing world* while psychoanalysts speak loosely of a first inner love-object, i.e. the experience of the care-taking person as a *coherent being*, who reciprocates one's physical and emotional needs in expectable ways and therefore deserves to be endowed with trust.

Hope, once established as a basic quality of experience, remains independent of the verifiability of *hopes*: for it is in the nature of man's maturation that concrete hopes will, at a time when a hoped-for event or state comes to pass, prove to have been quietly superseded by a more advanced set of hopes. The gradual widening of the infant's horizon of active experience provides, at each step, verifications which inspire new hopefulness. Even as the infant learns to renounce and to repress (with all the profound consequences uncovered by psychoanalysis), he also learns to dream of what is imaginable and to train his expectations on what promises to prove possible. All in all, then, maturing hopefulness not only maintains itself in the face of changed facts—it proves itself able to change facts, even as faith is said to move mountains.

The evolutionary character of Hope becomes apparent if we consider that it must help man to approximate that rootedness possessed by the animal world, in which instinctive equipment and environment, moment for moment, verify each other, unless catastrophe overtakes the individual or the species. To the human infant, his mother *is* nature; she must *be* that original verification, which, later, will come from other and wider segments of reality.*

All the self-verifications, however, begin in that inner light of the mother-child-world, which Madonna images have conveyed as so exclusive and so secure: and, indeed, such light must shine through the chaos of many crises, maturational and accidental.

---

* In what follows I must imply rather than spell out a number of self-verifications on which the strength of the ego depends; among them

(1) the *completion of growth-patterns*, and the successful exercise of physical and mental powers;

(2) the *consummation of significant relationships* to the point of a mutual engagement or a successful disengagement;

(3) the *resolution of maturational crises* with a reintegration of the unity of experience;

(4) the *confirmation of the individual's identity* as he gradually grows into his culture's technology and tradition.

4. *Will*

An exclusive condition of hopefulness, translated into various imaginable worlds, would be a paradise in nature, a Utopia in social reality, and a heaven in the beyond. Yet hope leads inexorably into conflicts between the rapidly developing self-will and the will of others. As the infant's senses and his muscles grasp at opportunities for more active experience, he faces the double demand for self-control and for the acceptance of the control of others: he must learn to *will* what *can* be, and to convince himself that he *willed* what *had* to be.

Here, no doubt, is the genetic origin of the elusive question of Free Will, which man, ever again, attempts to master logically and theologically. The fact is that no person can live, no ego remain intact without hope and will. Even philosophical man who feels motivated to challenge the very ground he stands on, questioning both will and hope as illusory, feels more real for having willed such heroic enquiry; and where man chooses to surrender his sense of having willed the inevitable to gods and leaders, he fervently endows them with what he has renounced for himself.

The rudiments of Will are acquired, in analogy to all basic qualities, as the ego unifies experiences on fronts seemingly remote from each other: awareness and attention, manipulation, verbalization, and locomotion. The training of the eliminative sphincters, too, can become the centre of the struggle over inner and outer control. A sense of defeat (from inadequate or over-training) can lead to deep *shame* and a compulsive *doubt* whether one ever really willed what one did, or really did what one willed.

If will, however, is built securely into the early development of the ego it survives, as hope does, the evidences of its limited potency: for the maturing individual gradually incorporates a knowledge of what is expectable and what can be expected of him. Often defeated, he nevertheless learns to accept the existential paradox of making decisions which he knows 'deep down' will be predetermined by events, because making decisions is part of the evaluative quality inherent in being alive: ego strength depends, above all, on the sense of having done one's *active part* in the chain of the inevitable.

It is the task of *judicious parenthood* to demonstrate that *goodwill* ensues from a mutual limitation of wills; it gradually grants a liberating measure of self-control to the child who learns to control wilfulness and to train his willingness.

5. *Purpose*

It is inherent in infantile man's prolonged immaturity that he must train the rudiments of Will in situations in which he does not quite know what he wants and why—which makes his wilfulness at times rather desperate. By the same token he must develop in 'mere' phantasy and play the rudiments of *Purpose*, a temporal perspective giving direction and focus to concerted striving. Play is to the child what thinking, planning, and blueprinting are to the adult: a trial universe in which conditions are simplified, and methods exploratory, so that past failures can be thought through, expectations tested. In the toy world, the child 'plays out' the past, often in disguised form, in the manner of dreams;[9, 20] and he begins to master the future, by *anticipating* it in countless variations of repetitive themes. In taking the various role-images of his elders into *his* sphere of *make-believe* he can find out what it feels like to be like them before fate forces him to become like some of them.

It may well be the evolutionary function of infantile play (and later, of drama) that it affords an intermediate reality in which the budding sense of purposefulness can disengage itself from the fixation on the past by giving it a mythological order and quality. It seems significant that play is most intense when the period of 'infantile sexuality' comes to an end and when that great barrier, the universal 'incest-taboo', is met. The direction of sexual drives and of purposeful energies must now be diverted from the very parental persons who first awakened the child's tenderness, sensuality, and amorphous sexual phantasies.

Play, in young animals, too, is predicated upon parental protection from hunger and from danger. In man it is, furthermore, dependent on the protection from unmanageable conflict.[9] The play age relies on the existence of the *basic family* in one of its exemplary forms, which must gradually delineate where play ends and irreversible purpose begins, where phantasy is no longer permissible and to-be-learned reality all-demanding: only thus is conscience integrated. It is not always understood that one of the main rationales for marital and familial loyalty and morality is the imperative need for inner unity in the child's conscience at the very time when he can and must envisage goals beyond the family: for the voices and images of those adults who are now internalized as an *inner voice* must not contradict each other too flagrantly, and, in fact, must speak *the same language*. Only the safe inner development of a rudimentary conscience, can, in turn, give the child the inner freedom to move on—to whatever school setting his culture has ready for him.

Purposefulness is now ready to attach itself to a sense of reality which is defined by what *can be attained* and by what can be *shared in words*. Thus, conscience, the consistent inner voice which delineates permissible action and thought, finds a powerful ally in the structure of *language*, which makes reality an order verbally shared and subject to joint mastery.

6. *Skill*

Ever since his 'expulsion from paradise', man has been inclined to protest work as drudgery or as slavery, and to consider most fortunate those who seemingly can choose to work or not to work. The fact is that man *must* learn to work, as soon as his intelligence and his capacities are ready to be 'put to work', so that his ego's power may not atrophy.

The rudiments of *skill* add method to hope, will and purpose. Now, what 'works' in the fabric of one's thought and in the use of one's physical co-ordination can be found to 'work' in materials and in co-operative encounters: a self-verification of lasting importance. All human environments, therefore, meet this stage with the offer of instruction in *perfectible skills* leading to *practical uses* and *significant achievements*. All cultures have their logic and their 'truth' which can be learned, by exercise, usage, and ritual. Where literacy is a common basis for all future specialization, the rules of grammar and of algebra, of course, form a more abstract demonstration of the workings of reality. Thus *workmanship* and the *reasonableness* which comes from convincing experience prepare in the child a future sense of *competency* without which there can be no 'strong ego'. Without it man feels inferior in his equipment, and in the hope to match an ever-increasing section of manageable reality with his growing capacities.

7. *Fidelity*

When man's sexuality matures in puberty, he is not yet ready to be a mate or a parent. His ego-balance is, in fact, decidedly endangered by the double uncertainty of a demanding instinctual machinery which must be kept in abeyance in some of its functions* while he must prepare for his own place in the adult order. The adolescent thus often appears to be a contradictory combination of shifting devotion and general perversity: at times more devotedly perverse, at others more perversely devoted. In all of this, however, an 'ideological' seeking after an inner coherence and a durable set of values can always be detected. I have, in a series of books and papers, described many aspects of this 'sense of identity',[7, 9, 10, 16] and I would now call the particular ego-quality which emerges with it and from it,

* By complete abstinence; by sexual release without the involvement of another; by emotional love without sexual involvement; by sexual license without genital involvement; by genital involvement without procreative commitment.

fidelity. This word combines a number of truths to which adolescents alternately adhere: high *accuracy* and *veracity* in the rendering of reality; the sentiment of truth, as in *sincerity* and *conviction*; the quality of genuineness, as in *authenticity*; the trait of *loyalty*, of 'being true'; *fairness* to the rules of the game; and finally all that is implied in *devotion*: a freely given but binding vow, with the fateful implication of a curse befalling the undedicated. When Hamlet, the emotional victim of his royal parents faithlessness, poses the question 'To Be or Not to Be', he demonstrates in word and deed that to him To Be is contingent on being loyal (to the Self, to Love, to the Crown) and that the rest is death. Cultures, societies, religions, offer the adolescent the nourishment of some truth in rites and rituals of *confirmation* as a member of a totem, a clan, or a faith, a nation or a class, which henceforth is to be his super-family; in modern times we also find powerful ideologies which claim and receive the loyalty (and, if demanded, an early death) from youth.

Thus one could say that societies 'meet the needs' of youth. Here, however, the principle of complementary needs must be stated more explicitly. As cultures, through graded training, enter into the fibre of the individual, they also absorb into their life-blood the rejuvenative power of youth. Adolescence is thus a vital regenerator in the process of social evolution: for youth selectively offers its loyalties and energies to the conservation of what feels true to them and to the correction or destruction of that which has lost its regenerative significance.

Loyal and legal are kindred words. He who can be loyal can bind himself legally (or decide to remain deviant in his insistence on new laws). As the young adult selects those who in turn will select him—as friends, mates, co-workers—he completes the foundation for adult virtues. His identity and his style of fidelity define his place in what history has determined as his environment.

8. *Love*

There must clearly be an important evolutionary function in the selectivity of sexual love: I think it is the mutual search for a *shared identity*, for the mutual verification through an experience of finding oneself, as one loses oneself, in another. While many forms of love can be shown to be at work in the formation of the various virtues, it is important to realize that only graduation from adolescence permits the development of that intimacy, that selflessness of joined devotion, which anchors love in a mutual commitment. Intimate love thus is the guardian of that elusive and yet all-pervasive power in psychosocial evolution: the power of cultural and personal *style*—which gives and demands conviction in the shared patterns of living and thus guarantees individual identity in joint intimacy. All of this, and, alas, no less, is necessary for the human equivalent of those rituals by which birds select each other for mating and nesting. That in man various kinds of 'love', rather than instinctive certainty, must animate his affiliations and associations, is at least one reason for his clannish adherence to styles which he will defend 'as if his life depended on them'. His ego's coherence, his certainty of orientation *does* depend on them; wherefore *ego-panic* can make man 'go blind' with a rage which induces him, in the righteous defence of an endangered identity (religious or national, racial or ideological) to sink to levels of sadism for which there seems to be no parallel in the animal world.

Entrance into adulthood is marked by genitality, the capacity for a full and mutual consummation of the sexual act. An immense power of verification pervades this meeting of bodies and temperaments after the hazardously long childhood, which, as the study of neuroses has revealed in detail, can severely prejudice the capacity for psychosexual mutuality. Freud observed that mature genitality alone guarantees that combination (by no means easily acquired, nor easily maintained) of intellectual clarity, sexual mutuality, and considerate love, which anchors man in reality.

The word 'affiliation' means to adopt somebody as a son—and, indeed, in friendships and partnerships young adults become sons of each other: but sons by a free choice which verifies a long hope for kindredness beyond (incestuous) blood-bonds. From here on, ego-strength depends on an affiliation with others equally whole and this means, by the nature of things, soon equally ready and able to share in the task of *caring* for offspring, products, and ideas.

9. Care

Care (in all the various meanings of *caritas*) is a quality essential for psychosocial evolution: for we are the teaching species. Animals, too, instinctively encourage in their young what is ready for release; and, of course, some animals can be taught some tricks and services by man. Only man, however, can and must extend his solicitude over the long, parallel, and overlapping childhoods of numerous offspring united in households and communities. As he transmits the rudiments of hope, will, purpose and skill, he imparts meaning to the child's bodily experiences; he conveys a logic much beyond the literal meaning of the words he teaches; and he gradually outlines a particular world image and style of citizenship. All of this is necessary to complete in man the analogy to the basic. ethological situation between parent animal and young animal: all this, and no less, makes us comparable to the ethologist's goose and gosling. Once we have grasped this interlocking of the human lifestages, we understand that adult man is so constituted as to *need to be needed* lest he suffer the mental deformation of self-absorption, in which he becomes his own infant and pet. I have, therefore, postulated an instinctual and psychosocial stage of 'generativity'. Parenthood is, for most, the first, and for many, the prime generative encounter;[21] yet the continuation of mankind challenges the generative ingenuity of workers and thinkers of many kinds.

Modern man, forced to limit his fertility, is apt to consider the matter of procreative involvement resolved by the technical possibility of making a conscious choice in the matter of fertilization. Yet an ever so 'safe' lovelife, if accompanied by a denial of generativity, can be the source of the specific guilt of playing with the 'fire of creation'. It is essential, therefore, that the control of procreation be guided not only by an acknowledgment of man's *psychosexual needs*, but also by a universal sense of generative responsibility toward all those brought more planfully into this world. Such care includes the guarantee to each child of a chance for such development as we are outlining here.

Generativity, however, in the form of a selfless 'caring' and a need to 'take care' of whatever one generates and leaves to the next generation, potentially extends to whatever a man creates and produces (or helps to produce). The ideological polarization of the Western world which has made Freud the century's theorist of sex, and Marx that of work, has, until quite recently, left a whole area of man's mind uncharted in psychoanalysis. I refer to man's love for his works and ideas as well as for his children, and the necessary self-verification which adult man's ego receives, and must receive, as he labours to change conditions, and changes himself under the impact of his labour's challenge. As adult man needs to be needed, so—for the strength of his ego and for that of his community—he requires the challenge emanating from what he has generated and from what now must be 'brought up', guarded, preserved—and eventually transcended. Man's creation of all-caring gods was not only an expression of his persisting infantile need for being taken care of, but also a projection on a super-human agency of an ego-ideal: this agency had to be strong enough to guide (or at least forgive) man's propensity for freely causing events and creating conditions which, ever again, prove to be beyond him. It is obvious, however, that man must learn to accept the responsibility which evolution has given him, and must learn not only to develop but also to understand and planfully restrain his capacity for unlimited invention and expansion.

10. *Wisdom*

Psychosocial evolution with its biological and technical advances has not only elongated man's childhood but also his life-expectancy beyond the period of procreative power. In man's family or community the toothless oldster lives next door to the toothless baby, and the signs and signals both of the beginning and of the end exert a deep influence on the search for meaning in those in between.

Ego-strength in the old takes the form of 'wisdom' in all of its connotations from ripened 'wits' to matured judgment, which constitute the ability to maintain the *wholeness of experience* even as the body's faculties gradually fall 'apart' and again become a conglomerate of parts which now weaken (as they once matured) at different rates. If vigour of mind combines with the gift of responsible renunciation, some old people can envisage human problems in their entirety (which is what *integrity* means) and come to represent to the coming generation a living example of the 'closure' of a style of life. Only such integrity can balance the despair of a limited life coming to a conscious conclusion.

Our society, taught by the 'century of the child' that it is not enough to keep children alive, now learns the same truth about its old people. As children were brought up, according to the maturation of their various parts, so old people must be relieved gradually, according to their declining faculties, while their wisdom and experience is recognized and cultivated. This is not just a humanitarian duty but a Humanist obligation; for the expectation, now aroused in many children by the evidence of daily living, namely, that man's prolonged life may only mean the return in old age of a new kind of childishness, can only weaken their own vital fibre. Any span of the cycle lived without vigorous meaning, at the beginning, in the middle, or at the end, endangers the sense of life and the meaning of death in all whose lifestages are interwined.

11. *Conclusion*

Our survey suggests an *evolutionary scheme*: the stages of childhood have evolved in a pattern which permits the maturing ego, under the protection of the adult environment, to integrate those part-functions (biological, mental, emotional) which secure a measure of psychosocial adaptation. Man, not guided by a comprehensive and conclusive set of instincts, must *learn* to *wish* strongly, learn to *control* himself securely, learn to give *direction* to his imagination, and learn to acquire *methods* for his direction; and he must finally learn to bind all these with *devotion*. All this, ego-defence must guard, and virtue fortify. Hope, Will, and Purpose provide the human animal with the initial strength to take part in the space-time of human existence: hope provides the long-range vision which replaces the animal's immediate certainty; Will, the psychological backbone for man's physical and moral 'uprightness', his 'standing on his own two feet'; and Purpose directs to a new variety of goals the energies of the bipedal hunter with special powers of visual perception. Finally, Skill develops man's tool-using capacities, his reason, and his speech. But if man had all this, and had not Fidelity, he would not be able to attain his specific integrity: therefore, his need for styles of truth.

The cogwheeling stages of childhood and adulthood are, as we can see in conclusion, truly a system of *generation* and *regeneration*—for into this system flow, and from this system emerge those social attitudes to which the *institutions* and *traditions* of *society* attempt to give unity and permanence. In the chart,* I have tentatively listed these social attitudes as reverent, judicious, moral, technical, ideological, interpersonal, productive, and philosophical.

Thus, the virtues, far from being ornaments to be reflected upon in front of the mirror, or traits easily accounted for in tests, are deeply rooted in evolution and in unconscious processes to which we are finding access only in our time. From here, we must gain new understanding of the virtues called *natural*, or *cardinal*.

It is probable that the vices corresponding to our schedule of virtues are to be found in the array of inner states which reveal themselves in psychopathological symptoms which in recent decades have been studied in so much detail. We would recognize, for example, an inner affinity between the loss of hope and the nature of delusion and addiction, between the impairment of will and the structure of obsession and compulsion. They spotlight the various ways in which ecological (or adaptive) integrity is forfeited: like the transgressions called *deadly*, the symptoms called *malignant* indicate the forfeiture of 'ecological integrity' in man.

An attempt to abstract any ground plan is an invitation to the reproach that one contributes to the fetish of norms, neglects diversities and thus undermines individuality. I must admit the neglect of one major diversity: that of the two sexes. Yet, as clearly pervasive as sex-differences are in all aspects of life,[20] the ego's development and function is relatively similar in the two sexes; which may contribute to the fact that old men and women look, think, and feel more alike than in any other period—except infancy. As to individuality, there is no need to worry: we cannot dictate deadly conformity to the life processes—they themselves will lead to more diversity than we can comfortably manage with our thoughts, our plans

* See Chart on page 152.

and our cures. And so will, luckily, man's reaction to the diversity of conditions: in an evolutionary setting, we can ascribe a long-range meaning to the idiosyncratic individualist and the deviant as well as to the conformist: for all healthy individualism and devoted deviancy contains an indignation in the service of a *to-be-restored wholeness* without which psychosocial evolution would be doomed—even as biological evolution would have been doomed without deviancy. Thus, one may say, *adaptation* has its loyal deviants who refuse to *adjust* to 'conditions'.

Neither a Humanist nor a psychoanalytic view, however, can overlook for a moment that so far in his history man has realized this blueprint only in fragments. There are many reasons for this. In this context we can only say that in the course of the individual's abandonment of his childhood he loses much of his creative childlikeness while he attaches his unresolved childishness to *personal* and *collective projections* on what is *beyond* and *ahead* of him. Guided and justified by what he calls 'great' men and ideas, he is apt to use history to play out past failures and to test the future in dangerous experiments with fate itself. His long (and much exploited) childhood dependence conditions him to an alternation between *total conformity* and *excessive diversity*, leading him to the Utopian expectation that, at last, some absolute wholeness may be secured either to a community that sets itself above the individual or to the individual who considers himself above all community. Thus, the psychological study of the residues of our evolutionary origins and of our infantile 'pre-history' must be extended to *recorded history*[16] and above all to those ideas which have exclusively dominated whole eras of the past:* for these ideas, as we can now dimly discern, may well owe their dominance to the fact that they promise masses of men a verification which, by each single individual, is truly experienced as 'eternal' because it lifts one of the ego's prime potentials for verification to the level of a promised historical reality. History justly records the triumphs of perfectibility thus attained in certain eras; but it has, on the whole, lacked both the method and the intent to demonstrate the dynamic relation between these triumphs and

---

* A glance at the ego verifications enumerated earlier (footnote, page 154) suggests, that in different historical periods one or the other of these verifications is lifted to the level of exclusive universal values. The ideal of the *perfection of growth patterns* we may recognize in the Greek idea of a *complete harmony* between an excellent body and an excellent mind. The *consummation of interpersonal relationships* in such Utopias as the idea of *perfect Christian love*, as well as the mystic consummation of the relationship with God, and, in modern times, in the idea of the all-healing power of the *genital union*. The idea of a *resolution of developmental crises* without any leftover of loose ends fits modern man's idea of a *perfect adjustment*, as if developmental crises were so many efficiency tests applied to an organism with accidental flaws in design and production. Finally, the *mutual fittedness* of personality development and social structure, in modern times, dominates the idea of the *perfect state*.

the ego-distortions and social sacrifices imposed both on the triumphant minorities and the vaguely participant masses.

Where do we stand? In our time, for the first time, one human species can be envisaged, with one common technology on one globe (and a bit of outer space). At the same time, psychological insight has made our consciousness wiser by the recognition of the body's wisdom, of the power of the unconscious, and of the ego's functions and limitations. This increased margin of consciousness, in itself a major step in evolution, enables man to visualize new moral alternatives, and to strive for a perfection both abundant and adaptive which mediates more realistically between his inner and outer world than do the fatal compromises resulting from the reign of moral absolutes. Outworn alternatives may eventually yield to an order, in which deliberate and creative *diversity* is anchored in a common *responsibility* for all of psychosocial evolution.

How this will change the bringing up of children, it is hard to predict and impossible to prescribe: effective pedagogic sentiment emerges from the strength of a lifestyle. Yet, our scheme suggests, for any future life-style, a morality based on the responsibility of each individual for the potentialities of all generations, and this in a more informed manner than has ever been possible before. But this means that the men of all fields who concern themselves with human destiny must take care lest their vision remain illusory through that exclusive emphasis on concerns of power, which has characterized the study of history so far; leaving pedagogics, the very powerhouse of evolution and tradition, to the educationists.

As we have seen, the individual ego can be strong only through a mutual guarantee of strength given to and received by all whose life-cycles intertwine; and it can transcend itself only where it has learned to engage and to disengage itself responsibly from others.

Thus the basic virtues—these miracles of everyday life—seem to provide a test for universal values, and to contain the promise of a possible morality which is self-corrective as it remains adaptive. The study of these virtues, therefore, is indispensable to an appraisal of the process man partakes in, of the stuff he must work with, and of the strength he can count on, as he charts his future course.

REFERENCES

(1) Roe, A., and Simpson, G. G., ed. *Behavior and Evolution*. New Haven: Yale University Press, 1958. See especially 'Evolution and Human Behavior', by Roe, A., and Freedman, L. Z., and the last sentence of G. G. Simpson's Epilogue.
(2) Huxley, T. H. and J. S. *Touchstone for Ethics*. New York: Harper & Brothers, 1947.

(3) Freud, S., *The Ego and the Id* (1923). London: Hogarth, 1947.

(4) Freud, A. *The Ego and the Mechanisms of Defense*. New York: International Universities Press, 1946.

(5) Hartmann, H. *Ego Psychology and the Problem of Adaptation*. New York: International Universities Press, 1958.

(6) Rapaport, D. 'The Structure of Psychoanalytic Theory: A Systematizing Attempt', in Sigmund Koch (ed.) *Psychology: A Study of a Science*, Vol. III. New York: McGraw-Hill, 1959.

(7) Erikson, E. H. *Identity and the Lifecycle*, Monograph, *Psychological Issues*, Vol. I, No. 1. New York: International Universities Press, 1959. With an introduction by Rapaport, D. 'An Historical Survey of Psychoanalytic Ego Psychology'.

(8) Rapaport, D. 'Some Metapsychological Considerations Concerning Activity and Passivity' (unpublished).

(9) Erikson, E. H. *Childhood and Society*. New York: W. W. Norton, 1950; London: Imago, 1951.

(10) Erikson, E. H. *Young Man Luther*. New York: W. W. Norton, 1958; London: Faber, 1959.

(11) Weigert, Edith. 'Human Ego Development in the Light of Animal Behavior', *Psychiatry*, 1956.

(12) Schiller, Claire H., ed. *Instinctive Behavior; The Development of a Modern Concept*. New York: International Universities Press, 1957. See particularly the contributions of Lorenz, K., and Tinbergen, H.

(13) For a parallel argument, see Buehler, Charlotte. *Der menschliche Lebenslauf als psychologisches Problem*. Göttingen: Verlag fuer Psychologie, 1959.

(14) Freud, S. 'Three Essays on the Theory of Sexuality.' Standard Edition. London: Imago Publishing Co., 1949.

(15) Erikson, E. H. 'Psychosexual Development', in *Discussions in Child Development*, World Health Organization, Vol. IV. London: Tavistock Publications Ltd. (in press).

(16) Erikson, E. H. 'The Psychosocial Development of Children' and 'The Syndrome of Identity Diffusion in Adolescents and Young Adults' in *Discussions in Child Development*, World Health Organization, Vol. III. London: Tavistock Publications Ltd., 1958; New York: International Universities Press, 1958.

(17) Inhelder, B. and Piaget, J. *The Growth of Logical Thinking from Childhood to Adolescence*. New York: Basic Books, 1958.

(18) Wolff, P. H. *Piaget's Genetic Psychology and its Relation to Psychoanalysis*. Monograph, *Psychological Issues*. New York: International Universities Press (forthcoming).

(19) French, T. *The Integration of Behavior*. Chicago: University of Chicago Press, 1952.

(20) Mead, Margaret. 'The Childhood Genesis of Sex Differences in Behavior', and Erikson, E. H. 'Sex Differences in the Play Constructions of Pre-Adolescents', in *Discussions in Child Development*, World Health Organization, Vol. III. London: Tavistock Publications Ltd., 1958; New York, International Universities Press, 1958.

(21) Benedict, Therese. 'Parenthood as a Developmental Phase', in *Journal of the American Psychoanalytic Association*, VII, 3, 1959.

FRANCIS HUXLEY

MARGINAL LANDS OF THE MIND

FRANCIS HUXLEY

Born 1923. Educated: Balliol College,
Oxford. Field work in Brazil, 1950; Sas-
katchewan, 1958; Haiti, 1959.

Publications: *Affable Savages*, 1956.

MARGINAL LANDS OF THE MIND

Scattered within the body of our civilization are what seem to be lost worlds of reason and imagination, whose continual existence is often a puzzle and sometimes an affront. These are the worlds of the fortune-teller, the spiritist, medium and occultist: worlds which came into being many centuries ago, and which show no signs of disappearing. On the contrary, in spite of its evasive pronouncements, and in spite of the opposing certainties of calculating machines and psychiatrists, the lure of the occult is as strong as ever. The rational mind may deride it as superstition, while our world goes roaring on with mechanical spirits Solomon would have been proud to command; but the occult, spawning horoscopes in the daily papers, battening on a rich diet of magic, gnosticism, yoga and obscured desires, steadily grows.

It is not really surprising that in this century, when we know so much about things, people should still wish to question that hidden something which is supposed to know better about purposes. What we have learnt about sudden discoveries and inspiration shows that there is indeed an imaginative process that leaps beyond logic, once it has been set going by a minimum of reasoned observation. This hidden process, with its purposive activity, has ever been the goal for seekers: shamans, yogis, alchemists, and fortune-tellers, besides poets and the mystic devotees of love who also desire that knowledge *toda sciencia trascendiendo*. The occult, in its way, is an attempt to formulate this transcendental knowledge and even to apply it—conclusions which, however, are often as erratic as the principles they are based on are misleading. The hope that there is a short cut to the Unknown is a standing temptation, but if we leave aside the actual formulation of this approach—which, in occultism, is a mixture of magic and metaphysics—what may still surprise us is the energy devoted to it. Here is a nether world which many, often brilliant, imaginations have peopled and nourished, offering a mode of thought and feeling which seems to be perennially attractive.

How is it that magic and metaphysics have become combined? This marriage, it seems, came about in an effort to bridge the age-old split between the moral imagination of man and his material circumstances. It is here, in this split, that the occult strikes root, turning into many curious forms in its continual attempts to make the hidden world visible: sometimes by magical practices that spring from an interest in matter, sometimes by that systematizing effort of the will which is always trying to prove its independence of matter. This very contradiction in the way the occult treats matter is perhaps what draws people to the occult, whatever the results of its practices or the truth of its system. If you are disappointed in the magic there is always the metaphysics to fall back on, and when the metaphysics become boring, there is the magic. The metaphysics, it must be confessed, grow increasingly boring the more involved they become, and the magic—from telling the future to speaking with the dead, practising telepathy, and healing by spiritual vibrations—has, by its very nature, an inconclusive quality. Luckily, however, we do not need to prove that the phenomena of occultism are real in order to be interested in them. There is another question that can be asked: what is there about this strange world, hidden though it may be under equivocations, that gives it a kind of Utopian significance?

The problem is well seen in a country like Haiti, where occultism is widespread in many forms. Famous for its voodoo, Haiti also has quantities of fortune-tellers, of magicians both black and white, and of herbalists. These fortune-tellers and fortune-changers—we might perhaps call them fortune-mongers—are consulted by everyone, for every imaginable reason. Their usual technique is to go into trance and become possessed by a spirit who then diagnoses what is wrong with the client, and—for an additional fee—carries out a cure either magically or with herbs. The trance is an integral part of the process, for it alters the character not only of the fortune-monger, letting him speak with the greater assurance and, sometimes, deeper insight, but also that of the client who easily succumbs to the sense of confidence the fortune-monger generates. It is, in one sense, a confidence trick: but since the client welcomes it, not necessarily a trick in the bad sense of the word.

A sense of confidence is of course essential if magic is to be believed in. In voodoo, this confidence is created through drumming, dancing and singing, so that in the end it is not only good entertainment but good theatre, the spirits possessing their servitors in a thrilling atmosphere full of energy, directness and drama. But the pleasures of this kind of activity are not shared by all: some Haitians think them demeaning, and when they consult the occult they go in for the more mechanical aspects of it, such as the casting of horoscopes or the reading of cards and hands. Even here, however, the diagnostic function of fortune-mongering is supported by an active and therapeutic one: the astrologer may make a talisman for his client, or the card-reader prescribe some necessary magical operation, by which the foreseen future may be amended and brought to pass.

Fortune-mongering, therefore, can be quite a complicated affair. It can also have enormous social consequences, as we may see from the history of Haiti itself. The revolt of the slaves, after all, was hatched and bred in voodoo, the leaders of the revolution met in a voodoo temple to hatch their plot, and the voodoo spirits afterwards descended upon the slaves throughout the revolt, giving them the fierce courage to confront their French overlords and overthrow them together with all their own bad fortune. Other nations too have been set aflame by fortune-mongering: the Indian tribes of Brazil, for instance, oppressed by war and slavery during the Portuguese conquest, were led on enormous journeys by shamans who prophesied the renewal of their fortunes on the other side of the ocean, in a Utopian land of abundance and immortality. In North America the plains Indians, in a similar situation, tried to fight back against the whites, and many of their efforts were inspired by shamans. Fortune-tellers change fortune: this was well known to the Roman emperors, who allowed only their own to practise, fearing that prophecies once uttered, no matter how unlikely, would be made to come true by an unruly populace.

Fortune-telling, it is plain, goes with frustration. Nowhere is this more obvious than in Haiti, where poverty, misery and ambition go hand in hand with endless magical practices. Misery can breed magic, as a way out of a desperate situation; but magic in its turn breeds misery, not only because it costs so much, or because it is addictive, but because it naturally makes play with real or imagined enemies and rivals, and so makes a man suspect his neighbours. Haitians know this well: 'on est bien nommé Haïtien,' they say, 'parce que tous les gens se haïssent'. Together, magic and suspicion do much to undermine the vitality of the country, and any sense of community.

The world of the fortune-monger is usually fragmentary and episodic. It spins itself out in fantasies, in stories of buried treasure, guardian demons who turn on their owners if not fed with the proper sacrifices, zombies, men turned into oxen and sold on the market, or sorcerers flying through the air. Like the occult everywhere, once it starts dealing with individual people and their separate desires, it begins to make a world of its own and has difficulty in finding its way back out of the imagination and into material reality. However, this ability of the occult to make its own world points to what the occult and fortune-mongering are always trying to be, and to what they eventually spring from. Devious as it may be, the occult yet aims to describe or bring about an optimum state of affairs, and to be the perfect theory of which society is the practice. We can see this most clearly in the fate of astrology, which arose at the founding of the first cities with sacred kings as their focus and representative. A very close system of correspondences between the city and Nature, especially the heavens, was formulated, the motions of the sun, the moon and the planets being thought to announce and create corresponding motions in the fortunes of the city. It was only much later that this system of correspondences was made to work not between the two collectives of Nature and the city through the figure of the king, the city's representative, but directly from Nature to the separate members of the city—in much the same way as, in Egypt, mummification and the hopes of immortality ceased to be the prerogative of the Pharaohs and became available to all who could afford it. From being the theory of the fortunes of an entire community and its land, therefore, astrology was secularized and became what it is now: a cross between a psychological classification and a game of snakes and ladders.

Psychological classifications are always useful, and occultism is full of them. They do not hide, however, the dramatic element which is of more real interest, and which can be found not only in the early days of astrology but also in voodoo and in other simpler forms of occultism. Whatever shape it may take, besides, this dramatic element is dependent on the force of one principal actor, whether he be voodoo priest, medium, or fortune-teller. He represents fortune in the acting-out of it, and he may be successful even if what he prophesies is vain and his magic puerile—like Madame Blavatsky, whose poor tricks did not stop her from generating an enormous confidence in her representation of the occult.

A fortune is thus an activity rather than a bonus, best manifested in a human being. The existence of such a human being is as important for the lower kinds of magic as it is for the higher forms of religion, as we can see among shamans or mediums. It has long been known that there is a relationship between mental illness and native doctoring, for example, and that among primitives certain of the insane can be thought of as those who have not managed to become doctors. This very interesting relationship can tell us a great deal about occultism. In Haiti it is commonplace: magicians and voodoo priests may only become aware of their calling after a seizure of madness, some trivial anxiety blossoming into such a pitch of uneasiness that the patient becomes either raging or dissociated. From this state he can be rescued if the upwelling anxiety is mastered by being transformed into a spirit capable of possession—that is, given the ability to manifest itself clearly. What might then have been an aberration or worse becomes the agent of a new activity which, since it has successfully transformed an ominous situation, is a fortune in itself, and can also be used to deal with the anxieties of others who wish their fortunes to be told.

The key to this curious sequence of events seems to be anxiety. The occult is of course consulted when people are anxious, and it is successful according to the amount of anxiety it is able to convert either into action or into knowledge. Voodoo turns anxiety into many forms of action: into dancing and singing, into ritual activity, into obligations of service; it also lets people shed their self-control and their rigidities, with the full support of everyone else. Naturally it is not always successful, but it does manage in its special way to transform anxieties into something positive so that the internal contradiction of the client becomes public property and indeed part of the social process from which his anxiety had estranged him.

Fortune-telling by itself, however—the diagnostic arts of scrying, or reading hands, or laying out the cards—does not turn anxiety into action, but into knowledge. It is a knowledge which may be neither exact nor true, yet it is sometimes enough to settle equivocating doubts and let action take place. With the spread of literacy, however, anxiety can equally well turn into the act of ratiocination, and one consequence of this is the large mass of occultist literature and metaphysics, whose endless, tortuous self-windings apparently try to allay anxiety by denying it a material basis. Since anxiety, however, can only be allayed by action, the occultist writers have to go on and on writing out their explanations which, like the later prophecies of William Blake, may be full of interesting symbols and occasional poetry, but which become increasingly murky in their attempt at a total explanation of everything. The only action possible, since action is evaded when things are explained, is to continue searching for the final explanation which will put the whole matter to rest. Before this, action is indiscreet; after, unnecessary.

Something similar has happened to astrology. A horoscope is cast by the use of systematized calculations, and some form of meaning is drawn out of the resultant correlations and contradictions. Because of its use of arithmetic, it counts itself as being the most scientific branch of the occult, so that the relationship of astrologer to client is of a curious nature. I discovered this one day in New York, when I got talking to an astrologer. He was an interesting man who owned an occultist bookshop, a store of fascinating and obscure matter, and he tried to convert me to his science by what to him were positive reasons. He told me, for a start, that certain psychiatrists were now casting horoscopes for their patients instead of using psychological tests, with great effect; and that a physicist had found that cosmic radiations waxed and waned according to the positions of the sun and moon. When I remained unconvinced by his reasoning, he shifted his ground. I made the common mistake, he said, of thinking astrology was fortune-telling rather than a form of spiritual discipline like yoga or the cabbala; though he himself played on this mistake by casting innumerable horoscopes, in doing which he confessed himself the greatest dispenser of illusion in New York City. His clients all turned to him, however, because they were frightened and impotent, in a futile effort to find some hope for their lives, while he practised astrology in order to gain power and wield it. He also practised a little desultory magic for his clients but, in contrast to any Haitian astrologer, he thought it despicable rubbish.

Thus the clients of the occult in the West seem to be becoming more and more passive and to rely increasingly on knowledge to allay anxiety, instead of action. Occultism pretends to be a science, which of course it is not; partly because of this pretence, however, it can borrow from science in surprising ways. For instance, the year after the Chicago planetarium was opened, there was noticed an enormous increase in the sale of astrological books throughout the city; or, to take a better known phenomenon, there is the wonderful mixture in flying-saucer mythology of planetary spirits, telepathy, science fiction and space flight. In spite of its weaknesses, however, occultism is spreading quite rapidly. Mediums, for instance, are increasingly consulted for the kind of problem that social workers, marriage counsellors and psychiatrists also deal with. The reason for this seems to be that, while social work and psychiatry aim at the virtues of responsibility and compromise, which are easily infected by pessimism, mediums—besides speaking with the authority of the Other World—not only offer an interesting entertainment, but generate a sense of optimism in the future. Thus the client, instead of feeling he is either a patient or a victim, can see himself as the hero of a drama yet to be enacted. A medium, indeed, is a dramatist—though, as with the more usual kind, there are more bad ones than good ones—and has to search out the source of anxiety in a client by discovering past acts or future situations which now menace him. This done, the knowledge has to be turned into a figure of possible action. It is this optimistic outlook that makes many people turn to the occult for advice: rather than search out the roots of a situation, they prefer to encourage themselves with the image of a possible and hopeful future.

Often, alas, the anxiety of the client is made use of dishonestly, the occultist making his final diagnosis of the case only after lengthy consultations. This is a confidence trick in the accepted sense of the word. But the most ingenious of these tricks is in answering questions to which there are no verifiable answers: questions about the Other World, in fact, about departed relatives and life after death. It is not that these questions are themselves inane and without meaning; indeed, the problem of death is the ultimate anxiety which all men have to face, whether willingly or unwillingly. Nor is it that the answers may not sometimes be valuable. The problem is rather whether such questions actually raise the problem they hope to have solved—whether, that is, the questioner has not misplaced his anxiety in wanting to know, for instance, whether some relative still 'lives', though dead in the body. It is possible that this is so: but the real doubt is perhaps not so much in the continued existence of the dead relative, as in that of the person who doubts it. The questioner is wanting continuity of himself, and he asks his question in this way because he cannot find it in his daily life.

Occultism thus provides something which official explanations about the nature of the world and of human beings do not: it is a shadow world made by orthodoxy, as well as being the system that attempts to deal with anxiety and to transform it. However, the more occultism and orthodoxy ignore each other, the more difficult is it for the occultist to transform anxiety into direct and public action. The result is that occultism tends to be a private matter, and to allow its clients various degrees of simulated action, in which the real anxiety becomes misplaced. The consequence of this misplacing of anxiety is that the functions appropriate to one process are thought to be inherent in another, quite different one. The division of Man into body and spirit is particularly interesting in occultism because of this: its tendency is to rationalize a spiritual body out of physical yearnings, and to deny in some way that matter is real. As Swift said in his 'Discourse concerning the Mechanical Operation of the Spirit', there are those of us who 'pretending by the lines and measure of our reason, to extend the dominion of one invisible power, and contract that of the other, have discovered a gross ignorance in the nature of good and evil, and most horribly confounded the frontiers of both'. So, in occultism, with body and spirit: their frontiers have been confounded, and their natures trapped in the resulting confusion.

There is one process in which this confusion seems to reign absolutely and yet in the end manages somehow to relate body and mind according to their proper natures. This process is represented by fertility cults in which anxieties and the desires they represent are acted out and fulfilled in wish and, in order to assure fortune, are put back into the earth—or,

among hunting peoples, into the principal game animal—in order to act
as a fertilizer of action. Used in this way, the waste-products of social life
and of the tensions of getting a living are continually turned to account.
There is, however, a principle involved in this process which magic and
occultism neglect; one's own waste cannot be used directly to fertilize
one's own actions, but has first to be transformed through the exchanges
of society. Occultism is therefore always strong when the waste products
of society are bottled up without outlet, or are let to run to waste without
fertilizing the ground from which action springs.

All kinds of distractions have been invented in order to pacify anxiety
by letting the energy it generates dissipate itself harmlessly; but the anxiety
itself then remains. Making use of occultism, anxiety can push the mind to
the fringes of consciousness where, it is hoped, the great questions about
human existence have their answers. Certain peculiar things often happen
at these fringes, such as clairvoyance or precognition, and somewhere
beyond, it is thought, lies that marvellous state of being which all men
secretly desire. The occult indeed is rich in promises about the marvels
there, the fortunes to be had and powers to be wielded: and these portend
something about human nature that it would be foolish to ignore. Science,
of course, foretells marvels also, and offers its own dreams of power, but
as yet these marvels and dreams are anonymous. Not so those of the occult,
which promises its clients that they will participate in the most intimate of
fortunes by which the desires at their very heart will be touched. Unfortunately, the desires at the heart of man are not always commendable, as a
glance at black magic will show us; nor is a seeking after signs and marvels
the way, it seems, in which the marvel will manifest itself.

On the one hand, then, is anxiety; on the other, the marvel. What the
marvel is has been the subject of endless controversy, and unhappiness,
and war; but experience, and not merely hope, testifies to its reality.
Religion has of course always been the official propagandist of the marvel,
and occultism, its shady sister, the unofficial one—a difference that springs
from the different use made of the mind's capacity to think magically.
According to the use of this faculty the world is seen in various guises—
illusory, material, fallen from grace, animistic, demonic or holy—which
we may see illustrated from the begininng of the Christian era by various
attitudes and movements, many of which have been pronounced heretical.
At any rate, the marvel is rightly felt to be the creative centre of the world,
whence, no doubt, the churches' fear that the cosmogony of science, in
replacing that of religion, will fatally injure their ability to interpret the
marvel at the centre of things.

The problem seems to be this. Where there is anxiety—as there is in

every human culture—the imagination is called on to destroy it by an act
of reconstruction. This reconstruction can take several forms: it may alter
the forces within the psyche, so allowing a more comprehensive relationship between people to take form; it may destroy things in the physical
or social worlds, to give long pent-up energies their outlet; or it may
create a phantasmal world to serve as a substitute for the real thing. In all
these cases the solution is made to glow with the promise of the marvellous which, since it is nearly always unfulfilled, later produces more
anxieties, of a new kind.

We must, however, accept the fact that extraordinary and marvellous
things do happen, caused apparently by the activity of the creative centre
in Man, either when it is free to play or when it is under particular forms
of stress. Extra-sensory perception, for example, occurs especially between
people who enjoy close relationship together, such as those between
parents and young children, between lovers, or—as is now being found—
between psychiatrists and their patients. In these relationships things may
happen which transgress the usual definitions of order and selfhood, and
which make possible forms of participation which the ego, inasmuch as
it is the organ of separateness, cannot experience.

The relationships brought into being through love and dependence are
one way of stopping the ego from cutting itself off from the marvels of
experience, whether exterior or interior. Occultism has of course discovered other ways which involve dissociation, in which the separative
ego with all its attendant physical tensions is unseated from its dominant
position; it is apparently as a direct consequence of this that possessed
people may become clairvoyant, or perform strange feats of strength or
endurance.

Something, then, is happening which is well worth looking at. It is of
little use directing people's attention away from the existence of occultism,
or what it implies, and trying to engage their longings for marvels in
things outside themselves: the existence of occultism shows that the
marvel is to be sought somewhere within. It is thus, like all other forms of
sublimation, the search for a lost life: a life which, if its necromantic and
scatological elements are anything to go by, is still locked up somewhere
in the body awaiting release. It is the enjoyment of life through the body
that occultism, with all its dealings in fortune and fortunes, murkily
attempts to realize, by making use of the anxieties and pent-up energies
that human society generates in every person.

We shall never be without anxiety: nor, as a consequence, shall we
ever be without the hope of the marvellous, since anxiety is that state of
mind in which a desire for a rewarding marvel is created. Where occultism,

like other forms of therapy, is successful, is in fitting the two states together and getting rid of anxiety through action. It is at this moment, however, that this fruitful process can become fraudulent and self-defeating. This is because occultism tends to promise an almost permanent success by projecting the marvel into the future, once the initial anxiety has been transformed. But the real marvel is this act of transformation, and not any consequent state of being: it is here, in this creative process, that imprisoned energies truly become fortune, and it is the continual experience of this creativity that is marvellous. The solution to the problem of the occult, therefore, does not depend on doing away with the wish for a fortune and the marvellous, which are quite proper desires, but on some new and practical way of dealing with the age-old oppositions of body and mind, image and abstraction, desire and repression, individual and society, which become, in fact, the Faustian cycle in which desire can never be fulfilled since it is continually being sublimated and changed into an idealized analogue of itself. This analogue, being out of reach of the original impulse that gave it birth, becomes part of that which is known to us as 'mind'; and since it is separated from bodily satisfaction, it is a perennial source of anxiety which creates yet more 'mind' around it, to support its own loneliness.

Occultism is only a minute part of a universal problem, and its search for the miraculous can be paralleled elsewhere on different levels. The Utopias of science and nationalism, the promises of politics and war, the gnawing belief in romantic love, are manifestations of the same disease—the creation of imaginary bodies whose desires are always disappointed, since there is nothing material that can properly satisfy them. In the case of occultism, the mediator between the desire and the imaginary body is magic, but this tends to disappear and its place may be taken by a form of metaphysics which, in dematerializing the world, becomes increasingly inefficient to do what it is supposed to. It focuses more and more, therefore, upon those fringes of consciousness where materiality has not yet penetrated, hiding its failures beneath its ambiguities. 'These arts are uncertain today', wrote Paracelus of what he called physiognomics—the arts of discovering what is within and hidden in man—'because man is uncertain in himself.' But these arts can have no value unless they make man certain in himself—and when he is certain, then they will presumably be unnecessary.

Yet this certainty—what is it? The dangers of thinking that it is a purely subjective conviction are obvious, both in religious and in political life. Nor, obviously, can it be merely a conviction about the truth of scientifically ascertainable facts. A study of the various branches of occultism suggests rather that it is a kind of confidence engendered by success in dealing with anxiety, productively and in dramatic form, so that that which is within and hidden in man can make itself known to things already in existence. Moreover, this certainty and freedom from anxiety come into being when the body-mind opposition (to put the matter very crudely) is in abeyance, thus allowing the whole organism to become capable of experience instead of only certain parts of it.

It is plain that our civilization has to a large extent lost the institutions which in other cultures deal with such problems, and the growth of occultism can be taken as an attempt to provide what is lacking. We must be allowed to dream, that is obvious; but the dreams of individuals must somehow be interpreted in the light of that larger dream which is mankind, and of the facts brought into being by the scientific imagination. There are many ways of interpreting dreams, of which psychoanalysis is but the latest, and many ways of inducing them, for instance, by mescalin —which, indeed, can produce experiences more marvellous than any dream. In psychiatry there are also such relatively new advances as group psychotherapy and psychodrama, by means of which the anxieties of a group are made to work together in order to transform them into a sense of possible relationships. And then, matter for a rapidly growing body of knowledge, there are those illnesses known as psychosomatic. Psychological stress affects the body in many ways, from allergies to ulcers; and one of these ways, which the phenomenon of dissociation suggests is highly important, is through the muscles. So far little has been done to deal with such somatic stress, except by osteopaths—many of whom have strange ways of diagnosis and equally remarkable successes—by such exponents of postural health as the late Mathias Alexander, or by that practical art known as Gestalt Therapy, which takes as much notice of tense muscles as it does of tense thoughts. It is perhaps through such developments that the wheedling voice of the occult will finally be stilled, for when these arts are perfected, and related to the problems of social life, then the certainty Paracelsus spoke of may be near at hand; and the marvel, whatever it is, will come of itself.

MORTON M. HUNT

LOVE IN A HUMANIST FRAME

MORTON M. HUNT, B.A.

Born 1920. Educated: University of Pennsylvania and Temple University. In 1949 became freelance magazine writer. President of the Society of Magazine Writers, 1956.

Publications: *The Natural History of Love*, and numerous articles.

LOVE IN A HUMANIST FRAME

Although the behavioural sciences are still in various stages of adolescence, they have reached a point at which, for the first time in history, the Humanist can reasonably attempt an integrated naturalistic approach to love. The lunatic, the lover, and the poet are scarcely likely to thank him for doing so. Such persons (and, I fear, a great many others) persist in the belief that understanding is the enemy of feeling, and that Beauty cannot survive examination by Intellect. The attitude was perfectly epitomized by Keats, who thought that when Newton studied the optical properties of rainbows, he somehow wrung the poetry out of them:

> 'Philosophy will clip an Angel's wings,
> Conquer all the mysteries by rule and line,
> Empty the haunted air, and gnomed mine—
> Unweave a rainbow . . .'
>
> *Lamia*, ii

No one can deny that thinking is a different process from feeling, or that analysis proceeds by means unlike those of sensuous perception. But despite this difference, do we really jeopardize love by trying to view it within a Humanist frame? Some experiences do disintegrate when so treated; Keats's 'haunted air, and gnomed mine' prove empty enough when illuminated by the light of understanding. But what man, except the born clod, does not rejoice in the sight of a rainbow, even though he studied physics in college? Each of us knows far more about nutrition and digestion than men did a century ago, but our delight in good food has not diminished; each of us understands something about the nature of the skies and the stars, but a starry night is no less wonderful to us than it was to men a thousand years ago. Quite the contrary: in many things, the more we understand of what we see, the richer our appreciation can be.

So, too, with love. If it can be made to vanish by merely shining light upon it, it is one with goblins and gnomes; if not, even poets and lovers may benefit from learning to understand it. As for lunatics, their case is even clearer: the *lack* of love is often the root of their troubles, but magical balsams, incantations, exorcisms, or sentimental treatment will not help them; it is, rather, through drugs and therapies that derive from an understanding of human behaviour that they may be taught to give and to receive love.

But what do we mean by the word 'love'? Had we not better define our terms? We ought at least to say what we do *not* mean, which, in this essay, includes parental love, filial love, or such peripheral loves as those of country, God, money, music, or pets; the subject here is the love of man for woman, woman for man, or the permutations thereof. But we ought not to try to define it in advance, for the word has been applied to such a variety of emotions, cultural values, and sexual practices that a single definition can hardly fit all the phenomena. Here, somewhat compressed, is a definition in an excellent current dictionary: 'LOVE, a strong, complex outgoing emotion, between persons of opposite sex, based on or affected by sexual attachment.' But the Greeks rarely felt it for persons of the *opposite* sex, Roman libertines weren't in the least *outgoing* about it, Christian ascetics stripped it of *sexual attachment*, and men of the Enlightenment did their best to keep it from being *strong*. Instead of linguistic and logical methods of arriving at a definition, we will understand love better if we employ description and taxonomy, the methods of the naturalist.

For it is only by observing and classifying a wide sample of specimens that one arrives at a scientifically valid position. Most of the theorizing about love in the past has proceeded on the principle of selective screening rather than wide sampling; one starts with a theory and finds cases to illustrate it, ignoring or overlooking those that contradict it. Consider the notion that love is simply a set of emotions contingent upon, and appropriate to, sexual courting and pursuit—a theory held in one form by nearly all the libertines in history, and in rather a different form by such a high-minded evangel of emancipation as Havelock Ellis. True enough, in many primitive cultures—and in many periods of Western history—love has been associated only with the sexual quest; it was supposed to exist only within premarital or extramarital relationships, but not within marriage, where it was quite unnecessary since there was no uncertainty about gaining one's sexual goal.* Yet such a theory quite fails to explain the transports and exaltations felt by lovers in certain situations where there has been no sexual chase or attempted conquest, such as the chaste 'spiritual marriages' of many early Christians, the keeping of *agapetae* or spiritual sisters by clergy of the early centuries, or the forms of 'true' or

* 'Uxoriousness' was even a term of derision to many Greeks and Romans, and ..1 Xenophon's *Symposium* Socrates mentions with astonishment the case of a man deeply in love with his own wife.

'pure' love variously advocated by Avicenna, the Albigensian poets and troubadours of the twelfth century, and the Neoplatonists of the Italian Renaissance.

Indeed, the very efflorescence of love in these unconsummated relationships is responsible for an opposite theory, namely that love is not the accompaniment of sexual pursuit, but the outcome of delayed, postponed, or repressed desire which is transmuted into idealized and romantic feelings. But this hardly explains why love existed in such non-Christian societies as those of the Polynesian island groups in which children were allowed relatively free sexual expression and experienced little repression, nor why many a pagan Roman and many a Catholic priest of the Dark Ages came to love his concubine long after possessing her body. And it quite fails to explain why Geneva, under Calvin, should not have been the most romantic and love-drunk of all cities.

So it is with many another special theory. Most ethical or religious views of love hold that it is not merely selfish desire, but a generous, nurturing, cherishing emotion; if so, Catullus, Caesar, Henry the Eighth, Casanova, and legions of others never loved. The psychological view of love sees it as primarily the product of familial relationships, and of the young child's inevitable incest-wishes, castration-fears, and sexual repressions; but family life in Athens, Samoa, Versailles, and many other places was quite unlike this psychoanalytic archetype and in them men and women still grew up and fell in love. The anthropological view of love is apt to see it as a mechanism involved in mate-selection, but in many periods mate-selection has been governed by lineage, status, and property negotiations without regard for love.

The Humanist approach, in contrast, is holistic. Love is an aspect of human behaviour, and human behaviour is the product of an interacting complex of forces ranging from the individual's blood-sugar level to the ethos of his civilization. Though it is not yet possible to assign commensurable values to the many factors involved, we can at least set forth a brief suggestive paradigm of them:

(1) *Biology (aside from the sexual drive) influences the shape and meaning of love.* Studies of the digestive and other processes in 'gentled' newborn laboratory animals versus controls show that warmth and gentle tactile stimuli promote the general health of the young. The gestures and deeds of love, and the need for affection, are deeply rooted in the autonomic nervous system, not only in the psyche.

(2) *Sexual desire is a major source of the power behind love,* but the relation between them is not inevitable, nor is one altogether included

within the other. Sometimes sexual activity does not involve the emotion of love, and sometimes love does not involve sexual desire. Affection, friendship, companionship, the need to nurture or be nurtured, are connected most of the time with love, but only sometimes with sex.

(3) *Family structure and childhood experiences mould love.* Biology and infant sexuality operate within the familial framework, but that framework varies greatly; its particular shape has some definite results—but not always. For instance, although incest between child and parent is universally tabooed, in the milieu of the small nuclear family the forbidden and repressed desires yield the 'one-person' theory of love or 'doctrine of affinity', in which a one-and-only lover (the image of the unobtainable parent) is sought; among primitive peoples, who spread their filial and paternal feelings out to a wide spectrum of relatives, the one-and-only theory of love is incomprehensible. Yet the milieu of the small nuclear family does not always produce the romantic result: witness the typically Gallic attitudes towards love. The family environment is thus important, but not completely determining, in the shaping of love.

(4) *Technology, productivity, or the acquisition of surplus income by conquest, plays a significant role in the development of love.* A society or class which lives on the brink of starvation has little time or energy for the elaboration of love. Typically, in Western civilization love first became culturally important with the appearance of leisure in classic Greece, waned during the Dark Ages, and reappeared in force with the elaboration of medieval culture, commerce, and leisure. Yet love has also flourished among hard-working accumulators of wealth such as the Victorians and modern man; it is not just idle time that counts, but an advanced human condition.

(5) *Various social institutions, values, and mores influence, hinder, promote, or colour love,* according to how it serves or disserves the social milieu they form. Among them are: religious or social attitudes towards concubinage, prostitution, and the social mingling of the sexes; the laws of marriage and divorce, the condition of monogamy or polygamy, and the presence or absence of dowry and bride-price; the prevailing concepts of beauty, taste, manners, and friendship; the status of woman, her education, and her position in the system of magical and supernatural beliefs; and many others. Not least is the general cultural expectation of what love feels like, for as La Rochefoucauld said, 'There are people who would never fall in love if they had not heard love talked about'.

This rudimentary set of directions (which the reader is invited to modify or add to, as he likes) bears about the same relationship to a proper map of love as does that typical piece of advice of the native to the bewildered traveller—'You can't miss it.' Still, even with so crude a diagram one can begin to see why men in different eras have been alternately pleased and discontented with love, or have sometimes praised and sometimes scorned it, but have rarely understood how and why they came to their own particular feelings about it.

The upper-class Athenians, for example, possessed both leisure and refined aesthetic sensibilities, and were nearly free of guilt feelings about sex. Modern man, looking back, may suppose that love must have been a pure delight for them, without the ambivalence and inner turmoil known to so many men of later ages. Yet as often as the Greeks rhapsodized about the joys of love, they also complained that it was a folly and a god-sent affliction. They found themselves enamoured either of courtesans—whom they discovered to be avaricious and unfaithful—or adolescent boys—whom they knew to be frivolous and impermanent; and wanting merely to enjoy love, they were frequently aggravated by it. No wonder they considered it a rather mean trick played upon them by a capricious and mischievous god.

As an explanation of their ambivalent feelings, however, this was merely primitive thinking. In actual fact, a series of far from supernatural social and economic forces was to blame. In the Homeric era, a man's wife had been important and useful to him, though not an equal or companion, but by the time of Solon, the well-to-do Athenian had servants to perform the wife's useful functions. She became the cloistered housekeeper—untutored, uninteresting, and basically unimportant except for the bearing of children. Yet all this coincided with social changes which made individual affections more important than ever to Greek men, for as they had become urbanized and sophisticated, the city-state replaced the clan, and men no longer were surrounded by that lifelong web of affections and loyalties they once knew. Sexual desire was nothing new, but now somehow it seemed important to *love*. But what on earth did love have to do with sex? The biology of man permits the two to intermingle, but does not require it. As far as Greek men could see, the functions of woman were three-fold, and could best be taken care of by a kind of division of labour among women. Demosthenes stated it clearly in a court oration against a courtesan: 'Courtesans we keep for pleasure, concubines for daily [sexual] attendance upon our persons, and wives to bear us legitimate children and be our housekeepers.'*

---

* 'Against Neaera'. The authenticity of this oration is doubtful, but scholars generally agree that it dates from the time of Demosthenes, is much in his vein, and gives a legitimate picture of the morals of the period.

Meanwhile, since even the best-trained courtesan was neither as well educated as the Athenian male, nor a companion in his daily life and in war, Athenian men were drawn towards each other. It was not any mere genital perversity that accounted for Greek homosexuality, but something far more complex and emotional. Although they often praised *paederastia* in sensual terms, they always added a heavy gilding of justification on the grounds of friendship, honour, and character-improvement. Retrospectively they even interpreted Homeric warriors as homosexuals, attributing their courage in battle to the sustaining force of that form of love. In the *Symposium* Plato carried the trend to its ultimate in the theory he sketched so poetically, a curious hodgepodge of aesthetics, logic, and metaphysics, which indicates that even this gifted man had almost no insight into the actual nature of homosexual love. According to Plato, love was the emotion caused by the appreciation of, and enjoyment of, beauty, at first in the individual and least valuable form of a single person; later on it mounted, by a logical and ethical ladder, to beauty seen in several persons and generalized as beautiful types, and thence, step by step, to the beauty of abstract Ideas—timeless, indestructible, and of ultimate reality.

This alliance of love to higher truth has greatly appealed to lovers through the ages, but the uses they have made of it have been curious indeed. The early Christian theorists turned it into a sour theology in which the world and the flesh were mean, corrupt, and temporary, while heaven and soul were noble, pure and eternal (Plato might have been irritated by this); Renaissance Neoplatonists borrowed the whole Platonic apparatus, but applied it to the worship of other men's wives rather than of boys (Plato would very likely have been amused); and the Romantics and Victorians somehow took 'Platonic love' to mean an intense romantic heterosexual attraction in which sexuality was totally inhibited (Plato would have been utterly perplexed). Thus is philosophy, like clothing, cut to the shape of the philosopher rather than to that of fact.

To take another example, love among the upper classes during the Roman Empire had two very divergent interpretations among those who saw it at first hand, though neither interpretation came to grips with reality. Roman love-mores were rather different from those of the Greeks: both men and women, married and unmarried, played the game of love; it was graced by little philosophy or deep emotion, but was frankly hedonistic, and on a par with banqueting or the enjoyment of *décor*. To readers of costume novels, pagan love looks in retrospect exciting, uninhibited, tempestuous and heady, but to the more objective eye it displays a syndrome of unhealthy and self-destructive symptoms, including compulsive dissipation, concubinage, the sexual exploitation of male and female slaves, the stimulating of jaded tastes by perverse excesses, the practice of infant exposure, the loosening of marriage bonds to the point where divorce required only a one-sentence written message sent by either spouse to the other, and so on. The poet Ovid and like-minded hedonists in succeeding generations believed that man is here for pleasure, that illicit love is capable of yielding a great deal of it, and that each person should therefore amuse himself as much as he can, while he can. The moralists and their alarm meant nothing to him. 'Let the past please others', he wrote. 'I congratulate myself on being born into this age, whose ways are so congenial to my own.'

A number of Romans, however, found this simple philosophy of pleasure unsatisfactory. Some lived moral family lives; some laboured and orated on behalf of older standards; and some, though reared in luxury and inculcated with hedonistic attitudes from infancy, were strangely drawn towards the asceticism gaining ground throughout the Empire from the first century on. Stoics and Neoplatonists spoke in new and oddly severe terms; pagan philosophers like Apollonius of Tyana criticized sensual indulgence and even the enjoyment of married love; Julian the Apostate, the would-be reviver of paganism, ate food plain as any monk's, slept on a hard pallet, avoided amusements, and let his beard go uncut and lousy. From all this it was only a short step to Christianity. Wealthy Christians like Ammon of Alexandria fled from city luxuries and the enjoyments of marriage to live in the Egyptian desert and struggle with the boiling lusts of their flesh. In Rome a circle of rich women clustered about Jerome and, at his urging, gave up their lovers and palaces, and took to fasting, weeping, filth, continence, and prayer. All this was by way of atonement for the sins of Rome which, according to the Fathers of the Church, were bringing the wrath of God upon the Empire and thus causing its decline, and instead of which the new and lust-free love of God and of mankind was called for.

Here, then, were two opposed interpretations of Roman love—the pagan and the Christian; yet both were alike incapable of reconstructing the Roman family, halting the dreadful decline of fertility, or introducing warmth and tenderness into human relationships. Listen to Ovid, jauntily asserting that the gladiatorial games are a fine place to seek love: while watching men slaughter each other on the sands below, he says, one is particularly apt to be smitten by some new girl. Listen to Jerome, four centuries later, telling Christians that even in marriage sexual pleasure is vile: 'It is disgraceful to love one's wife too much. . . . Let a man govern his voluptuous impulses. . . . He who too ardently loves his own wife is an adulterer.' The Christian, like the pagan, poisoned and defiled the marriage bed, though by totally different means. By their concepts of love, pagan and Christian alike contributed to the decline of Roman society; the pagans blamed fate, and the Christians blamed their own sinful desires, but neither saw that a complex of economic, political, and cultural factors had emasculated the Roman character, and that the parasitic life of the conqueror, living on tribute, had slowly worked terrible changes in the values Romans had once held. Roman love was both a symptom and a part of this disease, but without properly comprehending the nature of the disease, men had no more chance of treating it successfully than of curing a tumour by cupping.

Similarly, *l'amour courtois* of the Middle Ages—that most intriguing and significant invention in the history of Western love—remains a poetic mystery as long as we try to explain it by any particular theory, but a poetic fact when we use the humanistic method. Medieval knights and ladies stumbled upon, and then carefully elaborated, a compelling relationship which could exist only between a man and woman not married to each other, and in which the man was the pleading, humble servitor and woman the disdainful, cruel tyrant. It was compounded of quasi-religious exaltation, much public discussion of aesthetic matters and of etiquette, 'purified' and often unconsummated sex-play, and the queer fusion of chivalric ideals and concepts of good character with the practice of secrecy, deception, and illicit relationships.

Some scholars have tried to explain this curious form of love as an import from those Arabian poets in Spain who praised a chaste or pure love in which one did not actually possess the beloved. Even if alien ideas could have crossed the Pyrenees into Provence, however, that hardly explains why they caught on and swept through Christian Europe. Other scholars have thought that courtly love was a product of Mariolatry, pointing to the Mary-like qualities of the idealized lady-love, and even to the troubadour's use of the term 'Madonna' in their love-lyrics. But it is not at all certain whether Mary-worship gained more from courtly love or courtly love from Mary-worship, for they co-existed and grew together in importance. Still others, led by Denis de Rougemont, see in courtly love a form of the Catharist heresy, which held the physical world to be Satan's world, not the Lord's, and so turned away from marriage and procreation. Yet similar opinions on the flesh and the physical world had been available as the Manichean undercurrent in Christianity from the earliest centuries; why did they fail to produce *l'amour courtois* until the twelfth century?

The only sufficient explanation is a complicated one, which might go somewhat as follows. Neoplatonic and ascetic ideas were part of the cultural heritage of Arab poets and Provençal troubadours alike. More importantly, ascetic Christian theology had set up nearly impassable barriers between sexual desire and the emotions of love, and effectively made incest-fears not just a childhood problem, but a lifelong one. Even so, this institutionalized incest-fear did not burgeon into courtly love until many other forces conspired to make a suitable milieu. Courtly love *did* catch on first in Provence, where the tradition of Manichean heresy and of spiritual marriage lingered on; yet even there it waited upon the attainment of a degree of wealth and leisure in the eleventh and twelfth centuries, and upon the concomitant political changes which made possible court life in large castles. It spread across Europe because, in these conditions, it served a number of real needs, among them the need for a courtly amusement, for a set of duties to refine and tame men's manners, and for those affectional relationships not provided for within the marriage system. Its proto-romantic qualities of sadness, suffering, distance from the beloved, difficulty of attainment of desire, secrecy, and the like can all be explained in psychological terms—but they would never have been admired and idealized had love not been forced by property considerations, religious asceticism, and the subservient status of the wife, to remain outside and alongside marriage.

Less cumbersome ways of explaining the shape of love in a given era may appeal because of their simplicity, but they raise more questions than they answer. The rationalists of the eighteenth century viewed romantic love as an absurdity ('Love', wrote Swift, 'is a ridiculous passion which hath no being but in play-books and romances'), and one can 'explain' this by saying that rationalists believed in the superiority of reason and in the importance of using it to control the emotions. True enough, but why *did* they, and why did *not* other people both before and after them? Or, to put it on a different level, why should intense, idealized male-female relationships of the courtly love or Neoplatonic types have failed to suit the needs of the eighteenth-century aristocrats, while brittle, impersonal adultery did?

Again, the romantic conceptions of love which originated in medieval *amour courtois* originally pertained exclusively to illicit relationships, but centuries later most of its sentiments and ideals were absorbed into the marriage relationship, especially in Protestant countries. Was this merely imitation of upper-class manners by the bourgeoisie? Yet the bourgeoisie did not ape upper-class ways in many other things; what, then, was specific about romantic love? Try another simple answer: romantic love entered marriage because of the waning of medieval asceticism and its strict separation of love and sex. Yet the Victorians, with all their sexual inhibitions, made more of romantic marriage than any of their pre-decessors. And so it goes; one simply cannot give an adequate explanation of love in terms of any single variant; love is the resultant of a bewildering complex of interacting forces.

Well and good (the non-Humanist might say), but all this is only descriptive and explanatory, and fails to make any value-judgments; it is not enough; we want to know what modes of love have been good or bad, and whether there is any better mode of love for us than the one that now prevails.

The Humanist view, however, does *not* exclude the making of moral judgments. Cultural relativism, which holds that all forms of behaviour are equally valid and moral within the context of their own cultures, may have been a useful stage in the development of anthropology, but most scientists, sensibly enough, are not content with the mere accumulation of data, and relativism already looks rather dated.

Some evolutionary Humanists, looking at the broad trends of biological and psychosocial evolution, will wish to relate their values to goal-concepts such as fulfilment, enrichment of life, or greater realization of potentialities. Others, however, prefer to derive their value-judgments from more strictly scientific criteria in which they are implicit. While they do not speak of 'good' and 'bad', they may employ an objective dicho-tomy borrowed from biological evolution ('adaptive' versus 'mal-adaptive'), or one borrowed from medicine and psychology ('healthful' versus 'pathological'), or one borrowed from sociology and physiology ('functional' versus 'disfunctional').

To be sure, one must use even these antiseptic words with caution, since what seems healthful, adaptive, or functional for a given individual may be pathological, maladaptive, or disfunctional for his society, or *vice versa*. Ovid adapted himself nicely to the circumstances of Roman life, got a good deal of pleasure and fulfilment out of it, and suffered no serious ailments or deterioration of his abilities to function. But the viewpoint for which he was such an eloquent spokesman caused the Roman ruling class to exterminate itself by failing to reproduce; by the early part of the second century A.D., only one of the forty-five great senatorial families that had lived in Rome under Julius Caesar was still in existence, and other people were moving into the void to take their place.

Courtly love, during its early centuries, was ideally functional for both the individual courtier and the courtly class. But for the bourgeoisie of the Reformation it was disfunctional in that, among other things, it required more time, money, and cultivation of taste than the middle class possessed; moreover, it was in conflict with their general sense of morality. When, however, it was modified enough to be amalgamated with marriage, these disfunctions disappeared. Thereafter, romantic love leading to romantic marriage ideally suited the commercial and business classes; yet even so, what was functional in general could still be severely disfunctional in many an individual, for the nineteenth century—that high-water mark of romantic and sentimental feeling—was a time when many men were made impotent or masochistic by the prevailing love-mores, and many women were warped by frigidity or frustration.

In the past several generations, Western society has undergone violent and rapid changes, and the imperfect love-ways of Victorianism have become even more imperfect. Accordingly, a number of experiments have been made in the effort to devise a *modus amandi* better adapted to modern society and the needs of the modern individual. Free love has been advocated and tested, but in both the bourgeois milieu of Western Europe and the socialist milieu of Russia it has proved hurtful to social stability and frequently productive of discontent and despair for the individual. It has therefore been junked, along with other unworkable inventions.

Less radically, Havelock Ellis, Bertrand Russell, and others have urged married people to adopt a frank tolerance towards each other's extra-marital affairs, arguing that the child-rearing unit should be stable, but that such stability ought not to restrict the individual's right to agreeable and enriching relationships and experiences. Despite the plausibility of this viewpoint, Western man (especially in the United States) has not taken kindly to this proposed dividing-up of the several aspects of his love-life, and has chosen instead to develop an expensive pattern of divorce and remarriage. Though this is a high price to pay for love, he apparently prefers it to a system that would once again split the sexual from the emotional, or the sexual and emotional from companionship and procreation.

The accepted love-and-marriage pattern of our time—still vaguely puritanical, semi-romantic, demanding, and complicated—has been widely criticized by *avant-garde* thinkers; nevertheless, on balance it appears relatively well adapted to the needs of both the individual and for modern society. Viewing the long sweep of history, we see that as society has grown more complex, urban, and impersonal, love has progressively grown more important and evolved towards the modern ideal of a fusion of emotion, sex, friendship, and procreative home-life. When man lived in a primitive village, surrounded by intimates and relatives, he did not need to glorify one woman or put a high price on sex; when he lived in a medieval castle in continual contact with his fellow knights and their ladies, he glorified one woman but hardly needed to live with her or frequently express his sexuality with her; but when man lives in a rapidly changing world like ours, in towns and cities where all are strangers to us or at best friends of a few years' standing, man comes to want one woman to be, all at once, mistress, beloved, companion, adviser and comforter, frail clinging protégée, playmate, and mother of his children and himself. She, likewise, wants him to be lover, tender friend, supporter and defender, big boy in need of occasional comforting, constant companion, and father of her children and herself.

Margaret Mead, among others, has pointed out that this is an extraordinarily difficult and demanding totality of roles to play at one time; love becomes the more liable to fracture as it bears too great a burden. Nevertheless, the modern bourgeois ideology of love must be admitted to be reasonably functional. For the individual, it is a major source of many kinds of security, reassurance, and affection, as well as the major source of more basic satisfactions; for society, it is the principal cement holding the family together in an era when almost all of the ancient economic and productive functions—formerly the source of the family's inner strength —have been transferred to factories, schools, social agencies and the government. Indeed, wherever industrialism is remaking older cultures today, love seems to be moving in this direction. In the Moslem world, in the South Pacific, in Africa, in Latin America, in Japan, the trend is unmistakable; women and love are moving in the general direction they have taken during the past several centuries in Northern Europe and America.*

This is not to say that the present love-pattern of Western Europe is ideal. By almost any kind of measurement, it seems to be transitional and undergoing major change, though to what the transition is leading is far from certain. As to the functionalism of present-day love, the Humanist can see room for a good deal of improvement. In some countries, and in some of the United States, the religious and civil laws of marriage and divorce are still such as to make the dissolution of unhappy or unfulfilling marriages extremely difficult and costly; more than that, the need to lie under oath, in order to win a divorce on false grounds, is a disfunction to areas of social value other than those of love itself. A serious contradiction exists, moreover, in the mores and attitudes towards sex: sexual desire is considered evil in the infant, naughty in the adolescent, and normal in the adult—yet affectional love is treated as good and desirable from birth on. This disjunction between affection and sex, maintained in

* China may be a great and terrifying exception to the trend, but it is too soon to tell the outcome of the grisly experiments going on there.

the individual for twenty or more years, is not easily repaired by the mere ceremony of marriage; tensions, inhibitions, and fears therefore remain powerful pathological forces in the love-life of a considerable number of adults.*

How to improve or guide the evolution of love is no simple matter. It is fairly clear that the puritanical disapproval of infantile and childish interest in sex should be modified; this process is already a good way advanced. Not quite so clearly, the continuing disapproval of adolescent and pre-marital sexual expression ought to be moderated; the disjunction between affection and sex will be minimized to the extent that sex and affection are blended in the lives of young sexually mature people before marriage. This process, too, is well advanced, though it is not without its dangers and disfunctional possibilities.

The trend towards earlier marriage and the increase of the life-span now make it routine for bride and groom to expect to spend fifty years with each other, barring separation or divorce; but it is not so sure an expectation that they will retain sensitive emotional reactions, warm friendship, or sensuous delight in each other all that while, or even a major part of that while. But the answer here is not at all clear. The advocates of greater extra-marital freedom may be urging a cure for one ill at the cost of producing a number of new ills. No doubt a more generous and less restrictive attitude on the part of husbands and wives alike would permit marriages to continue even though one or both partners had had outside love affairs, but whether this more permissive attitude could really be brought about is uncertain. All the evidence from the Anglo-Saxon part of the world would seem to indicate that modern love, being as important as it is and consisting, ideally, of a fusion of roles and values, cannot be genially and light-heartedly parcelled out. Much as one might see the value in so doing, the forces of history do not, at the moment, seem to favour this direction of development.

Or at least not until society itself provides some new and yet-undiscovered mechanisms to embody the values now forced upon love, and to meet the needs it now satisfies. Conceivably some future social order may provide us, on a rational and orderly basis, with emotional reassurance and security, the satisfaction of our sexual drives, the fulfilment of our yearning for companionship and fellowship, and the yearly requirements of our social order for young. If so, love may become once

* Two specific indications: the late inquisitive Dr Kinsey found that a large proportion of American males completed the sex act in less than two minutes (quite likely an indication of guilty haste), and the Margaret Sanger Research Bureau finds that about one out of four married women feel at best apathy, and at worst outright revulsion, about the sex act.

again, as in the past, a frolic and an amusement, rather than an earnest and demanding business. I suspect that that time is a long way off.

SUGGESTED READINGS

In order to keep this list brief, I have omitted primary sources and given only those secondary sources which cover large areas and provide documentation.

Andreas (Andreas Capellanus, or Andrew the Chaplain). *The Art of Courtly Love*, trans. J. J. Parry (from *Tractatus Amoris*). New York: Columbia University Press, 1941. Parry's introduction is an excellent résumé of courtly love-mores.

Beigel, Hugo G. 'Romantic Love' in *Am. Sociol. Rev.* Vol. XVI, 1951. A sociological review of romantic love and its descent from the Middle Ages into modern life.

Briffault, Robert. *The Mothers*. New York: Macmillan, 1927. Massive, anthropological, mostly on primitive love and western love up to the Middle Ages.

Burgess, Ernest W., and Locke, Harvey J. *The Family*. New York: American Book Co., 1953. Love and marriage in modern America.

Bury, J. B. *History of the Later Roman Empire*. New York: Macmillan, 1923.

Carcopino, Jerome. *Daily Life in Ancient Rome*. New Haven: Yale University Press, 1940; London: Routledge, 1941.

Ellis, Havelock. *Studies in the Psychology of Sex*. Philadelphia: Davis, 1901–28. See especially Vols. I, III, IV and VI, new edition published in London: Heinemann, 1955.

Frank, Tenney. *Aspects of Social Behaviour in Ancient Rome*. Harvard University Press, 1932.

Hunt, Morton M. *The Natural History of Love*. New York: Knopf, 1959.

Krutch, Joseph Wood. *Human Nature and the Human Condition*. New York: Random House, 1959.

La Barre, Weston. *The Human Animal*. University of Chicago Press, 1954. Interdisciplinary study of human nature and culture.

Lea, Henry C. *Historical Sketch of Sacerdotal Celibacy*. Boston: Houghton Mifflin, 1884.

Malinowski, Bronislaw. *The Sexual Life of Savages in North-Western Melanesia*. New York: Halcyon, 1929.

Mead, Margaret. *Male and Female*. New York: New American Library, 1955; London: Gollancz, 1950. Anthropological view of primitives and of modern Americans.

Montagu, M. F. Ashley. *The Direction of Human Development*. New York: Harper, 1955. The multiple bases of love—biological, psychological, etc.

Myrdal, Alva and Viola Klein. *Women's Two Roles: Home and Work*. New York: Humanities Press, 1956.

Painter, Sidney. *French Chivalry*. Johns Hopkins University Press; Oxford University Press, 1940. Includes material on *l'amour courtois*.

Robinson, C. E. *Everyday Life in Ancient Greece*. New York: Oxford University Press, 1933.

Westermarck, Edward. *The History of Human Marriage*. New York: Allerton, 1922. First published in 1889, mostly anthropological and limited to primitives.

Winch, Robert F. *The Modern Family*. New York: Holt, 1952.

Wright, F. A. *Greek Social Life*. New York: Dutton, 1925.

WILLIAM HOLFORD

THE SHELLS OF SOCIETY

SIR WILLIAM HOLFORD

Born 1907. Educated: Diocesan College, Cape Town; Liverpool School of Architecture. Professor of Town Planning, University College London. Technical Adviser to Ministry of Town and Country Planning. Planning Consultant to City of London, County of Cambridge, etc. Member, Royal Fine Art Commission. President, Royal Institute of British Architects.

Publications: *The Future of Merseyside; The Great Baroque Masquerade; Town and Country, Reconstruction in the City of London; Cambridge Planning Proposals; Corby New Town*, etc.

THE SHELLS OF SOCIETY

Architects in all ages have tried to express in their buildings something of themselves and something of the men and the societies for whom they built. Even when expressing themselves most freely—as Gaudi did, for example, in Barcelona—the intractability of the medium and the fact that their buildings are used as well as seen, keeps the architects' imagination in social and economic bounds which do not confine other artists to the same extent. Building today is organization. Besides being an art it is also a science, a technique and a business. The individual mind selects and refines and imagines; but the architecture that results is a collective product.

Seen in retrospect, architecture can always be read as a commentary on the social system that produced it; and in that general term one can include economics and politics and religion. This is easily recognized in the monumental remains of antiquity, an architecture designed to last. For there in the Upper Nile and in Attica, at Zimbabwe or Stonehenge, is the physical evidence of an old way of life, the testament of a collective mind that has reorganized itself and moved on. The homes and the meeting-grounds, the pyramids and temples, the citadels and walls, and the town plans as a whole recall the shells of human societies whose beliefs and attitudes gave them life and meaning. Soft shells or hard shells, buried or broken, they show where people lived together, what they valued and worshipped, and how they organized, defended and advanced themselves. It is too simple to view a society and its buildings as cause and effect; old shells are sometimes adapted to the ways of new inhabitants; and the preservation of ancient structures beyond their natural span of life is one of civilization's most recently acquired skills. Nevertheless, when seen retrospectively, architecture is a form of social history.

In prospect, on the other hand, architecture is something different. While it is struggling to be born, a work of design is in a highly individual phase of its existence. Heredity and environment help to shape it, but because it is the result of what we call a creative act, it has an organic life of its own, distinguishable from others, and—partly by reason of this differentiation—able to contribute to a still richer form of association with them. The quality of a work of art, as of a culture, derives from the subordination of variety and contrast to an overriding unity of purpose and effect. No society is rich without individual personalities, just as no national system is rich without regional variations. It seems that the process whereby a schedule of building accommodation is changed into a three-dimensional design must first take place in the eye and mind of an individual designer.

Only in this way can the possibilities and precedents be fused together by a single intelligence, the selection and discarding of materials and methods be brought under one controlling mind, the fusion of experience with intuition take place, and a total effect of unity and correspondence be achieved—unity in the object designed and correspondence with its physical setting and with the formative ideas of its time. In matters of design, procedure by the votes of a majority is worse than useless. Architectural evolution does not result, any more than biological evolution does, from the mechanical application of means to ends, but by realizing a continuous extension of the ends themselves. Significant architecture does not automatically come from the working out of formulae, or from modular co-ordination, or from a theory of structures, useful as these tools are in measuring standards of building performance. Here, as everywhere in life, whether human, animal, or vegetable, we come up against the problem of organization—organization of the raw materials of existence, whether physical or psychological, into effective patterns in which a variety of parts are combined and interrelated in a unitary whole. Students of architecture learn from art historians, and from structual engineers, and from making measured drawings of historic buildings, that a work of art can be analysed into component and calculable elements: but the process does not work in reverse.

Biologists have also realized '. . . that living beings, however perfect their spontaneity, were always decomposable into an endless chain of closed mechanisms. From this they thought they could deduce a principle of universal materialism. But they overlooked the essential difference between a natural whole and the elements into which it is analysed.'[1]

The making of architectural plans is, in fact, a gathering together of strands into a new stem with a character of its own, which may later proliferate and ramify in the manner of a biological tree. Collective experience is re-born in an individual personality and emerges as a cultural enrichment; diverse and complex requirements are given formal unity in a building; and thus society grows another of its innumerable shells. Soon it will be material for the historian and the anthropologist. It may even be the subject of a preservation campaign. But by that time new shells will be evolving.

The arts have an even greater capacity than the sciences and technologies to rejuvenate themselves at their earlier sources of inspiration. In drawing and in sculpture, for example, something expressed or evolved thousands of years before the invention of writing can register with a modern artist and quicken his senses. Good painters today have an instinctive understanding of the primitive. The architectural use of the word *renaissance* refers to the re-birth in Western Europe in the early fifteenth century of a system of *Orders* in common use more than a thousand years before. The correspondence that is established is, of course, on the emotional and not the technical plane. What is flashed across the intervening centuries is the stimulus of beauty and pleasure, the sense of continuity and the knowledge that the mundane facts of life, animal and human forms, landscape and seascape, and the proportions of structures can be transformed by real perception into significant and moving works of art.

At the moment, in Western Europe, architecture is less significant than usual. The sheer growth of numbers to be housed at home and at work, their greater mobility, and the increase of mechanization and mechanical services, accounts partly for this. Moreover, the emphasis placed by governments and organizations the world over on the economic responsibilities of architecture has tended to diminish its cultural and symbolic importance in the life of communities and nations.

In Britain, since the war, the battle for modern architecture has not been a battle for a style of building; it has been a battle for programmes and opportunities, for the recognition of architecture as a social art and of the proper development of town and countryside as a major instrument of cultural evolution. Too long divorced from structural engineering in such fields as transport, civil defence and public utilities, architecture has tended to become a specialized trade which it is not always necessary to employ.

This is a far cry from the philosophy of men like Trissino, Barbaro and Palladio, in the middle of the sixteenth century, who

'. . . saw architecture not as an isolated discipline but as one of the innumerable manifestations of the human mind which all follow the same laws'.[2]

It is also a long way from Wren and the Royal Society a century later.

One of the results of the perhaps inevitable withdrawal of architecture in modern times into a smaller sector of the great range of human achievement has been a somewhat restricted and uneven performance. In schools, small factories, certain kinds of mixed housing development and the nuclei of new towns, architecture has risen to the occasion; but for most commercial buildings in this country, for Government offices and town halls and hospitals, for railway stations and airports, modern university buildings, the architecture and landscape of recreation and amusement and the centres of the big cities, it has not.

In the USSR the prestige value of public architecture and in the USA the prestige value of business architecture, are both high. In Finland and Brazil—one of the smallest and one of the largest countries in the world—architecture is not only strongly progressive but an integral part of national life and achievement. In many under-developed countries, on the other hand, the over-rapid spread of mechanization and mass-production has produced urban deserts in which architecture cannot flourish at all; and the same description could be applied to the fast-grown suburbs of cities such as Calcutta and Sydney and Chicago. In many countries of Western Europe and of the British Commonwealth, there is now an architectural lull. And during this lull many eyes are turned upon the past —on the primitive and the classical past, on the Middle Ages, on the Age of Humanism in Italy. In England they turn to the eighteenth century, to the Romantic Movement and the Picturesque Movement, to the preservation of the past for the sake of its history.

This backward glance may well be the necessary prelude to evolutionary change, particularly if the right lessons are drawn from it. If the historians and the teachers have got near to the truth, they must have revealed to us during this century, from their studies of the past, more about the *processes* of architectural thought and more about the social settings in which designs were created, than was ever known or coherently assembled before. They have traced in Greece the transfiguration of the rough wooden post into the marble column, the domestic megaron into the sacred temple, the hilltop cluster into the ceremonial acropolis. And although this phase of architectural evolution took place when the dimensions of space-enclosure, the sizes of populations and the techniques of building were completely different from what they are now, the archaeologists and historians have shown the correspondence between it and the whole social and idea-system of the ancient Greeks. They have established the part it played in the sense of individual reponsibility and fulfilment enjoyed, as of right, by citizens of the small city-states of the time.

Historians have also examined the aspirations and incentives that produced such building forms as the Cistercian foundations and the republican city of Venice, and have noted the organization by which individual dwelling units were built up into self-regulated communities, the parts being proportionately related to the whole. They have studied the walled city of Pekin, the temple-mountain of Angkor Vat and other Hindu and Buddhist temples, and explained something of their symbolic and hierarchical character. They have looked at architecture in the age of the Italian academies, when art and science and philosophy were a manifestly related system of ideas, and Renaissance Humanism was a guiding concept. They have told us something of the mind of Leonardo da Vinci, and Michelangelo, and Wren.[3] They have assessed the leasehold system of the ground landlords of the eighteenth century in London, the Roman methods of Napoleon I, and the plastic surgery of Napoleon III and Baron Haussmann in Paris. They have revealed some of the colonial contributions to estate and town development in America, North and South Africa, the East and the West Indies. In all this, and in the many new towns and ideal cities that have been planned—sometimes too rigidly— in every period from classical times to the present day, the importance of *ideas* is paramount. These ideas originally emerged at a specific time and place, often in association with a set of religious beliefs or social customs; but it is remarkable how quickly they spread across regional frontiers and how they were adapted to new circumstances.

The idea of conscious limitation of numbers, for example, particularly in relation to the growth of a community, which appears in Plato, reappears in many of the religious foundations of the eleventh and twelfth centuries in Western Europe. Then at the end of the nineteenth century it appears again as one of the principles governing the creation of a Garden City, as enunciated by Ebenezer Howard. It has always been clear that one cannot plan in advance nor achieve a successful and well-proportioned layout in anything as long-term as town building, if the numbers of houses and people and vehicles are subject to indefinite and irregular expansion; but the methods of *control* are not readily accepted at first nor easily maintained later on. The conception of organizing and building for a limited number, so as to preserve the character of the community and the quality of its environment, is common to the small Greek city-state, the medieval priory, the ideal town of the Industrial Revolution (such as James Buckingham's *Victoria* of 1849), an Oxford College, or a London satellite established under the New Towns Act of 1946.* This

* *Editor's Note.* Here the consideration of size in animal organisms is relevant. First, for any given type of organization, both excessively small and excessively large size is a disadvantage: in other words, there is an optimum range of size. Secondly, increase in size

main conception has been supported for a variety of different reasons; and since the penalty of all successful civic design has been its inevitable attraction of greater numbers, the initial idea has to be succeeded by further experiments in the shape of satellite settlements or comprehensive redevelopment in order to cope with the surplus. Gradually the idea has been taken from its purely local context and applied regionally; it is now seen to be world-wide.

The historians have also recorded the results of periods of social disorder when planning, rational layout, and standards of design all suffered a partial eclipse. There were periods that produced slums and rural wastes, when Disraeli described prosperous England as *The Two Nations*, and when a sort of economic and social schizophrenia developed in all the industrialized cities and countries of the world. Architecture and town planning, during these periods, produced individual works of substance and of fantasy and, in reaction to squalor, began a series of model tenements and factories and villages. But the main stem of patronage had been split in two, and the cultural tree lost its unified shape. Interest, talent and money flowed into the smaller branches, which tried to live for themselves, as privileged groups, and frequently became deformed. Engineering not only divided itself from architecture as a profession, but erected lines of demarcation which it is becoming increasingly difficult, in the twentieth century, to break down.

The fact has now to be faced that mediocre and unimaginative designs have become acceptable to a majority of people in the industrially more highly-developed countries, not as a modest second-best to those of acknowledged merit, but for their own sakes, as if no better existed. And although public corporations, town councils and Government departments have tried to exercise the talent for patronage which had once graced royalty, the aristocracy, the landed gentry and the privileged, they have sometimes been neither knowledgeable nor critical enough, nor could they often afford to be long-sighted enough, to employ patronage in the same way. It was not that cheapness, mediocrity and quick financial returns were new motives in the commissioning of public works; it was simply that in many countries, towards the end of the nineteenth century, there were

demands changes in internal organization; thus an animal above a certain size must have special systems for transport and for communication (the circulatory and nervous systems). Conversely, new features of organization may make new size-increase possible: e.g. the 'invention' of bone eventually made possible the evolution of large land animals. Finally, there is a limit to the size of any type of organization, though different types have different limits: it is biologically impossible for an insect to be much bigger than a mouse, or a land mammal much bigger than an elephant.[1]

All these considerations appear to apply, *mutatis mutandis*, to the size of cities.

fewer sanctions against them. An informed and articulate minority, once entitled to represent public opinion, no longer regulated nor approved the general taste in art, architecture and industrial design; nor did they control its markets. Worse still, the rapid spread of mass industrialization and technology to less developed countries occurred at the same time.

The twentieth century has thus inherited a legacy of formlessness, in every sense of the word. A decline in visual perception among the many has served to set apart as 'aesthetes' or 'highbrows' the few who have seriously cultivated it. There is an obvious formlessness, also, in the urban pattern almost everywhere, blurring the distinction between town and country, between the gregarious and the wild places, between centres and perimeters, between one town and another.

The whole story of art and architecture in the past, now being revealed to us more and more fully, shows that progress towards a more intense state of awareness, and thus to a life lived more fully, has been markedly uneven. Sometimes through external factors and more often by lack of knowledge, long stultifying periods of disintegration or abortive growth have occurred, followed by a coming together of the fibres of conscious-ness in a new stem growing along the main line of evolution. It seems to be a function of artists and architects, individually and collectively, to make this emotive and intuitive breakaway from an old growth that has flowered and holds no further powers of germination, towards one that has a new phase of life before it. The approach through feeling appears at first sight to be more random than the scientific approach based on reason and experiment. But both depend on observation, and on an awareness of the relationship of a detail to the main principle behind it, of the small symbol to the grand design.

As man discovers, in Julian Huxley's phrase, that 'he is nothing less than evolution become conscious of itself', what is he going to think of the individual and collective shells that society will continue to create, inhabit, and later on discard? Will architecture still have a role to play, as an art or as a technology, in helping to give mankind a sense of fulfilment and wholeness? Will it stimulate people to see more clearly and more deeply, both with their eyes and minds?

Humanist values in architecture and landscape have a great deal to do with proportion, not only in the Greek sense and as defined by the Humanists of the Renaissance, but also in the modern sense of the relationship between the individual intelligence and the collective and therefore more permanent framework of ideas.

Quality in design has always come largely from interest and variety of detail within the major unity of the design as a whole. What has occurred recently has been a considerable extension of the area over which that major unity is possible and comprehensible. In this matter the humanities are not as advanced as is science, which has already become global; but they are part of the same thought-system. Architecture and town planning are being carried on to greater comprehensiveness by a revolt against the monotony of thoughtless standardization. Mechanical repetition of detail can be made significant as well as useful by being incorporated in a larger plan or system comprehensive enough to achieve an eventual unity and balance. Stereotyped windows and pilasters and parapets, used for example in the regular house-fronts of the Royal Circus at Bath, are brought together to form a unified group of great distinction; and the standard glass panes of the Crystal Palace in 1851 were framed into halls of increasing size and scale to create a complete and highly original composition.

Moreover, groups of buildings may each be designed by individual architects and not necessarily at the same point of time. Only if a pre-liminary scheme has first been prepared for what one might call 'the public sector' of the operation (the circulation and access, the building lines, the working conditions, the amount of open space, the limits of density, and so forth) can the variety of design in detail become part of a larger unity of conception, and the competition of different intelligences become constructive rather than hostile.

The same problem arises on a larger scale in the organization of a setting for a group of buildings or for the central area of a town. Concentration and high building demand low building and open space by way of contrast —for practical as well as aesthetic reasons. The scheme must therefore comprise enough land and enough finance to cover both types of develop-ment. In any plan for a city, high rents, high development values and great social activity at the centres (both main and subsidiary) should be balanced by lower rents and values and comparative quiet in the residential districts; and the plan must be comprehensive enough to secure this balance. In other words a mind is needed to control the larger design as well as the component parts. The development of land and the building of new settlements is no longer a natural or a self-regulating process. The population explosion alone has completely altered that situation. Urban growth also puts a premium on undeveloped land. The larger the cities grow the greater is the need for the countryside and the wild places. Every acre in Britain that is added to the towns deserves its counterpart of ten acres in the country preserved against unsuitable development. This, in a sense, is what the National Parks Commission is after in designating National Parks and Areas of Outstanding Natural Beauty.

Unfortunately the comprehensive approach, which would include an appreciation of *all* the human values which planning aims to achieve, and which would use biology and the social sciences as well as engineering and the physical sciences, has not yet been adopted on a national scale. It has been applied in the past to individual institutions and estates, and is now being pursued in certain administrative areas, watersheds and regions such as the Tennessee Valley. It would not be a big step to apply it to the whole of England and Wales, comprising metropolitan London along with the Lake District, and manufacturing industry along with the tourist trade. At present the claims of land features such as motorways, fuel plants, housing settlements, defence mechanisms, forest parks or nature reserves, which are difficult to compare by the criteria applicable to any one of them singly, cannot yet be evaluated in a cultural or thought-system applicable to all of them—not even an economic system. Legislation gives them certain rights and there is even an attempt at cross-referencing (as for example in the Electricity Acts where the Boards are enjoined to 'have regard to amenity' in carrying out their functions of generation and transmission).[5] But their powers are not measured by the same standards. They therefore contend with one another in the market and in Parliament, at local enquiries and in the Press. This is useful and necessary, up to a point; but it would be far more useful if it were done against a background of Humanist values which included the non-material and non-quantifiable ones with the material and quantifiable.

The essential preliminary to the creation of truly Humanist values in architecture and landscape is the organization of knowledge about the physical background itself and its conservation. The land of a small country like Britain is like a keyboard on which all manner of urban and rural compositions have been played—formal themes such as those of Westminster or Edinburgh or Bath, picturesque and classical landscape pieces, the functional patterns of industry, and the accompaniment of small houses and gardens. Compared with larger countries that contain big mountain ranges or tropical forests, the compass of this particular keyboard is limited. But the instrument is true, well-tempered, and complete. Inability to sound a particular note in the scale would be a crippling handicap for future performers, and thus it is one of the responsibilities of trusteeship to keep the instrument in tune, throughout its full compass and in every key, for the benefit of those to come.

The next advances in architecture are likely to result, not merely from the invention of new structural techniques, but from better definitions of the psychological and social needs which structure and shelter are intended to satisfy. Symbolic and fantastic architectural forms have long influenced human behaviour, and being long-lived in comparison with human beings, many of them influence us still. But far more questions are now being asked about individual and social behaviour in relation to buildings before they are designed. The requirements of temperature and lighting, of sound diffusion and insulation, are calculated in advance; time and motion studies are made, models are constructed, and the psychological effects of enclosures—more particularly of movement from one kind of space to another—are analysed from historical examples, both in buildings and in towns.

Significant architecture represents style as well as form. The spark of imagination that gives it life comes from a continuous search for the true and full expression of human capacities and human awareness, both of the external universe and of the world of ideas. Beauty of design cannot be created to order, or by effort alone; yet it is closely related to certain kinds of order, particularly mathematical theory, and often results from a passionate identification on the part of its designer with some of the simplest of human needs—shelter, security, social companionship, and the pleasure that comes from seeing the inventions of the mind of man against the background of nature.

REFERENCES

(1) Teilhard de Chardin, Pierre. *The Phenomenon of Man*. New York: Harper & Brothers, 1959.

(2) Wittkower, Rudolf. *Architectural Principles in the Age of Humanism*. 2nd Edition. Hollywood-by-the-Sea, Florida: Transatlantic Arts, 1953.

(3) See for example John Summerson. *Architecture in Britain, 1530–1830*. Baltimore: Penguin Books, 1954. Part III: 'Wren and the Baroque'.

(4) Huxley, Julian. 'The Size of Living Things', in *Man in the Modern World*. New York: Mentor Books, 1948.

(5) Hinton, C., and Holford, W. 'Power Production and Transmission in the Countryside: Preserving Amenities', *Journal of the Royal Society of Arts*. February 1960.

MICHAEL TIPPETT

TOWARDS THE CONDITION OF MUSIC

MICHAEL TIPPETT, C.B.E.

Born 1905. Educated: Stamford Grammar
School; Royal College of Music. Composer.
Director of Music at Morley College,
1940–1951. 'A Child of Our Time' first
performed 1944.

Publications: *Moving into Aquarius*, 1959.

TOWARDS THE CONDITION OF MUSIC

There is a knowledge concerning art, and this knowledge is something quite different from the immediate apprehension of works of art, even from whatever insight we feel we have gained by perceiving and responding to works of art. A simple statement such as: art must be *about* something, is innocent enough till we want to give a name to this something. Then invariably we delude ourselves with words, because with our discursive or descriptive words we cross over into the field of writing or talking *about* art. We have reversed ourselves.

This fundamental difficulty has made all discussion of art, as indeed all discussion of quality, a kind of elaborate metaphor. And since all metaphor is imprecise, the verbal misunderstandings in aesthetics have always been legion. It is only when we remain deliberately in the field of enquiry concerning the facts *surrounding* art, that we amass knowledge of the kind we expect to obtain through such intellectual disciplines as History, Anthropology, Psychology or Philosophy. We can confidently say that we have vastly increased our knowledge concerning art during the last hundred years, chiefly of course the history of art. Anthropology has added further dimensions to our sense of history as a whole, and so to the history of art. Psychology, in my opinion, will eventually make much more precise the terms with which we discuss the processes of artistic creation and enjoyment. Philosophy, in the sense in which we speak of Platonic or Christian Philosophy, has often assigned limits or directions to art considered as a social function. At the present time, when the pretensions of Islam or Christianity to do this are everywhere receding, only Marxist philosophy and the Communist states make the attempt. The most disturbing feature of Stalinist aesthetic dogma was (in China *is*) the apparent fear of the spontaneous (including the ineffable) element in art, which is gravely endangered by extreme social systematization. Plato, for all his systematizing tendency, accepted this. Socrates says in the Phaedrus: 'There is a third form of possession or madness, of which the Muses are the source. This seizes a tender, virgin soul and stimulates it to rapt passionate expression, especially in lyric poetry. But if any man come to the gates of poetry without the madness of the Muses, persuaded that skill alone will make him a good poet, then shall he and his works of sanity with him be brought to nought by the poetry of madness and see their place is nowhere to be found.'

Plato names three other forms of divine madness besides the artistic, viz. the prophetic, the expiatory, and that of the lover. To understand Plato's term 'madness', we must recall the argument of the Phaedrus in more detail. Socrates considers first whether what we call madness might not really be of two kinds. One kind is clearly a disease—the rational mind being disordered and unamenable to the will—and even if we picture it as though the sufferer's personality has been possessed by some other and alien personality, yet this possession is unhealthy and often markedly anti-social. But the other kind might be a madness where the invading personality, though unaccountable and irrational, is yet beneficent and creative: possession not by a devil, but by a god.[1] It is this 'divine madness' of Plato's which I call the spontaneous (including the ineffable) element in art, and I think that the intuitions of Plato concerning this spontaneous element are upheld by the findings of psychology, especially depth psychology. From such psychology we have obtained a concept of apparently spontaneous psychic generation; of unconscious psychic drives and inhibitions; of, possibly, an inner psychic collectivity which is boundless and non-discrete. Yet to use the word concept for such notions is, surely, a paradox. In the same way, at the point now at which this discursive essay needs to consider the immediate experience of, and the insight (if that is the right word) obtained from works of art *in themselves*, then, as has been pointed out above, this paradox reappears.

We must begin with the fact of works of art existing objectively and created to be appreciated. And we must accept that even if a state of mind, or an artefact arising from a state of mind, is spontaneously generated and only to be experienced immediately, or even ineffably, it is none the less a natural phenomenon, a fact of human existence. In rare experiences of this sort, such as the states of mysticism, the number of human beings to whom the experiences spontaneously come (or who have desires and techniques to induce them) is, at least in the West, small. Yet the tradition is so constant and the phenomenon so well established that we all have reasonable grounds for accepting them as factual and natural even when we can never ourselves have known them. They can clearly be spiritually refreshing; and may yet turn out to be one of man's hitherto undeveloped social qualities. For if psychosocial survival depends, as it well may do, on correctives to the present overwhelming social valuation given to material welfare, then evolutionary necessities may begin to operate, in an admittedly as yet unimaginable way, on seemingly socially valueless meditative disciplines.

While it would appear that the mystic can only render to society the refreshment received personally from mystic experiences through the quality of his conduct, the creative artist, from whatever source or in whatever medium he receives the spontaneous element, must, by the nature of his mandate, create objective works of art. These works subsist then in society independently of their creator, and many thousands of human beings receive enjoyment, refreshment, enrichment from them. This is a commonplace fact. Perhaps indeed every human being alive has experienced immediately something of this kind. Because the experience is so common and yet capable of being heightened to embody our profoundest apprehensions, it has in every age demanded intellectual understanding of itself. Modern psychology has provided new counters with which to play this age-old game.

If I now proceed to play this game in an up-to-date mode, it must be remembered that all discussion of what art *is*, or what it is *about*, is semantically imprecise. (We are probably on safer ground when we discuss what art *does*.) So it is hardly possible to proceed without the danger of misunderstanding, although our modern counters for discussion are, in my opinion, an improvement on some of those of the past, i.e. are probably semantically less equivocal.

Works of art are images. These images are based on apprehensions of the inner world of feelings.[2] Feelings in this sense contain emotions, intuitions, judgments and values. These feelings are therefore generally supposed to be excluded from scientific enquiry. I make this statement, in so far as it is true, not as an implied judgment, but solely as a fact, in order to emphasize the semantic problems of aesthetic discussion. It is not an easy matter to pass over from language used in the observation of natural objects extended outside us in space and time, to language used to discuss or describe the inner world of feelings, where space and time (at least in certain states of mind) are differently perceived altogether. Even where we succeed in such an attempt the description is always at one remove. The images which are works of art, are our sole means of expressing the inner world of feelings objectively and immediately. If art is a language, it is a language concerned with this inner world alone.

As 'inner' and 'outer' remain philosophically extremely difficult terms, so the dichotomy I have (at least verbally) established between space and time considered outside us and space and time perceived within is certainly not rigid. Hence it often appears as though the raw material of artistic creation was obtained from observation of nature outside us, and that the creative activity resided in the organization and construction which the artist applies to this raw material. The danger of this way of considering the matter is that very quickly we come to talk of works of art as *derived from* nature, which is much too simple. It loses sight of the one absolute idiosyncracy of art, that works of art are images of *inner* experience, however apparently representational the mode of expression may be.

This difficult matter is best set out by considering first the extreme case of space in painting. (I use the word 'extreme' because the matter is not quite the same in architecture.) And secondly the opposite extreme of time in music.

The vital fact of all pictorial works of art is that the space in the picture is always virtual, not real. The space in the room and of the wall on which the picture hangs is real. Part of the means by which a picture becomes an image of the inner world of feelings is the contrast between the real space of the wall or the room and the virtual space in the picture. Hence it is not of vital concern to the art of painting whether the virtual space is constructed by representational methods or the reverse. We accept this, if we are gifted or trained to do so, without demur. We find it difficult if we consciously or unconsciously believe that art *derives* from experiences of outer nature and not, as is the basic fact, from the inner world of feelings. The representations of outer nature, if present, are always images of the inner experience, which the artist has organized.

At the other pole to painting, music offers images of the inner world of feelings perceived as a flow. As our concept of external time is itself an equivocal one,[3] it is perhaps less easy even than with space in painting, to realize that the time we apprehend in the work of musical art has only a virtual existence in contrast with the time marked by the clock-hands when the work is performed. Works appear short or long from other considerations besides that of performance time, and our sense of performance time will be markedly modified by them.[4]

Because music is concerned not with space but time, this method of artistic creation seems to by-pass the problems of representationalism, present in some degree in all the other arts. Hence the dictum: 'all art tends towards the condition of music'. This aphorism, wrenched from its original context in an essay of Pater, has nowadays been commonly used in this much looser and wider sense, precisely, in my opinion, to draw attention to this real tendency. For if the matter-of-factness of the outer world gets too much into the foreground of art, then expression of the inner world of feeling is probably correspondingly more difficult. By dispensing *a priori* with all the problems arising from expressing inner feelings through representations of the outer world, music can seem a very favoured art. This is not always a merit. Music's easiness quickly degenerates into escapism; escapism not only because music seems absolutely abstracted from real objects but also because the emotional content of music is both obvious and permitted.

To a certain degree all appreciation of art is escapism—to leave behind the world of matter-of-fact. The important question is always: escape into what? Escape into the true inner world of feelings is one of the most rewarding experiences known to man. When entry into this world is prevented, and still more when it is unsought, a man is certainly to some degree unfulfilled. Yet even escape into the simpler states of appreciation is often self-denied. Darwin wrote in his *Autobiography*: '. . . now for many years I cannot endure to read a line of poetry. . . . I have also lost my taste for pictures and music. . . . My mind seems to have become a kind of machine for grinding general laws out of large collections of facts. . . . The loss of these tastes is a loss of happiness and may possibly be injurious to the intellect, and more probably to the moral character, by enfeebling the emotional part of our nature'.

Darwin puts his finger unerringly on the danger. He uses the word 'machine'. In the vast social apparatus which modern science and technology demand the person often becomes lost in a 'machine'. Eventually there arises the danger of too great mechanization of the social life in every field.[5] At this point creative artists are sometimes driven to use the shock tactics of a genius like D. H. Lawrence—or in another field Kokoschka.

As I have already pointed out, within the dazzling achievements of the modern knowledge-explosion we must include the lesser portion of a greatly increased knowledge about art. But the contemporary explosion in the means and methods of art itself over the last hundred years is not of the same kind. The new art is not related to problems of the outer world at all but to apprehensions of the inner world. What can certainly be deduced from the contemporaneity of the two explosions, is that the psychosocial change and consequent adaptation demanded of modern man is without precedent in its totality.

It may in fact be misleading to speak of art as primarily or always responsive to social change—though in many obvious senses this is true. For art is unavoidably and primarily responsive to the inner world of feelings. And this inner world may be spontaneously generative (in the sense I attempted to define the term earlier) independently of, e.g., the social consequences of scientific technology. Or it may be attempting to restore some sort of psychosocial balance. I would say that it is all these things. Yet clearly changes (and these are constantly happening) in our ideas of human personality will be reflected in certain arts, if not necessarily in music. Music may always appear to by-pass such considerations, but literature and the drama in all their forms certainly cannot. It may be that changes in our ideas of human personality reflect changes in the inner world of feelings, and not *vice versa*. We are not yet able to judge properly what happens in this complex and interrelated field; we cannot yet be certain what is cause and what is effect.

At the present time, for example, we can only see that the knowledge-explosion in all the sciences is a challenge to psychosocial adaptation, while the violent changes in methods in all the arts are symptomatic of deep-seated changes in man's inner world of feelings.

Modern psychology is indeed beginning to produce a kind of relativity of personality, especially in personal relations. This is sufficiently far advanced in the West (it may be nothing new for the East) for it to be satirized by a cartoonist like Feiffer. Here is a caricatured conversation between a young couple suffering from this relativity of personality—i.e. valid uncertainty as to what is real in their notions of one another and what is projection.

She: You're arguing with me.
He: I'm *not* arguing with you. I'm *trying* to make a point.
She: There is a difference between making a point and embarking on a sadistic attack.
He: If sadism is your equivalent to impartial judgment then I admit to being a sadist.
She: How *easy* to be flip when one precludes responsibility.
He: How irresponsible of one so irresponsible to speak of responsibility.
She: Since you *must* project your own inadequacies into a discussion of the facts I see no point in carrying this further.
He: How like you to use attack as a disguise for retreat.
She: Ah, but if we were not arguing as you so heatedly claim, what is it that I am retreating from?
      (Silence).
He: I'm getting a stomach-ache.
She: Me too.
He: Let's knock off and go to a movie.

Behind this caricature is something real, to which art cannot be indifferent. The dénouement is also quite serious. We knock off to go to a movie. This is not merely an escape from the at present insoluble problems, it is a therapeutic necessity. We project our problems, whether of dual or multiple relationship, momentarily on to the movie—i.e. on to an objective work of art. Movies are generally works of popular art; and they are socially immensely valuable. For most of us there can be no objective examination of the constant and developing situation such as that caricatured by Feiffer, except by recourse to the movie or its equivalent: the splendid value of this recourse being that it is mostly un-selfconscious and indeed an enjoyment.

The enjoyment of popular art, in my opinion, is much more often of the same kind as the enjoyment of more serious art (though not of the same quality) than snob circles like to think. There is of course a vast mass of sentimental popular music (to take my own art) which is poor and dispiriting. But there is a great deal indeed of popular jazz where the dissonances and distortions of the voice or the instruments, the energy and passion and often brilliant timing of the performance, combine to produce an enjoyment which is of better quality, and is also expressive of the tensions produced in man by the inner and outer changes of his life. Carried on the pulse of this music we really do renew in a limited degree our sense of the flow of life, just because this music gives hints of deeper apprehensions through its qualities of style and even form.

As the purely emotional element recedes and the formal element comes forward the music ceases to appeal to vast masses: this is happening already in the world of jazz itself. When the limitations of popular musical harmonies, rhythms, melodies and forms are left entirely behind, as in music for the concert hall, then the public further diminishes. Yet symphonic music, in the hands of great masters, truly and fully embodies the otherwise unperceived, unsavoured inner flow of life. In listening to such music we are as though entire again, despite all the insecurity, incoherence, incompleteness and relativity of our everyday life. The miracle is achieved by submitting to the power of its organized flow; a submission which gives us a special pleasure and finally enriches us. The pleasure and the enrichment arise from the fact that the flow is not merely the flow of the music itself, but a significant image of the inner flow of life. Artifice of all kinds is necessary to the musical composition in order that it shall become such an image. Yet when the perfect performance and occasion allows us a truly immediate apprehension of the inner flow 'behind' the music, the artifice is momentarily of no consequence; we are no longer aware of it.

Music of course has a tremendous range of images, from the gay (and, if perhaps rarely, the comic) to the serious and tragic. On the serious side music has always been associated with religious rituals and been a favoured art for expressing certain intuitions of transcendence. That is to say, certain music, to be appreciated as it is, expects a desire and willingness on our part to see reflected in it transcendent elements, unprovable and maybe unknowable analytically, but which infuse the whole work of art. This quality in music has permitted such works as the *Matthew Passion*, the *Ninth Symphony* of Beethoven, or *The Ring*.

According to the excellence of the artist, that is to his ability to give formal clarity to these analytically unknowable transcendent intuitions, these works of art endure to enrich later minds when the whole social life from which they sprang has disappeared. Hence the enduring quality of a work such as the Parthenon, even when maimed and uncoloured. And it is these formal considerations alone which enable us to set the *Matthew Passion* and the *Ninth Symphony* above *The Ring*. Apparent from all this is the fact that art does not supersede itself in the way science does. Methods and modes may change, and of course, in music, instruments and occasions for making music. These are the things which can make it difficult for us to appreciate, e.g., Pérotin (Perotinus Magnus) now as the great composer his period considered him to be. We may have superseded Pérotin's methods, but we have scarcely superseded his imaginative intuitions. And yet, in another sense, we have. Because the material from the inner world is never quite the same. The extreme changes in the art of the present time are, I am sure, due to more than changes in techniques.

The techniques of music have always changed from time to time with the development of new instruments, e.g. the pianoforte; and even more through the changes of social occasion and means of dissemination, e.g. the invention of the concert hall, or of radio. At the present time there are new electronic methods of producing every imaginable sound known or as yet unknown, and these methods, if they do not supersede the older ways altogether, will certainly be added to them.

The techniques of musical composition change also. There is a widespread preoccupation at present with the new methods of serial composition. Changes in composition technique are more the concern of the composer than of the listener, who is usually disconcerted during the period of experimentation, as with serial technique now. The deeper reasons for this constant renewal of artistic techniques are still somewhat mysterious.[6]

The most striking novelty in music was the gradual invention of polyphony in the late middle ages. All known music up to that time, and right up to our own time in all cultural traditions outside the European and its derivatives, had been, or is still, monodic. This means that in general the melodic line, endlessly decorated and varied, is the essential (as in India and Asia; until the invention of polyphony, Europe). Or combinations of dynamic or subtle rhythms have been used to build as unending a stream of rhythmical variation as the unending line of monodic melodic invention (Africa, Indonesia). In both these kinds of music harmony is incidental and secondary. But European polyphony produced the combination of many ever more disparate lines of melody, and such combination immediately posed problems of harmony new to music. Over the centuries these problems have been resolved in one way or another, and there have been periods of European music when the harmonic element, initially derived from the practice of polyphony, becomes primary, and what polyphony the music contains has become secondary. We are at present in a time when European-derived music has experimented to an unprecedented degree with harmony. This has been pure invention. At the same time discs and tapes and printed collections of folk-songs and dances, and discs and tapes of African, Indonesian, Indian and Chinese music, have stimulated, or been used as basis for a considerable experimentation in rhythm. The melodic element on the other hand (and the formal element in my opinion) has been secondary.

Now European polyphony has proved so powerful an expressive medium that it is mostly sweeping over the whole world and carrying away much of the indigenous traditional musics with it. In this way Europe and America appear still as musical initiators for the globe. But this will not last. When the time is ripe the values of the non-European musical traditions, where they have been temporarily lost, will be rediscovered. The speed at which we are having to become industrially and politically one world would seem to be such that the problems of forging a unified expressive medium may be coming upon us faster than the European composers are as yet aware. This question may well, in my opinion, solve itself first through popular music, just because popular music is by definition and purpose music of the people. Popular music is an open music. In order to entertain it will take everything offered, from Bali to New Orleans, and whatever is successful will be amplified round the world. Popular music will become increasingly global rather than local.

In all the manifestations of music the enduring portion is the sense of flow, of the kind I have described above, organized and expressed formally. A wide-ranging Humanism will always seek to extend to more and more people, through education and opportunity, the enrichment of the personality which music gives. In our technological society we should be warned by Darwin: 'The loss of these tastes (for one or more of the arts according to our predilections) is a loss of happiness and may

possibly be injurious to the intellect and more probably to the moral
character, by enfeebling the emotional part of our nature'. These are wise
and serious words. We are morally and emotionally enfeebled if we live
our lives without artistic nourishment. Our sense of life is diminished. In
music we sense most directly the inner flow which sustains the psyche, or
the soul.

> 'O divine music,
> O stream of sound
> In which the states of soul
> Flow, surfacing and drowning,
> While we sit watching from the bank
> The mirrored world within, for
> "Mirror upon mirror mirrored is all the show".
> O divine music,
> Melt our hearts,
> Renew our love.'[7]

REFERENCES

(1) Tippett, Michael. *Moving into Aquarius*. London: Routledge, 1959; cf. the
chapter 'The Artist's Mandate' for a fuller discussion of this whole problem.

(2) For a full discussion cf. Susan Langer. *Feeling and Form*. New York: Scribner,
1955, and other writings.

(3) Cf. Bergson, *Durée et Simultanéité*, and the provocative essay of Jung, *Syn-
chronicity; An Acausal Connecting Principle*, in Jung and Pauli's *The Interpretation of
Nature and the Psyche*. New York: Pantheon Books, 1955.

(4) Stravinsky. *Poetics of Music*. New York: Vintage, 1956.

(5) Cf. Tippett. *Moving into Aquarius* [see (I)].

(6) For a provocative discussion cf. Ehrenzweig. *The Psycho-analysis of Aesthetic
Vision and Hearing*. New York: Julian Press, 1953.

(7) From the unpublished text of my opera, *King Priam*.

STEPHEN SPENDER

SOCIAL PURPOSE AND THE INTEGRITY OF THE ARTIST

STEPHEN SPENDER

Born 1909. Educated: University College
School; University College, Oxford. Co-
editor of *Horizon* magazine, 1939–41. Editor
of *Encounter* magazine.

Publications: *20 Poems: The Burning Cactus*,
1936; *Forward from Liberalism*, 1937; *Poems
from Spain*, 1939; *Life and the Poet*, 1942;
World Within World, 1951; *Collected Poems*,
1954; *The Making of a Poem*, 1955; etc.

SOCIAL PURPOSE AND THE INTEGRITY
OF THE ARTIST

———

Evolutionary Humanists hold that evolution, which has ceased to occur on a large scale in the world of nature, has become, or should become, the conscious and purposive aim of human beings. People must be awakened to the idea that there is an evolutionary obligation which has to be fulfilled not only through organs of government and public opinion, but also by every means of bringing such a purpose into consciousness.

In common with theories like those of Marx and Freud, which make behaviour conscious that was previously unconscious, this inevitably involves reconsideration of the past. Every advance in consciousness has to be confirmed by evidence that it realizes conditions already implicit in human nature, though not before stated. Conscious processes are unconscious ones made conscious.

If it is true that evolution has become the responsibility of which Evolutionary Humanists have to persuade their fellow-beings, then this task is all the more pressing at a time when the future of the human species seems itself in balance.

Here I shall discuss the visual arts as a function of evolving human consciousness. In a way such a discussion may seem superfluous. For obviously it would be simple to trace the evolution of art from the cave painting to the modern, and point out that as images, architecture and sheer accumulation of styles and objects, art expresses the growth of human awareness and even reflects history. Art is a central medium for the realization of man's search for significance in life. Art provides a record of the stored history of events, of rulers, of religions, of fashions. In the development of the artist himself from the primitive magic-man to the artisan and craftsman, and thence to the artist prince, Leonardo or Michelangelo, Degas or Picasso, the historic development of consciousness from anonymity to individuality is epitomized: hence, no doubt, our preoccupation with the biographies of artists. At a time when individualism is threatened, if not a lost cause, the artist tends to be regarded as a hero, his works his deeds.

Nevertheless, I think that to describe art as the realization of unconscious social evolution would be largely misleading. For if art represents such an unfolding it is of a consciousness that stands outside the society of which it is nevertheless a part and by which it is conditioned. Like the individual artist or spectator, art is both inside society and outside it, conditioned by it and yet sometimes opposed to it, expressing it and yet denying it, fulfilling it and yet frustrating it.

It is tempting to adopt a Marxist attitude and interpret art as history projected into a language of symbolism as on a lantern screen. But if one looks at art from the point of view of society one sees that on many occasions society has regarded the artist or his artefact as a subtle and satanic enemy, and at other times it has destroyed art by attempting to make artists propagandists. No one who reads the Old Testament can take the view that visual art is the expression of the same process of historic evolution as religion or the law. The Hebrews regarded graven images as dangerous to the one God. Perhaps they were right, because where there is monotheism there must always be one and only one idea of God, the goal of orthodoxy sought for with the single mind of religion. The visual arts tend towards the multiplication of images, which in effect means polytheism, as is evident in Hindu religion and the Catholic Church.

Art not only tends to multiply gods through multiplying images, and through the search of the artist for new interpretations to visualize, it also tends to invent objects which themselves become gods. In agnostic societies, where there is no religion, artefacts tend to become things in themselves, the objects of an art cult interpreted by aesthetic high priests. Here is evidence that art need not take sides in the dialectic of history, except in so far as for a great medium of expression, to be outside it, can be interpreted as taking sides. Free Art was annoying to the monotheists of the Old Testament as today it is a thorn in the flesh of social mono-ideologists.

The relationship of artistic to social consciousness varies from time to time and place to place. One must not forget the conditioning influence of society on the artist; but art and society have relations resembling those between separate powers. Not of course that art has worldly power, but it does have the power of being only able to exist on its own terms. Society is at liberty to dominate it, but at the price of there being no art. And where there is no art, the spiritual health of the community is in danger because the expression of perceptive sensibility has been over-ruled.

In the past priests and princes have, not without success, enlisted art to enhance their glory. In civilizations like the Egyptian, where the greatness of the pharaohs, and the mythology of the after-life were visualized, art was fused with the sacred, just as in Hebrew civilization laws and poetry were one, or in Greece, poetry and religion. In Egypt, art, although attached inseparably to the power of the State, remained imaginative, because the authority of the State itself rested on a powerfully imagined mythology.

There have been periods, like that of the Renaissance, when princes or popes, in their dealings with artists, have treated them as equals, and, in ordering their chapels, their statues, and their tombs, submitted their own judgment to the artist's.

There is a vital difference between the attitude of the State in the past, and that of rulers with ideologies today, to the arts. It is that in societies which were tyrannical but nevertheless superstitious, religion provided an escape from the view of life of the tyrant, perhaps even of the Church. The makers of tombs and monuments may have been carrying out the wishes of tyrants, but nevertheless they did so according to the rules and mysteries of their own art. They were not making an extension in stone or paint of a secular view of life which regarded all intellectual activities as interpreters of its single will. They were adding to the tyrant's limited realm of worldly power the transcendent qualities of their power.

Thus the Renaissance condottiere demanded that Verrocchio should make his image beautiful according to Colleoni standards, of which the artist remained the supreme authority. But the sculptor or painter who represented Stalin's or Hitler's image had to interpret in the work that branch of the dictator's ideology which could be realized by rules known to the ideologists in the sphere of artistic creation.

Of course, liberal humanists are not dictators, but for just this reason they should realize the danger implicit in attempts to persuade artists to realize in their work a directing social idea, however justified and urgent this may seem. There is no good modern art expressing a social purpose. Or if, as may happen, the artist conceives of himself as expressing a social purpose, as Leger was a communist, and Picasso painted pictures against Franco, this is not a vision which iedologists would accept, because it is expressed in quite other terms than those of social or political ideas.

The history of the development of art is, largely, the history of the attempts of the artist to create his own vision, with or without the approval of society. Historically the development of art has been mainly in the direction of greater realism: e.g. Egyptian and Greek sculptures and painters developing the technique to represent figures seen from the front and not only in profile, the spectacular growth of naturalism in Greek art, the exploitation of the laws of perspective in Renaissance art, etc. As E. H. Gombrich points out in his *Art and Illusion*, 'discoveries and effects of representation . . . were the pride of earlier artists'. Some of these developments ran counter to the superstitions, prejudices and conventions of the times in which they took place.

All art is and always has consisted of acts of individuation—though this is a view which may appear to be contested by the theory that 'individualism' was something which began with the Renaissance. But individualism was only the coming into self-consciousness of individual experience and individual craft, which exists even in the paintings on the walls of the caves at Lascaux. The fact that an artist does not think of himself as a conscious individualist whose work is evidence of his personal signature, does not mean that he is not an individual. When he uses his eyes he sees more sharply and originally than his neighbours see, and a bit differently from other artists; when he uses brush or chisel he realizes himself within the shared mystery of his craft. His interpretation of an orthodox tradition of work expresses something, however marginal, peculiar to himself.

It is not the threat to the individual that is a danger to art in modern times so much as the threat to the operations of individuation. This threat exists just as much in the democratic countries as in the ones where there are dictatorships, the difference being that in free societies artists are free to indulge in paroxysmic works of protest. But the threat still exists and it is to do with the undermining effects of the material aims and achievements of industrial society, stronger than the potentialities of any individual, and the diffusion of an orthodoxy in the way of seeing and feeling things without our having to use our imaginations, an orthodoxy more tyrannous than the imposed orthodoxies of the past, which nevertheless did leave room for the exercise of the imagination.

The Evolutionary Humanist, wishing to relate his conscious purposiveness with the kind of consciousness realized in art, will ask, 'What is art for?' When he looks back on history he will see a mass of objects embellishing cities and filling museums which were produced within various cultures which, in turn, existed within various histories. He may be disposed to think that art is an expression of historic consciousness in symbolic forms through the medium of the artist's sensibility.

In part this is true, but in part it is also untrue. The two parts, historic-social consciousness, and individualist-aesthetic consciousness, are not always easy bed-fellows in the lives of artists. Sometimes the individualist-aesthetic strangles the historic-social, and sometimes the historic-social alters, bowdlerizes, falsifies the unborn work which it does not allow the individualist-aesthetic to produce.

The nearest thing to art accepting the responsibility of social evolution would be perhaps Greek art which was influenced by the ideas and ideals which we recognize in Greek thought. The amazing development of sculpture in Greece was connected with the inventiveness, the curiosity, the 'modern' scientific spirit of the Greeks. All the same, Greek art can be criticized for being too conceptual. Although the sculpture of the Parthenon frieze is an immense step forward in representation, its reality is not that of particular faces, particular bodies, particular human beings. A great many bodies, wings, robes and horses are assembled in order to produce a procession of godlike figures which are not themselves particularized but ideal.

Classical Greek art provides the great historical example of art produced under the influence of ideas. In a society where the artist-craftsman was respected, even known by his own name, there was the goal of expressing the ideal which, in sweetness and light, aspires towards the linear, and idolizes physical beauty. All the same, in the presence of Greek art, one feels the ideals, as it were, shine through. There is something of illustration even about the Parthenon frieze. We admit that it is sublime, but it does not fulfil our idea of the material realized as well, perhaps, as negro sculpture.

Greek art of the fifth century represents the artist at his freest in a world in which art to some extent pays homage to philosophy. It seems to us today that the result is not as great as Goethe and Winckelmann claimed, though certainly not as contrary to the principles governing the art-object as Roger Fry argued. The Parthenon frieze expresses ideas with the utmost beauty, through conquest of material; and it has the transcendent clarity of those ideas and the skill with which they are expressed. But today we believe that art should come to terms with the material used—express not just the domination over stone of the sculptor but also his feeling for the stoniness of stone. And it is important that we should cling to this idea, because it is connected with the independence of art in the modern world, which rests upon the integrality of the medium with the sensibility of the artist. The material out of which it is made is the independent territory of the nation that is art.

Art whose lines meet philosophy on some graph of the ideal, enslaves the material to the Idea. This suggests that there are self-sufficient and independent elements in art. Such is the material—paint, wood or stone—of which the artefact is made; another, that part of the sensibility of the artist which is, as it were, the material of himself, of his own sensibility.

The artist's sensibility decides, for example, that the subject-matter and the style of his work cannot be imposed by anything but the direction of his talent and his sympathy, in a word his 'truth'.

The artist may be like his contemporaries in social attitudes and may very well share their interests. He may, like them, accept the beliefs current in his time. The medieval craftsman who builds the cathedral or sculpts the images on its façade, shares the faith of his contemporaries and undertakes in common with them the great social enterprise of his time—cathedral-building. Nevertheless, he is separated from them by his absorption in the qualities of stone; he may also feel that in his dedicated task of image-making he is creating faith in a way unknown to them, who take it for granted. In the course of this creation he may depict characteristics (in a gargoyle, for example) which criticize his fellow-beings and the society in which he lives in ways that they might find unacceptable. But the criticism might not be overt. It might be a secret of the art itself; part of a mystery.

At this point, the reader may, with justice, protest that there have been wars, revolutions and churches which have inspired art. Yet a certain reserve we feel when we speak of 'war artists' or even of 'religious art' reveals our sense that the intoxication of artists with a public cause does not necessarily produce aesthetically good results.

It is extremely important to bear these considerations in mind. For perhaps the greatest danger which threatens the arts today is not dictatorship, or even commercialization and those much-cited enemies the 'mass media', but the unified consciousness within modern societies which secretly unites everyone—even opponents—in striving towards the same goal of material progress. This unity of consciousness attacks us at several levels, in our altruism as well as our selfishness, in our hope that the world will be improved as well as in our fear that it will be destroyed. In a word, it is materialism; and perhaps what might be called 'idealist materialism' is an even greater danger to the arts than 'selfish materialism' which seeks benefits only for ourselves. For the selfish are at least in some sense individualists.

'Idealist materialism' is dangerous because it invites us to undertake the pursuit of social happiness, and having done so to sacrifice our own judgment wherever this seems to oppose that goal. Traditions, beliefs, tastes, all have to be washed out like stains in the laundry of necessity. If we need a philosophy which reconciles art with progressive ideas, it must do so in a way which respects the independence and integrity of art, treats art as a separate power, regards what it expresses—I shall insist— as a separate kind of consciousness. For art is concerned with individual feelings, mysteries of technique, stones and paints, and minutely observed particulars of experience which fascinate the artist however much they may obstruct progress or evolution. Art is not only clear vision, it is also the faithful record of the mote in the artist's eye, which becomes an integral part of that vision. Although, historically, art has built temples which the god inhabits, made images even of the god himself, built palaces for princes, recorded the pageants to flatter victorious monarchs, and might perhaps even celebrate the World State of Universal Brotherhood, it nevertheless pursues obdurately its own course. This may lead the artist at one time to notice, quite unnecessarily, that when feet are viewed frontways, toes look like little blobs or coins; at another, that in a landscape or street scene, lines receding from foreground through middle distance to distance are directed towards an invisible vanishing-point; at another, that the monarch is extraordinarily ugly, and has a pimple on the end of his nose; at another, that spatial relations enclosing objects can be painted without suggesting the objects themselves. We should remember that the ideal house, as conceived by Alberti, was one which no one could or would wish to inhabit, not even God.

Under the cover of the artist's historic usefulness, there is a world which may appear to coincide with historic development but which in fact is a vision of life having remarkable independence, concealed as it were under what is overtly history. What happens when society demands that art should imitate the view of life which seems necessary for society's salvation? The results are directly apparent in work produced today in the Soviet Union and China, propagandist art which is called Social Realism. Those elements that are intrinsic to the mind and vision of the artist—the delight in material used, the concentration on form, the observation of eccentric particulars—are suppressed. The social view of man regarded as a social unit is optimistically superimposed upon a literal rendering of visual appearances, and both the artist and his material have to become the media for advertising an ideology.

Modern dictatorships indirectly pay a compliment to the power of art. More than democrats, the ideologists realize its power to distract public attention from policy, by drawing attention to that which society wishes to ignore, by depicting values and aims which are not those of a central committee. Yet the vitality of art is dependent on those qualities in a work which, from the point of view of progressive society, may seem the most irrelevant, irritating and, above all, unnecessary.

Dictatorships, however, are only the logical extensions of the modern tendency, which I have already mentioned, to dissolve all traditional, religious and aesthetic attitudes into the constructive aims, reinforced by the destructive menaces, of materialism. The extreme subjectivism of certain movements of art in democratic societies is a reaction to the same situation that has produced social realists in other countries. Social realism and movements like tâche-ism are really opposite sides of the same medal. There is considerable evidence that if artists were free to express themselves in the communist countries, they would react to extremes of subjectivism as practised in Paris and New York; and among us, some artists reacting against an isolation into which they feel that they have been forced by the Western brand of materialism, are supporters of a society where they feel they would 'belong'.

We see in Asia and Africa today the effects on primitive unself-questioning traditional art of contact with Western conscious social purposiveness. Apart from the more obvious and superficial effects of such contacts, the deeper and less remediable cause of the collapse of the traditional supports of the Eastern tradition is the social corroding, not just of traditions, but of cultural activities, by the influence of aims which make everything that cannot be related to them seem backward, supersti-tious or irrelevant. Sociologists have discovered recently that primitive art in primitive societies does have a purpose—even if this consists only of giving people the illusion that they have one. So there are projects put forward by UNESCO and other organizations for re-teaching natives the arts and crafts they may have lost in the first rush of Westernization. But if the purpose of such teaching is utilitarian the last state of nurtured archaism will be worse than the first one of brutal disillusion. What has to be restored is not the utility value of art but faith in it as an activity which relates to, but does not have to justify itself in terms of, the social consciousness.

In 'advanced' societies, artists have learned to protect their mystery more cunningly than can those in backward societies. The esotericism of modern Western art, and of the critical schools that support it, the extremes of abstraction, the theories of pure form, the extravagant claims made for the artist himself as someone who should be completely outside society with no responsibilities towards it—are not all these symptoms of a sophisticated mystery-mongering which protects art from the flooding in of contemporary social consciousness?

Broadly speaking, today in the world there are two kinds of art: conscripted art, in those countries where art is simply regarded as a special area, appealing to the visual senses, to which the central political will of the rulers of the state extends; and the much more complicated phenomenon of 'free' art in supposedly free societies. In the countries where there are mono-ideologies the artist produces only official art unless he is a subversive, in which case his art will have no public; yet in the countries in which he is not directed by the state, he nevertheless may feel himself alienated from society.

In the West everything points to the fact that the artist, though free, feels that he has to resist social forces which in some way repudiate or do not require the values of his art.

He often uses his freedom either to express a complete subjectivity or to attack the society which has given it to him. Those who are conscious of the benefits which material progress after all does bring to humanity may regard subjective Western art as perverse and irresponsible. Perhaps they should ask themselves whether this art is not a social phenomenon after all: or rather whether the anti-social attitude of the modern artist is not a criticism of our kind of society, a manifestation by the artist that he feels his particular form of expression to be threatened by the values of the industrialist civilization, and that sooner than be integrated into the aims of such a society he would use his freedom to work in a self-willed social vacuum.

The Evolutionary Humanist, with his ideas for bringing forward social consciousness to the stage where man believes that society should be occupied with deciding and planning its own evolutionary future, should ask himself what role he expects the artist to have in such a future. Would it simply be an extension of socially conscious evolutionary purpose into the sphere of the visual arts? And if he does not desire this, how can he prevent art from becoming such an extension of the social consciousness, since it is evident that the dynamic ideas and the scientific methods of modern societies often have the effect, either of liquidating the arts or alienating the artists?

What is needed I think is a theory of art as the expression of a kind of consciousness which is different from the social, even though it functions within the society and is influenced by it and which may express its aspirations and record its history. The difference is essentially a difference of scale which puts society and art in a relationship to one another which may be complementary, and may also become hostile. It is essentially a relation in which each one has values which measure and criticize and judge the other.

Society—or rather its mouthpiece—thinks according to the scale of history. Art—or rather the artist—creates according to the scale of individual birth-and-death-bound sensuous living.

It seems strange that men can think according to the scale of history—but history proves that they do so. Whoever thinks socially or historically does not think according to the scale of his own life-span. He thinks in terms of a future which perhaps he will never see. Thus history achieves real progress: in fact, history *is* progress and countries without progress also have no history. Historic progress consists in the social development superseding itself, producing as the result of the efforts of those who think and act in social terms, situations which leave them, the instigators, far behind. The inmortality of the actors on the stage of history consists in their becoming the landmarks along a journey which has rendered them completely anachronistic. Historic figures are generals with armies that could be wiped out by one machine-gun, revolutionaries who, as the result of their posthumous successes in setting up new states, would, if they were alive today, be sent instantly to concentration camps, orators who, if they spoke today, no one would listen to.

But the immortality of art rests on the ability of one man quite to identify himself with the experiences of another man living at another time and place but absorbing that time and place, through his senses, into the measure of his individuality and expressing it in signs which that other perceptive spectator of that other time and place can share. Art makes of history a kind of geography, so that to the spectator the work of the artist which derives from his personal experience and which he makes with his hands, is the report of a traveller who expresses strangeness as a personal experience of coldness, heat and shock which the spectator can share in his imagination. We need a view of the relations of art and society that reasserts the scale of the human individual as a measure of the social consciousness. Art is supremely the realization of the individual human scale within and against the social scale. Art, working from the human individual scale, depicts the relation of the individual to the given society.

O. L. REISER

THE INTEGRATION OF KNOWLEDGE

OLIVER L. REISER, M.A., PH.D.

Born 1895. Educated: Ohio State University.
Chairman of the Department of Philosophy,
University of Pittsburgh, where he has
taught since 1926. Chairman of the International Committee for Scientific Humanism.

Publications: *Humanistic Logic*, 1930; *The
Promise of Scientific Humanism*, 1940;
Nature, Man and God, 1951; *The Integration
of Human Knowledge*, 1958, etc.

THE INTEGRATION OF KNOWLEDGE

―――――――

I. *The World's Cultural Crisis*

We live in a world of political sovereignties, with a variety of social, religious, national, and economic loyalties and doctrines. Such competing loyalties and creeds have existed for countless generations, and while conflicts arose between them, here and there and now and then, these clashes in the past were localized in scope and consequence.

As the world has undergone a mechanical unification through the telescoping of space and time-relations, it has become increasingly difficult to limit these conflict-patterns to local areas—as two world wars have demonstrated. Now with the military uses of atomic energy and biological warfare already at hand, it has become clear that it would be fatal to man's civilization, perhaps even to his existence, to permit these clashes of doctrines and faiths to get out of hand and cause conflicts, which may generate more hatreds, fears, suspicions—and even open warfare.

This is the dark side of the picture. Looking to the future, we find that there is a prospect of world unity and perhaps ultimately an effective *United Nations Organization* with a code of international law to formalize its civil relationships. But this new world of tomorrow, where peace and justice reign in dignity and security, is still in the future, over the horizon, luring us on. We hope it is not merely a mirage, but a reflection of some future reality. In the meantime, however, we must live in the world of the present. It is a world of angry and scarred horizons, the valleys in between filled with the rubble of dead hopes and the anguish of human frustrations. Here, in the restless present, the nations of the world find themselves in a kind of twilight zone between the world of the past, filled with the relics of an era that is dying, and a world of the future, with its embryonic proliferations of a social order yet unborn.

This interim period in human history finds the 'world that was' face-to-face with the 'world that is to be'. These two worlds rub elbows everywhere, but perhaps the contrast stands out in sharpest relief in such organizations as UNO, FAO, WHO, and UNESCO as they carry on their work in New York, Paris and elsewhere. Here the disappearing past and the emerging future come to grips; realism and social idealism clash; and despair and hope stare each other in the face. The problems are acute; the stakes are high; the rivalries are keen; and the tensions are electrifying.

As one surveys the many problems which confront mankind, one of the major issues which stands out is this: What is the place of cultural diversity in the world community which the member organizations of the United Nations are seeking to foster? In general, what place do ancient provincialisms and modern localisms have in our world of integrations?

Without doubt, the roots of such cultural diversities go back into the remote past. Varying environments have elicited varying responses to the challenges presented to the peoples of the earth, and the diversities of cultural patterns which were thus created are in a sense the results of environment turned into history.

But consider the consequences of this historical development: seemingly irreconcilable oppositions have been created which now threaten to precipitate the clashes we have referred to. It is no exaggeration to state that man's very existence is at stake. Men everywhere are impaled on the horns of a tremendous dilemma. On the one side, we wonder whether cultural diversity is not a divisive force in the world, setting peoples apart from each other. Why, then, show tolerance of diversity and regionalism, if such diversity separates peoples? Indeed, is not such regionalism nothing other than a kind of cultural infantilism? Are not ethnic provincialisms like the immaturities of those who, because of their age, should have put away childish behaviours? If so, is it not time for the human race to grow up and act its age?

On the other hand, one of the main assets of any group is its cultural achievements, its inheritance of traditions, its dreams and beliefs, its customs and folkways. These are intimately tied in with deep emotional drives. If you propose—in the interest of a 'higher culture'—to make men rational and receptive to new global values, will you not destroy the local cultures and values? Will you not destroy the great cultural achievements in literature, and the arts, in music and architecture and religion? And if you sweep away the past, induce social amnesia, so to speak—what then? What have men to live for, if you take away their traditions? And what remains to build upon? Here we have the dilemma of the modern world in a crucial form. If we keep our diversified and local cultures, how can peoples function as parts of a world civilization? But if we do function as a part of a world civilization, will we not kill off these local cultures and ideologies peculiar to regional groups? Will we not be creating world uniformity and cultural poverty? How can we obtain unity without destroying variety?

To some extent the issues here represent a clash between those who cling to the forms of the past and those who are reaching out to new and more inclusive thought-forms and culture-patterns of the future. This is an important aspect of the argument between those who favour an 'ideological pluralism' and those who advocate an 'ideological monism'.

II. *The Need for a General Ideology*

It appears, therefore, that at the present juncture in human history the world is caught between two opposing forces. The first force is a *vis a tergo*, an inertia binding us to the past. This is a conservative force which would maintain the traditional political and theoretical diversities based on regional and parochial patterns of thought and doctrine. At its best, this force is associated with an 'ethnic democracy', a cultural pluralism of local systems mutually 'tolerating' each other. At its worst, this force produces rivalries between religions, 'races', nations and ideologies, which periodically burst into open conflicts.

The second force is a *vis a fronte*, a suction drawing us toward unification, a synthesis of cultural variety in ideological unity. This social and intellectual integration of nations and classes will eventually culminate in a world civilization based on a commonly accepted world philosophy—provided the local groups do not destroy each other in the meantime.

It is my conviction that we humans no longer have much choice in the matter of whether we shall have an ideological plurality or an ideological unity. Economic and political exigencies, nuclear energy developments and the erosion of cultural barriers, are bringing us to the place where, if there is to be any world at all, it will have to be a more unified world. In that sense the only live option now remaining consists in the selection of the particular type of ideological unity we shall embrace.

All serious thinking today should be concerned with the methods for constructing a world civilization appropriate to man as the planetary species. The supreme problem of the contemporary world is how to bring into being a new simplicity, a unitary system of ideas based on the minimal core of beliefs, values, and institutions, which will do for our time what Scholasticism did for the Western medieval world and what Marxism allegedly has done for the Russian experiment. What is wrong with Scholasticism and Marxism is not that they aspire to the position of a world ideology, but that they go about it in the wrong way and are based on wrong and outdated presuppositions. Neither one conforms to the requirement of scientific method—democracy in thinking—but each is authoritarian and therefore unscientific in procedure. A world ideology is not to be attained through revelations, whether from Moses or Marx. Only science and the scientific imagination can provide the methods and the materials for philosophical synthesis.

That a planetary way of living is already on the way is shown in a paper by Oscar W. Junek.[1] Our problem now is to formulate the workable philosophy which may guide the embryogenesis of the coming world civilization. If we leave the processes of social synthesis to expediency, power politics, vested interests, or the survival of the militarily best prepared, we will get either the totalitarianism of the victor of World War III—or the complete chaos of a universal catastrophe. In any case, it will not be a world we co-operatively designed, and we humans will not like it if we are still alive to inhabit it. But if we can voluntarily and co-operatively fabricate the outlines of a general ideology, we may avoid the alternatives of destruction or a totalitarianism imposed through a chain of authoritarian controls. Indeed, *such an ideological unity is essential if we are to preserve our cultural diversity*. We must never regard cultural diversity and unity as antithetical. Both variety and unity are necessary ingredients of any organized field-pattern. The problem is how to integrate a reasonable amount of diversity into a unity which is dynamic and flexible.

III. *Cosmology and Ideology*

Those mental isolationists who are incapable of loyalty to the sum-total of human knowledge will shrink from this stupendous undertaking. But surely such a comprehensive integration of our human knowledge into a philosophical synthesis is preferable to the social epilepsy of the everlastingly splintered and embattled pluralisms of rival idea-systems. The mission of philosophy today is to furnish vision and guidance to a perplexed world. Those who have lost faith in a universally valid system of knowledge as the goal of man's search have abdicated the role of human intelligence; they have renounced the very function of philosophy—the pursuit of wisdom. The great heritage bequeathed us by Pythagoras, Plato and Aristotle—to mention only Western thinkers—is the tradition of a unified body of knowledge which is independent of 'race', nation, religion and other particularisms. It is in the spirit of this tradition that I sketch the outlines of a possible basis for a general world-view.[2]

Recently, in my seminar at our University, the members of the class explored the theme of the 'integration of knowledge'. To orient the discussions, the following problems were proposed:

(1) State the commonly accepted major generalizations in (*a*) the physical sciences; (*b*) the biological sciences; (*c*) the social sciences,

including aesthetics and comparative religion, where humanistic knowledge emerges.

(2) Give examples of situations in which scientific knowledge is not applied, or is misapplied, in contemporary society.

(3) Give examples of cases where social synthesis rests upon intellectual integration, and where the failure to secure the first is related to failure to produce the second, and conversely.

(4) How would you solve the major problems of modern man—such as freedom from mass destruction, mass unemployment, mass starvation, mass prejudices of 'racial', religious, and national origins, overpopulation, and illiteracy—in terms of the utilization of an integrated body of beliefs?

I do not have space here to discuss the results. The reader should, of course, work out his own answers to these problems, after which comparisons are possible.

To be sure, some scientists and religious leaders will object to this programme, arguing that *facts* and *values*, *what is* and *what ought to be*, are mutually exclusive areas and pursuits. In reply, I would seek to demonstrate how an ideology can be derived from a cosmology, so that the 'normative sciences' and the 'natural sciences' become subdivisions of one inclusive domain. This proposed synthesis finds some support in the proposition that we already have the basis for an objective theory of value in the democratic processes of problem-solving—as John Dewey has stated them[3]—which are the common denominator of our scientific methods and our political democracy.

If we are right in this, the supreme need today is to erect on this foundation an 'operational research' project on a planetary scale, sponsored and carried on by a World University, to produce the super-national, super-racial, and super-religious body of integrated knowledge which will constitute the world-level wisdom for mankind—the *World Brain* of H. G. Wells.[4] This is not impossible. The real problem seems to be to combine the cultural diversity of mankind—which is highly desirable —with the technological and ideological unity which is necessary to support the framework of a future civilization. I shall deal with this later. Meantime, we should be careful not to make the antithesis between cultural diversity and a unified civilization too sharp—though certainly *some* elements of diversity (e.g. 'racial' and religious fanaticisms) must be scrapped to make way for a general ideology adapted to our modern knowledge.

It is obvious that an ideology, as we use the term, refers to the ideas and beliefs about man's place and role in the universe and his consequent privileges, duties, and potentialities in that universe. The precise form of any given ideology is a function of (*a*) the past history of the culture, and (*b*) the state of knowledge about man and the universe which is available at that time. Our thesis is that present knowledge makes it necessary for us to develop a new ideology which centres about the fact that man is the agent for his own future and that of the entire planet. The current 'knowledge explosion' makes this imperative in our time.

IV. *The Knowledge Explosion*

A major objective of a scientific Humanism is the organization of human knowledge for the purpose of human progress, that is, guiding human development toward what might be called the 'fulfilment society' (as a successor to the 'welfare state'). Specifically, this means that we must integrate human knowledge around some overall conception of man's destiny. Scientific advances and the application of knowledge have always been the inciting agencies in man's unfolding history, the basis for anything that can be called progress. Since increasing knowledge always alters man's idea of his destiny (as for example, modern genetics and psychology spell the doom of 'original sin' in its earlier theological form), we constantly face the problem of finding new visions of man's future possibilities.

The 'knowledge explosion' of the last half-century—the accelerating accumulation of knowledge in all fields, from cosmology to social science, aesthetics, and religion—has produced an enlarged awareness of cosmic, planetary, and human evolution. The multiplication and piling up of our ever-increasing mountains of knowledge intensifies the need for finding integrating principles.[4]

One of the leading principles in the modern synthesis which we may employ is given by Julian Huxley[5] in his suggestions concerning the several types of evolutionary processes. I would enlarge his analysis to include physicochemical evolution, and then associate each of these patterns of causality with its own operative field. This would yield the following levels of study: (1) the *physical field;* (2) the *biological field;* (3) the *human* or *psychosocial field.* Here we use the term *field* to designate a relatively continuous medium within which entities interact with each other to produce new configurations. By a *technology*—as I shall use the term in a moment—is meant any operational procedure man employs for controlling the ongoing behaviours on any level of organization. Thus, on the level of psychosocial behaviour, an ideological field created by thinking men gives guidance control over institutional functions.

This way of looking at operative fields of integration calls attention to the fact that, as we move up the ladder of evolution, new patterns of causality become manifest. At the lowest level we have *physical fields*. Here, on this level, we deal with the total pattern of physical energy (nuclear and atomic). This physical or ground field is then modified as it enters into the successive phases of the evolutionary process.

Next we have the *biological field*. Within the organism, biological fields and gradients are important in ontogeny, as was pointed out by E. B. Wilson, then Huxley and de Beer in their volume.[6] Later these ideas were further perfected by Paul Weiss, C. H. Waddington, H. S. Burr, Henry Margenau, and others. We know that fields which control growth for aggregates of cells (as well as cells in mitosis) exhibit a formal integrity which cannot be completely mapped out in the geometry of cell structures; they are organizations with morphogenetic effects. Biological fields of this sort are characterized by a combination of unity and an increasing tendency toward differentiation of parts: they exhibit a total pattern (gestalt) within which a number of differentiated parts are interrelated.

In the biological phase we find in operation the total pattern of selective forces of living matter (involving self-reproduction and self-variation) as these change with the emergence of new properties and types of organization. On this level the action of natural selection culminates in what Pittendrigh calls *teleonomy*, the moulding of organisms in relation to the ends of survival and reproduction.[7]

The operation of biological evolution is a necessary precursor to the human or psychosocial phase of development. In this phase there is, however, an addition to the antecedent factors, the emergence of human emotions and ideas in an inter-thinking society—hence the term *psychosocial field*. On the human or psychosocial level, natural selection is now subordinated to the operations of man's psychosocial integrations. Man's superior mind is, of course, associated with the highest known elaboration of the central nervous system. The increasing cephalization seen in biological evolution makes possible, on the human level, the displacement of biological energies from overt behaviour into thought as an imaginative and symbolic substitute for muscular responses. With the coming of human psychosocial life and the media of social heredity, such as articulate speech and writing, the *symbol* takes on its unique importance. With the symbolic function, art, religion, science, and philosophy make their appearance in the evolutionary process both as resultants and as operative factors.

This philosophy of evolution appears to me to be in harmony with the views of Pierre Teilhard de Chardin[8] who proposes that human evolution depends upon an increasing complexification of the psychosocial field. This, of course, applies to the entire system of thought now operating in human society. Accordingly—to interpolate some personal reflections—tensions are not necessarily destructive: we must learn to turn tensions and conflicts to creative uses. Thus we will carry to new heights our social goals and ideals of self-development.

In all this we see how technologies take over the direction of operative fields. Just as physicochemical technology has already been succeeded by biological technology, so next we need a psychosocial technology for future human evolution. The humanistic ideology must function as an operative field guiding man's psychosocial development toward a richer world for him. This it must do without leading to more regimentation, cultural uniformity, or authoritarianism. Obviously, however, evolutionary advances must take place in relation to the satisfaction of man's universal biological (material) needs and the fulfilment of man's psychological nature—the increasing enrichment of personal creativity. We must plan for unity-in-variety, both individual and social, within a unitary ideological field. This planning—or ideological technology—brings us to the important problem of the relation of facts to values.

V. *The 'Dualism' of Facts and Values*

A crucial test of the utility of a naturalistic Humanism is its ability to overcome the alleged dualism of facts and values. One could begin a discussion of this problem almost anywhere: with Bertrand Russell's statement that the field of values is closed to science;[9] or the view of Robert Hutchins that science is more suited to the determination of means than of ends;[10] or the dictum of the Positivists that value-preferences, if considered in relation to the past, are cultural anthropology, and if considered in relation to present and future needs and desires, are only wishful thinking;[11] or the pronouncements of the clergy who claim that moral principles are outside the scope of science and belong to the domain of religion. This is a strange assortment of individuals to be found in the same camp. They all agree on the impotence of reason to build a science of ethics; but they agree about little else.

To get the full nature of the problem before us, let us examine more carefully the various aspects of the alleged 'dualism'.

The diagram (below) shows us that the *natural sciences* deal with the 'isness' of a world of facts, while the *normative sciences* (logic, ethics, aesthetics) deal with the 'oughtness' of a world of preferences and values as objects of human desires. That is:

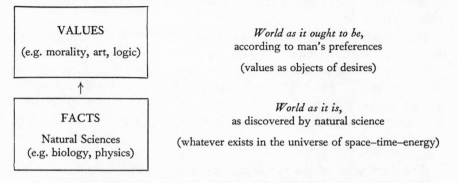

VALUES (e.g. morality, art, logic)	*World as it ought to be,* according to man's preferences (values as objects of desires)
↑	
FACTS Natural Sciences (e.g. biology, physics)	*World as it is,* as discovered by natural science (whatever exists in the universe of space–time–energy)

An example of this dualism would be this: Natural science can tell you how to get to the moon, if you want to go there; but it cannot tell you whether you should go to the moon. Again: natural science may eventually tell you whether smoking cigarettes does (or does not) cause cancer (or it will give a probability statement of the statistical correlation between them), but it cannot tell you whether you should (or should not) stop smoking. Our inability, up to the present, to resolve this dualism, i.e. find the answer to the problems of 'oughtness' in the 'isness' of things, seems to be responsible for a number of resulting difficulties, as follows:

(1) The dualism of objective, descriptive natural science and subjective, prescriptive human purposiveness seems to support the amoral attitude of those scientists who maintain, with the Positivists, that natural ('objective') science knows nothing of values, so that such preferences are incapable of rational justification. In his thoughtful volume, *Natural Rights and History*, Professor Leo Strauss[12] argues that the troubles of modern social theory stem from a dualism of non-teleological natural science and teleological social behaviour, with an accompanying irresponsibility thus made available to those amoral scientists who take refuge in the fact-value dualism and the persuasions of contemporary positivism.

(2) Confusion about the moral responsibility (or non-responsibility) of scientists for the application of scientific knowledge is only one aspect of the fact-value dichotomy. A second defect of the dualism is that it is correlated with an inability to provide a reasonable justification for value preferences. 'Truth', 'goodness', and 'beauty' are said to be our highest human values—but how can one prove that men should foster such values? The problem here is not so much which specific values are 'highest' as it is the question of the rational justification of any selected

values—why any specific values are 'best', and what makes them right. The diversity of viewpoints in the discussion of this question in the recent volume, *New Knowledge in Human Values*[13] is indicative of the lack of unity in the field.

(3) A third consequence of the fact-value dualism is that it appears to support the cultural relativism of those anthropologists and sociologists who can find no final and universal standards, though they do sometimes discover trends. Thus, by implication, if Nietzsche extols the tough virtues of the 'superman', and Jesus praises the virtues of love, charity, and mercy—who is right? Is it possible to prove that any preferred values are 'right'?

These are some of the problems created by the above dualism. In the course of the next several sections I hope to have something to say which may help to overcome this. Meantime, I would like to state some considerations which we should keep in mind as guiding principles.

VI. *Some General Considerations*

In the first place, it is obvious that the natural sciences are more fundamental (but not more important) than the normative value-disciplines, in the sense that our life is built upon material foundations. If our religious or aesthetic preferences are permitted to determine our models of reality as framed by the natural sciences, these lead to wishful thinking. Of course, such preferences are an important part of social reality and must be taken into account. In general, a knowledge of empirical facts and laws must provide a basis for moral reforms, if we are to have intelligently guided social change. To settle the questions of fact about the physical universe, natural science must eventually come up with a generally acceptable body of natural science propositions. Meanwhile we must act in the light of our most probable hypotheses as to what are the facts, laws, and principles of natural science. Applied to the problem of human social development, this means that what men *should* do, according to ethics, must be related to (1) what men *must* do, human nature being what it is according to the science of psychology; and (2) what men *can* do at the present time, human variability and social plasticity being what they are (also still to be determined).

Our second general observation is that values are facts. They are entirely natural products of man's psychosocial evolution, and as such they are modified as our knowledge increases. They are phenomena to be studied and understood like any other phenomena. A survey of the evolutionary process demonstrates that whereas in biological evolution natural selection operates as an ordering principle directing organisms toward greater adaptiveness for survival ('teleonomy'), in psychosocial evolution ideological factors operate in relation to consciously conceived goals and values. Morality must therefore evolve to keep pace with new circumstances and new knowledge of a changing world.

At any given stage in the process of human evolution particular problems will loom large and demand solution. The present moment in psychosocial evolution is a stage in which several issues are of overriding importance, e.g. the threat of atomic war, the threat of overpopulation, the harmful effects of radioactive fallout, and the immense problem of unifying the whole of humanity into some sort of single 'inter-thinking group'. Here man's knowledge of his own possibilities is the most powerful tool for his own future progress. We need research on human potentialities and a synthesis of the resulting knowledge about man's creative capacities. Then we require a wide dissemination of that knowledge. This is the ethical framework of a new and general ideology.

A third general observation is that while these two levels of science reflect a dualism of types of interest and study, we have not therefore created any necessary conflict in the sense of an unresolvable hostility. Nor is there any real 'paradox' residing in the fact that while our ideals come out of experience, as 'ideals' they go beyond experience. Our standards of what is 'best' in the world of ideals and achievements are based on human judgments of excellence in fields where men create and transform, and there is considerable agreement about standards and values among those who have made it their business to study in their chosen fields. There is not a paralysing scepticism, especially where common needs and mutual admiration of cultural achievements are evident.

Indeed, it is only a question of time before peoples everywhere, reduced to a common destiny by the coercions of science and technology (e.g. controlled thermonuclear power, automation in industry, the conquest of outer space), *and guided into co-operation through the overwhelming pressures of integrative psychosocial aspirations*, will accept the general ideology ('humanist frame') as the architectonic for an emerging planetary democracy.

Having thus sketched some general theses, I pass on to more specific items.

VII. *More Specific Guiding Principles*

(1) We humans never begin or carry on existence with a *tabula rasa* of values. Man, whether he be scientist, poet, peasant, or philosopher, begins with emotional and valuational commitments which are implicit in the

facts of organic existence, i.e. man's biological constitution and cultural heredity. Because of this inescapable inheritance, we all want a measure of bio-social security, balanced with more or less novelty and adventure.

(2) Science involves ethical commitments no less than religion, politics, art, education and other phases of human enterprise. The notion of the 'scientist as scientist' is a product of an abstraction. The 'objectivity' of science is itself an ethical imperative. The scientists of Nazi Germany may have prided themselves on their 'ethical neutrality'—until it was too late. Whether you have *taken* a side or not, you are *on* a side in every important social issue, even if it is only the side of 'non-resistance'.

(3) 'Facts' are of value, because a knowledge of the facts helps us solve human problems, i.e. enables man to survive and enrich his existence. In addition, knowledge is valued for its own sake as well as for its utility.

(4) Judgments of fact and judgments of value are not necessarily exclusive of each other. When a judge says to a vicious criminal 'you are an evil man', this may be both a judgment of fact and of value—it may be both true and right. When a Humanist says, 'it is good that men should be happy', this is both ethically sound and logically defensible. *Indeed, I think it may be possible to show that every judgment of fact presupposes prior value-judgments, and conversely.* There is here a feed-back between facts and values which resembles the servo-mechanisms of cybernetics.

(5) Historically what were once only value-preferences have occasionally become matters of social fact, and conversely what were once facts may have disappeared from the human scene. Thus social security, public hygiene, etc., which were once ideals to be realized, are now (in some parts of the world) matters of fact (or more factual). On the other hand, organized Fascism was once a social fact, but it is now socially extinct in some parts of the world where it formerly flourished. Our values help to determine the facts, at least some of the psychological and social facts. Moreover, alternatives are sometimes set up as exclusive of each other ('either-or'), which in fact are not exclusive. Thus to say that you can have either security or adventure, but not both, is to set up a false antithesis: perhaps we *can* have some of both. Such mutually satisfying values may be described as complementary.

(6) If we completely understood the facts, and the 'logic of events' which factual situations exhibit, we could frequently resolve conflicts which otherwise are unresolvable except by violence. Thus if one could demonstrate that happiness is incompatible with selfishness, as Erich Fromm asserts[14] or that 'race prejudice' is not only based on false-to-fact beliefs but will ultimately lead to injury to the supposedly 'superior' race, this should help to persuade reasonable men to abandon self-injurious

beliefs. If the claim to 'white supremacy' by some Western nations means that these nations will ultimately lose the respect and co-operation of the 'coloured' peoples of Africa and Asia and of the leaders throughout the world, would the opponents of social equity be willing to pay this price? This seems doubtful.

(7) To resolve problems which seem to involve conflicts of beliefs and values, we must try to find more inclusive value-systems. Thus Josiah Royce's 'loyalty to loyalty'[15] provides a higher plateau than, e.g., loyalty to 'capital' or 'labour'; and loyalty to mankind is higher than loyalty to this or that nation, 'race', or religion. Sometimes, however, higher loyalties can be fostered only through the media of existing institutions and values. Thus excessive nationalism is a social evil, but international friendships can be created only through nations. In other cases, for example, human slavery and religious fanaticisms, the institutions and associated values may have to be combated directly, or even destroyed outright.

(8) The problem of the modern world is to create planetary objectives, universal values for all mankind. This is the Humanist frame—with an ideological field—within which a cultural pluralism of diversifications may be protected. The process of choosing new ends and creating new values must of necessity maintain continuity with the fact-finding processes. On the human level there frequently are alternative courses of action each of which may be continuous with the history of the individual, or group, that faces the alternatives and must make a choice. The choices should favour those alternatives which promise results maximally advantageous to all who are affected by the consequences of the choice. In general, social and ethical progress has moved toward the fabrication of more inclusive societies, from the family units→tribal societies→villages→ city-states→nation-states→world community. In this process, differences of races, religions, nationalities, and social classes, are gradually submerged in higher social and ideological integrations.

VIII. *The Humanist Frame as Planetary Democracy*

The *Humanist Frame* is one in which the greatest mass of significant facts becomes the supporting foundation for the maximum satisfaction of human values. The problem is to achieve the optimum combination of both factual knowledge and value satisfactions. Perhaps it is only a question of time before the pioneering approach presented by Oskar Morgenstern and John Von Neumann in the *Theory of Games and Economic Behaviour*[16] is extended to the field of social ethics. Indeed, R. B. Braithwaite's study, *Theory of Games as a Tool for the Moral*

Philosophers, marks a beginning in this direction.[17] Here a word of warning is in order. Those who would use electronic calculators to solve moral problems must not forget that the value-judgments which the machine obeys are supplied by the external moral agent, namely man, who programmes the 'decisions' through the machine. On earth, man alone is capable of moral choices; this is a source of pride in man—though also his potential source of self-destruction. To prevent human tragedies, what is required is a synthesis of knowledge and benevolence, 'facts' and 'values', unified into a general ideology. In my own language, I would picture the situation in this manner:

$$(\textit{The Facts of all Sciences}) + (\textit{The Complementary Values for all Mankind})$$
$$= \textit{A General Ideology}$$

It is the faith of a naturalistic Humanism that people of the highest order of knowledge, ability and social environment, will agree on the next major objectives for psychosocial development. Indeed, human history reveals a number of such overall trends in social development. For example, the 'rights of man' as enunciated in the United Nations Declaration are now progressively being recognized, regardless of colour, nationality, or religion. Taken out of the field of revelation, tradition and authoritarianism, a humanistic ideology thus becomes a guiding field for the fabrication of a planetary democracy.

Obviously, if our 'general ideology' is to be meaningful in its content, it will be necessary to spell out in detail the objectives of a planetary Humanism. Before that, however, the initial task is for mankind to take stock of its position. First, we need to reach a proper definition of fulfilment in all its modes and aspects; secondly, we need a survey of human capacities and potentialities and how they can best be realized; thirdly, we require a survey of world resources as these are essential to man's aesthetic enjoyments as well as to the satisfaction of his needs for food, medicine, fuel and various raw materials; and finally, we need studies on how our knowledge of human potentialities could be utilized as a central motivating force for human action and social evolution. How the brains of mankind can be mobilized for such an integrated enterprise is not for me to discuss here. But the task is necessary in order to clarify the various objectives of naturalistic Humanism and relate them to overall plans.

IX. *Universal Ethics as an Ideological Field*

It is clear that the ethics of a naturalistic or scientific Humanism places a premium on intelligence—as opposed to an unintelligent morality which demands blind obedience to absolute commandments 'from above'. Man's duty includes the obligation to be as intelligent and well-informed as his biological heredity and social environment permit. As an 'ideological technology' an evolutionary Humanism thus aims at a universalist ethics which would become a guiding field for the fabrication of a planetary democracy.

From this it also appears that, operationally defined, *ethics is what ethics does*. And what it does is tell men what they ought to do. In today's world, therefore, ethics should labour to create an overriding conviction that knowledge can and must be integrated into a unitary ideological pattern with a central focus concentrated on the destiny of man, i.e. the conscious control of human evolution through the maximum fulfilment of the potentialities of man—both of individual men everywhere and of societies as groups.

Finally, before leaving these matters, I wish to reiterate that a 'planetary democracy' based on principles of this sort would not imply a mono-tonous standardization of human experiences and values. The most workable solution to the dilemma of *freedom versus order*, for the immediate future, is a middle-of-the-road programme: within the common framework of psychological and social uniformities required for living in the same world of peace and justice, each ethnic, cultural and professional group should be free to enjoy its own traditions, myths and cultural achievements. Regional groups should be free to act out their social heredity—the mimesis of their cultural patterns—and also create new achievements, provided there is acceptance of similar cultural 'deviations' from the norms of an emerging world community with a universalist ethics. Here, then, we have the answer to the challenge of cultural and ethical relativism. In an evolutionary framework social values are not absolute; they are relative, but they are relative to something—in the case of ethical values they are today relative to the greater fulfilment of present peoples of the world and to the welfare of future generations of mankind. Thus increasingly and progressively our social world becomes a self-integrating multiplicity of culture-patterns which move in a convergent march toward a world civilization.

REFERENCES

(1) Junek, Oscar W. 'What is the Total Pattern of Our Western Civilization?', *American Anthropologist*, 1946, 48, 397-406.

(2) Reiser, Oliver L. *The Integration of Human Knowledge*. Boston: Extending Horizons Press, 1958.

(3) Dewey, John. *How We Think*. Boston: D. C. Heath & Co., 1933.

(4) Wells, H. G. *The World Brain*. New York: Harper & Brothers, 1938; London: Methuen, 1938.

(5) Huxley, J. S. 'Three Types of Evolutionary Process', *Nature*, 1957, 180, 454–5.

(6) Huxley, J. S., and de Beer, G. R. *The Elements of Experimental Embryology*. New York: Macmillan & Co., 1934.

(7) Pittendrigh, Colin S. 'Adaptation, Natural Selection and Behavior', *Behavior and Evolution*, ed. A. Roe and G. G. Simpson, Yale University Press, 1958, p. 390.

(8) Teilhard de Chardin, Pierre. *The Phenomenon of Man*. New York: Harper & Brothers, 1959.

(9) *The Philosophy of Bertrand Russell* (The Library of Living Philosophers, ed. Paul Arthur Schilpp), Northwestern University, 1944.

(10) Hutchins, Robert M. *The Conflict in Education in a Democratic Society*. New York: Harper & Brothers, 1953.

(11) von Mises, Richard. *Positivism, A Study in Human Understanding*. Harvard University Press, 1951.

(12) Strauss, Leo. *Natural Rights and History*. Chicago: University of Chicago Press, 1953.

(13) Maslow, Abraham H., ed. *New Knowledge in Human Values*. New York: Harper & Brothers, 1959.

(14) Fromm, Erich. *Man for Himself*. New York: Rinehart, 1948.

(15) Royce, Josiah. *The Philosophy of Loyalty*. New York: Macmillan & Co., 1908.

(16) von Neumann, John and Oskar Morgenstern. *Theory of Games and Economic Behavior*. Princeton: Princeton University Press, 1944.

(17) Braithwaite, R. B. *Moral Principles and Inductive Policies*. New York: Oxford University Press, 1953.

PATRICK MEREDITH

THE FRAME OF HUMANIST
COMMUNICATION

PATRICK MEREDITH, M.SC., M.ED.,
PH.D.

Born 1904. Educated: Wolverley School;
University of Leeds; University College
and the University of London Institute
of Education. Professor of Psychology,
University of Leeds since 1949.

Publications: *Visual Education and the New
Teacher*, 1946; *Algebra by Visual Aids*,
1948; *The Modular Calculus*, 1956; *Semantic
Matrices*, 1959; *Learning, Remembering and
Knowing*, 1961, etc., and numerous articles.

THE FRAME OF HUMANIST
COMMUNICATION

Our experience of the Press, the radio and the television should warn us that what is said, even when true, can be truly judged only in relation to what is *not* said. Communication is always finite and a message can be no more than a sample of all that could be said on any event or issue. If we can trust the attitude of the speaker we accept his sample as fair. If an attitude to human affairs is of any significance it has both feeling and direction. It is a kind of momentum which moves its possessor to action. Thus the meaning of a message is determined by both the position and the momentum of the speaker. The recognition of this principle has an obvious bearing on the supposed neutrality of science. The late Lord Stamp once declared that 'to tell the truth to those who do not understand it is to propagate falsehood'. True, but not enough. We should add that to hear 'the truth' from one who knows too little, or who is known to harbour falsehood, is to make one doubt the truth. There is no need to spin further aphorisms to drive home the point, nor is this the place to argue the meaning of 'truth'. The principle behind this is that messages are (among other things) currents of social causation and must be judged by their relation to the knowledge and movement of society. 'Knowledge' tends to crystallize into frameworks and these determine the meanings of messages.

When we think of the so-called 'mass media' we see the need for what might be called a 'social oceanography'. Many sponsored researches and individual enquiries are sounding this ocean and glimpsing some of the currents. But research, like communication, is also determined by position and momentum. The questions asked, and the energy and resources devoted to answering them, help to decide what currents of communication will be looked for and how firmly they will be drawn on the map. We can be certain that the currents are exceedingly complex. Kavrin Dovring,[1] writing on 'the semantics of biased communication' refers to 'the jungle-like character of the field of influence and response'.

Whether ocean or jungle, it requires something more than naïve fact-finding if any usable interpretation is to emerge. One thing is evident: we are not dealing with a purely random process. Dr Dovring introduces the useful concept of 'communication realms'. There are clearly innumerable regional dominions in this jungle; areas dominated by a communicator, an ideology, a system of values. In these realms the communication of truth is seldom the only aim and in some it may even be regarded as expendable.

But there is a danger in letting the mass media dictate our thinking about communication. The problems then tend to be reduced to sociology and technology whereas they are problems of humanity and purpose. We live in groups. Each of us belongs to many groups, by no means always in physical proximity. Some groupings are imposed, some are accidental and some are freely chosen. Among the last are those whose members have some similarity of epistemic position and social momentum, forming psychosocial 'communicative tissues'. The Humanists of our present context should form such a tissue. They attach value to human knowledge, they wish to share it, and to apply it to relieve human need and to enrich life. Communication sustains what we may call the psychometabolism of such a tissue.

An essay on such an encyclopaedic theme as communication is an exercise in self-denial. Let me divide what can be said into four headings—Propositions, Problems, Principles and Proposals. The *propositions* provide a foundation of assertions on humanism and science, on language and communication, on the recent 'explosion of knowledge', on evolution and ecology, on the economy and adequacy of communication. The *problems* concern the obscurity of science, the multiplicity of frameworks, the flux of jargon, the mutual incomprehension not only of scientists and non-scientists but even of scientists and scientists, the failure of linguistic translation to remedy intercultural misinterpretation, the neglect of what is *known* in the excitement of what is *new*. The *principles* deal with communication as a causal process and with its efficiency, with Information Theory as revealing some of the determinants of efficiency, with 'transfer of training', with the importance of ideologies and 'world pictures', and with language-planning. Finally the *proposals* concern the recognition of global ecology, the application of knowledge to need, the organization of communication to this end, the education of scientists, the linking of communication with documentation, and the morphology of knowledge.

Propositions

The Industrial Revolution was grounded in coal and oil which are products of the earth, and the economy of the steam and electricity ages is the balancing of output against fuel consumption. In this context the laws of thermodynamics were discovered. They are laws of physics, but their present significance rests on the limited availability of energy to man. They relate to systems in which economy is a prime consideration.

The very fact that it is taking longer to release the full abundance of nuclear energy than was first hoped, testifies to the proposition that economy of time is as important as economy of energy. The knowledge needed to effect this release has been available since the first atomic pile went 'critical', but the knowledge of how best to apply it to human needs is spreading too slowly. Ask India. But the efficiency of communication is not merely a matter of improving cables and printing-presses. We have to improve language itself.

Will a more rapid spread of knowledge intensify our ulcerous modern tempo of living? Rather the contrary, for if we can learn more *with less effort* we can relax more often. Efficiency may be gained not by hurrying but by saving time. This should be one of the primary concerns of communication theory. Education shows, as yet, little appreciation of this principle. At present it seems that the more educated you are the less leisure you have. Human knowledge, measured by the sheer quantity of information, is increasing explosively. The brain is choked with the input. The congestion will not be relieved by speeding up the input, but by reorganizing the whole transmission of information, starting at the source. It is not enough for scientists to write their papers (and so swell the literature): they themselves are groaning under the pressure. Science itself must find the remedy.

In the communication-process there is always a brain at each end. The rate at which the receiving brain can handle information is a decisive limiting factor in the efficiency of communication. D. E. Broadbent has suggested[2] that the nervous system may act as a single channel with a limited capacity: this may be true in a narrow context such as the study of a skill in which only certain defined types of information are relevant. In any case, at any given moment the brain has only a limited focus. But there are many channels feeding it with information and it can range narrowly or widely over these sources. Language plays a vital role in guiding this scanning process. The brain's own incessant activity ensures that knowledge already stored is potentially active. The act of responding to a new idea may be thought of as a confluence of two streams, one from the communicator, the other from within the brain itself. The inner stream is determined by previous learning and experience. Hence communication and education must go hand in hand.

One of the principal tenets of Humanism is that man is not only taking a hand in evolution, but that his situation makes this obligatory. The congestion of population on the one hand, and on the other the acceleration of communication by which the living-habits of whole populations can be rapidly changed, make for increasing instability. Man has already gained a large measure of control (of a kind) over his environment, a measure which has become global since the time when a network of radio waves was added to the earth's field. Global ecology is not a fanciful phrase but a somewhat ominous fact, and man's activity is becoming the most potent single factor in this ecology. As Sir James Gray[3] has said: 'his environment has become world-wide . . . and he can begin to direct the course of his own evolution'. But this control depends on the actions of statesmen, and since brinkmanship has become too dangerous a game, statesmen, while they still have to haggle, are slowly perceiving that an increasingly important component in any bargain they may drive is the amount of fraternity they can dispense. Their difficulty is that this amount is incalculable, for it depends on their own policies. Financial aid to one area, machines to another, technical experts to a third, educational opportunities for a fourth, these are measures which have unpredictable consequences. A new serum can change the epidemiology of a whole region, and with it the man-power and economic potential. There is no clear quantitative relation between expenditure and results: it is the distribution of expenditure which counts. To decide this intelligently demands understanding: and understanding depends on communication.

Communication, by whatever the means or the medium, involves three essential ingredients: a sender, a message and a receiver. In the prolific research on communication there has been a marked tendency to concentrate on the middle term and to take the two end terms for granted—in fact literally to prefer means to ends. And unless technology is humanized this tendency will grow. True, with the mass media there is a growing attempt to assess the impact on the masses—to ask what the message does to the receiver. The answer, so far as science is concerned, does not seem very encouraging, according to a recent leading article in *Nature*:[4]

'Indeed, if one generalization is to be drawn from these reports, it is that the mass media are unlikely to prove a reliable method of increasing the public understanding of science unless the mass audience has itself already been prepared by its general formal education to understand what science is about and the place it takes in the world today.'

Scientists have not been unconcerned about the problems of communication. Many international conferences have discussed them, two of outstanding importance being the Royal Society Conference on Scientific Information in 1948[28] and the Washington International Conference on Scientific Information in 1958.[29] Not unnaturally these conferences have been primarily concerned with the problems of the working scientist in keeping abreast of the specialist information relevant to his own research. The world's army of research-workers produces a swelling flood of publications, but in this flood each individual worker has a highly idiosyncratic need. The modern technology of documentation[6] is applying modern logic, semantics and computer techniques in a strenuous endeavour to satisfy these multifarious needs. Librarians are finding their traditional training increasingly inadequate and are being forced to learn the new technology. This is a large and highly technical theme, involving many disciplines hitherto unrelated.

Nearly a quarter of a century ago the prophetic voice of H. G. Wells was heard urging the creation of a 'World Brain' and showing the crucial role of the documentalist in the communication process:[5]

'Few people as yet, outside the world of expert librarians and museum curators and so forth, know how manageable well-ordered facts can be made, however multitudinous, and how swiftly and completely even the rarest visions and the most recondite matters can be recalled, once they have been put in place in a well-ordered scheme of reference and reproduction.'

The dream was premature, not only because the will was lacking and the terminologies of the sciences were anarchic, but because the technology of data-processing was not yet ready. Today, according to J. W. Perry, the dream can be realized:[6]

'Just as the invention of writing and of pictorial representation made it possible to store knowledge outside of human memory, so these dreamers now argue, a further advance has become a necessity. Libraries must be converted from warehouses of knowledge to effective extensions of human memory. . . . The technological basis for realizing our dream is at hand.'

Problems

The obstacle to the dream's realization lies in the stubborn three-body relation of language, knowledge and culture. Some four hundred artificial languages have been invented without really facing this problem. The anthropologists and linguists throw important light on the relation of language to culture, Malinowski, Sapir, Whorf[7] to mention only three. Through the forms of language a culture imposes a world-view, a metaphysic, on the individual. A culture is a totality of experiences, concepts, beliefs and their consequences. It provides the determining context in which language finds its meaning. But cultures are no longer static. Man's increasing control of his own evolution is seen in the reshaping of his cultures. In this process the conceptual innovations of science are persistently eroding and transforming the metaphysical groundwork of ideologies. But of course it is not a one-way or a uniform process from primitive concepts of magic to sophisticated concepts of science. Intercultural communication in a language apparently accepted by both parties can be nullified by unformulated ideological discrepancies, as in many United Nations debates.[8]

We might suppose that science constituted an autonomous pattern of culture. It is something of an international fraternity, but scientists can sometimes be even more mutually incomprehensible than laymen, if only because their thought reaches so far from the rut of common sense. On the frontier of research intuition is often obscure yet compelling. New dimensions are glimpsed, used, found to work, and enshrined in new jargon, the forerunner of respectable terminology.

The organization of science today is so dominated by the needs of research, with its emphasis on novelty, that the tremendous span and volume of existing scientific knowledge tends to be taken for granted. The fact that this or that theory is modified or discarded tends to be generalized into a dismissal of all that was known up till about five years ago as out of date. The great conceptual network of principles still valid, stretching back to Newton and even to Archimedes, the historical insight and experience built into the design of all modern instruments and terminology, the evolutionary and synoptic perspectives inherent in the world-picture presented by science, the greater part of its vocabulary, and the increasing body of established fact, all contribute to the indispensable and continuing inheritance of modern science. The failure to communicate the latest news in science may be less serious than the failure to assimilate this common heritage.

In the past the great encyclopaedists such as Diderot satisfied this need.[9] Today the traditional multivolume encyclopaedia can no longer meet the need: it can serve for reference but not for education. We still have to find the answer to the question of Lancelot Hogben:[10] 'Will the accumulated scientific knowledge of the last century be made available for the satisfaction of common human needs?'

The difficulty of the problem was first appreciated, even before

Newtonian mechanics, by Bishop Wilkins, who in 1668 regretfully observed:[11]

'It must be granted that by reason of exceeding *comprehensiveness* of some notions, and the extreme *subtilty* of others ... that several things cannot be disposed of so accurately as they ought to be.'

Principles

An intuition of the inescapable relation between knowledge and language led the founders of the Royal Society, three centuries ago, to commission Bishop Wilkins to design a philosophic language for the communications of science. In 1668 his 'Essay towards a Real Character and Philosophical Language' appeared. The quaintness of his classification of 'things and notions', and the oddity of his stenographic ideography, must not be allowed to obscure the essential insight which he displayed into the relations between taxonomy and language, even though he failed to take account of the emotive overtones of words. For taxonomy represents not only the logic but the economics of classification. It is by the creating classifications that science systematically and economically stores its findings. In the biological sciences the accumulation of an ever-increasing variety of specimens forced the design of taxonomic systems from Aristotle onwards. In the physical and mathematical sciences the role of classification is less often recognized, but the supremacy of set-theory today testifies to the fundamental role of the class-calculus in the economy of deductive reasoning.

But here we strike a major failure of communication. It is the gap between those who move with ease and richness in the qualitative and meaningful regions of empirical knowledge and those who move with power and penetration in the mathematical and meaningless regions of symbolic abstraction from experience. The theory of sets, which is central for mathematics,[30] is also the logical key to taxonomy; but it is a key which needs two hands to turn it, the hand of the mathematical logician and that of the empirical taxonomist. These are groping towards each other in the modern science of documentation.[29] It is no accident that the two major synoptic triumphs of the nineteenth century—Darwin's theory of evolution by Natural Selection and Mendeléef's establishment of the Periodic Table of Chemical Elements—were both outcomes of the taxonomic approach. The classification of stars in our own century is a further triumph of insight.

Classification is not merely pigeon-holing. It creates order and leads to linguistic organization and new terminology. It represents the unification of a range of instances under a single term. The experiential *many* become the conceptual *one*. But taxonomy does not stand still. Julian Huxley[12] predicts an increasing elaboration of biological systematics:

'The Sabbath was made for man, not man for the Sabbath. Similarly systematics exist for human convenience, not in the interest of some Platonic *eidos* stored up in Heaven. . . . A few decades hence it will, we may prophesy, be regarded as necessary taxonomic routine to give the mean measurements, with their standard deviations, of at least five or six standard characters, as part of the description of a new form. . . . The new taxonomy, with the aid of its subsidiary terminologies and its quantitative measurements, will seek to portray this many-sided reality.'

The importance of Bishop Wilkins lies in his perception of the relation between the design of language and the structure of the 'things and notions known to man' to be communicated. There have been countless subsequent attempts to design artificial languages, but this essential relation has been largely overlooked and the principles of language design have been sought in language itself, or in logic. Meanwhile, science has thrown up a host of special symbolisms in chemistry, meteorology, electronics and the like, admirably adapted to their special fields of fact but unrelated to one another or to any master code. Of course the 'master code' is in a sense a dream, to be realized neither by information theory, nor by logic, nor by epistemology, nor by semantics. But science should keep this dream as one aim of its evolution. In my view, an indispensable contribution will come from information theory, which is itself 'a scientific body of knowledge'.[13]

I have given the name *Epistemics* to the embryonic science which concerns itself with the functional relation between knowledge and language. The planning of scientific language could give an economy of representation for information theory to work on. The problem, though massive, is finite. Colin Cherry's reply, as it were, to Bishop Wilkins is just this:[14]

'When we speak or write about anything, we can say only a finite number of things about it. We cannot describe and convey ideas with infinitesimal precision.'

We seem to be so free to say whatever we want that we overlook the inherently causal nature of communication. Language does real work; but the amount of physical energy involved is so extremely small that it hardly seems worth taking thought to economize our language. However, when we reckon the *time spent in the act of communication*, rather than the energy consumed, the scale of magnitude at once becomes significant. For the act of communication is completed only in the act of understanding. And economy of time in communication is the obverse of richness of understanding.

Information Theory in its deeper implications then becomes *an investigation of the conditions of mutual understanding*. Here we should note that communication does not depend on information alone. Dr Johnson once remarked that men need more often to be reminded than informed. But here we are passing over to a somewhat different concept of information, which D. M. Mackay[15] distinguishes from quantitative information by stressing its logical and evidential aspects. But the language of scientific communication must remind us not only of logic and evidence but of the world-picture which provides the context of its evidence.

Proposals

Logic and evidence are essential ingredients in any positivist representation of knowledge. All good scientists would go farther and add 'imaginative constructions', 'models' or some equivalent term. Whatever we call them, they play a decisive role in the coherence of science, and it is by virtue of coherence and imagination that we can speak of a 'world-picture'. Without such a picture it is difficult to see how we can speak of a 'frame of Humanist communication'. But modern man has lost the implicit cosmic security of medieval and Elizabethan man. The Elizabethan world-picture is well described by E. M. W. Tillyard.[16] Shakespeare (in *Troilus and Cressida*) declares that

> 'The heavens themselves, the planets and this centre
> Observe degree priority and place
> Insisture course proportion season form
> Office and custom, in all line of order'.

His hearers all knew and accepted this scheme. But the vision which gave coherence to their thought was soon to be demolished by science. Humanism must meet the challenge thrown out by Dennis Gabor:[17]

'It is a sad thought indeed that our civilization has not produced a *new vision*, which could guide us on into the new Golden Age which has now become physically possible, but only physically.'

This vision must be more than an aspiration, it must be an instrument, a systematic structure, a *morphology of knowledge and belief*. F. Zwicky[18] has shown that a 'morphological' approach to astronomy opens new vistas of discovery. Even the visible pattern of a constellation (to take a trivial example) cannot yield its meaning until placed in the co-ordinate framework of the celestial sphere. Morphology is the indispensable basis for the documentation of global knowledge. But this new documentation must make its impact on scientific education. For communication depends not only on organization at the source but on the conceptual preparation of the receiver, as shown, for example, in relation to agriculture by Emery and Oeser.[19]

There are three distinct criteria by which communication can be judged—*adequacy*, *accuracy* and *economy*. These are represented by the three questions—Have I said enough? Is it correct? Have I said it in optimum time? They are not inherently incompatible, but each has its own field of relevance. Critics and scholars, logicians and methodologists have all conspired to erect *accuracy* into the position of prime criterion, often overlooking that accuracy is relative to the means of knowing, to the capacity of the knower and to the purpose in knowing. In the context of rapidity of understanding *economy* is supreme; while in that of global ecology, as well as of philosophy and poetry, *adequacy* in the scope and depth of knowledge is all-important.

At this point a fuller treatment of the problems of communication would extend beyond the confines of science as ordinarily understood. For man does not live by bread alone. The ecological environment must include messages from musicians, painters, sculptors, poets and dramatists.

Taxonomy is the methodology of classification and classification demands the establishment of systematic categories. The importance of this, which has long been appreciated by scientists, has recently been given a psychological interpretation by Brunswik, Bruner and others. As Bruner says:[20]

'The object of systematic categorization as compared with *ad hoc* categorizing is that one seeks to find a minimum set of reliable attributes capable of guiding one to a series of categorizing decisions about many forms of identity.'

This is not only a matter of economy. When the Copernican revolution led to the reclassification of the earth as a *planet*, the whole cosmic picture was changed. Categories are organizers of thought, though intellect often resists the reorganization. As classification becomes more adequate our world-picture becomes richer. As insight into its structure spreads, the mind depends less and less on the multiplicity of fact: the pressure on the means of communication is reduced.

This principle underlies the educational doctrine of 'transfer of training' which, in the words of John Locke, signifies 'that having got the way of reasoning . . . they might be able to transfer it to other parts of knowledge'. Experimental psychologists have thrown doubts on this doctrine, but as many studies have shown, e.g. Meredith,[21] Olsen,[22] a morphological analysis of topics is needed for it to be successful. All knowledge involves general principles as well as specific facts, but the principles must be *explicitly* generalized for transfer to take place. Gestalt theory with its concept of 'prägnanz' confirms the principle.

Education tends to be thought of solely in terms of children and undergraduates, and to be divorced from research. Not only the scientific education of the 'arts man' but the working scientist's continued need for education is overlooked. True, many people from sheer love of knowledge continue to read widely, even at some peril to their specialist advancement. Also they are often defeated not only by the sheer mass of knowledge but by the incomprehensibility of other specialist languages. The problem would be insoluble were it not for the neglected phenomenon of *isomorphism*;[31] i.e. that if two concepts, though differing in expression and qualitative reference, are structurally identical, then a single effort of understanding can replace two distinct efforts, provided that a common language is used. This transfer-principle, systematically exploited (but with adequate safeguards against the misuse of analogy), could revolutionize the psychological economy of scientific education. It is bound up with the development of a scientific *interlingua* grounded in the objective structure of science itself. This interlingua, however, will not be like any spoken language, whether natural or artificial: it will be more like an atlas. Languages have to be *learnt*: an atlas is *consulted*.

When we have designed this novel and powerful atlas for our ecological-evolutionary world-picture, our own everyday language will not lose but gain as Woodger[23] has suggested.

In this 'science of the transmission of knowledge'[24] many disciplines will be needed. *Semiotic* studies will contribute to its morphology, as Charles Morris points out.[15] The mathematics of matrices,[26] sets, measure and probability will find many new applications. The far-reaching insight of Ogden and Richards[27] in their epoch-making *Meaning of Meaning* are needed more than ever. The frame to be constructed must needs follow their prescription that 'every referent has a fixed place in the whole order of reference'. This order will be displayed in the 'atlas'.

But just as any world-language will require a multitude of dictionaries to relate it to the existing separate languages, so any systematic world-picture will need a multitude of inter-dimensional dictionaries to relate it to the independently evolved disciplines of the different sciences. To this task the methodologists, the mechanical translation specialists, the professional interpreters, the documentalists, as well as the psychologists, educationists and natural scientists, need to apply their energy and their Humanism.

It is not Utopianism which drives Humanists to explore the future. Nor, as the nuclear deterrent cancels itself out, is it any longer the fear of extinction. It is love of their children and a dread of their degradation. It is also a concern for the millions still condemned to lives which are 'nasty, brutish and short', and for the whole future of evolution. These considerations provide the context for what I have had to say about Humanist communication. Communication is a factor in evolution and man can no longer leave evolution to chance. Our thoughts about randomness and probability must needs be revised when we impose a direction on events. A direction can be defined only in reference to a frame. This frame decides the context, and hence the meaning, of Humanist communication. In this brief space I have only hinted at the nature of this frame, this atlas of knowledge. When we have it open before us our language will suffer a sea-change.

Language is so much a part of us that we passionately resist external efforts to change it. Yet each generation assimilates changes, rather delighting in the shocks to their fathers. And although some of the changes are degenerative others lead to wider horizons of thought. The young of today, thanks partly to space-technology, take naturally to a global language. The *mappa mundi* of the Humanist world-picture will enable the new generation to sail on the high seas of human knowledge with confidence and courage.

REFERENCES

(1) Dovring, Karin. Road of Propaganda. New York: Philosophical Library, 1959.

(2) Broadbent, D. E. Perception and Communication. New York: Pergamon, 1958.

(3) Gray, Sir James. Presidential Address, The Advancement of Science, Vol. XVI, No. 62, 1959.

(4) Nature, Vol. 184, No. 4687, August 29, 1959.

(5) Wells, H. G. The World Brain. New York: Doubleday, 1938.

(6) Perry, James W. 'Co-operative and Centralized Information Processing'. Documentation in Action, ed. J. H. Shera, Allen Kent and J. W. Perry, from the proceedings of the 1956 Western Reserve Conference on Documentation in Action. New York: Reinhold, 1956.

(7) Whorf, B. L. Language, Thought and Reality. New York: Wiley, 1956.

(8) Glenn, Edmund S. 'Semantic Difficulties in International Communication'. ETC: A Review of General Semantics, Vol. XI, No. 3, pp. 163–180, 1954.

(9) Morley, John. *Diderot*. New York: Macmillan.

(10) Hogben, L. *Science for the Citizen*. New York: Knopf, 1938.

(11) Wilkins, John. *An Essay Towards a Real Character and a Philosophical Language*, 1668.

(12) Huxley, Julian. *Evolution, the Modern Synthesis*. New York: Harper & Brothers, 1942.

(13) Brillouin, Leon. *Science and Information Theory*. New York: Academic Press, 1956.

(14) Cherry, Colin. *On Human Communication*. Massachusetts Institute of Technology, 1957.

(15) MacKay, D. M. *Meaning and the Human Senses*. Information Theory; Third London Symposium, 1955.

(16) Tillyard, E. M. W. *The Elizabethan World Picture*. New York: Macmillan & Co., 1944.

(17) Gabor, Dennis. *Electronic Inventions and their Impact on Civilization*. London: Modern Books, 1959.

(18) Zwicky, F. *Morphological Astronomy*. New York: Springer Pub. Co., 1957.

(19) Emery, F. E., and Oeser, O. A. *Information, Decision and Action*. New York: Cambridge University Press, 1958.

(20) Bruner, J. S., *et al*. *A Study of Thinking*. New York: Wiley, 1956.

(21) Meredith, G. P. 'Transfer of Training through the Application of Topic Analysis', *Researches and Studies* No. 2, 1950. Institution of Education, Leeds University.

(22) Olson, Harry F. *Dynamical Analogies*. Princeton: Van Nostrand, 1944.

(23) Woodger, J. H. *The Axiomatic Method in Biology*. New York: Macmillan & Co., 1937.

(24) Meredith, G. P. 'The Transmission of Knowledge'. *Brit. Jour. Psychol.*, Vol. XLII, Part 4, November 1951.

(25) Morris, Chas. W. *Foundations of the Theory of Signs*. University of Chicago Press, 1938.

(26) Meredith, G. P. 'Semantic Matrices'. *Proceedings of International Conference on Scientific Information*, Washington, November 1958.

(27) Ogden, C. K., and Richards, I. A. *The Meaning of Meaning*. London: Routledge, 1946.

(28) The Royal Soc. Scientific Information Conference, 1948. *Report*.

(29) National Science Foundation. *Proceedings of the International Conference on Scientific Information*, Washington, 1958.

(30) Fraenkel, A. A., and Bar–Hillel, Y. *Foundations of Set Theory*. London: Holland Press, 1958.

(31) Andree, R. V. *Selections from Modern Abstract Algebra*. New York: Holt, 1958.

H. L. ELVIN

AN EDUCATION FOR HUMANITY

LIONEL ELVIN

Born 1905. Educated: Southend High School; Trinity Hall, Cambridge. Principal Ruskin College (Oxford), 1944–50; Head of Education Department UNESCO, 1950–56; Director, University of London Institute of Education since 1958.

Publications: *Men of America*, 1941; *An Introduction to the Study of Literature (Poetry)* 1949.

AN EDUCATION FOR HUMANITY

It is still difficult to think of human civilization without thinking of a series of particular civilizations, each in its own time and place. Up to the stage of recorded history we now tend to see Man as a single evolving species, but we are only just reaching the point where we can see civilized man in comprehensive and unified terms. This is because civilizations until now have necessarily been local.

People living in the great civilizations of the past naturally supposed that to be civilized was to organize social life as they did, to behave according to their norms, to hold the beliefs that all right-thinking people held in their time and place. Yet, since the Stoics at least, to be civilized has implied a feeling that transcends local limitations, something that belongs to humanity as a whole. We ourselves feel this common humanity in the works of the different great civilizations, especially through the arts.

There is really a double shift taking place in our attitude to past civilizations. On the one hand we feel we have to see them as more local than we used to think necessary. We realize that it is misleading to respond to Greek thought in the abstract: we need a thorough knowledge of the Greek city state and of many other relevant local matters if we are to make sense of Greek thought on any subject. [1] The same is true for a great deal of the literature and philosophy of the past: the enjoyment of Dante demands understanding of the politics and religion of the Italian civilization of his time, we can make little of Confucius without knowledge of the social structure of traditional China, and Arab thought is a closed book to us without some knowledge of Islam.

On the other hand, because of the growth of comparative studies and because of the shrinking of the world through modern communications, we think of these differing civilizations as less local, as simply differing forms of something common to mankind. In a scholarly sense this realization of community may be limited to comparatively few people, but in terms of general sympathies it is increasingly a sign of our age. It has to be, as a condition of our living and working together. It has developed enough for us to feel that we are on the way to a culture that will rightly retain local forms but that should be more broadly and consciously human in its outlook than any civilization of the past.[2]

Here we meet the great cultural dialectic of our time. On the one hand, threatened by a cosmopolitanism that washes away local roots under a flood of mass-production, we cry out for preservation of local variety. On the other hand, since humanity must now be one society for many of the most important purposes of our lives, we feel that any picture of the civilized man that imprisons him in a local framework is inadequate.

Two features of the present stage of history reinforce the movement towards a view of humanity as a whole and lead us to ask which local characteristics of civilization we should try to retain and which we must redefine in larger terms lest the present stage of human development end in disaster. The first of these features is political, though it comes in turn from material and technical advances. We begin to see pretty plainly that we cannot preserve peace without controlling the use of ultimate force, and that for this no unit smaller than mankind will do. And since political plans are of no use if they do not sink deep into men's consciousness we realize that the educational and cultural means at our disposal cannot remain geared to an earlier stage of human society. In the second place, through the progress of comparative studies, the different idea-systems by which men have explained the universe to themselves begin to look much less exclusively true at the expense of all the others (which were by definition false).[3] Nor are so many people now disposed to consider any of their formulations as final, in contempt of the knowledge of man and the universe that we have gained and are continuing to gain. These two features of our time impel us to think less of a number of different civilizations, each with its local name, and more of the quality of being civilized, whatever the local modulations of this may be.

The change in outlook that this implies is a general one and may well be only true in part at this moment or in this place or that. What we still find it useful to call the Renaissance in Europe did not happen in a day and is not easy to define.[4] Historians may argue as to what centuries they should have in mind when the term is used, as well as what features of European life. But the term remains indispensable to describe a real shift in the way in which men regarded themselves and the universe, even though it was nowhere quite the same and even though historians have to warn us to be on our guard against the unanalysed use of the term.

The major cultural shift of our time follows the working of forces that may similarly be identified in broad terms. But it is not only a question of forces operating upon us. The role of our own ideas may be decisive. We can decide—indeed have to decide—what form the ultimate resolution of forces shall take. All the forces that are making us into 'one world' will not take us into one happy world unless we will both the end and the means. Among the means themselves there is choice, for instance between a monolithic solution and one that is politically and culturally federal, leaving a rich diversity within the unity.[5] To some extent we have it in our power to control our own evolution. Since man now has such immense powers in his hands it is not too much to say that he ought to regard himself as custodian for the future of all life on this planet.

Now all this does constitute a major shift as compared with even thirty or forty years ago. Like the Renaissance and other cultural shifts, but on a much more important scale, it must be seen to involve corresponding changes in the education we give to those who will live in this changed world. Unfortunately, if the Renaissance is any guide there will be a melancholy time-lag between the need for such educational changes and their coming about. Bacon, and Milton after him, were still crying out for them when they were long overdue. But once educational methods and systems have made their reorientation they become a positive force helping to establish the society and the ideas that until then were only beginning to make themselves felt. It has been said that the 'Public Schools' of the type of Arnold's Rugby were a response to the need of nineteenth-century England for a new administrative and governing class, with values and beliefs that were significantly different from those of the eighteenth century. It has also been said that the young men formed in the Public Schools played a major part in creating Victorian England and its empire. Both these statements are true. There was an interplay between the first Industrial Revolution, with its consequential change in the English social balance, and the system of ideas that, when established, helped to consolidate Victorian society. If a parallel may be drawn with the transition we are now experiencing, more quickly and on a larger scale, the forces at work are already plain. Thinking has begun about the changes that should be consequential in education. But the decisive establishment of an education that will consolidate the change has yet to take place.

It has been noted that men are being forced to consider closer association for political reasons. These are not only reasons of protection from annihilation. There are also reasons connected with the desire for a common prosperity. We would like to think that these come in part from our altruism. Certainly the idea that the technically developed countries owe some help to the less well developed is increasingly winning acceptance.[6] But, helping slothful altruism forward, there is a sense of common need. We have to co-operate in health measures because diseases ignore passports, in air transport because planes are over frontiers in no time and have to land on foreign fields, and so on through all the spheres of association so modestly 'covered' by the United Nations and its Specialized Agencies. These activities are already modifying our habits and our view of mankind.

The economic, social and political forces which have produced an embryonic world order are gaining support from what is happening in the world of scholarship and ideas. Through the growth of comparative studies of all kinds we are being impelled to think more and more of humanity as a whole. The sense of the musician and the artist that national boundaries were irrelevant to their work, and especially the sense of the scientist that his professional community was world-wide, have been reinforced by the students of comparative sociology, comparative religion and social psychology. Whereas even fifty years ago, for instance, it would have been natural for an adherent of one religion to say to an adherent of another religion, 'We worship different gods', he would now almost certainly say 'We worship God in different ways'.[7] That is a considerable improvement. Indeed, if one travels about the globe now one must feel how odd it was that people should have oppressed, killed and 'converted' one another with such zeal on the ground of the differences between their religious creeds and practices when they were obviously much more like one another than they were different. (The greater danger now is that they may do this over differences in political creed.) There are more significant differences between the philosophic and the vulgar forms of a single religion than there are between any two major religions as such.

To the Humanist it seems a natural step to move from these comparative studies to a realization that the invocation of supernatural powers, in all its varied forms, like the equally widespread former belief in witchcraft, belongs to an earlier stage of human development. It does not really explain anything, and it darkens understanding more than it helps it. However that may be—and the Humanist is content to leave it to the free play of thought, so long as thought *is* kept free—he recognizes the considerable liberalizing of religious thinking that has taken place in recent years, and feels that he may count on the agreement of liberally minded believers with much of what he would propose in education.

What kind of education would be appropriate to the present age? In answering this question it would be well to recall that our educational predecessors are by no means to be written off as foolish. Some of them were wise and enlightened men and women and what they did often served their own societies well. When innovation is in the air it is worth remembering that there are perennial purposes in education, however form and method may be adapted to different times and places. The important thing is to re-interpret these purposes as a changing society and a changing climate of ideas make necessary. But what are these perennial purposes?

Last year I read an account by a man now in his fifties and living in the United States, of the education he had had as a boy in the West African bush. The day after I happened to read an account by a man who had been a county education officer, of the education he had had at the same time in a well-known London secondary school. The comparison was instructive. The African[8] explained how with other boys of his age-group he had been sent away to the 'school' in the bush where he had learned that he was now part of the tribe. Before, if he had done wrong, he had been responsible to his family. Now if he did wrong he had injured the whole tribe, and especially his own age-group. Secondly, they learned practical things in the bush school, like tracking game and the medicinal use of plants. And lastly, they learned to listen to the silences of the forest and to become attuned to the rhythm of the earth 'so that the nature within ourselves found unity with the nature of the earth'. The Englishman[9] had a very different story to tell, and admittedly he was so critical that he should not be taken as quite representative. He says that he left school 'a short-sighted, introspective lad', with no feeling of responsibility to his fellows, useless with his hands and knowing nothing of the workings of the machines that made his life swift and comfortable, and having learned neither to trust himself nor to believe in God.

Allowing for the fact that the African's education was utterly unsuited to any but a static pre-technical society, which of these two felt he had had the better education? There can be no doubt of the answer. Within the limits of the needs of his society the African's education had done what the Englishman felt his had failed to do: helped him to make the transition from the family circle to the wider community, given him the skills and knowledge he needed, and encouraged him to respond imaginatively to the mystery of life. These are the perennial purposes of education. How should we interpret them in terms of what young people need today?

Take first the equipment of young people with necessary skills. Our discussions of technical education are still bedevilled with the antithesis between technical and liberal education that goes back to the fifth-century Greeks. They believed that most technical skill was hardly proper to free men, but only to those of servile status. And, as has often been pointed out, this was a direct reflection of their own society. The African, on the contrary, was taught to hunt and he learned some botany. There is nothing necessarily liberal or illiberal in either of these things: hunting may be a prestige-conferring exploit for the well-to-do or it may be for food. Knowledge of plants may be the basis of a science, as it is for us. It has its uses, though we do not teach it for that, as the tribal Africans did. The difference turns on the approach and the social setting. In modern society we are not divided by status into men of free condition who have the leisure to take part in government and to cultivate the mind and men of servile condition who because they have to do the heavy work cannot be expected to take part in either of these things. In status at least we are all free, and virtually all of us have to work. Like the tribal Africans, and unlike the Greeks, we have to have a positive attitude to education in the skills that are necessary to maintain life. Yet our educational philosophy in Europe (though much less so in the United States) has been largely coloured by a Greek attitude that is quite inappropriate to our own society.

There is a case for caution in the teaching of industrial skills in school. But it is not that such studies must of necessity be illiberal: they become liberal in so far as the teaching brings out the knowledge that lies behind them. It is of course true that some mere skills do not lend themselves to this. But the real case for caution is that the detailed skills needed in industry are now changing so rapidly that it is much wiser to teach the principles behind them, and a general machine-mindedness, than to train more narrowly. This is vocational education rather than vocational training, a very different thing and one much more appropriate to schools.[10]

This leads us to a need that we have and that the tribal African did not. We are concerned with basic knowledge, and for two reasons: first, because it is necessary for further technical advance; and second, because without it we cannot understand either ourselves or the universe we inhabit. This leads us to the apparent paradox that in an age of rapid technical change what we need most is a revitalized general education, with a better command of the basic skills of reading, writing and calculation, a good understanding of fundamental scientific principles, facts and methods, and a sense of individual and social values without which their application is sterile.

It would not be true to say that in England leaders in technical education or in industry are insensible of the need for better general education. But particular short-run pressures work against it. And it is true that the excessive and premature specialization that runs through our whole educational system makes it extremely difficult to give a good enough general education. Unless we reverse this tendency we shall be unable to do the two things that in theory everyone wants: to equip our young people to function in a rapidly changing technological scene, and, even more important, to liberalize our industrial society.

Our search for knowledge to understand ourselves and the universe better is something that a member of a primitive tribe could hardly conceive. But here too we have come to a point where serious consideration of what to include in our teaching and what to leave out is very necessary. In recent years in many subjects developments have been so rapid that we cannot just go on adding new matter to the syllabus as it used to be taught. The additions are too many; and some of them have seriously modified the whole shape of thought in a given study. Our African said they were taught all the elders thought they needed to know. We cannot hope to teach all of that in the span of school or even university. Our hope for an educated adult generation must lie more and more in nourishing the desire to go on studying, and therefore in introducing the young to the methods of the distinctive disciplines and in giving them the basic tools for study in each. It cannot lie in cramming in yet a few more pieces of information measurable in tests of attainment at the appropriate points.

This is especially important for us because we are educating for change. For this, shaping a mind is more important than stuffing it. We need to sit back and think through each syllabus freshly, so as to bring forward the key concepts that will continue to work vitally when the particular applications of today belong to the past. We have to educate so that young people will think of man as an evolving species in an environment that he himself is changing and should change only with consciousness of what he does.

It is here that the imparting of technical skills links up with the broader purposes of education, especially with the desire for knowledge for its own sake and with the 'world view' that is suitable to our stage of history. In other words technical education must become part of a humane education. We depend far too much on technical skills for the antithesis between liberal and technical to persist with its old divisive force.[11] The antithesis is useful only in so far as it may remind us that techniques are a means, not an end.

The African to whom I have referred clearly felt that his 'school' had done more than give him the skills he needed. It had helped to 'socialize' him. Of course this was easier in the bush than in modern London, for society there was both self-contained and stable. It is precisely because this is no longer so that tribal societies are losing their force in Africa and the traditional ways of training the young are giving way to schools in our sense of the word. But our Western societies are in rapid transition too. We also are enjoying (or suffering from) a far greater social mobility than was known in the nineteenth century. The transition from family to wider community is more difficult than it was when the lines were more clearly laid down for people in every station in society. We realize the need for concerted action between the schools and the various other agencies that are concerned with this transition. Schools are indeed not the only agency responsible for the good social upbringing of the young, but education is one very important factor in it. We have to think out in terms of new situations what the school ought to do in relation to other agencies while remaining faithful to its own distinctive purposes.

There is one particular respect in which we may see an analogy between the changes in our society and those in tribal society where the tribe still exists but is not relevant to the changed situation. We are still educating the young for the nation-tribe. No doubt the modern schools that are succeeding the bush 'schools' in West Africa will draw on much local material for their teaching; and in the same way we may expect our national cultural traditions still to work vitally in the schools of the modern world. But in a larger sense, and especially politically, we know that the nation-tribe must become a thing of the past. We have the difficult task of socializing the young for a community that has become world-wide.

For us, as for any African tribe, the change has to be in our mental as well as our physical boundaries. This has obvious implications for our teaching, especially of history and geography, and the need is greater in history. For some reason, while it has always been thought proper to teach world geography (after all the globe is the geography teacher's symbol), it has not been thought respectable to teach world history. Why? Whatever the shortcomings of H. G. Wells as a historian (and he freely admitted them) he performed an immense service when he wrote his *Outline of History*. For the first time we saw biological evolution and human history as a continuum; and when Wells came on to recorded history he saw it as that of humanity as a whole. Now we are in need of a more authoritative basis for teaching world history in the schools, and the Scientific and Cultural History of Mankind that UNESCO is preparing should give an agreed basis for school books. In carrying such a broadened history teaching into the classroom there are real problems to be faced, of balance and of method and of time-tabling, before we can say that we know how to teach history with a due feeling for local life, with a proper sense of the 'ancestral spirits' of the nation, and with an imaginative acceptance of the much more significant community of mankind. These are teaching problems that we should set ourselves to solve.

There can of course be no effective induction into a wider community without a sense of a strong moral bond. This means that we must strive for an extension of the range of recognized obligation. Hitherto it has been felt that, after certain formalities, to kill a member of another nation-tribe was not the same as murder. One could argue that this was in a way rational in so far as the social bond between nations was not as positive as that between the citizens of a single nation. But good men have always been uneasy about this. In peace-time we recognize moral obligations to persons from a different nation-tribe. The virtual cessation of such moral obligations in war could not be regarded as good, even though under-standable; it was at best a regrettable necessity following a social breakdown. And from time to time men have tried to establish limited codes even for the conduct of war.

We have now reached a point where these tentative recognitions of the oneness of mankind must be given force. So profound a change in our laws and in our habits of mind cannot be introduced overnight. Yet we must set ourselves now to break down the attitude that there cannot be a common and enforced law over Capitalist and Communist alike. We must break down the assumption that there are either lesser breeds without the law, or higher breeds, ourselves, that can flout it with impunity. To accomplish this it is necessary to widen and deepen the understanding of different ways of life, of different religions and philosophies, and of different social systems; and above all to bring understanding of what the different peoples have in common.

I suggested that the third of the perennial purposes of education was to give the rising generation a 'world view'. This is the one whose reinter-pretation for our own time is likely to cause most controversy. By a world view I mean a view of man and his nature, of the earth and its history, and of the universe of which it is a minute part. I mean also a total response, at once scientific and imaginative and in a sense also moral, to what we know and to what we are unlikely ever to know. (Some, like the African writer to whom I have referred, think of this as a religious response. I would be reluctant to argue too long about a word, but I should make it clear that I mean a kind of response that for some people takes place in association with their religious beliefs but that *per se* is not dependent on any religious creed or dogma and is felt equally by those who are in this sense without religion.)

Now it is really of importance that the different elements in this response to the universe (the scientific, the imaginative, the moral) should not fight each other but should fuse in a total personal synthesis. The intellectual framework of such a world view should be sound, being based on the best knowledge that we have. It is the contention of Humanists that the leading concepts as to the nature of things handed down to us through religious dogmas do not afford us elements for a world view that we can regard as satisfactory for our own period of human history. It is here of course that the Humanist parts company with many of those who up to this point would have gone along with him happily enough in discussion of the kind of education we need.

Of course some of those who would regard themselves as religious (though indeed not those in the central citadel) would say that they set little store by dogmas and formulated creeds but believe in religious education because of the moral guidance it gives. Here it is necessary to be clear on what is essential definition. Religious and moral education are commonly associated. But it is wrong to suppose that they are the same thing. They are no more identical than theology and ethics are identical, for the simple reason that whatever else it includes, religious education must include the inculcation of some religious beliefs.

There is at present considerable dissatisfaction with the state of religious education in English schools. Those who are ill at ease with the credal implications try to turn it into an occasion for the discussion of what is right and what is wrong, and of course no one, least of all a Humanist, would deny that this in itself is an essential part of education.[12] But this attempt to turn religious education into something that is different from religious education in one quite crucial respect does not deal with the difficulty at its root. The difficulty is that only at a level of comparative sophistication can the world view given by the Bible and by Christian tradition be made to appear to harmonize with our knowledge and with the increasingly prevailing climate of ideas.

What started the once famous Bishop Colenso on the path of doubt about the historical accuracy of the Pentateuch was the question asked him by the Zulus for whom he was translating it: 'But, sir, is it true?'[13] That question, in one form or another, still confronts the teacher in his class. It is difficult for an honest and thinking Christian to reply except in the phrase, 'Well, not all of it is to be taken literally, of course'. That 'not literally' takes a lot of explaining to young children. When children ask if a story is true they mean, is it true in the sense that the statement that the Battle of Waterloo took place in 1815 is true? Here it must surely be right to follow the Colenso logic to its conclusion. Even if it is agreed (as it reasonably may be) that the Bible is a collection of unusual historical interest, with exceptional moral and imaginative power in places, it is still in the same class as other great books of the human tradition. This no more takes away its value than declining to believe in the existence of Apollo or Poseidon takes away the value of the Iliad or the Odyssey. One can reconcile enjoyment of the Greek classics with the concepts of science because one does not need to accept these apparent belief-statements as true in the sense in which I am using the word.

Now the increasing number of those who are liberal in religion do not take credal statements in a simple factual sense. They agree that stories of the sun standing still or of devils entering into men or animals belong to a stage that we have passed beyond. But the real difficulty goes deeper. It is that the very idea of an originating or intervening supernatural power is ceasing to have the force that it formerly had. The liberal theologian may feel that his religion is as real and as important to him as it ever was but his idea of a supernatural power is undoubtedly distanced: it has become something more like a philosophical ultimate. If as many people as ever believe in a supernatural power it is a fair statement that they believe in it, or him, less immediately and less continuously than they did, and that there is a wider and wider realm of daily experience in whose working the conception is not invoked. The Humanist simply goes one stage farther. He suggests that though of course individuals who have grown up in a tradition may have made a kind of working synthesis for themselves, feeling that to do otherwise would be to give up too much, nevertheless the time is coming when we shall see that this world view based on the postulate of supernatural powers, immediate or distant, intervening or merely originating, does not fit our present time.

Yet it is important that there should be a framework of leading ideas that will really help young people to see life steadily and see it whole. It must be one that does sort with our present knowledge, incomplete though that may be and incomplete though it will remain. What should these leading ideas be?

What the young need to know as soon as they pass from the earliest years of childhood is what they are, what mankind is, and how mankind fits into the universe around us. The leading idea here should surely be the continuing story of humanity, continuing back into the past through the history of evolution of life to the story of the evolution of the universe, and continuing forward towards the idea of one humanity conscious of its unity and of its collective responsibility for life on this planet. Both in going back and in going forward scientific knowledge and imaginative response should meet in the wonder of what we know and the mystery of what lies beyond knowledge.

If one were to work this general concept out in terms of school subjects one would see it as implying a general background of science, drawing on astronomy and physics, then on geology and biology, and leading on naturally to social studies like history, geography and international affairs. And man's response to his situation would be felt, with no conflict between the sciences and the humanities, in literature and the arts. This is not the place to go into details of curricula that might be devised but to point out the kind of leading concept that alone now can give the unity to education that educationists have been crying out for. This concept is the concept of man's evolutionary history and future in his environment.

In his book *Authority, Responsibility and Education*,* Mr R. S. Peters refers to Professor Piaget's account of the stages children pass through in their attitude to rules. There is the 'transcendental' stage when rules emanate from the unquestionable authority of parents and teachers. Then comes the more 'autonomous' stage when it is seen that rules may be questioned, depend not on authority but on mutual consent, but yet are indeed necessary. Mr Peters then says: 'Piaget's distinction between the transcendental and autonomous stages of the child's development is as a matter of fact a paradigm of our social development. We have gradually emerged from the closed, traditional, patriarchal sort of society when our lives were governed almost entirely by external unquestionable authorities. Science and morality are two of the most important manifestations of this stage. And they are connected not because the scientist is a new authority to replace old ones, but because they are both *anti-authoritarian* in character.'

What the Humanist asks for is an education which, in what it teaches as knowledge, in its moral and imaginative response to life, and above all in its leading theme of the evolution of mankind, is seen to be appropriate to the twentieth century.

REFERENCES

(1) See Sir Ernest Barker's Introduction to his translation of the *Politics of Aristotle*. New York: Oxford University Press, 1946.

(2) See Lionel Elvin, 'Nationalism and Internationalism in Education', Foundation Oration, Goldsmith's College, 1959.

(3) Ruth Benedict's *Patterns of Culture*. Boston: Houghton Mifflin Company, 1934, was one of the first anthropological works to stress the relativism of culture and beliefs.

(4) See W. D. Wall, 'A Child of Our Time', National Children's Home Convocation Lecture, 1959.

(5) The Constitution of UNESCO refers both to the 'intellectual and moral solidarity of mankind' and to its 'fruitful diversity of cultures'.

(6) See Professor P. M. S. Blackett's Presidential Address to the British Association, Dublin, 1957.

(7) Rank, Otto. *The Myth of the Birth of the Hero*. New York: Vintage Books, 1959.

(8) Prince Modupe. *I Was a Savage*. New York: Harcourt, Brace & Co., 1958.

---

* Allen & Unwin: London, 1960

(9) Burton, H. M. *There Was a Young Man*. London: Bles, 1958.

(10) See Ministry of Education Circular 323, May 13, 1957, H.M.S.O.

(11) For the disproportionate attention given to 'applied' science see W. H. Whyte, *The Organization Man*. New York: Simon & Schuster, 1956.

(12) For an interesting example of the embarrassed desire to turn religious education into moral education see the Crowther Report, paras. 174 and 175 (15 *to* 18: *Report of the Central Advisory Council for Education*—England, H.M.S.O., 1960).

(13) See Sir Geoffrey Faber, *Jowett*. Harvard University Press, 1958.

(14) See C. P. Snow, *The Two Cultures and the Scientific Revolution*. Rede Lectures, New York: Cambridge University Press, 1959.

(15) See Sir Julian Huxley's 'The Two Cultures and Education', *Encounter*, June 1960, and Professor H. J. Muller's 'One Hundred Years Without Darwinism are Enough', *School Science and Mathematics*, April 1959.

(16) Peters, R. S. *Authority, Responsibility and Education*. New York: Taplinger, 1960.

MICHAEL YOUNG

SOCIOLOGY AND PUBLIC POLICY

MICHAEL YOUNG, PH.D.,
B.SC.(ECON.)

Born 1915. Educated: Dartington Hall
School. Director of P.E.P. (Political and
Economic Planning), 1941–45. Research
Secretary of the Labour Party, 1945–51.
Founder of the Institute of Community
Studies, 1954, Consumers Association, 1957,
and the Advisory Centre for Education,
1960. Lecturer in Sociology at Cambridge
University, 1961.

Publications: *The Rise of the Meritocracy*,
1958.

SOCIOLOGY AND PUBLIC POLICY

If a sociologist professes deep anxiety about the use to which his work is put, suspect him of posing as more powerful than he is. But as long as his look is not too haunted, do not completely dismiss his fears. For, slight as it still is, the knowledge he has accumulated could in the wrong hands be peculiarly obnoxious. It could be used, even though at present it is only in small doses, to manipulate people who remain quite unaware of what is happening to them. The sociologist's special problem is only an example of a more general dilemma—wherever there is use, there is also the possibility of misuse—but it is a real enough problem all the same. In the first part of this essay I will consider this problem as it arises in the relationship between social research and public policy in Britain.[1] In the second part I shall be concerned with the relevance of sociology to some aspects of world development, and especially to the structure of social classes.

*　　　*　　　*　　　*

The House filled rapidly yesterday afternoon when the Prime Minister spoke in the debate on the Address. He began by repeating his pledge that no change would be made in Central Africa until the wishes of the people there had been consulted. This welcome statement was received with applause from the Government benches and silence from the Opposition. Order papers were waved in the air and shouts were heard when he said that he had listened to the Leader of the Opposition with dismay. Why raise again these absurd demands for abolishing capital punishment and the licensing laws when it was clear that public opinion was not ready for them? This led to a spirited exchange with the Leader of the Opposition who suggested in forcible language that the Prime Minister was completely out of touch with what the public was thinking, especially the youth of the country. The Prime Minister made a shrewd thrust (greeted with laughter from the benches behind him) when he said that the claim of the Leader of the Opposition to be an expert on public opinion must of course be taken very seriously in view of his Party's performance at the Election. It was after all the Government 'which had gone to the country and had renewed its mandate'. The debate continues.

This imaginary account of a parliamentary debate is very close to the sort of thing that appears regularly in the newspapers. Political leaders talk about public opinion as though they have private knowledge of it, although on many questions neither they nor anyone else have ever asked people for their views. At a general election a thousand issues are jumbled together, from steel nationalization to nuclear disarmament, from provincial repertory theatres to old age pensions. The electors are not given the chance to say what they think about particular items in the party portmanteau. Until recently this was not only the way things were done, it was the way they had to be. Apart from the clumsy device of the referendum, there was no way of discovering what people thought about any particular political question.

Techniques of sampling have changed this situation. It has often been said that democracy could work in Greece because the State was so small, and that in a vast modern society it cannot work in more than a symbolic way. This overlooks the fact that the social sciences have from one point of view made the largest societies as small as a City State. A random sample of a few thousand citizens can now be selected so as to represent adequately the entire population from which they are drawn. As a result, it is comparatively easy to find out whether the electorate favours, say, the abolition of capital punishment or the introduction of decimal coinage: you have to ask not everybody, but only a small body chosen from the whole. You can be confident that their answers will, within calculable margins of error, reflect the views of everybody. For the first time in history it would be practicable to have government of a large society according to the popular will.

A boon to mankind? A means of making democracy effective by reducing not just a national government but even a world government to the scale of a Greek City State? It is not, I think, such an attractive prospect as it may sound. The reason is the obvious one that government according to the popular will would often be very bad government. The majority of the British electorate was in favour of the Suez attack. But that does not mean it was right. The electors did not have more than a tiny part of the information needed about, say, the strength of the British forces or the attitude of the Russian or United States governments, in order to make up their minds wisely. If they had, many of them might have come to a quite different decision. What if the great majority were in favour of abolishing income tax? That would not make it the right thing to do.

Indeed, the danger is that governments will pay too much attention to public opinion, now that they can so easily find out what it is, and use their information in order to stay in office as long as possible. Using social research for this purpose is not just an academic possibility, at least not in Britain and other countries with similar constitutions where the Government can choose its moment for a general election. Polls are able to predict within fairly close margins of error how people would vote if there were a general election at any particular time. As a result the party in power enjoys a big new advantage it did not have when trends in public opinion had to be guessed from by-elections. It can avoid the valleys when the polls show that it would be defeated, and (as long as there are some) choose only the peaks when a majority is certain. In the years after 1955 there were only two peak periods—the autumns of 1958 and 1959—when the polls gave the Conservatives a decisive lead over Labour. It was not too difficult for the Prime Minister to choose the right moment.

It would be far-fetched to expect that, as a consequence of opinion sampling, parties would now be able to stay in power for a hundred years. At some point any government will in its last years of office make irretrievable mistakes or be beset by bad fortune not of its own making. But the new research techniques will probably make the pendulum swing more slowly. Governments will win a row of elections more frequently than they have done in the past, and Opposition parties, deprived of power for longer periods, be more liable to demoralization. I can see only one reason for welcoming this development. If Government leaders did not know that when it came to choosing the date for a general election they would have a considerable advantage over the Opposition, they might be too inclined to play for popularity, as measured by the polls, between elections.

So one cannot, on balance, expect public opinion polling to bring any great advantage to society. People's opinions on complicated questions are of little weight unless they appreciate the nature of the complications. But another kind of more intensive study, of people's experience rather than of their opinions, can, I believe, be of great value to government. Traditional methods of enquiry are no longer adequate. Royal Commissions invite people and organizations to give evidence. But they may not get any. The Wolfenden Commission was set up partly to enquire into prostitution. Naturally enough, it invited prostitutes to give evidence: naturally enough none of them did. Since no researchers were sent out to gather the facts, recommendations were made and laws changed without those in authority ever having heard from the people most closely concerned.

This is an extreme instance. Some other Royal Commissions, such as the last one on taxation, have employed sociologists, and some Depart-

ments do so as well. There is a special organization, the Government
Social Survey, which conducts enquiries for them. For the Treasury it
finds out from samples of consumers how they spend their incomes in
general, and for the Ministry of Agriculture how food consumption
varies between rich and poor. It has collected information (which is being
acted on now) about incomes in the main professions in order to show
how much force there is in the complaint by doctors that they are under-
paid; about the postal practice of business houses in order to advise the
GPO on the possibilities of electronic sorting; and about the views of
deaf people on the hearing aids given them by the Health Service. But
the Social Survey is still a small affair, its total cost being less than
£200,000 a year.

On the whole the Government has better information about economic
movements than about anything else. On the impact of the social services
hardly any research has been done, although the need for a good intelligence service is here especially great. The Government spends many
hundreds of millions of pounds on health, education, housing, on security
in old age or sickness, and spends virtually nothing to find. out the
experience of the people who are supposed to benefit. No one knows
whether or not a policy achieves its objectives. Schools are for teaching
children—how much of what they learn is valuable to them in adult life?
Which is the most economic way of teaching mathematics or English or
carpentry?[2] There is hardly ever any controlled experiment in education,
almost everything is done according to rule of thumb. Houses are subsi-
dized for families to live in—but no one ever asks the families whether
they are satisfied or would have suggestions about changes in design.
Prisons are supposed (amongst other things) to reform the unfortunate
people who are put into them, but research to find out whether prisons
succeed, or rather with whom, under what conditions, is only just
beginning. Hospitals 'belong' to the nation since the National Health
Service was established; but who ever tries to find out whether the
patients are satisfied with them, or have any ideas for improvement?
Payments are made to people when they are old, or sick, or widowed.
Are the payments too small or too large? Do some people still suffer from
crippling poverty despite all that is done? The authorities almost never
try to find out.[3] A few enquiries have given some idea of what could be
done.

A study was made of manual workers and their families resettled on a housing
estate outside London. One of the main complaints of the wives was that they
could no longer see their mothers and other relatives or get help from them in
time of illness or other need. A high proportion of the lonely young wives had

to be treated for 'neurosis' by local doctors and hospitals. The study suggested that more small houses suitable for elderly couples should be built on the estates so that they could accompany their children if they wished.[4]

A comparison of two hospitals showed that at the first there was a much lower turnover of nurses and a higher turnover of patients. People who had had appendicitis operations recovered much more quickly than at the second hospital. At the second hospital the nurses complained that their tasks were 'unintelligible'. The enquiry suggested that there was a great need for better communication between the hierarchy of medical professions.[5]

A widow receives financial help from the State. But her subsistence benefit has been reduced if she earns any sizeable amount herself. A study showed that this earning rule was intensely resented and, generally, that the poverty into which widows of manual workers were forced accentuated all the tendencies of grief, the isolation, the bitterness, the apathy, the sense of being rejected. The regulations were subsequently revised.[6]

These examples show how much more fully the Welfare State would be able to meet people's needs if policy-makers tried to find out what these were before they made their decisions. Despite (or perhaps because of) their good intentions, they so often seem to believe they *know* what is good for people. They are in a pre-scientific age, prepared to see the spirit of enquiry let loose in the world of technology but not in the world of administration. I can imagine a Welfare State that was really in tune with the needs of ordinary people. I can imagine that the public would be consulted, by means of social research, about the ways in which their money was spent. But this will only come about when administrators are persuaded that the best way to become more efficient is to begin finding out about the objective needs and the subjective reactions of the people whom they administer.

I return now to the same question that arose over public opinion polling—is there a danger that a government which used social research to bridge the gap between itself and the experience of the electorate would become unassailably popular, even if it paid no attention whatsoever to polls? This particular danger does not seem to me yet a very serious one. Probably the chief reason why more research is not done at present is that the results would so frequently be embarrassing to the Government. Politicians have to defend the policies of their Departments. If those policies are mistaken, as they often are, it is much easier to defend them if there is no evidence available by which to assess the magnitude of the error. In other words, research would be of great use to critics of the Government, as well as to its defenders.

I think that a programme of research on public administration should be welcomed, subject to two safeguards, firstly about publication, and secondly about independent institutions. At present few of the reports of the Social Survey are published. This is quite wrong. The reports of this body and of all enquiries paid for by the Government should be published, for use not only by one party, but by other parties, and by anyone else interested. This would be all the more necessary if, as I believe it should be, the scope of the Social Survey and other official research agencies were greatly expanded. The danger of misuse of sociology (as of any other research) would be far greater if its findings are kept secret.

The second safeguard is even more important—that research should be conducted not only by official teams, not only on behalf of the Government, but by independent institutions as well. I do not mean that all surveys should be made in parallel, officially and unofficially, but that public experience on the same kind of issues should be tapped by other bodies than the official ones. Official research is always likely to be muted in its criticism of government—a scruple from which independent research need not suffer. Independent research can underpin and inform the criticism from which no government should ever be free.

Which are the independent bodies? Universities, of course. They are and should remain the main centres of research as well as teaching, responsible for 'applied' research conducted from an independent point of view as well as for more 'fundamental' research on human behaviour which may be of no direct or immediate use to policy-makers. There is also a need for institutes, within and without universities, which will employ people whose primary responsibility is research rather than teaching. The person whose main job is teaching is often at a disadvantage. The sociologist is like the geologist or the archaeologist in that the subjects of his enquiry are not congregated together—they may be scattered over thousands of square miles. In these circumstances the person who is tied to a university by teaching may have no alternative except to employ interviewers to scout the country and the world for him. If he is absolutely sure what he is looking for, this division of labour may not be a disadvantage; otherwise he is almost bound to be handicapped by having to rely on second-hand observation. More full-time research posts are therefore an urgent requirement.

*   *   *   *

If sociology became the eyes and ears of public administration, a great deal of detailed information would be accumulated. It would soon become unmanageable unless it was blended into a general picture of human society, not just in one country like Britain but in all countries undergoing to some extent similar development. This is one of the main concerns of sociologists. They are attempting to build up a differentiated yet global view of social change, especially in industrial societies.

Anthropologists have studied (and compared) pre-industrial societies in great depth. The surprising thing about their research is that they can generalize so little. All societies have some sort of family, all have some economic, religious and political institutions, but after that, there is not a great deal more to say about the things they have in common. One cannot show that, say, matrilinear kinship systems usually go with a particular type of economy or religious institution, for they do not. The variety to be found in pre-industrial societies is immense.

All that is changed by industrialization. Once machines appear, societies everywhere converge. They become more complex internally; at any rate the occupational system becomes a great deal more diverse even if what people do in their leisure seems to become more standardized. At the same time industrial societies everywhere become more like each other. One of the jobs of the researcher is to discover the consistencies between them. This can be done in two complementary ways, by the historical method and by the comparative method.

Each of the more advanced countries is to some extent a microcosm of all, and if you could find out enough about the social history of any one of them, many of the secrets of the whole would probably be revealed. Although countries coming later to industrialization can skip some of the stages passed through by Britain, as the first with the new powers, it is still true that the newer countries have to pass through many of the same stages. In the eighteenth century Britain had by means of enclosures to increase the size and capitalization of farms, and to improve agricultural methods generally; it had to produce more food *before* it could support industrial workers in towns and cities. So did Russia. So does India. In the nineteenth century the early industrial operatives of Lancashire had little sense of time or acquisitiveness. To become efficient, they had to be dragooned into obedience to the clock so that they at least started work together, and persuaded to want more than their accustomed standard of life. So it was in Russia. So it is in India.

The other method, which belongs more to economics and sociology than to history, is to compare contemporary societies which are in different stages of development. In this way we may be able to throw further light on the regularities observed in historical change. Eventually, we can hope it will be in time to be of some use to the societies just embarking on industrialization—a comprehensive description, historical, sociological, economic, psychological and technical, will be pieced together. To show the kind of thing that should become more and more practicable I shall draw, for an example, upon the studies that have been made of social mobility. By this term sociologists refer not to movement of people between societies but to movement of people between social classes within societies.

In pre-industrial societies it seems that there is relatively little movement between 'classes'. A person's class, and often occupation within it, is usually determined by his parent's class. The squire's son becomes a squire too; the cultivator's son a cultivator. With the coming of industry this pattern is changed. Class, although to some extent ascribed by birth, becomes to a greater extent achievable on merit. More able children from the bottom classes get a chance to rise to the top, and more of the stupid children from the top classes fall to the bottom. This type of movement up and down has for long been the concern of sociologists, and since 1945 they have attempted to measure its rate. Individuals drawn from random samples in various countries have been asked about jobs held during their lifetimes and about their parent's jobs too. The results have been compared in a recent book by two American Professors of Sociology, who have themselves been active in the research for many years.[7] Many of the sociologists who have taken part in this work have wanted to highlight the social obstacles to mobility and, maybe, to show how low mobility was in their own countries compared to those industrially more advanced. The results do not bear out their hopes; they are all the more interesting for that.

Upward 'social mobility' is measured by the proportion of the sons of manual workers who became non-manual workers. International research shows that as many do so in Germany and France, in Britain and Japan as in the United States. In each country something like a third of all sons make this jump up. In each country, too, the same kind of proportions—around about a quarter—fall in their occupational class. These are all comparisons between countries which are in various degrees industrialized. The rates of mobility in most predominantly agricultural countries taken as a whole are less, but even in them there is the same sort of mobility in their cities as in cities elsewhere. Studies show that Poona is in this respect much the same as Tokyo, São Paulo much the same as Kansas City, Aarhus much the same as Indianapolis.

The conclusion, that in this vital respect societies all converge, rests on comparisons between two generations of the same family. Another kind of comparison is possible, of the amount of social mobility achieved in one generation. How many people whose first job is manual get white-collar jobs later? Once again there is a startling likeness between the countries where the relevant facts have been collected—the United States, Britain and Japan. Most people not only change their jobs very frequently, but in all three countries the proportions of manual workers who move upwards during their lifetimes are roughly similar. The same goes for marriages. As many daughters of manual workers marry upwards in Britain or Germany as in the United States.

Some historical comparisons can also be made, though more tentatively. It seems that social mobility in the United States may be no greater or less than it was a century ago, and the same goes for Britain too over the last fifty years. Whether the approach is historical or not, the story always seems to be the same. Despite their differing levels of productivity, their differing rates of economic expansion, their differing ideologies, in their social mobility countries turn out to be not different but similar.

Now that so many facts have been assembled, the next step is to try to explain them, and this will not be adequately done without drawing on other disciplines besides sociology, particularly genetics. What is now needed is more evidence about the mode of inheritance of the innate factor in 'intelligence' and of such human qualities as are partly innate and also relevant to social mobility. What proportion of the sons of fathers with more (or less) than average intelligence are less (or more) intelligent than their fathers? It may be that the pattern of inheritance is one of the chief reasons why there is a more or less constant amount of occupational mobility, from jobs requiring relatively less to jobs requiring relatively more intelligence. But a full explanation obviously cannot be cast merely in terms of genetics. Social and economic factors must also be taken into account—notably, the ratio between non-manual and manual jobs in any given society, all the educational and other social barriers to mobility, and the strength of motivation to rise in the ocupational hierarchy. I should point out that the facts cited are about mobility at a low level in the occupational hierarchy, at the junction of manual and non-manual work. Different countries would not necessarily show the same amount of mobility into professional and managerial jobs. My guess is that at this level a society, in trying to concentrate its intelligence in its 'head' as it were, will only bump against the limits set by the supply of intellectual ability when it has become highly industrialized. The more economically developed a society is, the more it tends to become a 'meritocracy'.[8] Whatever the explanation of social mobility may turn out to be, there is no doubt about the importance of the subject for public

policy, particularly in education. All countries embarked on industrialization are short of talent; all are making some effort to mobilize it.

*   *   *   *

Social mobility is only one subject out of many which have to be
mastered before a more general picture can be drawn. In time we should
be able to piece one together, combining a multitude of observations
from many different countries into a theory, if only a partial theory, of
social change in the setting which is becoming increasingly common all
over the world. This work will, I believe, only be supported on anything
like the required scale if it is continuously related to issues of public policy,
if it enables public administration to become more and more sensitive to
human needs, if it plays some part in achieving Bacon's ideal of using
science for 'the relief of man's estate'. The dangers are there plain enough.
The new knowledge could be used to degrade mankind. But it could also
be used to open up new human possibilities. The knowledge which
sociology is trying to build up is 'self-knowledge', self-knowledge of
ourselves in the social groups to which all of us belong.[9] Groups of one
kind and another, from families to churches, from nations to the slowly
evolving international communities, are the means of human fulfilment
as well as of human frustration. Although man is the creature of these
social groups, he is not absolutely so: he also creates new kinds of groups
and constantly changes those he inherits. As knowledge grows of the conditions under which groups of different sorts are formed, maintained and
dissolved, man will be able more and more to choose between them with
a full knowledge of the implications of doing so.

The limits within which we can choose are now so narrow. Council
tenants cannot even decide that they would like a different sort of house-
design or layout of streets. Patients cannot suggest a different kind of
hospital administration. But even if they could these would only be details.
Most of us cannot choose something different in place of the major social
groups to which we belong, one reason being that by the time we have
grown up most of the decisions have been taken for us. In the process of
maturing we have absorbed the values of our society so fully, at an age
when we have had little power of discrimination, that we do not, except at
the margin of our existence, even see the possibility of choice. Family and
school, as the chief civilizing influences upon children, can do their work
too well, civilize too thoroughly, and suppress too much of the emotional
vitality and openness to experience which is the outstanding mark of young
children. As the amount of knowledge increases, and with it the amount
which growing children are expected to absorb in and out of school, so

does the danger of reducing people's emotional vitality and the spontaneity of their response to life. What social research can do is to throw more light not only on the many great benefits conferred by family and school but also on the neglected subject of the harm they do, of the situations in which they contribute not to human fulfilment but to human stultification. The hope is that in time more people will remain more malleable to experience right into their adult lives. In so far as they do, the limits of choice will be widened, both for them as individuals and for the society which is their collective expression. Eventually man should be able to choose not just the house and the hospital but the society which will make possible human fulfilment on a higher level than ever before. He should be able to choose his social destiny, instead of accepting it.

REFERENCES

(1) For a general account of the relevance of sociology to public administration see Shils, E., 'Social Science and Social Policy', *Philosophy of Science*, Vol. 16, 1949, p. 219.

(2) Such research on education was urged in Thomson, Sir George, *The Foreseeable Future*. New York: Cambridge University Press, 1955.

(3) This kind of study was more often made before the Hitler war. See Rowntree, B. S., *Poverty and Progress*. New York: Longmans, 1941.

(4) Young, M., and Willmott, P. *Family and Kinship in East London*. The Free Press of Glencoe, Illinois, 1957.

(5) Professor R. W. Revans in a report not yet published.

(6) Marris, P. *Windows and their Families*. London: Routledge, 1958.

(7) Lipset, S. M., and Bendix, R. *Social Mobility in Industrial Society*. Berkeley: University of California Press, 1959.

(8) Young, M. *The Rise of the Meritocracy*. New York: Random House, 1959.

(9) Homans, G. *The Human Group*. New York: Harcourt, Brace & Co., 1950.

ROBIN MARRIS

HUMANIST ECONOMICS

ROBIN MARRIS

Born 1924. Educated: Bedales and King's
College, Cambridge. At present Director of
Studies in Economics at King's College and
a lecturer in the Economics Faculty at
Cambridge.

Publications: *Economic Arithmetic*, 1958
and (in preparation) 'The Economics of
Managerial Capitalism', also a Fabian
pamphlet 'The Machinery of Economic
Policy', and a number of articles.

HUMANIST ECONOMICS

Man's economic environment is largely of his own making. The majority of significant economic 'laws' express the behaviour of man-made institutions and are not immutable. If we choose to regard an economic system as a rigid framework, and suffer thereby, it is our own fault—the product of conservative ideology rather than scientific analysis.

This proposition is fundamental to the Humanist position. For, as medieval religious sentiment inhibited experiment in natural science, modern political sentiment often inhibits experiment in economic organization. The Humanist believes in purposive social evolution: therefore he cannot agree to treat the behaviour and development of economic systems as passive, mechanical processes: he is bound to visualize these matters as problems of deliberate collective choice.

As a matter of fact professional economics was never as dismal as its image. The 'classical'* writers did not, as is often asserted, believe in unchangeable economic laws, nor did they base their 'science' on purely *a priori* reasoning. They observed the institutions and behaviour of capitalism, they deduced theorems, and often expressed overt political approval. Some did not approve: Marx was one of the classical writers and John Stuart Mill has authoritatively been described as a Socialist.[5] Neither Adam Smith nor Malthus believed that man's economic chains were unbreakable. Smith set out to discover how the wealth of nations may be increased; Malthus, influenced by contemporary population statistics, deduced his theorem from a reasonable interpretation of their implications, then searched for ways in which the 'law' might be prevented from operating: there have been plenty of sniggers at his suggestion that

* There are several accepted definitions of the classical period in economics. In this essay, by 'classical' we mean main-stream writers from Adam Smith (*Wealth of Nations*, 1776) up to and including Karl Marx (*Das Kapital*, 1867):[1] the writers from Jevons (*Political Economy*, 1871), Walras (*Etudes*, 1896) and Marshall (*Principles*, 1898)[2] up to but not including the later Keynes (*General Theory*, 1936)[3] are referred to as 'post-classical', and subsequent work affected by the Keynesian revolution as 'modern'. However, Knut Wicksell, whose first 'Lectures on Political Economy' were published in 1901, anticipated much of modern economics.[4]

clergymen, in conducting marriages, should be compelled to preach on the immorality of conceiving children who cannot be supported, but today we can see that if every priest at every wedding in every country not only preached this sermon but endorsed contraception, the world would be a much better place.*

Adam Smith, faced with only the rudiments of industrial Capitalism, concluded that decentralization and the Invisible Hand[10] would best encourage the growth of wealth. This was a pragmatic argument. He did not say that economic institutions were natural phenomena with immutable laws: he said that the institutional structure implied in the doctrine of *laisser-faire* was a *desirable* structure, on account of inherent properties which, he believed, favoured prosperity. In other words, Adam Smith's advocacy of *laisser-faire* was just as conscious as is, for example, the Socialist advocacy of alternative systems today. Both, in principle, are consistent with the Humanist tradition.

Nevertheless, the popular impact of classical economics was indeed dismal. Whatever the classical writers may or may not have intended, all (except Marx!) contributed to a middle-class ideology of institutional conservatism. And there is considerable force in the accusation that their style of argument encouraged misinterpretation. They seemed to imply that the supply of coal will fall if the price is reduced with the same inevitability as coal released from a height will obey the law of gravity. The fallacy lay in failing to recognize that the relation between price and supply depends on a particular pattern of human institutions and behaviour. This can be changed, and, if we so desire, economic 'laws' be conquered: the conquest of such laws is different in kind from the conquest of gravity by the heroes of science fiction. No professional writer has overtly denied this; but, as already suggested, methods of argument have sometimes implied otherwise.

Throughout social science, the difficulty of conducting controlled experiments (and the difficulty of interpreting uncontrolled observations) both tempts and requires the practitioner to rely on heavily intuitive inductions. Thus introspection suggests that people like to be rich. How then should businessmen behave, we may reasonably ask, if they wish to *maximize* their profits over a finite period? On the single assumption,

* Malthus, himself a priest, regarded contraception as evil, but nineteenth-century neo-Malthusians, such as J. S. Mill, were definitely sympathetic. It has to be admitted that Malthus's first version of the *Essay on Population*, 1798[6] is open to most of the technical criticisms which have been made of it, and the potentialities of abstinence were only recognized in the second version, 1803.[7] Among the *cognoscenti*, Malthus is more respected for his work on a general theory of economic growth than for his specific theory of population.[8, 9]

treated as an axiom, that the aim of business is profit maximization, the analyst can erect an extensive deductive framework—extensive, sophisticated and difficult to test. The scheme's originator may have known what he was doing, but recipients are likely to be persuaded, not only of the internal consistency of the system, but also of the validity of the initial assumption: the latter is supposed to be based on intuitive 'observation', but if it is shaky, the fact is concealed by a glitter of deductive logic, verbal, mathematical, or both.[11]

Modern economics is more empirical than classical and post-classical economics, but some influences from the classical tradition remain: Keynes himself was by no means above criticism in this respect. The university student spends much of his intellectual energy in analytical exercises which embody specific behaviouristic assumptions which he is entitled in principle to question: in practice he rarely does so, for the main object of a training in theoretical economic analysis is to acquire facility in testing logical models for internal consistency. It is possible to show, for example, that the institutions of a society in which supply does *not* tend to fall when price falls must have peculiar properties. This is valuable; but the ideological effects, if not strictly guarded against (and they rarely are), can be dangerous: in particular, from the Humanist point of view, there is considerable danger of fostering pessimism as to the possibilities of reorganizing economic systems or changing economic behaviour.

Can we then delineate a specifically Humanist approach to economics? I believe we can, and suggest that it could be summarized in three principles, which I would call the principle of involvement, the principle of logical realism, and the principle of scientific integrity.

We have seen that although the classical writers did not believe social institutions to be unchangeable, the effect of their work was to rationalize middle-class conservatism. Furthermore, not only classical economics proper, but also post-classical and much of modern economics is fundamentally utilitarian—utilitarian and rationalist, but not necessarily Humanist. People's 'wants and desires' are to be accepted as given data, and the only problems of economics are those of satisfying them. Modern economists, to do them justice, do not deny the possibility of changing wants, but they tend to define their subject in such a way that these questions lie outside it.

This raises two fundamental objections. The first is the scientific objection that the psychological and sociological assumptions are often bad ones, based on inadequate consideration of individual psychology on the one hand and of general sociology on the other. The second, more specifically Humanist objection is that the effect is to suppress discussion of deliberate social change, of the question 'How should man mould his institutions in order to improve his evolution?' When economists suggest policies to governments their prescriptions generally relate to a given set of institutions (Capitalist or Communist as the case may be); they seldom propose new ones. The few professionals who do advocate radical institutional changes are rarely favoured with the highest academic honours, however much they may deserve them. Much is written on the desirable behaviour of central banks, but little as to whether central banks are themselves desirable.

Humanist economics, by contrast, because of the Humanist's concern with psychosocial evolution, will be especially interested in institutional and behavioural development. In this field, Humanist economics will inevitably be tinged with socialism in a very broad sense. Humanist economics, in contrast with purely utilitarian economics,* may share something with the doctrines of certain minority religions, for example with the economic doctrines of primitive or neo-primitive Christianity. The Humanist cannot regard the economic system as outside the sphere of ethics, although he need not, of course, follow the actual practices of the neo-primitive Christian, of the Kibbutz, or of the orthodox Socialist. Indeed, if he believes that any of these practices involve enormous loss of technical efficiency, he may judge that on balance they do not indicate desirable paths of evolution: what he continues to share with these philosophies, however, is their positive approach to the subject. It is this that distinguishes Humanist economics from mere logic, and may be summed up in the principle I have described as 'involvement'.

The principle of involvement carries a corollary. The conscious development of social institutions is impossible without conscious social experiment. At the present time, social experiment is usually regarded in the West as rather shocking—a kind of mass human vivisection. In practice, large-scale social experiments have mainly occurred under dictatorship, but even here the policies have seldom been overtly admitted to be experimental. (Contemporary China may be an exception.) In Western democracies the contrast between the value-tone of the adjective 'experimental' as applied to social and to technical policy is remarkable. In time, social experiment may become as respectable as laboratory experiment; for the Humanist, this time should already have arrived.

The principle of logical realism means no more than that Humanist thinking should always be both logical and realistic. Because we know that by moulding their institutions and behaviour men and women can determine their future, we must not fall into the error of assuming that any

* It is not intended to imply that all modern economics is purely utilitarian.

particular future has only to be striven for to happen, or that any plausible solution will do. The institutions and the behaviour needed to produce the desired results must be precisely specified, and the resultant models, as intellectual creations, be analysed to see that they would in fact possess the properties supposed. And only when viable institutions have been specified can the magnitude of the organizational task be appreciated.* In order usefully to change the environment, it is necessary to have a sense of direction. 'Formal' economic and social theory is therefore an essential weapon in the armoury of the Humanist social scientist, and the Humanist economist must be as vigilant against woolliness, unrealism or *naiveté* as any other. But in being realistic we do not say 'human nature can't be changed'; we try to find out scientifically and logically the ways in which behaviour can be changed usefully. It follows, among other things, that Humanist economics should pay more attention to psychology than economics has hitherto done.

Finally, the principle of scientific integrity. In all social science this requires particular emphasis. Our typical subject-matter has three characteristics which, in combination, create unique difficulties: social systems are structurally complex, structurally unstable, and not readily susceptible to experiment in the laboratory sense. All complex systems, social or natural, are difficult to define and analyse, and if in addition the complex structure is unstable, the problems are redoubled. Nevertheless, provided laboratory-type experiments are possible, some hypotheses about such systems can usually be verified, as the results of population genetics, microbiology and general biochemistry demonstrate daily. At the other extreme, astronomers, although unable to manipulate their objects, can adequately test many of their theories by uncontrolled observation alone, because macro-spatial relationships are relatively stable and relatively simple. In social science, experiment is inhibited not only by the political objections of the potential subjects, but also, more than in any other field, by the fact that even if subjects agree to participate, the experimenter cannot avoid interference: people who know they are subjects of experiments tend to behave unnaturally.

Methods for overcoming some of these difficulties have been successfully developed for a limited range of problems in social psychology, but it is not easy to envisage corresponding solutions in economics. Economics, therefore, is bound to be mainly an observational and analytic discipline. And, almost self-evidently, the observations are mainly statistics, and will

* In other words, experiments in action should be preceded by experiments in thought. But the latter are not substitutes for the former; theory, to be adequately tested, must be practically applied.

need to be interpreted by statistical methods. The statistical method of testing hypotheses has been very successful where the causal relations under study are simple or, if complex, are comprehensively understood, so that extraneous factors can be controlled. But where these conditions do not apply, the results obtainable, although often suggestive, are inevitably inconclusive.[12] Such cases are, unfortunately, typical in social science. In the various natural sciences, problems which appear similar often turn out not to be so, and only relatively rarely does the natural experimenter face up to unstable complex systems, every one of whose variables is outside his control. When he does, he is often just as embarrassed as the social scientist: he finds hypotheses not only difficult to 'prove' but, more serious, impossible to disprove. Thus, not long ago, a geneticist and statistician of world distinction publicly questioned the significance of the statistical association between smoking and lung cancer on these grounds: in economics, analogous situations arise daily.

This position places a considerable strain on scientific integrity. There are two temptations—one evident, the second less obvious. Because of the difficulty of testing, empirical investigators in the social sciences are subject to unusually strong temptations to find what they are looking for, while theorists are equally strongly tempted to set up hypotheses which are inherently untestable. And where tests are carried out, and prove negative, the results can be discounted by recourse to the argument that the situation (of necessity) was incompletely controlled. The history of many sciences demonstrates an early phase of obscurantism, of domination by theories which in retrospect are seen to have been absurd. But in the majority of these histories, at least since the end of the seventeenth century, the source of error was usually to be found in the demands of some individual scientist's ego. In economics, because of the evident political implications of economic theory, the desire to rationalize whole ideologies has been even more compelling. The position has some similarity to that of natural philosophy before the age of reason; lacking the empirical facts and technique for explaining phenomena, people turned to religion: the modern social scientist is not usually religious, but almost as bad, he is often implicitly ideological.

The alternative offence against scientific integrity is an exaggerated reaction to the first, and it too has some affinity to religious evils. Because few hypotheses in social science can be conclusively 'proved', suggestive results can always be derided, and the sceptic left in undisturbed possession of his preconceived ideas. He wishes to believe that flogging is good for offenders, or that unemployment holds down wages, and he remains totally unshaken by the evidence, if any, of 'cold statistics'. Men created theologies because they could not understand the natural world. Today, many people do not want to understand social phenomena for fear of what they may learn; they escape by denying the validity of all types of probabilistic reasoning. This exaggerated scepticism of social and economic hypotheses is totally sterile, except as a source of much practical inhumanity; by rationalizing inertia, it often sanctions cruelty or starvation.

Humanist economics, following the principle of scientific integrity, must attempt the difficult task of steering a true course in a sea strewn with dangers from bad theory, phoney experimentation and exaggerated scepticism. Such a course does not involve the rejection of political value-judgments; indeed, it must often employ these, but the political values must be frank and open, and not, as is frequently the case, concealed in deductive apparatus. Humanist economics will fully employ mathematics, but will not restrict their application to models based on the assumption that institutions and behaviour can be treated as given, and therefore exogenous to the problem. For Humanist economics must observe above all others the principle of involvement, and will accept the duty to investigate desirable directions in which institutions and behaviour may be changed. Even today it is not conclusively proved that smoking causes lung cancer, but the data now available create a sufficient degree of probability in favour of the hypothesis that a reasonably intelligent person, familiar with them, is committing statistical murder if at any time he abets in the initiation of an addict: a person who repeatedly initiates addicts will eventually be responsible for one or more actual murders. By the same token, an economist, for instance one who is not a Humanist, who asserts that *laisser-faire* is the best policy for contemporary under-developed countries is as culpable as the priest who exhorts the governments of these countries to discourage birth-control.

It will be obvious that we have been describing Humanist economic principles against the background of thought and organization of industrial Capitalism. Much of what we have been saying might appear to have little application elsewhere: it is difficult to decide whether this impression is correct. Clearly the Humanist economic sermon is of great importance in the uncommitted, undeveloped countries. In Russia and China, it is an open question whether, at the *economic* level, an important part of the code we have suggested is not being followed. Obviously in these countries there is at least *prima facie* evidence of belief in the principle of involvement.* In Russia, also, there is evidence of application

* Although it is one thing to engage in social experiment in a spirit of collective institutional adventure, and quite another to do so at the hands of autocratic government.

of the principle of logical realism, but, in the social sphere, the principle of scientific integrity is still paid little respect. The quasi-religious outlook in social thought may have waned since Stalin, but is still prevalent. Nevertheless, these are countries where far-reaching re-appraisals of whole systems of social and economic organization really happen, where programmes for organizing millions of peasants into rural communes can be initiated one year and drastically modified the next, and where desk workers can never be sure they will not suddenly be sent to work in factories: in such countries, it cannot be denied, potentially Humanist social experiment is far in advance of the West. This emphasizes that economics represents only a small part of the Humanist frame: inhuman and outrageous political systems, which happen to follow some Humanist economic principles, do not make a Humanist society.

How will a Humanist economist, then, see the West? I do not think there is a definite answer, for different individuals may apply the same set of principles and reach different results. What follows is personal, and I make no secret, socialistically biased. Western Capitalism has evolved a system of economic organization based on a considerable degree of decentralization. The institutions which undertake the greater part of direct economic activity are operationally autonomous: each Capitalist 'firm' plays what amounts to a game with other firms and with the economy as a whole. The character of the game is ill-defined. In classical and some post-classical economics it was assumed that the result could be described by a theoretical model involving intense price-competition. Only if the players 'cheated' by forming combinations would the system fail to behave in an ideal fashion. No one any longer believes all this. The autonomous organizations compete, and fail to compete, in many different ways: relations between them are better described as a condition of rivalry rather than strict economic competition. Part of the system remains classically competitive, but the other part consists of a few hundred giant corporations controlling half the industrial assets of the whole Capitalist sector. The result, in a narrow sense, is not inefficient, and these economies have been able to display rapid economic growth in political conditions which for all their drawbacks were far more reasonable than those of Stalin.[13] There are people who believe that the whole represents a masterpiece of social organization, reached by something akin to a natural evolutionary development. At the other extreme are those who regard the system and its results as little less than a perversion of human destiny. These critics include various types of neo-Marxist, together with others whose complaints are less precise and more variable in severity— they complain of excessive materialism, of 'commercialism', of a 'machine age', of 'admass' and of a general decline in the quality of economic life. Many are also concerned about new and unpleasant stratifying tendencies, new class tensions and conflicts, closely associated with the emergent economic pattern of the 'affluent society'.[14] Much of this has a Humanist flavour, although a good deal offends Humanist requirements by being woolly, naïve, often prejudiced and often (a personal objection this) rather puritan. At its best, however, the criticism is powerful, and seems to rationalize a general disquiet at the inability of Capitalism to organize *purposive* development. The disquiet is currently stimulated by fear of material competition from the successful Communist countries. For example, Professor Kennan, speaking in 1959, is reported as saying:

'If you ask me—as a historian let us say—whether a country in the state this country is in today, with no highly developed sense of national purpose, with the overwhelming accent of life on personal comfort and amusement, with a dearth of public services and a surfeit of privately sold gadgetry, with a chaotic transportation system, with its great urban areas being gradually disintegrated by the headlong switch of motor transportation, with an educational system where quality has been extensively sacrificed to quantity, and with insufficient social discipline even to keep its major industries functioning without grievous interruptions—if you ask me whether such a country has, over the long run, good chances of competing with a purposeful, serious and disciplined society such as that of the Soviet Union, I must say that the answer is "no!" '[15]

Kennan here throws everything but the kitchen sink, but the particular significance of his outburst, and of similar tirades by J. K. Galbraith,[14] is that they have no Socialist origins. The central theme clearly deserves investigation, for Kennan particularly implies that contemporary Capitalism is incapable of purposive evolution.

The character of 'managerial' Capitalism is moulded by the logic of the corporate system. For while it is true that a large proportion of the national capital—roads, schools, hospitals, public offices and much public housing—is administered collectively, most of the dynamic power remains in the 'private' sector: the behaviour of the private corporations sets the tone for behaviour in the economy as a whole. Up to 1950 the balance of power between the private and the collective sectors was probably moving in favour of the latter: both in Britain and the United States the period from 1930 to 1950 saw considerable extensions of public enterprise. The us Tenessee Valley Authority, the British National Health Service, and the development of atomic energy in both countries are outstanding successful examples. But in the last decade, the trend has been reversed. The very considerable financial success of private enterprise has enabled the large corporations almost to take over the State: more precisely, they have collaborated with government to such an extent that it is increasingly their directors, rather than professional politicians, who determine the pace and character of economic change.* Their type of economic activity and their economic ethic is increasingly dominant, and valuable collective activities such as the organization of education, public health, public housing and the arts become national Cinderellas. The tendency may be only incipient in Britain but, Galbraith argues, is already well advanced in the United States.† 'What's good for General Motors is good for the country' has become a serious political philosophy.

It is possible that the theme is exaggerated. Perhaps the relationship between public and private consumption has got out of line simply because, while standards generally have risen, public expenditure has temporarily lagged. That the imbalance cannot be corrected without radical political reorganization is not self-evident. And, from the point of view of Humanist economics, there is no *a priori* presumption against private pleasures, or against uneven development. The mechanics of managerial Capitalism require considerable further analysis before we can confidently assert that they are inevitably deleterious to human evolution. Furthermore, the fear of being 'buried' by Mr Krushchev is only partly relevant: if our chosen methods are in the long run superior, it is our task to defend them from short-run aggression, economic or military.

The industrial units of managerial Capitalism are of all sizes, but the most significant are large. The giants are of course generally subdivided into smaller units—factories and subsidiaries where the majority of people work. The 'firm' is essentially an administrative entity, and, following the familiar history of separation between ownership and control, it is an institution with an autonomous dynamic of its own: it grows, or fails to

---

* I do not discuss the effects of Trade Union power, because I am convinced that in contemporary conditions this is largely negative.

† A celebrated passage deserves quoting in full:

'The family which takes its mauve and cerise, air-conditioned, power-steered and power-braked car out for a tour passes through cities that are badly paved, made hideous by litter, blighted buildings, bill-boards and posts for wires that should long since have been put underground. They pass into a countryside that has been rendered largely invisible by commercial art. (The goods which the latter advertize have an absolute priority in our value-system. Such aesthetic considerations as a view of the countryside accordingly come second. On such matters we are consistent.) They picnic on exquisitely packaged food from a portable icebox by a polluted stream and go on to spend a night at a park which is a menace to public health and morals. Just before dozing off on an air mattress, to the stench of decaying refuse, they may reflect vaguely on the curious unevenness of their blessings.'

grow, much in the manner of a tree, and this behaviour can no longer be explained exclusively in terms of the financial ambitions of a single individual. Typically, Capitalist firms are both technically efficient and financially dynamic: the greater their financial success, the more rapidly they grow in terms of both capital and manpower; this characteristic is conducive to good internal morale. Because the organization grows on the basis of its own success (a process which has many analogies to biological selection) there is a tendency for the most effective administrative structures to be developed: it is efficient administration as much as anything else which creates morale.

Where then lies the criticism? It lies in the fact that the corporations, though individually efficient, are collectively aimless. They have evolved by organic growth in a system which requires them to create the demands for their own products. This they do very well. In effect, they create their own environment, but they create aimlessly. Given their size, and given the proven effectiveness of advertising, the idea that in playing this game the companies can do no more than react passively to the exogenous desires of society is as dead as Queen Victoria: they succeed by creating wants, not by meeting them. The role of the consumer is rather like that of the oval ball in a rugby football game: we know that its movements are entirely determined—although in a complicated way—by the actions of the various players, however much, to the players themselves, it may seem to have a mind of its own.

This analogy is good only up to a point. For although we can say that the objective of scoring goals corresponds to the objective of corporate financial success, sporting games differ from this economic game in possessing relatively clearly defined rules, rules which are designed for the conscious purpose of creating a stimulating competition; both public and players have a fairly clear idea of what constitutes a 'good game' even though they may argue about the best rules for achieving it. By contrast, in the economic game not only are the important rules ill-defined and frequently changing, but the players (the directors of the corporations) seem to be making up many of them as they go along. This fact enhances the overall sense of purposelessness. To put it another way, social systems which behave like badly controlled games are unlikely, in the modern world, to foster human evolution. There is no reason to suppose that the 'market' will evolve a pattern of 'behaviour' which is desirable even in the narrowest biological sense,* let alone one which represents a pattern consistent with our broader aims. More serious is the substantial political power in the hands of the corporate players: the control of

* Again one cites lung cancer.

corporate wealth has become considerably more important than control of
the ballot-box; also, with modern methods of promotion, the control of
corporate wealth provides significant influence on ballot-box results.
Consequently, not only are we over-concerned with maximizing the
production of refrigerators, we are conditioned to oppose the doing of
anything much else.

The corporations have great power, yet, in the political sense, little
responsibility. In general they are of course run by 'responsible' men,
i.e. men who behave reasonably according to their own lights. But in the
political and social sense these men are responsible to no one, neither (for
all practical purposes) to shareholders, nor to any other individuals, nor
to society. That they behave decently at the local level is no answer: for
they certainly do not interpret their duties as comprehending general
human development; and, if they did, there is no particular reason to
suppose that their scale of values would necessarily be acceptable. It is
therefore at least arguable that a reorganization of economic power is a
necessary, if not a sufficient condition for progress.

This is not the place to specify programmes, but it is essential, before
concluding, to emphasize that a society which has once been Capitalist
can never be the same as one that has not. Communism, as it developed in
Russia and China, was an alternative to the Capitalist phase of development, not a successor. The Communist method is extremely crude, and
has permitted rapid economic growth in Russia not because of any
superior technique in the detailed allocation of resources, but solely
because of the political power of the Communist State to restrain total
consumption and to free large *quantities* of resources for investment: the
use made of these resources has been clumsy, but the quantities involved
have been so great that important results were almost inevitable (it is true,
however, that predictions of total irrationality in resource allocation, and
hence ultimate breakdown, prove to have been exaggerated). It follows
that the imposition of what are evocatively called 'state monopolies' on an
already highly developed Capitalist industrial structure will do very little
good. The correct solution seems to lie in a radical alteration of the legal
and social basis of the basic Capitalist units of industrial organization—
the public companies—designed to maintain their present internal
advantages while reducing their irresponsible powers. If the autonomous
firm were deprived of its indirect political power, the State—expressing
the collective ideals of society—would much more effectively be able to
manipulate the environment in which the corporations operate and the
people live. The State, regaining its independence, would be able to
restore the prestige and quality of collective consumption, and become

able, purposively, for the first time, to guide economic development. Long-term general economic planning, an almost forgotten idea in the West, does not require total nationalization of industry, but it does require a favourable political milieu. While directors are nominally responsible to shareholders, and while shareholders (who are naturally concerned only with the value of their investment) are nominally the owners of industry, a favourable milieu is impossible. The solution would seem to lie in the abolition of shareholders, and in the creation of a legal structure in which directors of companies were made overtly responsible to their employees and to society at large.[17]

Successful institutional reforms must, of course, express a definite popular intention. They rarely occur in an unfavourable climate of opinion. 'Imposed' reorganizations usually fail. Unless an influential minority actively wants purposive development, and unless the majority is prepared to be led in this direction, no amount of tinkering with organizational machinery will be successful. Social organizations are collectives of individuals, and therefore depend intimately on the outlook and character of their members. It follows that the Humanist economist has to be a propagandist just as much as the Humanist specialist in any other field.

But although a favourable climate of opinion is a necessary condition of progress, it is not a sufficient one. Machinery does matter. Good institutions are better than the sum of their members and a people passionately desiring progress will not necessarily succeed in evolving suitable institutions. With the best will in the world, they may fail to find solutions which, to the objective analyst, might seem obvious. The proper contribution of the Humanist social scientist is a combination of analysis and propaganda. At present, there are not many practitioners.

REFERENCES AND SELECT BIBLIOGRAPHY

(1) The following is a list of relevant classical texts. They are mostly available in numerous editions and are therefore here dated by year of first publication alone:

Smith, Adam, *An Inquiry into the Nature and Causes of the Wealth of Nations*, 1776.

Malthus, Rev. T. R. *Essay on the Principle of Population*, 1st edn. 1798, revised edn. 1803.

Ricardo, David. *The Principles of Political Economy and Taxation*, 1817.

Malthus, Rev. T. R. *Principles of Political Economy with a View to their Practical Application*, 1820.

Senior, Nassau. *An Outline of Political Economy*, 1836.

Mill, John Stuart. *Principles of Political Economy*, 1848.

Marx, Karl. *Capital: A Critique of Political Economy*, Vol. I, The Process of Capitalist Production, 1867.

(2) Jevons, Stanley. *The Theory of Political Economy*, 1st edn. 1871, revised edn. 1879.

Walras, Leon. *Etudes d'economie politique appliquée*, 1896.

Marshall, Alfred. *Principles of Economics.* 1896.

(3) Keynes, Maynard. *The General Theory of Employment, Interest and Money.* New York: Harcourt, Brace & Company, 1936.

(4) Wicksell, Knut. *Lectures on Political Economy*, 1st Swedish editions 1901 to 1906, 1st English translations, ed. Lionel Robbins. New York: Macmillan, 1934-1935.

(5) See Schumpeter, Joseph, *History of Economic Analysis.* New York: Oxford University Press, 1954.

(6) See Malthus, *op cit.*

(7) Malthus, *op cit.*

(8) See for example Benjamin Higgins. *Economic Development.* New York: Norton, 1959.

(9) Malthus. *Principles of Political Economy with a View to their Practical Application,* 1820.

(10) Smith's celebrated reference to an Invisible Hand leading the individual in the right economic direction as a result of market forces can be found on p. 385 of the 1925 (London) edition of the *Wealth of Nations,* edited by W. R. Scott.

(11) For example, see Nassau Senior, *op cit.*

(12) See R. A. Fisher, *Statistical Methods for Research Workers.* London and Edinburgh: Oliver & Boyd; first published 1938, p. 193 (7th edition) *et seq.*

(13) See Edward Crankshaw, *Russia Without Stalin: The Emerging Pattern.* New York: Viking, 1956; and Alexandre Métaxas. *Russia Against the Kremlin.* New York: World Publishing Company, 1957.

(14) The following is a selection of readings on these themes:

Galbraith, John Kenneth. *The Affluent Society.* Boston: Houghton Mifflin, 1958.

Hoggart, Richard. *The Uses of Literacy.* New York: Oxford University Press, 1957.

Keats, John. *The Insolent Chariots.* New York: Lippincott, 1958.

Krutch, Joseph Wood. *Human Nature and the Human Condition.* New York: Random House, 1959.

Mackenzie, Norman (ed.). *Conviction.* New York: Monthly Review Press, 1959.

Mills, C. Wright. *The Power Elite.* New York: Oxford University Press, 1956.

Packard, Vance. *The Hidden Persuaders.* New York: McKay, 1957.

Packard, Vance. *The Status Seekers.* New York: McKay, 1959; London: Longmans, 1959.

Packard, Vance. *The Waste Makers.* New York: MacKay, 1960.

Riesman, David. *The Lonely Crowd.* Yale University Press, 1950.

Whyte, William J., Jr. *The Organization Man.* New York: Simon & Schuster, 1957.

And articles by Edward Hymans, J. B. Priestley and others in the London *New Statesman,* 1950-60.

(15) From an address to the Women's National Democratic Club, U.S.A., October 22, 1959, reproduced in a pamphlet obtainable from 'Towards an Enduring Peace Inc.', 112 Beech Avenue, Woodmont, Connecticut.

(16) Galbraith, *op cit.,* p. 196.

(17) For further reading see George Goyder, *The Future of Private Enterprise.* New York: Macmillan, 1951; and Robin Marris, articles in London *Encounter,* September 1958, and London *Socialist Commentary,* December 1959.

SUDHIR SEN

NEW HORIZONS FOR UNDER-DEVELOPED
PEOPLES

SUDHIR SEN, B.A., B.SC., PH.D.

Born 1906. Educated: Calcutta University; London School of Economics and Bonn University. Director of Programme Division, Technical Assistance Board of the United Nations.

Publications: *Conflict of Economic Ideologies in India*, 1941; *Land and Its Problems*, 1943; *Tagore on Rural Reconstruction*, 1943; and numerous articles.

NEW HORIZONS FOR UNDER-DEVELOPED
PEOPLES

I

In its long evolutionary process mankind has been moving towards a higher pattern of values. The progress has been neither smooth nor uniform; there have been many setbacks, and some cruel lapses; but the general trend is unmistakable—on balance, man's humanity to man has been on the increase, and, in very recent years, thanks to a unique combination of social and historical forces, it has received an unprecedented impetus.

Since the dawn of history every age has been marked by exploitation and persecution, at the hands of tribal chiefs, feudal lords, monarchs, dictators, capitalists, and churches. In the most flourishing ancient civilizations large-scale exploitation was taken for granted. The pyramids provide a massive proof of the skill and workmanship developed in Egypt five thousand years ago, but also of the forced labour extracted from the people on a staggering scale.

Post-Aryan India, with all its transcendental philosophy, found it necessary to justify and uphold a cruel caste system. The Greek cities, which did so much to enrich and beautify life, were constantly waging ruthless wars among themselves, and relied heavily on the institution of slavery. And we need hardly recall the Mongol invasions under Jenghiz Khan and Timur, with their orgies of devastation, slaughter and wanton destruction which caused a permanent setback to civilization in the Middle East.

2

With the discovery of the New World and of a new route to the Orient, the era of modern colonialism began. In the wake of exploration came exploitation. Many tragedies were enacted, including the slave trade and the destruction of the remarkable civilizations of the Incas, the Aztecs and the Mayas.

The colonial policies pursued by the European colonial powers showed striking differences in political administration, but economically they had an identical core. Colonies were valued for their precious metals, rare spices and raw materials, for their man-power and markets or their strategic value; they were treated as possessions whose sole business was to promote the greatness of the mother-country. Given this major premiss, three conclusions followed: a colony must trade only with the mother-country; it must not develop manufactures that would compete with 'home' industries; and it must concede a monopoly of its carrying trade to 'home' shipping. This one-sided arrangement was sanctified by the Mercantilists, who raised it to the status of an economic doctrine.

Exploitation continued as the keynote of colonialism until very recently. Yet the colonialist record was by no means uniformly dark. Thus a major impulse behind British power in Africa was humanitarian—to abolish the slave trade. The Western colonial authority curbed inter-tribal rivalry, unified small tribes or princely states, and created more viable units capable of developing into independent nations. Western democratic institutions were often introduced, and became the basis for government after independence. Although Europeans brought new diseases, they also introduced modern medicine and public health measures. Capital investments, though made primarily for the benefit of home interests, also produced economic and social progress in the colonies; as a by-product, they stimulated the growth of nationalism.

British rule in India stands out as an example of complex motivation. Adventure, empire-building, power politics, economic exploitation, all these were assuredly involved; but inextricably mingled with them was the urge to establish peace on the sub-continent; to foster trade and improve communications; to introduce democratic institutions with an independent judiciary; and set up an efficient administration which, at least partially, endeavoured to fulfil the responsibilities of a modern state, and to train Indians to play a significant part in that administration. Even when the national movement for independence was at its peak, the best Indian minds were not oblivious of the weighty entries to be made on the credit side of the ledger. The severest charge levelled against the British rule by men like Gandhi and Tagore was also the most revealing: that, in governing India, Britain had failed to uphold her own cherished principles and belied the hopes she had herself engendered; that, in short, she had let *herself* down.

There is another extenuating factor. Colonial exploitation went hand in hand with exploitation within the mother-country. The difference, though significant, was one of degree. This was most clearly seen in the early phases of the Industrial Revolution, when, to use Goldsmith's words, wealth accumulated and men decayed.

Even today in the economically developed countries, we find under-developed areas where people have to eke out a precarious living. In the USA the South was for long virtually a colony of the industrial North, overwhelmingly dependent on the cultivation of three crops—cotton, tobacco and corn. In the last twenty-five years the balance has been largely redressed, owing primarily to the imaginative lead given by the TVA. Pockets of such internal colonialism persist in parts of Latin America and many other lands, where people suffer from chronic economic neglect or downright exploitation, or from racial, religious, or ideological intolerance.

3

Before the Second World War, about one-third of the world's population and its land area was under some kind of colonial rule. Since then no less than thirty-nine new states have been born, with a total population of over 800 millions. In 1960 alone, eighteen countries, containing some 82 million people, came into existence, and several more will have done so during 1961. The end of traditional colonialism is definitely in sight.

Freedom for almost a billion colonial people within two decades is something unique in human history. This political breakthrough is all the more striking as it synchronizes with breakthroughs in almost every aspect of human life—in industry and agriculture; in transportation and communication; in health and nutrition; in weaponry and space exploration; and in all fields of natural and human science. Suddenly, in one generation, new vistas of possibility have opened up, launching the world in general and the under-developed peoples in particular on what has been called the Revolution of Expectation.

The dynamism of our times has been heightened, but also distorted, by the explosive growth of population. The under-developed countries are now caught in a fateful race between population and living standards, thereby reviving the old Malthusian nightmare. Population is increasing at a 'geometric ratio', especially in the under-developed countries, but living standards are creeping up in an 'arithmetic ratio', if not remaining static.

This situation stems from a glaring imbalance in harnessing the forces of progress. Advances in science and technology have created the means to liquidate mass poverty and to achieve all-round progress all over the globe. But their applications have been largely confined to two major fields.

The continuing revolution in transport and communication is penetrating into all corners of the earth, spreading new hopes among the under-developed peoples. And these hopes are stimulated by the examples of Soviet Russia and China, which are compressing into decades the industrial progress that the Western countries took centuries to achieve.

It is, above all, in medicine and health that the under-developed peoples have tasted the fruits of scientific progress. The mass killers or cripplers, like malaria, smallpox, cholera, and tuberculosis, are now rapidly in retreat, or even in process of being completely eradicated. The result is a steeply falling death-rate and a marked lengthening of life-expectancy; and since the fertility rate has remained practically stable, populations have explosively increased. But the application of medical science has remained one-sided. It has almost completely neglected a crucial subject —birth-control.

4

Current thinking on birth-control often lacks realism, as was highlighted by the recent controversy on the wisdom or desirability of giving assistance to under-developed countries in this field. First, to give or not to give is not the main issue. For assistance cannot be forcibly imposed; it can be given only on request. Secondly, contrary to widespread impressions, the opposition to birth-control on religious or ideological grounds is often stronger in Western countries than, say, the East. Ten years ago the need for limiting population was almost ignored in India: today, it has become an urgent matter of high national policy. By the end of 1961, India should have 2,500 clinics established to help check the growth of population. The real obstacles in India are not religious but administrative, educational, and economic.

It is sometimes argued that the first task before an under-developed country is population-control and that, without this, economic development would be fruitless. This sounds plausible, but it contains a treacherous pitfall. A population policy standing by itself can never succeed; to be really effective, it must be integrated with a broad-based programme of economic development. To disseminate the main facts about population and its control among the masses of people in a country like India, and to bring the means of control within their reach, physically and financially, is a gigantic task; it can never be tackled adequately without a high development of transport and communications, of education, and of a wide range of industry.

Concentration on population-control to the neglect of economic development is certainly not the answer: but neither is concentration on economic development to the neglect of population-control. The right balance between population and resources can be achieved only if a bold population policy is integrated with an equally bold policy for economic development.

5

What, then, is the magnitude of the effort needed to stage such an economic blitz? Let us take a brief look at the effort being made by the United Nations and its Specialized Agencies for promoting economic development. Judged by magnitude of capital investment, the World Bank takes pride of place. By the end of 1960 it had made 270 loans to 53 countries for a total of $5,454 million.

The Bank has already been of unique service to the under-developed countries. At a time when they were threatened by a capital famine, the Bank has been funnelling funds for long-term investment into them on an increasing scale. The authorized capital of the Bank was raised last year from $10,000 million to $21,000 million. This accretion of financial strength will enable the Bank to step up its loans considerably.

The establishment of the new International Development Association (IDA) as an affiliate of the Bank, which should soon commence its operation, is an important landmark. Its loans will carry less stringent terms than those of the Bank. The interest charged will be lower; the period of repayment will be longer; loans will be repayable in soft currency where necessary; most important of all, projects will be eligible for loans even if not 'revenue-producing or directly productive'. Every project must satisfy one decisive test, namely, that it will make 'an important contribution to the development of the area or areas concerned'. IDA will give soft loans; but it will not be a soft lender.

The International Finance Corporation (IFC) was established in 1956 as an international source of equity capital, primarily for financing industries in under-developed countries. Its total capital is now $97.0 million, subscribed by 60 member countries; it has already made 37 investment commitments totalling $45.0 million in 17 countries. Although IFC has so far been operating in low gear, it has high potentialities.

The International Monetary Fund plays an important role in this context. Its task is to promote exchange stability as a basis for the growth of world trade, to give temporary help to nations seeking to stabilize their currencies, and to maintain or achieve currency convertibility, all essential prerequisites for economic development. By October 31, 1960, the Fund had made available a total of $3,871 million for these purposes.

The provision of long-term development loans from the World Bank and its affiliates is paralleled by the provision of technical assistance through the United Nations and eight of its Specialized Agencies—ILO, UNESCO, FAO, WHO, ICAO, ITU, WMO and IAEA.

First comes the so-called Expanded Programme of Technical Assistance, which has just completed its tenth year of operation. The Expanded Programme is financed by voluntary contributions which now come from 89 governments. The bulk of them are from the economically advanced countries of Europe and America; but the under-developed nations also figure at the contributing end. The Programme, which began with a budget of about $18 million, now involves about $40 million a year. In the last ten years something like $260 million has been spent by the UN and its agencies on it. To this should be added the counterpart support from the receiving governments, which should easily add up to twice this amount.

The most interesting feature of the Programme is not its size but its content; not the amount of money spent, but what it is spent on. Nearly three-quarters of the funds go to finance the services of experts in various fields; some 10 per cent is spent on equipment to make the experts' work more effective; the remaining 15 per cent is used for fellowships for training nationals of the receiving countries so that they may in due course step into the shoes of international experts.

There is a two-way flow of experts. Naturally most of them are drawn from the economically advanced countries, but by no means all. Thus in 1959 Chile both received and supplied 41 experts; India received 146 and supplied 109; the United Arab Republic received 129 and supplied 56. The fellowship programme shows a similar feature: last year 70 Mexicans were awarded fellowships to study abroad and 64 nationals of other countries were placed at training centres in Mexico. At present there is a task force of some 2,300 experts serving in various parts of the under-developed world on behalf of the Expanded Programme.

Some activities of the Programmes are aimed at creating the prerequisites of progress—for example, expert services in public administration, fundamental education, and teacher-training, or in pre-investment activities.

Many of its projects are immediately productive. In the heavily populated countries of Asia, it is customary to speak of 'labour-intensive' or 'capital-intensive' projects. To this conventional classification we might add another category: 'know-how intensive' projects where progress depends on the acquisition of a new skill or technique. The best hopes of the under-developed world lie in such projects, where small expenditures can yield big results. As the Secretary-General of the UN,

Mr. Hammarskjold, has said, 'a technical assistance programme may generate great results from small beginnings. It is a spark and a catalyst.'

A few examples may be noted. In Afghanistan, the substitution of a locally manufactured scythe for the traditional sickle enabled farmers to double their grain harvests. In Thailand, a vaccine developed by a British veterinarian has almost eliminated the Newcastle disease which was threatening the poultry flocks (the vaccine had to be administered by medicine dropper in order not to wound Buddhist susceptibilities). In Indonesia, experts evolved a substitute for milk from vitamin-rich soya bean. In Egypt, a Chinese expert stimulated the introduction of new strains of rice, which led to a tremendous increase in rice production: today rice ranks second only to cotton in Egypt's exports. In Haiti, a Belgian expert introduced better agronomic practices which led to a sevenfold increase in the potato harvest.

Apart from participating in the Expanded Programme, the UN and its Specialized Agencies provide sizeable amounts of assistance under their Regular Programmes—last year to the tune of $14 million. The United Nations Children's Fund, as a rule in close co-operation with WHO, with an annual budget around of $28 million, is currently assisting 387 projects in 106 countries and territories.

The UN itself, through its Office of Public Administration, has been giving assistance to strengthen the administrative machinery in many countries. Its budget for this purpose is only $300,000 a year, but is now being increased. The creation of the so-called OPEX programme in 1958 marks another step in the same direction. It authorized the Secretary-General to assist governments, on request, to obtain international administrators for operational or executive duties.

Finally, there is the Special Fund, established in 1959. It falls far short of the original proposal to set up a billion-dollar capital development fund to be called SUNFED—the Special United Nations Fund for Economic Development. It exists primarily to carry out pre-investment activities in order to facilitate the inflow of development capital. Like the Expanded Programme, it is financed by voluntary contributions, and the present goal is that the two, taken together, should reach an annual total of $100 million as soon as possible. The Special Fund swung into action with remarkable speed. Within two years it approved 115 projects costing $227 million, including $131 million of local expenditures by governments.

In spite of its limitations, the establishment of the Special Fund is a significant accretion of strength to the United Nations programme of aiding under-developed peoples. Its efforts are concentrated on three key areas—training, research, and surveys of natural resources; its emphasis is on creating opportunities for capital investment to raise production and productivity; and it seeks to assist only those projects which can make quick and substantial contributions towards that objective.

To complete the picture, mention must be made of programmes outside the UN. The largest is the US programme, operated through the International Cooperation Administration (ICA), though the bulk of its money is spent for military objectives. The Export-Import Bank and the Development Loan Fund, through their bilateral lending, play an important role as additional sources of finance. Most of the industrially advanced countries, including Britain, France, the German Federal Republic and the Soviet Union, have their own programmes of bilateral assistance. Lastly, there are the regional programmes: the Colombo Plan for South and South-East Asia, and the recently created Inter-American Development Fund.

During the last decade the idea of assisting the under-developed peoples has struck firm root in the world's conscience and in its economic systems. The main ideological battle has been won; and with the establishment of the Special Fund and of IDA, *institutional* adequacy has been achieved. The big question now is how to attain *financial* adequacy.

6

The volume of assistance currently provided to the under-developed countries is estimated at around $2,400 million a year. The inflow of private investment capital amounts to about $1,600 million, making a total of $4,000 million a year, as against an annual inflow of only about $500 million during the 1920s. But today's inflow must be related to today's prices and to today's needs, which are incomparably higher than three decades ago. Assuming a total population of 1,250 million in the under-developed countries, excluding China, $4 billion means an investment of just over $3 a head. This gives an increase of about 1 per cent a year, not enough to make an effective dent in the problem of raising their living standards.

Can this rate of growth be raised appreciably in the near future? And how much additional capital would be needed? The figure most frequently cited is $3,000 million. This is supposed to represent the optimum amount of new foreign capital which the under-developed countries could effectively absorb each year; and it would double their present rate of capital growth. This should enable the under-developed countries to be given their first sensation of real progress. Moreover, capital pumped in at this rate for ten or fifteen years should be enough for perhaps a dozen among them to break through to the state of dynamic self-propelling economies.

Many under-developed countries still lack the rudiments of a rational development policy. Projects may be launched without enough thought about their economic or their administrative feasibility, or because they appeal to the national ego. The development policy of most under-developed countries needs greater emphasis on production, coupled with stricter screening of projects.* For fixing priorities among projects three criteria need to be consistently applied: how large are the benefits, in terms of extra income units, expected from a particular project; how soon can these be realized; and at what cost.

7

In judging the question of how much at what cost, it is essential to consider not only the *money* cost, but also the *resource* cost. The emphasis must be shifted from exploitation of resources for immediate profit accompanied by a reckless disregard of the future, to their rational development, conservation and utilization.

In nature, water, air and soil minerals work in continuous harmony to support plant and animal life on earth. In spite of all the technical miracles achieved by science, man must respect this basic ecological balance. Yet in many parts of the world, out of ignorance or from immediate material necessity, man has been working at cross-purposes with nature. He abuses land by burning forests, excessive lumbering, ploughing up grasslands, cultivating row-crops on steep slopes, mining the soil's fertility. The result is accelerated erosion, often with irreparable loss of the top soil. Erosion leads to poorer crops, poorer cattle and poorer men on the one hand, and faster run-off, silted-up river-beds and aggravated floods on the other. This spiral of waste must be halted and reversed. It can be done: the cardinal principles for developing entire river basins on sound lines are now well known, though too often they are ignored in practice.

A rational resources policy should aim at increasing wealth and income, employment and enjoyment. It has two important implications. First, exhaustible natural resources such as coal, oil and other minerals, and also slowly renewable resources, like forests, must be husbanded, and wherever possible, non-exhaustible resources substituted. Secondly, it points to the need for rapid industrial development.

* It also needs to be tied in with a policy of population-control, as stressed by G. C. L. Bertram, C. M. Nicholson and H. J. Muller in their chapters. (Ed.)

Industries must be established to process mineral wealth and the produce of the land: where these are continuously exported as raw materials, opportunities for additional wealth and employment are lost.

Scientific resource-use is often immeasurably complicated by sociological factors, as is well seen in India. The first principle in dealing with soil is that it should have a protective and productive cover of vegetation. But the Indian peasant tends to grow what he himself needs, irrespective of what is best for the land. Solution of this problem will depend largely on the speed of industrial development and on the effectiveness of family planning.

'Family planning' is also needed for India's cattle population, which is estimated at over 200 million (including nearly 50 million buffaloes), or one-fourth of the world's total, and is increasing substantially from year to year. Between a third and a half of this cattle population is surplus in relation to the feed-supply. Cattle, like men, live on the land and consume the same minerals and organic matter, so that in many cases the choice is clear-cut: man or cow? The appalling practice of using cattle-dung as fuel, and so burning up soil fertility, has to be stopped. Yet to stop it, some cheap alternative fuel will have to be found.

Food habits are also involved. As Arnold Toynbee has stressed, the diet of most peoples 'is determined by ancient habits fortified by prejudice'. Millions of people will have to be persuaded to change their habits 'in order to bring their diet into conformity with the progressive findings of science'.

In the past, the march of industrial civilization has been frequently accompanied by thoughtless destruction of culture; there has been a rapid erosion of values as well as of soil. Material progress, to be meaningful, must go hand in hand with a wide range of cultural pursuits. As the forces of industrial revolution are let loose in the under-developed countries the need for the conservation and revitalization of culture acquires a new urgency.

Enough has been said to show why the search for adequate investment capital must be accompanied by unrelenting effort in other directions. The under-developed countries need an all-round mobilization—scientific, educational, economic and cultural—for the integrated development of their resources, both physical and human.

8

The under-developed countries are entering the race for higher living standards with two formidable handicaps. They are almost two centuries late in taking the first steps towards industrialization; and they are saddled with vast populations growing at frightening rates.

As late-comers, however, they can also count on some advantages: they can profit from the experience of other countries. They have at their disposal the findings of modern science and learning, pure and applied. And they have the possibility of obtaining large-scale development finance from the prosperous industrialized countries.

This third factor is crucial. The biggest problem before the under-developed countries is to find the substantial capital needed for their economic and social infrastructure—for roads, communications, schools, hospitals, irrigation and other basic facilities. These, not being directly revenue-producing, are normally not eligible for long-term loans.

The Western countries which pioneered modern industrial development had to build their infrastructure with the surplus capital accruing from a growing domestic economy, a process that took a good many generations. The Soviet Union followed a different line—a policy of belt-tightening and forced saving to accelerate capital-formation, regardless of the enormous sacrifices it entailed. Our Western views on the ethics of capital formation should not blind us to the advantageous economics of Soviet capital investment. When the dust of ideological controversy finally settles, we shall be able to see more clearly that the remarkable rate of progress achieved by the Soviet Union was due to its early effort to build up a broad-based infrastructure.

Can the under-developed countries attain a similar rate of progress without paying the same heavy price? They *can*, provided the industrialized countries are *willing* to come to their aid in a really big way, which they are certainly *able* to do.

9

Clearly, most of the capital needed will have to be supplied as long-term loans on very easy terms or as outright grants. Why should the industrialized countries make such a sacrifice?

Attempts have often been made to justify economic aid on grounds of national security, but the result has not been happy. It confuses the issue and hinders the best possible use of the funds. It has also been suggested that the question should be viewed in historical perspective: by present sacrifice the developed countries would be making amends for past exploitation. Such historical bookkeeping, however, is not enough as a basis for action. Neither are the promptings of conscience among the more fortunate peoples. Nor is enlightened self-interest: though it is true that capital and other aid will eventually benefit donors as well as recipients, this alone can never provide the necessary dynamic.

The advance of knowledge and the march of events in a shrinking world are forcing us towards a truly Humanist pattern of thought and system of ideas—global and evolutionary—directed towards increased fulfilment and focused on improvement through fuller realization of possibilities. It is in the light of this new Humanism that we must seek guidance for policy.

It is no longer possible to ignore the common mooring of mankind with its dependence on the available physical resources, some of which, like phosphates, are not only vital but are also scarce and arbitrarily scattered over the earth; the consequent interdependence of peoples and their evolution towards a common goal. We must recognize the fact that humanity is an indivisible entity, a continuing whole, inhabiting a planet that is no less indivisible.

One must admit that the very tempo of events in this revolutionary age has created an immense psychological problem—the problem of burying the past fast enough and deep enough. This was recently underlined by an African leader when, referring to the idea of creating a French Community, he labelled it as 'the union of the rider and the horse'. The colonial era is fast coming to an end, but its memories are still lingering, or rankling, in many minds. The result has been both awkward and unfortunate. There are many examples where the new-born nationalism of the newly independent countries is hurting their own national interests.

Progress in the under-developed countries hinges on the ability to establish new and harmonious relations, on the basis of equality in partnership between the erstwhile ruler and ruled. Such a radical adjustment in attitude is not easy to accomplish in so short a time. However, it should be powerfully aided by the realization of one important fact. The march of science which has given mankind the tools to create abundance for all has yielded a remarkable by-product: it has made exploitation obsolete, of the weak by the strong, both at home and abroad. It is no longer necessary for the former colonial powers to exploit the less developed countries in order to build, or maintain, their greatness. The rulers and the ruled of yesterday have moved tantalizingly close to this truth, but they have yet to grasp it fully and firmly.

Some thinkers, like Dr Blackham in his chapter in the present volume, believe that present economic and political trends, under the mounting pressure of Humanist ideas, will culminate in a truly comprehensive and unitary programme of world development under the guidance of a world organization, under which all the various projects of technical aid and assistance would be co-ordinated or combined.

Meanwhile the need for immediate and generous aid is urgent. As Sir Oliver Franks recently said, 'If twelve years ago the balance of the world turned on the recovery of Western Europe, now it turns on a right relationship of the industrial north of the globe to the developing south'. The most challenging task of our generation is to redress this global imbalance with speed and imagination.

The Western countries now accept as commonplace that national economic prosperity depends not on the privilege of the few, but on the welfare of all. This could be no less true of world economy. Capital properly channelled into the under-developed countries can in the end more than pay for itself, both in terms of widening production and trade and of an increasing fund of international goodwill. Humanist investment is good world business.

Further, as Millikan and Rostow put it, 'American society is at its best when we are wrestling with the positive problems of building a better world'. These words have validity also for other industrially advanced countries. 'Affluence', Walter Lippmann reminds us, 'is not greatness.' One may go farther and add that unless affluence is harnessed to creative objectives, it is likely to erode moral and spiritual values and, in the end, real happiness in life.

In the last analysis, have the developed Western countries any real choice in the matter? Probably not. To bring the fruits of science and technology to the depressed or backward areas of the world has all the lure of a great adventure; the Western countries cannot by-pass it without being untrue to themselves. The challenge is also an opportunity—higher living standards for the poverty-stricken half of humanity will raise world economy to higher levels of prosperity. This is a Humanist challenge which neither the West nor the world can ignore.

BIBLIOGRAPHY

Annual Reports:
    Technical Assistance Board, United Nations, New York.
    International Bank for Reconstruction and Development, Washington, D.C.
    International Monetary Fund, Washington, D.C.
    International Finance Corporation, Washington, D.C.
Brown, Harrison, James Bonner, John Weir. *The Next Hundred Years*. New York: Viking, 1958, p. 193.
Ford Foundation *Report on India's Food Crisis and Steps to Meet It*, issued by the Government of India, New Delhi, 1959, p. 259.
Hartford, Ellis F., *Our Common Mooring*, University of Georgia Press, 1941, p. 83.

328 THE HUMANIST FRAME

Hoffman, Paul G. One Hundred Countries—One and One Quarter Billion People. How to Speed their Economic Growth and Ours—in the 1960's. Washington: Albert D. & Mary Lasker Foundation, 1960, p. 62.
Lilienthal, David E. TVA: Democracy on the March. New York: Harper & Brothers, 1953, p. 294.
Millikan, Max F., and W. W. Rostow. A Proposal. New York: Harper & Brothers, p. 170.
Population Council. Population: An International Dilemma, New York, 1958, p. 97.
Sady, Emil J. The United Nations and Independent Peoples. Washington: Brookings Institute, 1956, p. 205.
Toynbee, Arnold J. Population and Food Policy, McDougall Memorial Lecture, 1959. Rome: Food and Agricultural Organization, 1959.
United Nations. Measures for the Economic Development of Under-developed Countries. New York, 1951, p. 108.
—— The Future Growth of World Population. New York, 1958, p. 73.
—— The First Ten Years of the World Health Organization. Geneva, 1958, p. 538.
—— The State of Food and Agriculture, 1959. Rome, 1959, p. 197.
—— International Economic Assistance to the Under-developed Countries in 1956–57: Report of the Secretary General. New York, 1957.
—— The International Flow of Private Capital 1956–1958, New York, 1959, p. 107.

H. KALVEN JR., and H. ZEISEL

LAW, SCIENCE AND HUMANISM

HARRY KALVEN JR., A.B., J.D.

Born 1914. Educated: University of Chicago. Admitted to the Illinois Bar in 1939. Since the war has been a member of the Faculty of the Chicago Law School.

Publications: *The Uneasy Case for Progressive Taxation* (co-author), 1953; *Cases and Materials in the Law of Torts* (co-author), 1959; and *Delay in the Court* (co-author), 1959, and has written widely in the field of civil liberties.

HANS ZEISEL, DR. JUR., DR. RER. POL.

Born 1905. Educated: University of Vienna. Co-founder of the University Institute for Social Research. Went to USA in 1948. Since 1952 Professor of Law and Sociology at University of Chicago Law School.

Publications: *The Unemployed of Marienthal* (co-author), 1933; *Delay in the Court* (co-author), 1959; author of *Say it with Figures*, 1947.

LAW, SCIENCE AND HUMANISM

Sir Julian's prospectus for Humanism opens before us the awesome and exhilarating vision of a world in which man has chief responsibility for the evolution of life on this planet. Man without the crutch of supernatural religion is to stand alone with only his scientific intelligence and his humanist values, to guide him to a better world. A better world we hasten to note, but not the brave new world that brother Aldous frightened us all with a generation ago. The Humanism is to be co-ordinate in importance with the Science.

The lawyer, invited to participate in this symposium and to review his field from the perspective of scientific Humanism, finds that the two key terms pick up familiar echoes. The law has had an interesting and complex relationship to both.* The purpose of this paper then is to reflect on these relationships.

Humanism appears to involve at least two related notions: respect for human values, notably those of dignity and individuality, and a concern with the aesthetic side of life, as reflected in art and literature. In both these senses the law is deeply humanistic. It is not an accident that the most revered American legal heroes such as Justice Holmes or Judge Learned Hand have been cultural heroes also. They have not only been distinguished as judges but have style as men and in particular as writers. If one wanted to locate the best image law has of itself he might well study the values implicit in the law's extraordinary admiration for Justice Holmes. For the American lawyer he is the beau ideal, and the lawyer quotes his aphorisms as the literate layman quotes Hamlet. This fascination with wit, style, felicity of phrase suggests that for those who have made it their life-work, law has a strong aesthetic appeal, and is at its best a kind of literature.

Further, law deals with the full range of human problems which with

* The joinder of Science and Humanism is particularly arresting in view of the thesis of C. P. Snow's recent Rede lecture, 'The Two Cultures and the Scientific Revolution', where he argued with force that in contemporary English and American society Science and Humanism have become two separate non-communicating cultures. It is encouraging to recall that in the Snow novels, it is the lawyer hero Lewis Eliot who moves easily between the two worlds.

all their variety and colour have been the domain of the novel and the drama. As Justice Holmes once put it: 'Law is as good a window as any through which to look at life.'*

To draw on but one example, consider the problem before the distinguished English judge, Lord Justice Scrutton, in the libel case *Watt* v. *Longsdon* which was decided by the King's Bench in 1930. The defendant had shown the plaintiff's wife a letter describing various infidelities of the plaintiff husband. The act of showing the letter to the wife was the publication complained of, and the court's task was to decide whether it was privileged, that is, whether the defendant had a duty to inform the wife. Beneath the technicalities of the law of libel with which the case is burdened there is the exquisitely delicate social issue with which Justice Scrutton manfully deals as follows:

'It cannot, on the one hand, be the duty even of a friend to communicate all the gossip the friend hears at men's clubs or women's bridge parties to one of the spouses affected. On the other hand, most men would hold that it was the moral duty of a doctor who attended his sister-in-law, and believed her to be suffering from a miscarriage, for which an absent husband could not be responsible, to communicate that fact to his wife and the husband. . . . If this is so, the decision must turn on the circumstances of each case, the judge being much influenced by the consideration that as a general rule it is not desirable for anyone, even a mother-in-law, to interfere in the affairs of man and wife.'

Legal education, too, is conscious of its debt to the values developed in the humanities, even in the professional law schools of the United States. The law teacher is fond of recalling that the first Vinerian lectures at Oxford, which became Blackstone's *Commentaries*, were given as part of the general liberal education of the English gentleman. Dean Edward H. Levi of the University of Chicago Law School recently spoke of the bar 'as a profession of public affairs broadly conceived' and of legal education as having 'the refreshing marks of an education for an élite, comparable to the position once held by classical education'.

Law is also sensitive to history, because in one way law is history. The English and American system of precedent requires the careful preservation and carrying forward of the history of prior adjudications. And although the great multiplicity of modern precedents has blunted the practice, it is routine for the lawyer, judge, or law student to cite a case which may date from the early eighteenth century.

* This is what we mean by the temptation to quote Justice Holmes.

Finally and foremost law is always engaged in translating the values of society into legal norms. All laws involve the resolution of issues of policy, and under the American system of a written constitution and judicial review, adjudication of constitutional issues brings the larger issues of the day into dramatic focus.* The law is thus a remarkable repository of dramatic debate over values. At its best, this debate will be as good as anything written on these themes. We shall pause for but one example, the so-called flag salute case, which, we believe, captures the drama and intensity of the individual conscience in opposition to state power, a perennial issue for a free society, as vividly and effectively, to risk a hyperbole, as Sophocles' *Antigone*.

The case arose during World War II in 1943 because a West Virginia school board had adopted a regulation providing for a patriotic ceremony every morning in which the pledge of allegiance to the flag of the United States was to be taken by the children. Refusal to participate in the ceremony warranted expulsion from the public schools. The plaintiffs were Jehovah Witnesses who hold seriously as a matter of dogma that a flag is an image and that it is sacrilegious to bow down to 'any graven image'. The legal issue was joined by the plaintiffs suing to enjoin the state school board in the enforcement of the regulation. The case thus poses the issue of the conscientious objector but in a poignant form because the objectors are children and because the country is engaged in a great war. The problem of the Supreme Court was complicated by the fact that it had dealt with such cases before. In fact it had had five of them, all involving Jehovah Witnesses. In the first three, the court declined to take jurisdiction over the case, in the fourth it upheld the compulsory flag salute in a brief *per curiam* opinion, and in the fifth, in a careful review, it again upheld the salute by an eight to one vote with Mr Justice Frankfurter writing for the majority and only Chief Justice Stone dissenting. This time, the court explicitly overruled its prior decision and found for the plaintiffs in a six to three decision. Without more, the case is thus a notable example of the power and willingness of the court on constitutional issues to reverse itself and correct errors. And when we remember the war situation and the distinctive reverence for the American flag even in tranquil periods,† the case emerges as a supreme reaffirmation of the rights of the

* Since the American constitution invests the courts with the right and duty to judge the constitutionality of legislation, it is in the courts, and particularly through the judges, that the great social and political issues are given expression. In England, where the courts have no such right, the great debates and the great heroes of the law are more likely to be found in Parliament.

† The salute to the flag is a ritual reaffirming in the words of the traditional text, '. . . allegiance . . . to the republic for which it stands'.

individual. And it becomes an important democratic ceremony and symbol.

But there is more to it than this. The majority opinion was by Mr Justice Jackson and the dissent by Mr Justice Frankfurter, and the collision between them produced a passionate debate and restatement of certain basic values. There is no way of conveying the flavour of the debate without quoting a few instances from it. Justice Jackson, who was another judge with a gifted pen, flicks off angry epigrams with almost every sentence. 'Compulsory unification of opinion', he tells us, 'achieves only the unanimity of the graveyard.' And again: 'The case is made difficult not because the principles are obscure but because the flag involved is our own.' And again: 'If there is any fixed star in our constitutional constellation it is that no official, high or petty, can prescribe what shall be orthodox in politics, nationalism, religion, or other matters of opinion or force citizens to confess by word or act their faith therein. If there are any circumstances which permit an exception, they do not now occur to us.'

We prefer Justice Jackson's resolution of the issue but there is much in Justice Frankfurter's dissent to command respect. For him the issue is not the merits of this little patriotic ceremony but rather the scope and propriety of judicial review by the judge who under the ambiguities of constitutional phrases is in fact substituting his judgment of what is wise for that of other more democratically selected public officials. This has long been an issue in American constitutional law but the conservative endorsement of judicial self-restraint receives perhaps its most eloquent exposition in this case. The Frankfurter dissent begins strikingly: 'One who belongs to the most vilified and persecuted minority in history is not likely to be insensible to the freedoms guaranteed by our Constitution. Were my purely personal attitude relevant I should wholeheartedly associate myself with the general libertarian views in the Court's opinion representing as they do the thought and action of a lifetime.' One senses in the opinion an almost puritanical refusal to go where his heart would lead him because of an austere commitment to a limited role for the judge in a democracy. Many pages later the dissent concludes: 'Of course patriotism cannot be enforced by the flag salute. But neither can the liberal spirit be enforced by judicial invalidation of illiberal legislation. . . . Reliance for the most precious interests of civilization . . . must be found outside of their vindication in courts of law.'

Thus a trivial issue has precipitated discussion of two great themes: that of the power of the majority to command conformity from the individual, and that of the democratic method of curtailing the majority.

Further, the case is a notable instance of the protection of minority beliefs, a point relevant to the new society of evolutionary Humanism in which traditional religions will, as Sir Julian predicted in Chicago, evolve out of existence. For the belief on behalf of which the state's arm was checked in the flag salute case was not a conventional religious belief colliding with scientific intelligence but an eccentric notion which collided with organized religion. Finally, the case is instructive on the law's recognition of its limits. The debate over judicial restraint might well be phrased in terms of the limits of law, the point being that if the majority of society is passionately on the move there may be little the judge can do to slow them down; thus it is possible to argue dismally that the society's finest libertarian norms may be inherently beyond the power of law to implement.

The flag salute case illustrates the operation of yet another legal institution congenial to the values of Humanism. It is the institution of the dissenting opinion, particularly at the level of the Supreme Court. Early in its history the American Court departed from the English custom of each judge writing an opinion seriatim. The dissenting opinion is a conspicuous gesture, wonderfully anti-authoritarian, for at the very moment the majority view becomes law it is joined by a public dissent carefully seeking to impeach it. It is recorded for all time along with the majority view so that on any future day he who has recourse to the majority decision will perforce be confronted with the considerations against it. The dissent is, as Chief Justice Hughes once put it, an 'appeal to the intelligence of some future day'. And on several important occasions it has been a source of the law's growth as the dissent grew into the majority view.

Such a role fell to Justice Stone's dissent in the earlier flag salute case. And such was, to cite but one other important example,* the fate of Justice Harlan's dissent in the *Plessy* case of 1895, which arose over the segregation of negroes in public transportation: 'The arbitrary separation of citizens on the basis of race . . . is a badge of servitude wholly inconsistent with the civil freedom and equality before the law established by the Constitution. . . . The thin disguise of equal accommodations will not mislead any one, nor atone for the wrong this day done.' Sixty years later the lone dissent was to become the unanimous opinion of the Court.†

* Plessy *v.* Ferguson, 163 US 537 (1896). Yet another is the evolution of the constitutional doctrine of freedom of speech, which comes almost entirely from the dissenting opinions of Justices Holmes and Brandeis.

† Brown *v.* Board of Education, 347 US 483 (1954). The school segregation decision is usually cited as major evidence of a social science contribution to the law. In the trial, social scientists testified as experts on the consequences of discrimination, and the Supreme Court

Before we move from the law's relationship to Humanist values to its relationship to science, it may be useful to consider for a moment another important legal institution—the jury. *A priori*, the jury would seem to be the supreme instance of the law's unscientific bent. Indeed, *a priori* it is a preposterous institution, as some of its critics like the late Judge Jerome Frank have insisted. A random group of laymen, inexperienced in law, momentarily invested with great powers of adjudication, is asked to listen to complex and conflicting evidence, the natural presentation of which is chopped up by the adversary system of putting in evidence one side at a time. And after the judge has read the relevant law to the jury, it is sent away to a private room to dispose of the matter. While the practice in the United States and England differs markedly on the degree of control exercised by the trial judge, in America at least, the judge tends to play the role of a passive umpire only, and in the majority of states is not even allowed to summarize the evidence neutrally, much less to comment on its weight. The critics thus argue that the jury's role is to apply rules of law which it will not understand to complex facts which it will not get straight, and to do all this on weighty matters with a *de facto* freedom to do what it wants regardless of the law. The whole enterprise looks like a travesty of the ideal of a rule of law and not of men, and in the day when expert administrative agencies are in fashion, it looks like an anachronism, only slightly less anachronistic than the trial by battle or ordeal which it replaced. And a cynical critic would add that we permit the jury to deliberate in private not so much for its sake as to conceal from ourselves the shambles it is making of the law's pretensions.

But this sketch has been advisedly overstated in order to make a point. For several years now at the University of Chicago we have been engaged in a large-scale empirical study of the jury system, the results of which will soon be published in a series of books. And the picture that emerges, as many defenders of the jury among experienced lawyers and judges already know, is quite different. First, neither the law nor the evidence are as unintelligible to the jury as the critics surmise. This is due primarily to the fact that the jury is a group of twelve, and much of the criticism has implicitly compared the ability of a single layman to that of a single

opinion has a famous footnote citing several items of social science literature. But on closer study, it is doubtful whether the scientific evidence added much to a conviction which had already found perfect expression in Harlan's dissent half a century earlier. In fact the segregation case has proved so little a happy example of science aiding law on a great issue, that Professor Edmond Cahn, a widely respected legal scholar, who felt that 'the decisions have added to the dignity and stature of every American', nevertheless felt moved to argue that it would be a 'genuine danger' if it were to be thought that this constitutional issue rested on the science offered in evidence.

trained judge; the group moderates the eccentricity of the individual and enormously improves its recall of the law and the facts. And what may appear as deficiencies of the jury are really difficulties in the law itself—the vagueness of its norms and the gaps and ambiguities and contradictions in the facts of the particular case. Consider the basic requirement in the criminal case of 'proof of guilt beyond a reasonable doubt'. It is often said the jury does not understand this formula, but it would be closer to the truth to say that no one understands it. It is not an exact standard that an expert would know how to apply, but rather an expression of the deep aspiration of Anglo-American society that it is better that some guilty men go free than that one innocent man go to prison. All trials on close examination involve the management of doubt, and the jury is likely to be as good a method as any for handling it in the serious criminal case. As Lord Justice Devlin recently said at Chicago, 'Trial by jury is not an instrument for getting at the truth; it is a process designed to make it as sure as humanly possible that no innocent man is convicted'.

We now know from empirical study* that juries decide cases somewhat differently than judges do. In the main their deviation, in criminal cases, consists in greater regard on occasion for the total human situation before them. Accordingly, to say, in the words of the ancient legal formula, that the jury's function is to be the trier of the facts, is to overlook its more essential function: of bending the letter of the law, where necessary, so as to bring the result in line with the community's sense of justice.

The jury thus works as a kind of built-in check on the rigour and inflexibility of the law. It is, as we are fond of saying, the law's most interesting critic. And its achievement is to insure a legal administration that is flexible, equitable and democratic. The jury system is then the last item we need cite on the law's roster of Humanism.

We turn now to our second basic theme, the relationship of law to science. While the law is not a science in the strict sense, the scientific stance is congenial to the legally trained man. Law has respect for evidence, and experience in weighing it; it places extraordinary emphasis on rational argument and requires that evidence be offered in support of any assertion of fact or law. Law has developed a sharp sense of what is relevant and of when a precedent is in point; law is a systematically organized set of rules, and there is interest in the coherent architecture and structure of the whole.

As we turn more directly to the law's use of science, a distinction will be

* As part of our study of the jury system we have made an intensive survey of the differences in the way juries and judges decide criminal cases. The results indicate that the differences are systematic and turn more on values and sentiments than on issues of fact.

helpful. Science may bear on law in one of two ways. It may provide information about the underlying human behaviour which law seeks to regulate. In this sense almost all sciences of human behaviour are relevant to law and can contribute to it. But the law may also study itself; in this sense it provides a special field for scientific investigation which can tell the law much about how in fact it is operating.

On the whole, though, law's approach towards science is hesitant and perplexed. To illustrate this we have chosen some issues where scientific insights into human behaviour, the most novel area of scientific development, have affected or tried to affect the course of the law. We begin with the efforts to change the law's definition of insanity as a legal defence in a criminal case.

For over a century in Anglo-American law the definition of insanity has been that furnished by the House of Lords in M'Naghten's case: was the accused so mentally disordered 'as not to know the nature and quality of the act he was doing or if he did know it that he did not know what he was doing was wrong'.

Psychiatry, conscious of half a century of unprecedented development, claimed that the old formula did not any longer fit the new knowledge. In 1953 a Royal Commission recommended, unsuccessfully thus far, replacing the old rule by instructing the jury to determine whether 'the accused was suffering from disease of the mind or mental deficiency to such a degree that he ought not to be held responsible'.

But in the United States, in 1953, the Court of Appeals for the District of Columbia did discard the test for a new one, couched in terms of whether the defendant's act was 'the product' of a 'diseased mental condition'.*

The case has aroused much attention and was hailed as a celebrated instance of the law's rapprochement to science. But on closer reflection one may doubt whether the law has here substituted a psychiatric test of insanity for a legal one. The law has not incorporated psychiatric categories so as to declare, for instance, that schizophrenia is legal insanity, but still proceeds by way of a general formula; nor does the new formula say when the crime is, in fact, 'the product' of the disease. To see the problem clearly, we might assume for the moment that the psychiatrist could do, what in fact he cannot, lay bare before the court the whole set of

---

* There is significant irony in the fact that the new rule is really not new but was adopted in New Hampshire in 1871. The history of that rule is the history of the influence a pioneer in psychiatry, Dr Isaac Ray, had on a distinguished New England judge, Charles Doe. The collaboration was successful but the New Hampshire rule was ignored and had no impact on the development of legal doctrine.

causes and motivations that led to the criminal act. Obviously, even such comprehensive knowledge would not be of decisive relevance to the law in its present state. With the judge in *Erewhon*, the defendant would be told: 'There is no question of how you came to be wicked, but only this—namely, are you wicked or not?' Our law is not yet quite ready to look at crime as a disease, hence insists on punishment for evildoing.*

Official punishment involves official and public condemnation as well, and the law is unwilling to give up whatever deterrent effect this defendant's punishment may have on others. The law operates on the theory that it does deter the rest of us, although this is a proposition about human behaviour on which scientific evidence would be welcome and relevant.† The fear of tampering with punishment and official blame by redrawing the line between the criminal and the sick is that it will upset the equilibrium of forces that keep most people from committing crimes. Presumably the public will not understand or accept the more lenient treatment of the criminal implied in holding that he is insane and to be the beneficiary of therapy rather than the subject of punishment, unless it can see the difference between him and themselves; just as in the war the healthy soldier who was to face the perils of combat had to see the distinction between himself and his fellow soldier who was released from service to safety with a psychiatric discharge. Thus all these difficult and obscure judgments and not merely a factual classification of disease are involved in the determination of insanity as a legal defence. The community, in other words, reserves the right to itself or to the jury by which it is represented, to decide whether the defendant was insane enough. And for this purpose the M'Naghten Rule probably provides as good a vehicle as the new rule which, we would suggest, represents a victory of science only at the level of ceremony.

But the psychiatrist could say something else about a defendant that is of interest to the law, not about his past but about his future. He might and sometimes does say that by putting this defendant through medical treatment rather than through prison, the chances of his becoming a recidivist would be greatly reduced.

* Butler's ironic joke of course was that the crime in *Erewhon* was a disease—the contraction of tuberculosis. Some American students of criminal law have argued that one risk of making prisons like hospitals is that hospitals may become more like prisons.

† Again, one must not overestimate this relevance as the example of another embattled issue, capital punishment, shows. Here, a great amount of evidence indicates that capital punishment has not the deterrent effect claimed by its defenders. But this does not settle the argument, because those who want capital punishment want it instinctively or emotionally, not so much for its deterrence as for what are believed its intrinsic values of desert and expiation for great evil.

The criminal law might conceivably re-define responsibility in terms of the defendant's future rather than his past, reorienting itself around the distinction between the curable and the non-curable. Although there have been some tentative moves in this direction, there are at least four formidable obstacles in the way of such a development.

The first is the psychiatrist's present inability to convince the law that he can indeed cure by therapy, and in some instances the psychiatrist's unwillingness to take the responsibility for declaring a defendant cured.

The second obstacle is the extraordinary expensiveness of the therapeutic apparatus. Society at this point is obviously unwilling to devote major resources to the treatment of the criminally sick or insane, especially since it is far from devoting such resources to the mentally troubled who have not committed a crime.

The third obstacle is that therapy would necessarily involve, at times, committing the defendant into indefinite medical custody until he is cured, and the law hesitates to entrust the psychiatrist with the formidable power of indefinite commitment. In proposals for compulsory psychiatric therapy, the law tends to see not the benevolent intention but the threat of compulsion, of coercive custody for an indeterminate period. Here, the law's Humanism is a barrier to the scientist's narrower view.

Lastly, the law is frightened by the ultimate implications of such a future-oriented responsibility. We know, for instance, that even without therapy murderers hardly ever become recidivists, and pickpockets almost always do. Are we then prepared to release the murderers, and keep the pickpockets in permanent custody? And what if our scientists could point out individuals who are very likely to commit a crime, although they have not committed one yet; is the law to act upon such counsel? Such thoughts come dangerously close to the aseptic visions of a 'brave new world'.

It is this last point, the concern with individual freedom, which the law's experience with compulsory sterilization reflects. About twenty-six American states have compulsory laws in some form and thirteen of these reach the criminal as well as the insane. The case of sterilization of the insane is the strongest that can be put for the response of the law to genetics and eugenics. The purpose is the impressive one of preventing the procreation of defective children. Again, the story of the legal reception is instructive. Initially the legislative efforts to sterilize the insane were held unconstitutional. Then in 1927 came a decision by the United States Supreme Court upholding such a state statute. The opinion by Justice Holmes which observed 'Three generations of imbeciles are enough' was hailed as the epitome of a liberal judicial attitude toward science. The story does not end here, however, and today we are likely to regard the Holmes opinion as more a tribute to his wit than to his wisdom. For what seems to have changed is not the law but the science on which it rested. Whatever the early hope, the promise of finding the key to insanity or to mental deficiency in human heredity seems to have largely dissipated. Modern genetics is so cautious and perplexed in its assertions as to the hereditary nature of mental disease that one is tempted to say that the scientific basis has evaporated. Sixteen years later the sterilization issue came back to the Supreme Court and the statute which involved the sterilization of habitual criminals was held unconstitutional by a unanimous Court, although, to be sure, only on a narrow technical point. But a distaste for the law, a recognition of the scientific perplexities, and a concern with the libertarian aspects permeates the majority opinion of Justice Douglas and the concurring opinions of Chief Justice Stone and Justice Jackson. 'We are dealing here with legislation', says Justice Douglas, 'which involves one of the basic civil rights of man. . . . The power to sterilize if exercised may have subtle, far-reaching and devastating effects. . . . In evil or reckless hands it can cause races or types which are inimical to the dominant groups to wither and disappear. There is no redemption for the individual whom the law touches; any experiment which the state conducts is his irreparable injury. He is deprived forever of a basic liberty.' And Justice Jackson adds: 'There are limits to the extent to which a legislatively represented majority may conduct biological experiments at the expense of the dignity and personality and natural powers of a minority—even those who have been guilty of what the majority defines as crime.' And the opinion, significantly, cites a report of the American Neurological Association Committee on Sterilization which, given the current state of knowledge about human heredity, favoured limiting the procedure to voluntary sterilization. Thus three generations of imbeciles may no longer be the prediction and even where it is, it may no longer be enough.

This last sequence of cases foreshadows an issue which is certain to be with us again as population pressures force a re-examination of the basic liberty of families to have as many children as they wish, and it furnishes perhaps the best example of the sources of the law's conservatism. There is no real difference of opinion here between law and science. Some day the scientific predictions may be high enough to outweigh the invasions of personal dignity involved. But they do not do so yet, and in the law's view we can afford to wait.

But while the law is reluctant to surrender its old formulae, the new thinking has nevertheless taken deep roots in our penal system. As one distinguished criminologist summarized it: 'The last fifty years have seen the acceptance of three major legal inventions: the juvenile court, parole and probation. . . . These developments have been accompanied', he continues, 'by nothing less than a revolution in public conceptions of the nature of crime and the criminal.'*

Our new knowledge of human motivations has seeped into the law and deepened its concern with the causes of crime and the possibilities of its cures. And the more we become aware of both, the more precarious our traditional notions of guilt become. Lastly, the law has been made conscious of the aggression in all of us and of the possibly suspect motivations behind the urge to punish. Thus, the rehabilitative ideal has imbedded itself strongly in modern criminal law.

The law, then, emerges as a body that is on the whole cautious, perhaps overcautious, in responding officially to scientific progress. One reason lies with the sciences. It is the social sciences which are of primary relevance to the law, and the certitude of their findings is relatively low compared to those of such exact sciences as physics or chemistry. This is so partly because of the irreducible complexity of social phenomena (sociology is more like meteorology), and partly because of the difficulties of investigating human behaviour. The other reason for the law's slowness lies with the law: often it appears to discuss scientific issues, when in fact it stands on value-judgments. Our laws, after all, have two functions: they prescribe means towards ends, but they also set forth the ends, incorporating the values of the community as they are or, at times, as they ought to be. The law thus does not always permit itself to be explicit about its goals and therefore sets limits to rational debate. The relationship between law and science will depend, in the end, more on the climate of mutual understanding rather than on the power of specific evidence.

Much encouragement should come from the law's growing interest in the investigation of its own peculiar problems through modern scientific methods. We have mentioned our own study of the jury system which integrates the findings from such a variety of investigative procedures as experiment, re-analysis of administrative statistics, and surveys. Also, the procedural and administrative problems of the law become increasingly subject to scientific investigation.†

Even the very paradigm of scientific method, the controlled experiment,

* Francis A. Allen, 'Criminal Justice, Legal Values and the Rehabilitative Ideal', *Journal of Criminal Law, Criminology, etc.*, Vol. 50, 1959.

† The first volume of the jury study is *Delay in the Court*, Little, Brown & Co., 1959, an analysis of the managerial problems of the American courts as they struggle with court congestion.

has gained a foothold in the law. The state of California, for instance, is now in the process of testing the effects of earlier parole, and of intensive parole supervision, by releasing a random sample of prisoners three years before their normal time and supervising only half of that sample. And recently, when the wisdom of certain court rules became doubtful, the courts of the state of New Jersey co-operated in a controlled experiment that is to provide the answer. And a distinguished Australian criminologist, Professor Norval Morris of the University of Adelaide, went so far as to suggest an experiment designed to throw light on the relative merits of various sentences for juvenile offenders.

Interestingly enough, the court's general hesitancy to approve official controlled experiments, ill-reasoned as we believe it is,* derives again from the law's humanistic values. The controlled experiment involves by definition that the experimental treatment be applied to only part of the population, the other, as 'control group', is to be excluded from it. The law, ever hesitant to sanction discrimination, hesitates here too.

The law's knowledge is largely what Michael Polanyi calls personal knowledge, a mixture of knowledge about values and the craftsman's knowledge of how to proceed, a knowledge of the scope and limits of the law's usefulness, and of the perplexities it has to face. As time goes on, more and more of this personal knowledge should become transformed into explicit knowledge, and thus expand the law's wisdom about itself.

As we review law then from the perspective of scientific Humanism, the record is uneven. Law is more closely linked with traditional humanistic values than with the scientific method and outlook. But the promise of evolutionary Humanism as a philosophy for modern man is a promise for law too, for it is a science integrated with a Humanist system of values that will be most readily and gratefully received by the law.

BIBLIOGRAPHY

Blum, W., and Kalven, H., Jr. *The Uneasy Case For Progressive Taxation.* University of Chicago Press, 1953.
Cahn, E. N. *The Sense of Injustice.* New York University Press, 1949.
Cardozo, B. N. *The Nature of the Judicial Process.* Yale University Press, 1921.
Cohen, M. R. *Law and the Social Order.* New York: Harcourt Brace, 1933.
Frank, J. *Law and the Modern Mind.* New York: Coward-McCann, 1949 (1930).
Freund, P. A. *On Understanding the Supreme Court.* Boston: Little, Brown, 1949.
Fuller, L. L. *The Problems of Jurisprudence.* Brooklyn: Foundation Press, 1949.
Hand, L. *The Spirit of Liberty.* New York: Knopf, 1952; London: Hamish Hamilton, 1954.
Holmes, O. W. *The Common Law.* Boston: Little, Brown, 1881; London: Macmillan.

---

* See 'The Case for the Official Experiment', Chapter 10, in *Delay in the Court.*

Holmes, O. W. *Collected Legal Papers*. New York: Harcourt Brace, 1920.

Kalven, H., Jr. *The Law, the Jury, and the Personal Injury Damage Award*, Vol. 19, Ohio State Law Review, 1958.

Kalven, H., Jr. A *Commemorative Case Note: Scopes v. State*, Vol. 27, University of Chicago Law Review, 1960.

Levi, E. H. *An Introduction to Legal Reasoning*. University of Chicago Press, 1948.

Levi, E. H. *Four Talks on Legal Education*. University of Chicago Law School, 1952.

Llewellyn, K. N. *The Bramble Bush*. New York: Oceana Publications, 1951.

'Symposium on Insanity and Criminal Law', Vol. 22, *University of Chicago Law Review*, 1955.

'Symposium on Morals, Medicine and the Law', Vol. 31, *New York University Law Review*, 1956.

Zeisel, Kalven Buchholz. *Delay in the Court*. Boston and Toronto: Little, Brown, 1959.

Zeisel. 'Law and Social Research', in *Law and Sociology*, Harry C. Bredemeier edit. Rutgers University Press, 1960.

Zeisel. 'Some Reflections on Legal Experiments', Vol. 8, *Stanford Law Review*, 1956.

BARBARA WOOTTON

HUMANISM AND SOCIAL PATHOLOGY

BARBARA WOOTTON—BARONESS
WOOTTON OF ABINGER, M.A.,
L.H.D.

Born 1897. Educated: Perse High School
for Girls, Cambridge; Girton College, Cambridge. Principal, Morley College, 1926–27;
Professor of Social Studies, University of
London, 1948–52; Nuffield Research Fellow,
1952–57; Member of the Royal Commission
on the Press, 1947, and a Governor of the
BBC, 1950–56; JP on the Panel of Chairmen
in the Metropolitan Juvenile Courts.

Publications: *Twos and Threes*, 1933;
London's Burning, 1936; *Freedom Under
Planning*, 1945; *The Social Foundations of
Wage Policy*, 1955; *Social Science and Social
Pathology*, 1959, etc.

HUMANISM AND SOCIAL PATHOLOGY

I

All societies have their misfits. Between one society and another, however, wide differences exist in regard to the code of behaviour to which people are expected to conform; to the degree of deviation from this code which is socially tolerated; and to the methods adopted to bring any misfits back into line. In illustration of the first of these divergencies, we may remind ourselves that somewhere at some time practically every imaginable pattern of marriage has been regarded as proper. Marriage can be polygamous, polyandrous, monogamous, indissoluble, dissoluble on specified terms, or by agreement, or at the wish of either party: all these arrangements have actually been operative. Moreover, even in communities which agree in their disapproval of certain types of conduct, the emphasis laid upon a particular deviation from recognized norms is by no means necessarily the same: attitudes towards infringements of property rights on the one hand and towards personal violence on the other are, for instance, extremely variable; while in highly developed communities a whole mass of social obligations has grown up, such as traffic regulations or factory laws, none of which exists at a more primitive level.

The degree to which deviations from social norms are tolerated seems to be to some extent a matter of the stage of technical development reached. In officially Christian, monarchical, monogamous Britain, for example, you can profess any religion or none, drink to excess, refuse military service, practise successive (but not simultaneous) polygamy, speak in derogatory terms of the Government, the Church and the Monarchy, and, short of actual nudity or what is technically known as exposure, indulge in any eccentricity of dress. True, some of these activities if carried too far may involve social disadvantages which are not wholly negligible: but none of them is criminal. By contrast, in tribal societies such as prevail in much of rural Africa, a higher degree of conformity appears to be expected. Nevertheless too much should not perhaps be made of this, since deviations from social norms are in the nature of the case difficult of detection by foreign anthropologists, who, after all, have enough to do to appreciate what constitutes proper behaviour in unfamiliar environments; and one has only to travel eastward across Europe to observe that there are significant variations in the degree of deviance countenanced even in communities that have reached a relatively high level of technical development.

More remarkable are the variations from one country to another, or from one age to another, in the methods used for dealing with deviants. Here a broad distinction may be drawn between measures which are embodied in a legal code and those which are purely social. Even within each of these categories, endless variants have been tried. In the history of Britain, for example, penal methods have ranged from transportation, press-ganging or imprisonment to psychiatric treatment; while the contemporary instruments of social pressure range from exclusion from court circles to loss of trade union membership. At a less advanced stage of social evolution legal measures are, as is to be expected, less highly developed; but their place is taken, sometimes by direct personal violence, and sometimes by—often extremely subtle—forms of social pressure.

To the issues posed in each of these three spheres the Humanist has a distinctive approach. Here as elsewhere the Humanist attitude implies on the one hand a distinctive set of values; and on the other hand a characteristic reliance upon the methods of scientific investigation. Humanism is thus, on both counts, at variance with traditional attitudes. Traditionally in the Western Christian world the whole field of social pathology has long been permeated by religious ideas—by concepts of taboo, sin, punishment and atonement set in the supernatural framework of the Christian dogmas; whereas the Humanist's standards are earthly, in a broad sense utilitarian, and, where possible, scientific. In determining the foundations of morality and the ultimate objectives of social policy, the Humanist is concerned with man's happiness and welfare in this life alone, and with the development of each and every individual's maximum potentiality for the good life conceived in these terms. All arguments that are derived from religious dogmas, or that rest solely upon appeals to the will of God, pass the Humanist completely by. Admittedly such phrases as 'potentiality for the good life' are far from being precise terms, and can be shot to pieces by professional philosophers: but for practical purposes it is clear enough what they mean. Indeed, in the present state of the world, even if we did not go beyond the purely negative definition that the Humanist is against hunger, poverty, ignorance, cruelty and bloodshed, we should have a sufficient basis for social policy.

So much for values. Meanwhile in the approach to his goals the Humanist looks to scientific investigation both to provide a measure of his success and to devise techniques for accelerating his progress. In one sphere after another—in the treatment of criminals, or in the selection of civil servants—he substitutes measurement for guesswork, objective recording for subjective judgment; and utilizes the knowledge thus gained to improve future performance.

In the present century the influence of Humanist attitudes upon every aspect of social pathology has indeed been remarkable. The norms of behaviour have been modified to suit Humanist conceptions of morality; toleration has been correspondingly extended; and—most striking of all —scientific method has invaded the field of penology, and perhaps even threatens to undermine traditional methods of dealing with malefactors.

In the present context, the changes that have occurred under the first two of these heads can be dealt with fairly briefly; but they have, none the less, created something of a social revolution, particularly in the sphere of sexual behaviour. In Britain, so far as divorce is concerned, the grounds for dissolution of marriage were greatly extended by the Matrimonial Causes Act of 1937: and what is more important, the social disadvantages suffered by divorced persons have, over a great part of the world, been reduced out of all recognition. The story of the Dilke tragedy of the eighteen-eighties, for example, has an extraordinary air of unreality in an age in which a divorced Prime Minister can advise the Queen as to the choice of bishops in a Church which still apparently upholds the lifelong indissolubility of marriage. Similarly in the matter of homosexual behaviour, although nothing has yet been done in Britain, there has undoubtedly been a great movement of opinion. The Wolfenden Committee's recommendation that homosexual acts committed in private by consenting adults should cease to be criminal would have been unthinkable fifty years ago, even though this has long been the law in many European countries.

These developments are both clear expressions of Humanist values; and they have their parallels in many other parts of the world. In sexual as in all other matters the Humanist thinks only in terms of the happiness and welfare of all persons who are or may be affected in a concrete case. In safeguarding the rights of children he will be second to none; but the private lives of adults he will regard as their own affair. Apart from the principles of integrity and mutual consideration, there are for him no absolutes. Contemporary developments therefore represent a considerable victory of Humanist over religious ideas: the changes that have occurred could not have occurred had not dogmatic religious belief been on the wane. At some points, it is true, the Christian Churches have come to terms with contemporary developments, while on others their opposition is still bitter. But in no case have they been the prime instigators of any relaxations of the prevailing sexual code. In regard to divorce, while the Anglican Church, as has been said, apparently maintains that the sanctity of marriage as an institution overrides considerations of the happiness of all the persons affected by a particular marriage, the pronouncements of some clergy are at the least equivocal; though the position of the Roman Church is still clear and uncompromising. In regard to homosexual acts, on the other hand, both Protestant and Catholic Churches take the view (which many Humanists do not share) that these are in themselves evil; but prominent churchmen, again both Catholic and Protestant alike, relying on a (possibly shaky) distinction between private and public morality, have accepted the view that, though sinful, homosexuality need not also be criminal. Plainly, what is actually happening in the world is the result of the accommodation of religious to evolving humanistic ideas and not *vice versa*.

The same is true of the growth of toleration—in those areas where it is growing. It may sound cynical, but undoubtedly the growth of toleration is the expression of weakening conviction and a declining belief in the importance of what is tolerated. No one is tolerant in what he believes to be both true and vital. No one who really believed that eternal hellfire was the price of unbelief would allow his child to be exposed to agnostic propaganda. Both in opinion and in behaviour we are only tolerant, either in areas in which we suspect that we could be wrong, or in those which we do not think matter very much—only tolerant of what is not felt as a serious threat. Even the most uncompromising upholders of freedom of speech do not think it necessary to allow believers in the flat earth theory or psychopathic murderers to ventilate their opinions on the air. The growth of sexual toleration is itself simply due to the spread of the Humanist belief that there are no absolutes in sexual morality: that in every instance sexual behaviour, equally with conduct in other spheres of life, must be judged in terms of its effect on the happiness, welfare and dignity of individuals. Religious toleration, likewise, results from the erosion of religious conviction under the accumulating pressure of Humanist ideology, while toleration in political matters is equally the expression of a growing sense of political and social security. When this sense of security is lost—as in wartime or in the McCarthy epoch in the USA—tolerance evaporates with remarkable speed and thoroughness. But the truth that toleration extends only to what is not felt to be a matter of vital concern loses its cynical ring if translated into the statement that toleration grows as fear declines. For centuries intolerance has been the result of the fear which man has made for himself—fear of the Almighty, fear of Communism, fear of witches; and for centuries intolerance has restricted the potential variety of human experience. Only as man becomes master of himself as well as of his environment can he afford the luxury and enjoy the fruits of tolerance.

The familiar changes that I have described have not been brought about by the direct propaganda of avowed Humanists. They are not the result of any militant Humanist movement. But it is impossible to believe that they could have come about, had it not been for the spread of a morality that is based upon human rather than upon supernatural values. Nothing perhaps separates this century so sharply from its immediate predecessor as the loss amongst educated men and women of conviction of the literal truth of the basic dogmas of the Christian religion and of the certainty of individual survival after death. As a result of this loss, a tremendous, though generally silent, shift has occurred in the bases of morality. We ask no longer what is pleasing to God but what is good for man.

II

It is, however, in the methods employed to deal with those whose behaviour goes beyond the limits even of contemporary tolerance that the influence of humanistic conceptions is, potentially at least, most radical. Here it is the scientific rather than the moralistic elements in the Humanist philosophy that are important. Granted that the purpose of penal treatment is to discourage antisocial behaviour, then to the Humanist the choice of techniques for achieving this objective is a proper subject for scientific investigation: and it is in the light of such investigations that penal policy must be shaped. Wishful propositions as to the effects of leniency, of severity or of any other attitude towards the socially recalcitrant must stand or fall by their empirically demonstrated consequences. In this field, however, wishful propositions are exceptionally prominent. In particular the demand for vindictive penalties or for the use of physical violence such as flogging persists without any regard to the evidence as to the effectiveness of such treatments—largely, in the view of many psychoanalysts, because it is itself the expression of the repressed desire of law-abiding people to commit criminal offences.

Nevertheless, even into this field science has already made a formidable invasion; and this invasion has proceeded in more than one wave. The first inroads came from the science of medicine led by the psychiatrists. From this have emerged entirely new ways of thinking about unacceptable behaviour as well as an entirely new vocabulary, comprising such terms as 'emotional disturbance', and 'psychopathic personality'. Up till now, it is true, the revolution in thinking has been more pronounced than the revolution in practice: the part which psychiatrists play in the actual treatment of offenders is still relatively small. In England the proportion of those admitted to prison who are regarded as suitable subjects for 'major psychotherapy' is said to be low. Nevertheless in many European countries and still more in the USA, troublesome or naughty children are frequently treated by psychiatrists; and in England recent legislation, for which there are parallels in Denmark and elsewhere, has created a new category of psychopaths who can be diagnosed and treated, and if necessary compulsorily detained, purely on medical advice and without recourse to any judicial procedures. Under such legislation antisocial behaviour is in fact transformed from a penal into a medical problem.

Unquestionably the primary effect of this contemporary tendency to regard antisocial behaviour as a symptom of mental abnormality has been to humanize penal procedures and penal institutions. A doctor seeks to cure his patient: not to punish him. He chooses, not the treatment that his patient 'deserves', but the one that he thinks most likely to effect a cure. Guilt and blame are not his concern. If medical treatment in any sphere can sometimes be unpleasant, in conception and aim it is always fundamentally humane.

As things are, however, the attempt to combine the new and the old methods of dealing with antisocial persons may well lead to somewhat formidable difficulties. For example: much the same sort of conduct may today be classified on the one hand as an expression of mental disorder and therefore suitable for medical treatment, or on the other hand as morally reprehensible and therefore punishable. This might not matter very much if the line between the normal and the disordered mind was both clear and absolute. But it is not. In any case mental abnormality is always a matter of degree, and in actual instances the opinions even of experts are frequently contradictory. Moreover, with the advance of medical science, new types of case are continually being transferred from the one category to the other. A man who is held by one psychiatrist to be fully responsible and punishable may be diagnosed by another as suffering from the mental abnormality known as psychopathy: or one who today is judged to deserve imprisonment might a year later in exactly similar circumstances be regarded as a subject for medical, rather than penal, treatment. The resulting contrasts are not unnaturally liable to be regarded as unjust.

Still greater anomalies follow when a diagnosis of medical abnormality is used, not to substitute medical for penal treatment, but merely to diminish the severity of the punishment inflicted upon an offender, as happens under the laws now in force in England and many other countries in regard to diminished responsibility. Under the contemporary English law an accused person who admits to having committed homicide may plead that his responsibility was diminished owing to some mental disorder. If the plea is successful, his offence will be reduced from one of murder to one of manslaughter, with the result that the judge, instead of being obliged to pass sentence of death in capital cases or of life-imprisonment in others, may in his discretion impose any sentence that he thinks fit. From the point of view of the protection of society this seems crazy. Whereas the wholly responsible, mentally normal person is put out of harm's way permanently or for a very long period, the mentally abnormal, and therefore presumably more dangerous, offender may be released after a comparatively short spell of imprisonment.

These paradoxes merely illustrate the incompatibility of the new and the old approach. In the long run, the new must, I think, win—at least in the sense that in the treatment of antisocial persons, the emphasis will be shifted away from considerations of guilt, deserts and punishment towards the search for what can be empirically shown to be effective treatment. In that sense the psychiatric approach to problems of unacceptable behaviour is undoubtedly an expression of the scientific attitude inherent in a Humanist or rationalistic philosophy; for such a philosophy in face of any social catastrophe—a murder just as much as a flood—asks not who is to blame, so much as what can best be done to repair the damage and to prevent the repetition of a similar catastrophe.

As to the effectiveness of psychiatric treatment, as judged by this criterion, no conclusive answers can yet be given. Controlled observation of the results of such treatment can and will eventually settle the question. But in the meantime the practitioners of scientific method are developing a second line of attack upon the problem of dealing with antisocial behaviour, by exact observation of the lessons of experience over a wide field. In the present century, thanks to the development of the social sciences, we are for the first time seriously addressing ourselves to the question of whether, or how far, the various methods employed by the courts and similar agencies do in fact succeed in producing the results desired; and whether the choice of such methods in particular instances might not be improved by systematic recording of the results of past experience.

At the best of times this is bound to be an extremely complicated matter. It arises, however, in its simplest form in cases in which only two alternatives are available between which choice has to be made; as when under court sentences of indefinite duration, a choice has to be made to release or not to release a particular prisoner. In the United States, where such indeterminate sentences are extensively used for adults as well as for juvenile offenders (as they are in this country), it has been found possible, by following up the after-careers of released prisoners and relating these to particular features of each man's personality and background, to build up a considerable body of knowledge as to the traits in a prisoner which make him a good or a bad risk for release on parole; and on the basis of these results it is possible greatly to improve the proportion of parolees whose release proves to have been justified.

Where choices are more numerous, the techniques involved are necessarily more complex. Even so, follow-up researches have provided material on which predictions can now be made as to the relative prospects of success of different offenders in a given type of penal institution or under a given type of penal treatment. The traits which give a good prognosis for, say, probation or Borstal training are in process of being identified; and already it is clear that in regard to specific treatments the judgments made on the basis of these investigations are significantly more accurate than the hunches even of those who have the closest contact with the persons concerned. Nevertheless, in order to make a rational choice between one sentence and another it is necessary to locate the comparative chances of success, not only of two men exposed to the same treatment, but also of the same man under alternative treatments. We need to be able to predict not only that Borstal training has a 70 per cent chance of success with A and only 50 per cent with B, but also whether B would do better or worse on probation or in prison than at Borstal. Technically the collection of data on this point presents no new problem of principle: all that is necessary is the extended use of existing techniques: in each case the records of past experience are the basis on which the chances of future success must be calculated. It is, therefore, only a question of time before we can expect sentencing and other decisions affecting antisocial persons to move from the field of art to that of science.

In New York even more ambitious projects are afoot, under the auspices of the City Youth Board and Sheldon and Eleanor Glueck. There an experiment is in progress designed to identify the potentially delinquent child even before he has declared himself by getting into serious trouble. Observations of seriously delinquent children suggest that certain characteristics occur amongst them with more than average frequency. An unusually high proportion of them, perhaps, comes from broken homes, or has suffered some serious family upset in early life. In so far as this is so, such experiences, it is argued, must be regarded as prognostic of future trouble. Verification of this hypothesis, however, must inevitably take some time, and no definite answer is yet possible. In any case, the fact that the seriously delinquent child is still happily quite exceptional and that delinquents have no monopoly of their own special characteristics creates a risk that any predictions made on this basis may prove grossly over-pessimistic. If more delinquents than well-behaved children come from broken homes, we may in one sense be justified in regarding the broken home as a danger sign; but at the same time it may equally be true that the vast majority of children whose homes are broken in infancy make a perfectly satisfactory adjustment to the world in which they have to live. How far this is or is not the case, researches such as these now in progress in New York will in due course help to show.

It will be noticed that in these pages no reference has been made to the possibility of scientific exploration of the *causes of* unacceptable behaviour. Obviously if science could establish what these causes are, we should be well on the way to a world in which criminality and near-criminal behaviour no longer presented any problem. Such, however, is the complexity of human behaviour that problems of causation will almost certainly be the last to be solved. In this field hypotheses abound: anti-social behaviour is said to be the product of unfavourable social environment, of an unfortunate genetic make-up, of separation in infancy from the mother or of other forms of family disturbance; but it cannot honestly be said that any of these hypotheses is yet validated—probably because, though many contain some part of the truth, all of them are far too simple to take account of the subtleties of human motivation and experience.

What we can say, however, is that Humanist philosophy would eliminate from social codes all those prohibitions and injunctions which are justified only in religious or supernatural terms rather than for their contribution to human welfare in this life; and that it would make for a tolerant and unexacting society, in which, within the framework of the common welfare, each individual would be free to develop his talents to the utmost. For the few who cannot or will not adapt themselves even to such a society, it would employ in each case the most effective treatment known to science, subject only to the limitations of its own moral premises. And we can indeed congratulate ourselves that already something has been accomplished along these lines—enough, at any rate, to feed the hope that the methods of patient observation and unswerving faithfulness to fact by which man has gained such astonishing power over the physical world may eventually win for him like mastery both of himself and of his social environment.

BIBLIOGRAPHY

For further reading:
Glueck, S. and E. T. *Unraveling Juvenile Delinquency*. Harvard University Press, 1950.
Grünhut, M. *Penal Reform*. New York: Oxford University Press, 1949.
Mannheim, H. *Group Problems in Crime and Punishment*. New York: Humanities Press, 1955.
Mannheim, H., and Wilkins, L. T. *Prediction Methods in Relation to Borstal Training*. H.M.S.O. 1955.
Mays, J. B. *Growing up in the City*. New York: Gregory Lownz, 1958.
Wolfenden Committee on Homosexual Offences and Prostitution. *Report*. H.M.S.O. Cmnd. 247 of 1957.
Wootton, Barbara. *Social Science and Social Pathology*. New York: Macmillan, 1959.

ROBERT PLATT

THE NEW MEDICINE AND
ITS RESPONSIBILITIES

SIR ROBERT PLATT, BT., M.D.,
F.R.C.P.

Born 1900. Educated: Sheffield University.
Professor of Medicine Manchester Univer-
sity since 1945. Editor *Quarterly Journal of
Medicine* since 1948. Medical Research
Council since 1953. President, Royal College
of Physicians since 1958.

Publications: *Nephritis and Allied Diseases*,
1934, and numerous papers to the *Quarterly
Journal of Medicine*.

THE NEW MEDICINE AND
ITS RESPONSIBILITIES

Introduction: The New Medicine

Somewhere in his autobiography Benvenuto Cellini says how convenient it was for him to have been born in 1500, for he never had to calculate his age. Equally convenient has it been for me to have been born in 1900. My excuse for this autobiographical opening is that I want to emphasize what Julian Huxley has called the 'knowledge explosion' of the last half-century; and to make and defend the statement that almost all that is valuable in medical treatment today has been discovered during my lifetime, and indeed since I graduated.

I remember when motor-cars were rare enough in Hampstead for my brother and me to walk on the other side of the road if we saw one in case it would blow up; and I well remember spending a morning in a field in Hendon in 1910 waiting to see Paulhan set out on the first flight from London to Manchester, for which he won a prize of £10,000. Of course the machine age was already more than a hundred years old and our annual train journeys from London to Scotland were accomplished in much the same time as they would take today. All discovery has its roots in what went before; the real change is in the speed with which progress has occurred. The unhappy thought is that the speed was enhanced by the stimulus of two wars.

The methods of clinical observation and interrogation on which medical diagnosis initially still rests go back to Hippocrates, and after a long period in which much of medicine was again governed by magic and superstition, the clinical method was revived and developed by the great physicians of the seventeenth, eighteenth and nineteenth centuries; men like Sydenham, Heberden and Richard Bright. It is true that modern methods of medical research started with Harvey (whose *De Motu Cordis* is still worth reading as an example of scientific method), and that the medicine of my time rests on the physiological and bacteriological discoveries of the nineteenth and early twentieth centuries, with which we associate names such as Claude Bernard, Pasteur and Koch and more recently Starling,

Bayliss, J. S. Haldane and Sherrington.[1] Preventive medicine, though in a primitive way it goes back to prehistoric times, started on its modern course over a hundred years ago, with Chadwick and Snow. Modern medical thought, moreover, has been greatly influenced by discoveries in physics and chemistry too numerous to mention (X-rays are an obvious example) and also more recently by biological, genetic and statistical enquiry initiated by men like Darwin, Mendel and Galton. The great importance of the evolutionary point of view in physiology and medicine was but slowly recognized. Modern surgery was made possible in the nineteenth century by the discovery of anaesthesia and by Lister's application of bacteriology. The glimmerings of knowledge about vitamins go back to James Lind and Captain Cook, and replacement therapy in disorders of endocrine glands to Murray's administration of thyroid gland in 1891. Yet for all this I hold that modern medicine is a matter of the last forty years or so and that during that short time the daily work and thought of a physician has undergone a revolution such as has never been known before.

Looking back to 1920 when I was a medical student the striking thing was the discrepancy between what a physician knew and what he could do for his patients. Bacteriology had already led to a much clearer understanding of disease than was possible in the mid-nineteenth century. It had led also to the introduction of important preventive measures through hygiene and vaccination, but in the treatment of bacterial disease, vaccines had already proved to be useless and antisera rarely effective. Pneumonia in the elderly was nearly always fatal, in young subjects always dangerous and often complicated; and such was still the case until the introduction of sulphonamides about 1935. For tuberculosis no such word as cure could be used, though early cases recovered after prolonged treatment in sanatoria: with streptomycin (1947) and other drugs an early case of pulmonary tuberculosis may now return to work in a few weeks. Infections such as acute tonsillitis, septic wounds and osteomyelitis could in 1920 readily give rise to fatal complications; even a pricked finger would occasionally cause death from septicaemia. Aseptic measures had made puerperal sepsis a rarity, but when it occurred it was deadly. Diphtheria, cerebrospinal meningitis and bacterial endocarditis are other microbial disorders in which the outlook has been completely altered since the introduction of sulphonamides and antibiotics in the last twenty years. Only in syphilis, because of the introduction of Salvarsan by Paul Ehrlich, was chemotherapy already a success in my student days; even so it required months or years of treatment which many patients were unwilling to undergo.

In 1920 the surgeons were somewhat more advanced than the physicians, for their aseptic technique enabled them to open the abdomen and more rarely the cranium, or even the joints, without much fear of the prolonged and often fatal sepsis which had been the enemy of surgery before Lister. Successful operations were carried out daily for emergencies such as intestinal obstruction and appendicitis, for the removal of diseased organs, for the repair of hernia and, less successfully, for the attempted cure of such conditions as gastric and duodenal ulcer. The modern surgery of the lungs and heart were unknown, although of course pioneer attempts had been made. Intracranial surgery was very limited in scope and rarely successful. Removal of the thyroid gland for hyperthyroidism was so hazardous as to be rarely practised.

It was not only in bacterial disease that the physician's therapeutic powers were so meagre. Almost all metabolic and endocrine disease is today treatable, either by medical measures alone or by combined attack from physician and surgeon, but with the exception of the treatment of myxoedema by thyroid extract, none of this was possible in 1920. Even insulin, one of the earliest of modern advances in medicine, dates from 1923. To the young man of today it seems unbelievable that only forty years ago a physician's influence on disease was so limited.

The Patient's Mind

It is extraordinary how very recent is the introduction of the psychiatrist into the general hospital. Many teaching hospitals even had no psychiatrist until the late 1930s. Good doctors throughout the centuries have realized the importance of the patient's mind in relation to illness, and that many illnesses have no basis at all save in the mind. No doubt the greatest successes of physicians of past centuries were due to their ability to manage, soothe, and persuade, and to apply to their patients a psycho-therapy which was often intuitive rather than deliberate. But in 1920 and for many years afterwards, the average physician tended to divide his patients into those who were suffering from organic disease and were therefore interesting, and those whose complaints were psychological and who were therefore neurotic and uninteresting, with the implication that they ought to know better. The role of the psychiatrist was to deal with madness, and, like his patients, he was segregated to the asylum, where his duties were largely custodial. This mechanistic view of medicine with its preoccupation with visceral disease was no doubt based on the fact that the advances of the nineteenth century had come from the laboratory and the post-mortem room. Of course there were pioneers in this country such as Ernest Jones, and physicians like Arthur Hurst, who under the influence of Freud and others had already begun to investigate and treat neurotic illness by psychological methods, and a further stimulus to this was provided by the large numbers of cases of neurosis from the 1914–18 war. That they were usually called *shell-shock* was further evidence of mechanistic thinking. Alongside the greater realization today of the importance of the patient's mind in all illness is a new awareness of the role of his whole environment, his work, his income, his food, his family, his children, his living conditions and his habits. This again was something which good physicians had known intuitively for centuries.[2]

It is still too early to say how far this outlook will take us. Most problems of the mind are impossible to measure in the present state of knowledge, and are more difficult to define and analyse than disorders of the body. Thus psychiatry tends to be dubbed as unscientific and is still at a stage of being divided into a number of schools of thought between which experts disagree. Although it is now quite proper and reputable to study the patient's mind whatever his disease, and there is a new realization of the importance of psychological factors in minor illness, there are differences of opinion as to how far the study should go, and by what means it should be pursued. Perhaps it is fair to say that one of the major contributions of psychiatry to medicine is that it has driven doctors to a position where they must recognize it, and the very recognition that symptoms may be psychological is an advance over the days when every ache and pain was thought to be the result of visceral disease.

The art of medicine always recognized that man was the product of his genetic endowment and his environment, that he had a psyche as well as a soma, that he must be treated as a whole, that he had spiritual as well as material needs, to speak in an older terminology. The new emphasis is only in part due to psychiatry, and has been greatly accelerated by the social revolution of our time. In 1920 there was a hospital population, grateful but undemanding, convenient material for the medical student, and another population of paying patients whose personalities were important. Today the two are less clearly segregated.

Ignorance Remains

I have not exaggerated the advances in medicine which have taken place in my professional lifetime, but I must not leave the impression that there is little left to learn. In every branch of medicine there is still far more ignorance than knowledge as we get nearer to fundamentals, and many problems will have to wait until more is known of processes which go on at cellular or sub-cellular level. The very nature of viruses is not yet really known, and against virus diseases we have few if any effective remedies, though we know something about prevention. Some disorders, often classed as psychosomatic, intimately bound up with personality, with allergy, and auto-immunity, such as ulcerative colitis and asthma, are still a challenge, as are also some serious neurological disorders like disseminated sclerosis, and some inherited diseases, especially those due to recessive genes. Then there are the constitutional diseases from which most of us will sooner or later die; arterial disorders, including high blood-pressure and coronary thrombosis,* and cancer. These mostly attack people beyond the reproductive age, though occasionally malignant conditions like leukaemia and certain tumours attack children, and constitute some of the most piteous conditions which parents, doctors and nurses have to witness. Although we know a great deal more about the cancer process than we did twenty or thirty years ago, and that certain malignant states are amenable temporarily to specific remedies, the main problem of cancer remains unsolved.

Arterial degenerative disease raises wide biological questions as to whether an ageing process, rarely if ever reached in the normal wild state of animals, is inescapable under conditions of domestication. Presumably we have to die some time of something, and we cannot put off indefinitely the ageing processes which eventually make the organism run down. The main preoccupation of medicine and psychiatry should be to find ways of keeping ageing people independent and useful as long as possible, and giving them the kind of occupation most suited to their talents. Researches with these ends in view are active at the present time.[3]

The Doctor's Responsibility

The new medicine, still so young, makes our profession far more satisfying and interesting than it has ever been before, but brings certain new responsibilities and new conflicts. Until quite recently when all you could do for most medical complaints was to look wise and sympathetic, to give advice about rest in bed and diet, and prescribe some harmless mixture, it did not really matter whether your diagnosis was right or wrong, except of course for your own reputation. Nature rather than the doctor would determine the outcome. Prognosis mattered rather more, especially to the doctor's reputation. Today this is altered, for there is usually a specific remedy to be prescribed. Moreover it *is* specific; the treatment for tuberculous meningitis is quite different from the treatment of cerebro-spinal meningitis. Both are curable diseases if the treatment is started early; diagnosis therefore must be swift and accurate, or a life is lost.

* The more accurate term for the condition which arises as a result of a sudden obstruction to cardiac blood-supply is myocardial infarction: here I use the term more familiar to laymen.

Not only in acute diseases has medical responsibility immeasurably increased; there are now many chronic diseases amenable to treatment either by medicine or by surgery, but only if an early and accurate diagnosis is made. The new medicine has had a salutary effect upon medical humbug which was, until quite recently, one of the assets of many practitioners. In the days when one knew so little one had to pretend to know so much.

Old problems of medical ethics remain. The doctor must often act on evidence which would be insufficient to the scientist. Herein still lies the value of experience, the art of medicine. Medicine has not yet reached a stage where a blood-test performed by an automatic machine can make the diagnosis and determine the treatment, nor will it ever do so, for treatment and advice must still be tempered to the patient's personality.

The question how much a doctor should tell still finds no universal solution, and must be answered individually in each case. Faced with incurable disease there are some who honestly wish to have pre-knowledge of the end. The majority seem to prefer not to face the question, although unconsciously or privately they may already have answered it: others are clearly making every effort to deceive themselves.

Human Experiment

Medical science has brought other responsibilities and raised new ethical questions. Human experiment has for long been amongst the responsibilities of the medical profession; every operation has once been performed for the first time; every new remedy has passed through a stage of trial, when its dangers were unknown; many of the more advanced diagnostic measures, essential in the investigation of serious disease, carry with them their own dangers, and these also have been used for the first time during some stage of their development. The answer as to what is justifiable must depend on all the circumstances. There is no easy or universal solution such as to say that the experiment must be explained beforehand to the patient, because one cannot expect the patient to have a medical or scientific background, and most patients will say yes to almost anything if explained in a certain way: neither is it as simple as asking 'would I have this procedure done on myself?', for we are trained people with a scientific curiosity and have been known to do experiments on ourselves which would not be appropriate to a patient who comes to a doctor full of trust.

State Medicine

The tremendous cost of modern diagnosis and treatment has raised acutely the question of State provision of medical services, and has led to the establishment in this country of the National Health Service.[4] This has raised difficult questions of State interference with professional independence, and it has to be acknowledged that the solution reached is in some ways an uneasy compromise. However, anyone who knows how in America a lengthy illness can reduce a middle-class family to bankruptcy must be convinced that some form of State medical aid is inevitable. It seems regrettably necessary to warn the American reader against certain quite false statements which are put out in his country by those who have financial or other reasons for opposing the establishment of a health service. It is known to the writer that American medical men have come to this country with the acknowledged intention not of studying our health service, but of meeting only a few extremists who still bitterly oppose it in all its aspects. Thus they take back with them a grossly distorted picture.

The Future of Individual Medicine

With expanding knowledge and the development of new techniques, specialization in medicine is bound to increase. This gives rise to certain difficulties but most of them can be overcome if specialists in different branches of medicine work closely together, sharing their skills. The main work of most doctors is likely to remain as it is today, the personal care of individual patients; this is what attracts most people into medicine. The practising doctor's first loyalty is to his patient and it should triumph even though it is in conflict with other loyalties such as the public health or medical research, for the practice of medicine, more than that of any other profession, is based on a system of ethics.

The growth of specialization is in some respects inimical to general practice as we have known it in the past. This has led to a situation from which there are two possible developments. One is the virtual abolition of the general practitioner, as has happened in some American and South African cities where every patient makes his own first step in diagnosis, and consults a cardiologist or an allergist, a paediatrician or an endocrinologist, according to what he conceives to be his need. Every doctor becomes a self-styled specialist, often quite inadequately trained but possessing most of the latest equipment. The other alternative is what I believe and hope is happening in this country, namely a recognition of the real scope of general practice and a change in undergraduate and post-graduate education so that men and women can get a proper training in this very important branch of medicine. For in general practice special skills are required in the treatment of patients in their own homes, in seeing them through minor illnesses, in dealing with the lesser but extremely important emotional disturbances, in caring for the chronic sick, and above all seeing disease in the earliest stage, and making the decision quite honestly as to whether it falls within the scope of the general practitioner or the specialist, and if the latter, which specialist. These difficult skills are exercised at the present time by the bulk of the profession who get no extra reward for being good at their jobs, and who vary in efficiency between the ultimate extremes of good and bad doctoring. Many of the best general practices of the day are run as group practices in which each doctor has his own particular interest such as children or minor surgery, so that between them they can treat a greater range of illnesses with added skill and competence.

Positive Health

Can doctors, working as individuals or in groups, do more for individuals than attend to their ailments, mental or physical? Clearly by seizing the opportunity for health education they can do something towards keeping people well. This has worked satisfactorily in the case of maternity and child welfare services and in the school clinics. Is there a case for the regular inspection of adults?

Most acute illnesses cannot be prevented except by community measures (clean air, clean food, housing, sanitation, preventive inoculation and so forth). When they occur, acute illnesses usually announce their presence in no uncertain way by pain, fever and so on. Now that everyone in Britain has a family doctor, opportunities for early and efficient treatment need not be lost.

Chronic illness is more subtle. Some internal cancers might be earlier diagnosed if everyone were exposed to a comprehensive series of X-rays at three-monthly intervals: at present the radiation hazard would probably greatly exceed anything gained by early diagnosis of a few cases, but this may be overcome by the development of image intensification so that smaller exposures can be used. In the present state of knowledge coronary thrombosis cannot be predicted. A man might come out of his medical inspection pronounced healthy and drop dead the next day. High blood-pressure could be discovered but in its milder forms it causes no symptoms and is compatible with a normal life-span. As soon as the subject is told about it he is liable to develop headaches, dizziness and other symptoms and become an invalid. Blood-pressure neurosis is extremely common. Cancer-phobia is common enough and might become commoner.

Health education should make people conscious of the necessity for seeking early advice about certain symptoms, and in some industries of course, regular routine inspection (e.g. for silicosis or lead poisoning) is necessary; but to invite regular preoccupation with the symptoms of disease in otherwise normal persons is doubtful wisdom.

Co-ordination between body and mind can of course be trained to a high degree of efficiency. This is one form of bodily fitness which in most people is accompanied by a sense of well-being. It does not, however, render the subject immune from illness; the young commando developed no protection from dysentery or malaria.

By far the greatest load of preventable illness and subnormal health comes from the mind, and better understanding and prevention of the factors which lead to maladjustment, frustration and unhappiness, is probably the most hopeful line of attack.

It is possible that new drugs may be developed which will temporarily increase mental efficiency without ill-effect. But it seems unlikely that any lasting improvement in human capacity will be achieved except by the selection and recombination of genes: the possible place of eugenics in the further evolution of man is considered elsewhere in this book.

The Future of Community Medicine

As the individual practice of medicine develops there will be further developments in preventive and social medicine, and above all in the study of environmental factors which influence non-infective diseases such as cancer and coronary thrombosis. This too is already happening, though vested interests still sometimes stand in the way of action. At the time of writing, cigarettes are advertised widely on posters and television, although the relation between cigarette smoking and cancer is clear beyond reasonable doubt.

It has long been accepted that certain doctors, usually working quite separately from those who treat individual patients, have a responsibility for the health of the community. Although this division of function has often been considered regrettable it has developed in response to a need, and provided that each group willingly co-operates with the other, it has great advantages, for the duty to the community is sometimes in conflict with the duty to the individual, and the doctor attending his patients is often too busy and too untrained to interest himself in problems of the public health. There is, however, a borderline exemplified by child welfare clinics and antenatal services where preventive medicine and individual medicine meet. There are many who think that these services should properly be the responsibility of the family doctor, and there is at present in Britain a movement towards the establishment of group practices operating from centres equipped to give this type of service. Nevertheless it must be recognized that the need for the provision of such services by the health departments of local authorities arose because the general practitioner was not providing them, and that on the whole women are more interested in infants and young children than are men. The existing child welfare clinics are largely staffed by women.

Medicine's Part in the Further Evolution of Man

The amazing progress in medical science described earlier in this chapter has only been due to a small extent to practising doctors; most of it comes from medical scientists in laboratories, from chemists, pharmacologists, physicists: even the new techniques of surgery would be impossible without modern anaesthetics and antibiotics. This combination of science and medicine has enabled man to be very largely master of his environment as far as the ravages of epidemic disease are concerned, with the result that the dangers from over-population are only too clear.[5] The doctor's duty is not, however, affected by this. He must continue to control disease, and other measures must be found for the relief of over-population. Of these there could only be two which would be acceptable in a truly civilized world, namely, increased food-production (which could only be a temporary remedy), and birth-control. The development of an efficient and harmless orally administered contraceptive tablet and the breaking down of superstitious and dogmatic prohibitions of its use are amongst the greatest needs of the present day. Recent experiments with steroids which inhibit ovulation seem to suggest that the medical part of the problem is nearer solution than it was a few years ago.

If man's environment is already very largely under his control, no doubt his heredity could be if he so wished. There is no doubt that by careful selection he could breed better scientists, better artists, musicians, mathematicians and with artificial insemination and the possibility of storing human sperm and even ova in deep freeze for years, the potentialities are boundless and exciting. They are also frightening in the extreme. The recent history of the world shows how far wisdom lags behind knowledge. A civilization which developed the atomic bomb before the atomic power-station does not seem fit to be trusted with experiments in human heredity.

Although human genetics is of great interest and importance, as stressed in the chapter *The Human Future*, man's future evolution will depend largely on the dissemination of ideas but in combination with the slower processes of biological variation and natural selection.

Mather[6] has made an analogy between genes and ideas and points out that they both influence evolution through the processes of variation and selection; but whereas genes are only conveyed vertically from generation to generation, ideas can spread laterally and much more quickly. To play some small part in evolution by the dissemination of ideas is the real purpose of this book.

Postscript: Medicine and Religion

A hundred years after Darwin and T. H. Huxley it seems remarkable that in conventional British society a disbelief in religious doctrine is something which has to be concealed or covertly explained lest the speaker or writer be thought odd, blasphemous or otherwise socially unacceptable, and expose himself even to open attack. I must therefore explain that in this postscript I write solely for myself and because of the strictures still imposed on free speech I do not even know whether I voice the views of a substantial proportion of my profession.

A large number of those who still claim adherence to their Christian faith would probably be embarrassed if you thought that they ever went to church save for christenings, marriages and memorial services; a way of life currently known as C of E, and regarded as respectable. But the acceptance of a scientific way of thinking in one's professional life and of the apostles' creed at memorial services seems to require a dichotomy of mind with which some are not equipped.

Systems of religious belief and doctrine have often proved an impediment to evolution by the dissemination of ideas in the past, and as they may still do so in the future, it is perhaps a duty to say something of a point of view which a life dedicated to medicine has helped to mould. Much has been written on how medicine and the Church can work together: less has been heard of the outlook of what has been called scientific Humanism in its relation to medicine.

The fact that there are moral, spiritual, emotional, ethical and aesthetic values not amenable to measurement does not argue for or against any final cause. If the churchman is to seize upon the compassion and dedication of nurse and doctor as evidence of a benign deity he must also be prepared to be asked why the laws of heredity are the same as the laws of chance, and why suffering seems to be distributed fortuitously and widely throughout the human and animal kingdom. These are no new questions, but there is no escape from them, especially for the doctor, and they still remain unanswered by theologians although readily explained by evolution.

Man's suffering is now being alleviated by man himself; or if man is only working through some benign supernatural power, then how is it that it was God's will that children suffering from tuberculous meningitis should die until about 1947 since when it is his will that they should live?

—a strangely capricious deity whose sudden change of heart coincided remarkably closely with the discovery of streptomycin. I would never take any step to lessen a patient's belief in his god, but I ask myself privately, if a god exists have I not been working against him rather than with him, for I have tried to use the means put into my hands by medical science to save the lives of those who were destined to die, while my paediatric and orthopaedic colleagues have tried to repair some of the handicaps which the dice of heredity serve out to little children. I cannot pass unchallenged the Church's tacit assumption that all that is good, moral and beautiful is its own exclusive right, and something which the unbeliever is unqualified to experience, for I have been trying to teach the ethics of medical practice for most of my life, and in another field of human experience I can, after years of endeavour, and in all humility, begin to understand the late Beethoven quartets.

Finally, I must assert in the clearest terms that the Humanist and scientist is not a man deprived of feeling. Indeed he may, as I know only too well, be most uncomfortably endowed with a talent for sharing the grief of those who suffer the slings and arrows of outrageous fortune.

REFERENCES

(1) Singer, Charles. *A Short History of Medicine*. New York: Oxford University Press, 1928.

(2) Stafford-Clark, David. *Psychiatry Today*. Pelican Books, 1952; Strauss, E. B. *Psychiatry in the Modern World*. London: Joseph, 1958; Lewis, Aubrey. 'Mental Disorders', *Chambers Encyclopaedia*, 1950, Vol. 9, p. 258.

(3) Comfort, Alex. *The Biology of Senescence*. New York: Rinehart & Co., 1956.

(4) Eckstein, H. *The English Health Service*. Harvard University Press, 1959.

(5) Rolph, C. H., ed. *The Human Sum*. New York: Macmillan, 1957.

(6) Mather, K. *The Listener*, October 8, 1959, p. 566.

G. C. L. BERTRAM

WHAT ARE PEOPLE FOR?

G. C. L. BERTRAM, M.A., PH.D.

Born 1911. Educated: Berkhamsted School; St John's College, Cambridge. Chief Fisheries Officer, Palestine, 1940–44. Fellow and Tutor of St John's College, Cambridge, since 1945. Director of Scott Polar Research Institute, Cambridge, 1949–56. General Secretary of the Eugenics Society since 1957.

Publications: *Arctic and Antarctic: The Technique of Polar Travel*, 1939; *A Prospect of the Polar Regions*, 1958; *Adam's Brood: The Hopes and Fears of a Biologist*, 1959, and many articles.

WHAT ARE PEOPLE FOR?

This question, 'What are people for?', is a supreme example of a fundamental question which is almost never asked. In the past the struggle to
survive, both specifically and personally, was so intense that the first
object of survival—reproduction—seemed sufficient in itself. Yet now,
surely, the changed circumstances of today must force us into further
thought. Today—already in advanced nations, soon we hope in all—the
expectation of life at birth is high; the physical struggle for specific and
personal survival recedes into the background, except for the heavy
shadow of nuclear or biological warfare; reproduction becomes deliberate;
and many intelligent people have already become conscious of today's
appalling population surge. The question may still be over-simple, yet the
answer is both elusive and all-pervasive.[4] [5]

There must be few indeed among us—atheists, theists, mystics,
agnostics and Humanists alike—who do not feel that there is an element
of direction in our personal lives and in the life of our species. Some will
feel that 'direction' has two meanings in this context, some that it has but
one. Again, there must be few who truly have no familiarity with
conscience and duty, love and altruism—few whose actions are guided
solely by external pressures within the social framework. Such attributes
are surely connected with matters of human direction and purpose. But
absence of clear purpose, in the sense of explanation, does not remove the
validity or the propriety of attempts to define objectives in human life and
living.

To clear the argument, it is perhaps easy first to agree what are *not*
among human objectives. Obviously we do not believe that humanity's
proper destiny is the breeding of cannon-fodder; nor the production of a
multitude who will have to live in squalor and hunger; nor the production
of an enlarged environment for human parasites; nor is our human
objective the production of the largest possible market for the manu-
facturers of material objects.

No. Our jointly agreeable objectives are in the realms of the 'good life',
the fulfilment of individuals, the achievements of societies and cultures,

and the perfection of humanity in terms of biological evolution. There may, indeed, be a large measure of agreement if we attempt to define the objectives in human life in some such terms as these: that every individual shall be born a loved and wanted child, in an environment which will, in liberty, allow the full development of all the attributes with which he is endowed, physical, mental and spiritual. We desire, at the same time, a continuation of human evolution, both genetic and psychosocial, such that gradually may be produced a population in which the many shall possess a stature which is rare indeed today. So may there be progress from primitive poverty and survival, through the Welfare State, towards Huxley's 'Fulfilment Society'.

If that is indeed our worthy aim, what are the chances in the matter of approaching it? The answer—to anticipate the argument—is discouraging indeed unless there is speedy global action—in Muller's words—'by the introduction of social conscience into reproductive practices'.

In this last half-century, an earlier growing stream of knowledge has suddenly expanded into a flood of factual detail rather than of under-standing. The glamour of the physical sciences, the marvels of manu-facture, the bombs and the rockets, the transport and the communications, have caught the attention of an astonished and now apprehensive public. Yet, truly, it is the biological changes of recent times which have most modified the prospects for our way of life. These are the conquest of major diseases, the removal of much pain, the extension of individual expectation of life at birth, and overwhelmingly the population explosion—a doubling of human numbers in eighty-five years and a further doubling in the next forty.[6][8] The world already contains 700 million more people than at the beginning of World War II, and the next twenty years will add a further 1,000 million and more. The present world figure is above 2,800 million, and among recent United Nations estimates[9] for the year 2000 is 6,270 million, based upon 'the medium assumption' for a variety of factors.

For any sensible consideration of human aim, purpose or destiny, the many must realize not only the explosion of knowledge, but this explosion of people, in the very heart of which we live today. An explosion of comprehension and intelligent action now is essential or we smother all that is worthy by our own proliferation.

This present frightening and unprecedented proliferation of population, made possible by the use of knowledge, is the supreme problem of the human world. If nuclear warfare becomes commonplace the aims of all but the mad are wrecked. If the nuclear danger is conquered—and it can be conquered by the decisions of the few—the dangers inherent in the human surge predominate.

The factors concerned in the population explosion are plain to see. First in time came the spread, in the last few centuries, of European dominance over much of the world—often a so-called colonialism which, whatever the mixture of motives involved, in fact and in large degree abolished that petty local strife which was a powerful check upon multiplication. Secondly, there has been the revolution in transport and a consequent power to alleviate famine. Thirdly, population-increase has sprung from the progressive control of diseases by large-scale improvements in water-supply and in sanitation. Fourthly, there is medicine at the personal level. And progressively and in parallel there have been all the population-sustaining improvements in crop-production which compose the agricultural revolution—increase of area cultivated, genetic advance, provision of fertilizers, control of pests, mechanization, and so on. All these are the children of the new knowledge.

A large part of these tremendous changes has been brought about by the mediation, or indeed under the spur, of man's compassion. If man had no ethical sense, no lively conscience, world population would be a small figure in comparison with what in fact it is today. Conscience, kindness, medicine, science—an astonishing conglomeration—have brought about widespread and still spreading death-control. Further, the consciences of many individuals have already begun to merge into the political activities of nations, the richer deliberately helping the poorer to develop.

Death-control, by deliberate effort sprung from an active conscience, has impinged most powerfully upon the formerly near stable or only slowly multiplying population. Yet how many, even of delegates to the United Nations, are really conscious of the facts today? How many of them yet realize—despite the statistical efforts of the United Nations Demographic Unit—that world population today already exceeds 2,800 millions; that world population will double well before the turn of the century, within the lifetimes of half of those already alive today?[6] Those delegates in the General Assembly would surely flinch if brought to recognize that every year in fact there is added the total of all the present people of Canada, Australia, New Zealand, Sweden, Denmark, Finland and Norway, and each year progressively still more. Yet that is how today the population of our world explodes.

Further, and shockingly, it is not only the absolute numbers of humankind that mount but the percentage rate of compound increment itself which grows inexorably: 0·53 per cent in 1800–50, 0·64 per cent to 1900, 1·04 per cent to 1950, 1·68 per cent to 1955.[7]

We now live under totally new circumstances, the product of our own compassion for others exercised through death-control. The essential surge of biological comprehension and action have yet to come. As in Biblical days the numbering of the people caused trouble, so today do matters of population study and control arouse depths of emotion as dangerous as they are ultimately absurd. The existing variety of mankind, in both the genetic and the non-genetic sense and both within and between nations, serves but to exacerbate emotion and endanger rationality and the possibility of solution.

If the maximum of coexistent human flesh were indeed the objective of human existence we are well on the way to achieve it. But most certainly no 'good life' would result.

Those who have biological education—and indeed any who understand simple arithmetic—recognize of course that all species are ultimately limited in their population-growth. At all times the number of any species represents the uneasy temporary balance between the forces of growth and reproduction on the one hand, and of destruction and death on the other. The availability of food is commonly the arbiter: it is the core of what we can call the population and resources complex. The total picture is blurred for the undiscerning by the deliberate activities of men and the products of new techniques. The food-providing capacity of our world increases with the aid of increased areas of cultivation, increased use of fertilizers, new crop varieties and so on. At the same time food-producing capacity tends to be decreased as a direct result of our wrong management of much of our environment, of which the over-cutting of forest, the over-fishing and pollution of water, the over-grazing of land, are simple examples. The net product of these two sets of processes is the annual yield of foodstuffs. The total has gone up enormously, but so has the total of mouths to be filled. So the normal pattern persists: between one-half and two-thirds, of all the people of the world alive together, regularly exist, decade by decade, on diets which are internationally agreed to be inadequate in terms of clinical observation. The surplus production of North America is almost negligible in proportion to the total need elsewhere.

The immense under-provision of biologically-produced materials—such as fibres, paper, timber and so many more competitors for productive land—is less discussed because there is no internationally accepted measure of the minimum desirable. The same is true of minerals and energy, even of water too. And, further, let it be recognized, even the availability of food and all the other biological and mineral resources, which we seek, are mere helpers on the road. Their provision is not an adequate end in itself. To think in terms of a race between population and food supplies is to have the wrong approach to reality.[3][4]

Today the fundamental priority is the decrease of the actual rate of annual human increment. We must achieve a substantial reduction of the accelerating rate of compound interest at which world population surges upwards. A clear example is afforded by a recent economic survey[2] of India which demonstrates that unless the incremental rate can effectively be halved within, say, thirty years, then there is slender hope indeed of wide-scale economic betterment—and with that goes nutrition too.

There is a particular aspect which needs attention here. There are those who urge that the potentialities for much greater food-production are immense, and that there is folly in fussing now about the total of consumers. Potentialities for increased food-production indeed are great, but there is, too, the awkward disregarded fact that the realization of potentialities so often needs the use of force, the power of dictation. The change from peasant agriculture to collectivization or plantation agriculture is a simple case in point: more food could often be produced from the same area of land as a direct consequence of the change. But in the West, Humanist or not, we love freedom; we hate coercion; we have faith in the virtues of individuality, the family unit, and personal effort. The use of force is utterly distasteful: potentiality, we argue, must be realized by technical guidance and education, leadership and co-operation. But force is quicker, and more can be done before the population mounts so high; there is possibility perhaps of gaining temporarily in the struggle against under-provision. Here is a crucial dilemma. Yet fundamental throughout is the necessity of reducing the rate of population-growth.

Now regard the problem in a broader way. There simply are *no* real and admirable advantages in any great further increase in world population. It cannot sensibly be argued that numbers must mount in order that the mass market may increase for particular material objects. The increase of a mass market is not a true measure of advance. Likewise, reproduction so as to build bigger armies, whether of infantry or technicians, is *not* admirable advantage.

Not only are there no discernible and admirable advantages in further population increase, but the disadvantages are so real and many, quite apart from poverty and under-nourishment. What is the correlation between mounting numbers and national pugnacity? It is surely all too often positive. Was not World War II initiated in the name of *Lebensraum?* Is India perhaps exceptional? We hear now, too, of stress syndromes which are known to afflict our fellow mammals under conditions of high population-density and resultant struggle. And urban man himself most certainly is not immune: neurotic symptoms multiply.

The despoliation of the natural environment, the extinction of other species of strange and beautiful animals and plants, the fouling of rivers, the oiling of birds and beaches, urban sprawl and traffic chaos, these are all direct consequences of excessive increase in numbers. Space itself already becomes a rare commodity as the conurbations grow, and cities become places of frustration rather than of culture. Even worse, for the full development of important aspects of the individual, is the progressive difficulty of finding solitude. Likewise, as local numbers mount so too diminishes the feeling of personal 'relatedness' with the majority of those one sees.

Indeed the population explosion jeopardizes whatever worth, development and evolution—whatever happiness, opportunity and enlargement of personality—we may cherish for our children and future generations.

What then may we, must we, do? Self-interest, knowledge and compassion, all urge action. Knowledge and kindness alone have developed death-control to an astonishing degree. The inevitable consequence is this population explosion—this overwhelming human surge—for which we must now take full responsibility. Indeed responsibility is our lot whether we act for good or ill. We have the future of our species in our keeping and doubtfully are we good husbandmen.

Problems, at least biological problems, rarely have one simple solution, for many factors interplay. If the nutritional state of the many is lastingly to be improved, not only must there be great increases of the food available, but limitation too of the mouths to be fed. As yet there is still the chance of limitation by deliberate contraceptive effort with the hope of avoiding the inevitable alternative, limitation by natural means—strife, disease and under-nourishment—which our compassion teaches us so strenuously to avoid.

Contraception is a vehicle of freedom and responsibility in the Western world. It is a blessing so far spread to only a small fraction of the world's population. In some areas its further dissemination is rapid: in other areas, lacking effort, it is nil. Japan affords an example where even government-sponsored dissemination of contraception has been too slow, and harsh environmental pressure upon a highly intelligent island race has resulted in a large-scale return to the locally traditional limitation by abortion. Thus has the birth-rate been halved, in less than a decade. But even that drastic action has still left an annual population-increment of about one million or $1 \cdot 2$ per cent, a heavy incubus indeed.

We cannot be certain that even the widest spread of personal contraceptive effort, exercised in freedom, will by itself necessarily succeed in halting the population explosion. But contraception most certainly could blanket and encompass it: and the explosion certainly cannot be contained without it in any manner which can be remotely acceptable to kindly, freedom-loving, human beings.

An immense awakening is essential, in speedy action and in understanding. We have already come far. It is only forty-three years since Margaret Sanger's trial and imprisonment in New York because of her pioneer advocacy of humanitarian contraceptive help for American women in poverty. And last year contraceptive controversy in relation to American overseas aid played a part in the contest for the Presidency. President Eisenhower has recently stressed that the problem of the under-developed nations is more lasting, more important, to Western civilization than Soviet-Western differences. The United States—in its wealth and benevolence so abnormal in world history—together with the United Kingdom and other nations, can surely now give a vigorous lead both in contraceptive research and in the provision of contraceptive aid on request from countries in poverty and demographic travail. Most promising research is already advancing, yet much more still is needed quickly, more especially with regard to oral contraceptives. Development of these is promising but all too slow, lacking as yet that degree of official encouragement and sponsorship which would be the hallmarks of effective and responsible national leadership.

International zeal is already manifest in such organizations as the World Bank, the World Health Organization and the Food and Agricultural Organization of the United Nations. International scientific, technical and cultural co-operation likewise grows fast today. Yet, in matters demographic, the time-factor is now of such transcendent importance that, whatever the good-natured zeal, wide success in human betterment is not truly attainable unless the percentage rate of population-increase is swiftly checked over a large part of the world. Already 3 per cent per annum is not rare. High rates of population-increase are now the measure of approaching disaster, rather than of medical and sanitary success. The greatest present numbers, poverty and danger to themselves, all lie in Asia, but the turn of the West Indies, Africa and South America will soon arrive.

Whatever nation leads, the immediate need is an international merging of effort, under the United Nations, so as to produce a World Development Organization with a truly global programme, aiming not only at the production of material wealth but also the conservation and development of 'enjoyment resources' like natural beauty and wild life, and on the balanced development and realization of man's own cultural and spiritual possibilities.

The policy contours of such a programme will only emerge clearly as the world evolves. Some of them are, however, unmistakable even now. For example, in giving aid to a country it would be essential to take into account its general ecology; the need not only to develop and utilize all its resources, but also to conserve them for future use and enjoyment; and finally its demographic situation, so that the rising tide of population may not wipe out the benefits of economic aid.

Thus one important function of the Organization would be to foster and provide demographic control as an integral part of development and human betterment. The huge and widening divide between the haves and have-nots of today, is impossible of reduction without world-wide control of population-increase. It is the have-nots, the people of the under-developed areas, who are most directly menaced by the highest rates of population growth, both present and potential.

The argument that industrialization and higher standards of living will by themselves solve all problems by cutting down the birth-rate auto-matically, is simply false. Industrialization and higher standards of material living may tend in that direction, but the present experience of the United States—with $1 \cdot 6$ per cent per annum increase and a doubling in forty years—amply demonstrates the possibility of the opposite tendency too. Furthermore, to be effective, industrialization would have to be so swift that it could only occur by the imposition of an unacceptable degree of force.

Deliberate checks to the fantastic present world-population increase are imperative if our children and our grand-children are not to lose much of what we hold dear, in the realms of beauty and freedom, opportunity and advancement and, if the majority are not to suffer more, even in health and strength.

We must then agree to limit total human numbers for these two desperately important inter-connected reasons. The first is plain biological good sense and foresight: excessive numbers ultimately crash in disaster. The second is that we are progressively less likely to achieve any aims beyond mere survival, let alone any ideals, as numbers further multiply.

Necessarily therefore numbers must be limited. The spread of contra-ception is certainly gathering impetus, but almost wholly on the personal level, as a method of increasing freedom, responsibility and dignity in parenthood. That is entirely valid personally, but totally inadequate globally, in relation to the fundamental urgencies and dangers which remain as yet entirely unshackled. Here indeed we have, by analogy, an example of an ineffective fine adjustment preceding the coarse adjustment which is essential. To operate an effective coarse adjustment without an excessive restriction of freedom is the heart of the problem. The mere passage of further time and the gathering momentum of population-increase make the problem not only more urgent but more intractable every day.

In this chapter there is no space to extend beyond the quantitative aspects of the population surge and its eventual control. There can be no more than mention here of the qualitative problems set by the inherent diversity of mankind, and their varying rates of increase. From the 'yellow peril' to the 'spawning of the English', from the spread of Indians into East Africa to that of Chinese into South-east Asia, here are facets of an age-old evolutionary process which continues today and certainly will not have ended tomorrow. How can the need for overall limitation of world population be correlated in peace with these racial and cultural problems? Surely by global action alone. There can be no peaceful solution without much education, much thought and much goodwill. Human population-control and human evolution alike have come to be our immediate joint responsibilities which we can neglect to our own detriment alone. There can be no important advance without co-ordinated international action—scientific, technical, educational and political together.

Yet the fact must be faced that there are the unthinking multitude, together with the part-thinking many, who feel no need for action. They assume or contend that the present world demographic problem will solve itself in the fullness of time. They fail to recognize that the process of 'solution' will involve economic disasters, great falls in the standard of living, progressively ever more under-nourishment than already exists today, even starvation and strife. The variations in well-being and in poverty between the haves and the have-nots will become even greater than they are today. Time alone *will* settle the demographic problem, but in a way which cannot be acceptable to any who possess a compassionate spirit, and desire further human advance.

Some, including those who take the Communist Party line, assert that there is, and will be, no demographic problem if the potentialities in science, agriculture, transport and the rest are allowed to develop to the full. There are two replies to that mistaken view. The one is that even hateful physical coercion would be inadequate to convert potentiality to practice at speed enough both to catch up with insufficiency and to raise standards so long as rates of population-increase continue to accelerate. The other is the complete absence, as we have seen, of admirable advantage in further great population-increases, and many disadvantages which are inescapable.

Others, on doctrinal grounds, condemn all limitation by contraceptive means. Those are pre-eminently the Roman Catholics. Others may find social or emotional, traditional or other difficulties, but not often those of actual doctrine. Yet even the Church of Rome appears to the outsider to allow a gradual revision of doctrinal interpretation with the passage of time and change of circumstances. It is a curious paradox that today the main impediments to the faster world-wide spread of contraceptive facilities are ignorance and emotion, Communism and Roman Catholicism.

The United Kingdom, under adverse economic conditions, is an example of an advanced population, with full contraceptive facilities available to a large part of its people, deliberately limiting its reproduction to much lower levels. That was true between the wars, when the net reproductive rate fell below unity and there was an expectation of a long-term decline in numbers. That took place entirely by personal choice aided by financial stringency and not by governmental encouragement.

In contrast there is the astonishing volatility and present buoyancy of the United States birth-rate under conditions of national optimism and material affluence. The United States has now, at $1 \cdot 6$, a high percentage population-increase. The United Kingdom, despite the post-war baby boom, still is not above replacement level, its unfortunate increase being the result of increased length of life alone. Yet even the United States population plus that of the United Kingdom together make less than 8 per cent of the world total.

However, these are examples of the actions of advanced nations, though still with only moderately good contraceptive facilities. So far in fact contraception has become a normal part of personal freedom and responsible parenthood for far less than one-tenth of the world's people. Lacking such facilities, voluntary male sterilization, with a State payment to hasten the new fashion, now spreads in parts of India.

Population limitation *must* indeed be brought about on the widest scale, and yet we desire that personal freedom shall not be excluded. If today's contraceptive spread and knowledge had come some eighty years ago, before the last doubling of world population took place, how much more promising would have been the present demographic outlook. With world population expected more than to double again by the close of the present century, the resultant pressures will not be favourable to freedom, either in reproduction or in wholesome democracy. Yet with leadership and education, persuasion and economic pressure through taxation, so much can still be done. The United Kingdom and Japan are diverse pointers towards what can be achieved.

However, the gloomy prophet must not restrain but must stimulate the present effort. Only thus is there hope for a worthy future in which the varied capacities of individuals shall have the opportunity to develop freely. Only thus may draw nearer the stimulating and fascinating goal of man deliberately perfecting himself by evolutionary process, in full freedom and within the framework of responsibility which in fact is already his.

Global population policies and programmes, racial or national quotas, government planning for optimal densities, are not far-fetched fantasies simply because today few people think of them. Such policies become essential if not inevitable. The assumption is that, once their eyes are opened by education and the harsh facts of environmental and demographic pressures, even the many will seek the promise of a fuller life at lower population densities. That is the only hopeful alternative to frustration and struggle, hunger and strife. However much we may be wary of an excess of regulation, consciously accepted discipline is far better than dictation on the one hand or chaos on the other. Whether the pride of nations and national sovereignties will promote national population quotas, or whether the need for quotas and limitation will stimulate wider and world organization, is not for prophecy here. The generality of governments must see the writing on the wall and not those of Japan, India and a few others alone. The United Nations itself, together with WHO and FAO, must cease to shirk the reality which so many of their leaders can already see. As yet they shirk simply because of Roman Catholic and Communist pressures. That would seem to be religious and racial discrimination in reverse.

Those who think and care, both the religious and the Humanists, the teachers and the leaders, surely must come to recognize that reproduction and survival cease to be the central and sufficient core of human endeavour. Under modern conditions, reproduction and survival to old age come to be deliberate and expected: no longer are they matters of chance and struggle except where so far we have failed in present efforts. That being so, the future heart of our lively endeavour must surely become the complete development of individuals and the evolution of the species— in wider fulfilment and cultural achievement—struggling to that end to retain our appreciation of freedom and of quality. Yet time is of the essence: urgent conjoint action on the global scale is the world's necessity today. It is in that setting that now the thoughtful must persuade the many to ponder 'What are people for?' As they strive to answer that question so will they react at last against the horrors of excess, both of materialism and of people.

REFERENCES

(1) Teilhard de Chardin, Pierre. *The Phenomenon of Man*. New York: Harper & Brothers, 1959.

(2) Coale, A. J., and Hoover, E. M. *Population Growth and Economic Development in Low Income Countries*. Princeton University Press, 1958.

(3) Brown, Harrison. *The Challenge of Man's Future*. New York: Viking, 1950.

(4) Huxley, Sir Julian. 'Population Planning and the Quality of Life', *Eugenics Review*, Vol. 51, 1959.

(5) Huxley, Sir Julian. 'What are People for? Population versus People.' Address on November 19, 1959, at the Annual Luncheon of the Planned Parenthood Federation of America.

(6) P. E. P. (Political and Economic Planning). *World Population and Resources*. New York: Oxford University Press (Essential Books), 1955.

(7) *Population Bulletin*, Vol. XV, No. 8, December 1959. Population Reference Bureau, Inc., Washington, D.C.

(8) *United Nations Demographic Yearbook*. New York, 1958. Annual Editions.

(9) United Nations Department of Economic and Social Affairs. *The Future Growth of World Population*. 1958, p. 23.

(10) United Nations Population and Vital Statistics Report. *Statistical Papers* Series A, Vol. XI, No. 4. New York, 1960. (Figures to October 1, 1959.)

(11) See H. J. Muller's chapter in the present volume.

E. M. NICHOLSON

THE PLACE OF CONSERVATION

THE PLACE OF CONSERVATION

Man, like other animals, began life in a natural habitat. Unlike other animals—except a few which have become dependent on him—he has outgrown and almost forgotten it. This basic fact has much to do with many present-day human problems, economic, social and psychological. Unfortunately, most of those who have been most aware of it have been heavily influenced by sentiment and nostalgia towards the Yeomen of England, or even the Noble Savage. They have neither had the wish, nor possessed the mental training, to rethink what it means in terms of the future of our increasingly technological civilization. On the other hand those able to grasp the historical, economic, social and technological evolution of mankind have often been illiterate in terms of the life and earth sciences: at best they have expressed strong aesthetic misgivings. The problem, therefore, has slipped through one of the cracks in our education.

It is, for obvious reasons, an almost universal rule for animals to satisfy their everyday requirements for food and shelter by 'cropping' current surpluses of plant or animal life without imperilling their sustained yield in future years. Animals unable to adapt their habits and regulate their numbers to this end are heading for extinction. Many cases are indeed known, and countless others must exist, where animals indirectly enrich the soil or the fauna and flora of their habitat while directly exploiting a part of it. Mites, nematodes (eelworms) and innumerable other tiny animals help to make soil by such activities as breaking down dead leaves and releasing their stored nutrients, while millipedes and earthworms generate or regenerate soils by passing them through their guts. Some earthworms, in turn, can exist only where they can find dung of grazing animals. On oceanic islands herbivores such as sheep are sustained on plants fertilized out of the sea through marine birds living on a diet of fish or plankton and spreading some of the nutrients in their rich droppings, so that biological productivity is enhanced.

Just as evolution has produced higher forms of life, so the ecological interplay of different plants and animals has often raised the biological potential of their common home, and has thus enabled more complex and more specialized communities to develop out of simpler or poorer ones. The tall tropical rain-forests exhibit an amazing array of exotic and specialized plants and animals maintaining a living web which rises a hundred feet or more above the surface over thousands of miles. Yet these forests are often growing on poor soils which, once stripped of their original cover, prove incapable of yielding any economic crop.

Sometimes natural catastrophes such as storms, floods and droughts may temporarily and locally set the clock back. Occasionally also the natural regulation of animal populations fails to prevent a local plague or epidemic. Often these setbacks bring compensation by opening opportunities for development in new directions. At worst they are hardly significant exceptions to the general tendency for living things to maintain or improve opportunities for equally or more advanced living things to follow them.

Man is the main violator of this law. It now appears that at quite early stages in prehistory, man stumbled on means of over-exploiting his habitat for short-term gain, especially by the lavish use of fire. Other techniques followed, bringing in their train soil-erosion and loss of woodland cover over rather extensive areas of early human settlement. From the Indus Valley to Greece and Italy the regions which cradled civilization are with few exceptions deforested, with degraded and relatively infertile soils, eroded slopes and wrecked systems of natural drainage and water-supply. This is man's mark as it used to be before he acquired his recent mastery over larger-scale instruments and techniques of destruction. He can and does step up the impact now.

Until the past five centuries, although damage was done to a disturbingly high proportion of the earth's limited resources of good cultivable land, it was limited by the rather small numbers, restricted mobility, and rather feeble equipment and technology of the human species. As lately as some three hundred years ago the entire area of European settlement in the Old and New Worlds had to support only just over 100 million people at fairly low consumption standards, against ten times as many today, making immensely higher demands per head on both renewable and non-renewable resources. World population, now close to 3,000,000,000, has increased some six times in just over three centuries, but more than half this immense increase has occurred within the memory of many people now living.

With the discoveries in other continents by European explorers, the improvements in navigation and seaborne trade, the rise of invention and the consequential exploitation of food and raw materials in other lands, the need for restraint, or in other words for conservation, became increasingly acute. Unfortunately few of the emigrants, or of those most influential in this great change, recognized the problem or knew the techniques. A sense of responsibility towards posterity over these matters could hardly be expected in view of the poor ethical standards too often exhibited by the builders of new countries towards their fellow-men. Conservation had next to no part in the philosophy of even the more enlightened. Cultures such as those of India and China, which contained elements of conscious and universal reverence and respect for the earth and its creatures, and even taboo on the killing of some animals, were themselves encroached upon by supposedly more advanced cultures without any such inhibitions. It was both an irony and a catastrophe of human history that, the more desperately world-wide conservation was needed, the more the leadership passed to those who least understood and valued it, until the need for it had to be learned again the hard way.

The mining of the land, and the destruction of biological capital, happened fastest in the newly occupied white man's countries. It was in these, and particularly the United States, that the shock of sudden extinctions of abundant animals such as the passenger pigeon and (very nearly) the bison, together with the spectacle of the dust-bowl and the catastrophic floods released by the devastated watersheds, brought the earliest revulsion from unreflecting exploitation towards deliberate, scientific policies of conservation. President Theodore Roosevelt, by his outspoken leadership and example, converted this feeling into something almost like religion among public-spirited Americans.

The course of the industrial revolution and of early colonialism tended to perpetuate local customs and so to delay the full impact of technology in what we now call the under-developed countries, while hastening and accentuating it in industrial Europe. Here nineteenth-century invention and materialism proliferated immense mounds of mining spoil and urban refuse, sewage (and later chemical) pollution of rivers and estuaries, smoke pollution of the air and of everything exposed to it, clumsy and thought-less canalization and diversion of waterways, subsidence through mining and pumping, and the creation of many types of blighted or devastated areas. These became regarded as normal accompaniments of nineteenth-century 'progress', and if they were complained of, it was rather because of their dirt, smell or other inconvenience than as a violation of trusteeship.

All these abuses continued throughout the first half of the twentieth century, with the addition of toxic chemical pollution of the air in the form of smog, massive oil pollution not only of fresh but of tidal and even marine waters, wholesale killing of fish and other aquatic life through deoxygenation (for instance by heated water pumped out from electrical generating stations), drying up of rivers or mingling of biologically incompatible streams through diversion tunnels for hydro-electric schemes, destruction of wild life through spraying land and water with chemical poisons, and the beginnings of pollution of the deep ocean by radioactive waste and of the upper air by radioactive fall-out following nuclear tests.

This second wave of modern devastation of life and its habitats differed from the first in being much less localized and in having more pervasive and widespread indirect and cumulative as well as direct and immediate effects. Early in the second half of the century even pollution of the moon was brought within reach. The impact also spread to regions of the earth hitherto relatively immune from exposure to advanced industrial technology, including many of the industrially under-developed countries. At the same time accelerating capital-formation and greatly improved communications called for much more land per head of population for housing and for utilities such as roads, airfields and reservoirs, industry and recreational needs. Another result was the building up of long stretches of shoreline for seaside resorts and the indiscriminate spread of week-end and vacation dwellings, ski-lifts, car-parks and many other sources of interference with landscape, fauna and flora over hitherto inviolate country. These last-named blots and encroachments on nature were uniquely unfortunate, and absurdly symptomatic of human perversion and perversity, because they were deliberately located in places of special beauty and wildness, which qualities they were bound to destroy, thus triggering off a similar process elsewhere among the frustrated seekers for the rest and peace which they themselves had already eliminated in the developed areas. The persistence and vigour with which so many people take every opportunity of fleeing from modern cities in order to seek out (and thus almost inevitably desecrate) anything resembling wilderness is perhaps the most telling evidence for the hypothesis that the conservation of wilderness and its natural scenery and wild life is, although often unconscious and inarticulate, one of the fundamental and essential needs of mankind.

A slum is a neighbourhood reduced to squalor through too many people seeking to take too much out of it and to put too little in. A pest is an animal which finds means of flourishing at the expense of its environment, and accordingly becomes a nuisance or a menace to others. Why is it—for there is no denying the plain fact—that modern man is rapidly turning the earth into a slum and himself into its only serious pest? And why is it that ostensibly enlightened people, and advanced governments and international agencies, are united in pressing forward towards this squalid and unworthy goal? How can evils so evident to every eye, ear and nose be so often ignored, as if they did not exist, or were of no account? How can it be taken for granted, as something not even needing to be argued, that the permanent, general and irrevocable destruction of what has taken millennia to create is automatically justified in order to make room for any fashionable ephemeral technological project? Can any moral progress be claimed between the earliest savage who managed to set a forest alight to get himself an easy meal of panic-stricken game and the latest international development project which drowns thousands of wild animals in order to flood an African river valley for what is, perhaps only for a decade or two, the cheapest source of power?

History shows plenty of examples of the astonishing capacity of the human mind to close itself against situations which it may be convenient to ignore. Awakening follows only when the warnings of the far-sighted are reinforced by compelling evidence of evil results. Thus the unwisdom of excessive emphasis on the sacred right of the individual or group to make a quick profit, or of the sacred right of nations to disregard ordinary morality in their dealings with one another or with their people, has become fairly generally accepted in sophisticated societies. Yet the plain need for family limitation is still blocked by blind belief in a sacred right of unlimited and irresponsible reproduction. The urge to self-deception is abetted by the genuine incapacity of most minds to grasp such vast processes as the build-up of the total human biomass from a mere twenty-five million tons of seventeenth-century humanity to a present burden on the earth of perhaps 150 million tons of seething, hungry, restless human life. Only on small islands such as Mauritius or Barbados can the cause and effect of unbridled population-increase be visibly demonstrated beyond all possibility of evasion.

Yet there is no escape from the truth that the more the world's human population grows the longer it will take and the harder it will be to end the tragic hunger and poverty in which most people at this moment spend most of their days. This is the most optimistic formulation which is reasonably defensible. A perfectly arguable more pessimistic view is that continuation for only a few more years of the present net increase of over a million people a week or a hundred a minute will lead to a situation in which widespread starvation and violence will become unavoidable. Moreover, that is only the problem on the level of animal needs. There is in addition a colossal deficit of everything which civilized nations look on as essential. Every new mouth to be fed takes, and must take, priority over the provision of schools and universities, of playing-fields and theatres, of libraries, and in fact of all that distinguishes civilization from mere existence. Moreover, the control of capital expenditure, of production and distribution, of imports and exports and even at times of movements which are necessary in order to keep too many people alive on too few resources or on too little land can only mean increasingly drastic and unpleasant interference with individual liberty and dignity. The citizen of a modern metropolis experiences this in a crude simple everyday form as he finds it either impossible to move along the roads in his car or to get out and leave it safely, because there are now too many others trying to do the same thing. Human intelligence applied to engineering gives him a carriage such as kings would have envied; lack of human intelligence applied to human numbers forces him back into a modern counterpart of slavery. All over the world we see at work the inexorable law that the more people there are per square mile the less liberty there can be per person.

As long as this problem of world population remains unsolved—and it can still be solved with intelligence and goodwill—the outlook for conservation of the earth's resources must become increasingly grim every day. Each new noon the world's burden is the heavier by the equal of a new Dundee; every Sunday morning the last week's newcomers to the global housekeeping equal the inhabitants of a Manchester and a Leeds, and every couple of months a new Greater London. Those who still neglect or obstruct the way to a solution bear a grave personal responsibility for helping to deprive their children of much of the natural inheritance which this generation has enjoyed and is squandering. The moral position of the churches on this problem, sometimes flatly reactionary, often equivocal or evasive, at best recognizing the problem without doing anything active about it, is likely to prove embarrassing to them as the truth becomes understood and prevails. As the true threat of sheer weight of numbers not only to material standards but also to freedom and spiritual values becomes manifest the churches may have some awkward questions to answer.

Here religion touches conservation, often unhelpfully, because it is above all the influence of churches, exerted through pressure upon governments and through international agencies, which inhibits the logical and scientific matching of birth-control or family planning with death-control or medical aid. Thus resources intended to raise standards of living are diverted so as to lead to stimulation of fantastic and impractical rates of natural increase of human population, in some cases exceeding 2 per cent annually. The neglect and avoidance of the conservation and family planning issues in most serious discussions about the under-developed countries is a sign of moral irresponsibility as well as intellectual failure.

Conservation is indeed a testing-point for civilizations. Societies which are either scientifically enlightened or imbued with a moral sense of responsibility conserve. Those which are steeped in ignorance over the consequences of their actions, or are too greedy or irresponsible to care, do not conserve. Ours today falls perilously near to the second group.

The reasons for this are worth discussing further. Conservation calls for restraint, and in so far as the benefit accrues to our fellow-men it is mainly to posterity, who have no vote and will not be able to take us personally to task if we leave them in a mess. It is difficult enough to pacify the anxieties and demands of the living. If we can make it easier at the expense of the unborn, why worry? It needs character and objectivity to act as a trustee, and to tell those present that the absent are not always wrong. Yet whatever part such factors may play in contemporary attitudes they are not the whole explanation. There is an extraordinary lack, even among intelligent and well-informed citizens, of any lively and persistent awareness of the continuity of living processes and of our dependence on our ecological base. They do not understand, as every farmer must on his own farm, that present decisions about the land can do much to make or mar the earth for posterity, and that it is therefore incumbent on this generation to know how to exercise a wise trusteeship of that which does not belong to us, but is only at our present disposal as tenants for life. This points to something seriously wrong at least in British educational and religious teaching. Other democracies, such as Sweden, Switzerland and the United States, do far more to open the eyes of the young to the continuing national heritage and to the duty of conserving and preserving it. None, however, has hitherto been more than moderately successful.

Whether or not there is any sound theological reason why the Christian churches should have shut their eyes to the unwisdom and immorality of handing down a spoiled earth to our children, it is to be feared that the attachment to dogmas tending to that end is too rigid to offer any hope of church leadership, or even of effective and vigorous church support, for a more responsible attitude within any time that can help. Individual churchmen see clearly what is wrong, yet in practice it seems that nothing short of a new reverence and respect for the fulfilment of mankind's destiny can provide the foundation for adequate measures of conservation, and that for this we must look to Humanism to lead the way. It is through that sense, and through awareness of the continuing spiritual need for the wilderness in which Christianity itself was born, that the importance of permanent and strict trusteeship for the earth's wonder and beauty and its remaining natural monuments and resources of wild life and scenery, can best be grasped. If a Humanist religion of any sort ever emerges, this must be part of it. It is indeed impious by any standard to desecrate and destroy those inherited possessions of us all which have the power suddenly to exalt the mind of the human beholder, or to convey, like the groves of giant sequoias in California or the oceanic cliffs of St Kilda, a sense of each man's insignificance in time. Yet, as wise men for centuries have known, wilderness even at its least dramatic possesses this power for those who have eyes to see it. A civilization which turns to using psychiatrists instead of wilderness is not rich, but poorer than it will ever understand.

Conservation, however, deserves a place in the Humanist frame on other grounds as well. Conservation is applied ecology, and ecology is the relation of plants and animals (including man) to their environment and to one another. Few even among supposedly natural habitats have escaped experiencing at some time some change through human influence. Few even of the most sophisticated and artificial human activities are entirely divorced from nature. Many of these, indeed, depend on manipulating natural processes without attempting to understand them, except just so far as is essential for successful exploitation. Conservation therefore draws us towards not only a scientific but a philosophical and historical approach to the problems of the earth and our place on it. It propounds from a different angle the question raised elsewhere in this volume 'What are people for?' The questions with which it challenges us take us, like evolution in the nineteenth century, into the domain of morals and religion, yet they are scientific questions and must have scientific answers. Although the life sciences and the earth sciences are today less fashionable than physics and chemistry, their potential is immense. Every glance cast towards outer space reminds us how very little we know yet about the planet which is our home, its rocks, soils, waters and atmosphere, and the plants and animals which have to share it with their selfish and destructive dominant neighbour.

Scientifically, there is at our disposal an immense storehouse of material for research, which is annually being depleted by short-sighted projects whose promoters do not begin to understand their long-term consequences. Reservoirs of special genes lost when a species or local stock of wild or domesticated animals or plants is wiped out can never be replaced: any contribution which they might have yielded when we come to understand many times more than we now do about breeding from such material will have been closed to us forever. Methods of working with, rather than against or regardless of, nature cannot be successfully studied except in the field, in flourishing living communities which have not become warped or diseased through thoughtless interference by man. Often these need to be large if they are to be securely self-perpetuating, and to avoid relapsing to a state when it becomes necessary to manage them like zoological or botanic gardens. They must be free also from invading pests and diseases encouraged by civilization, and from the intrusion of polluted air and water. Some must be kept utterly undisturbed, while others must be available for scientific investigations and experiments, and others again more generally accessible for the education and enjoyment of visitors of all kinds.

Far from 'sterilizing' large areas, and aggravating the problem of feeding human population, a bold and comprehensive programme of conservation and research can contribute much towards the attainment of harmony between world resources and population. Spendthrift attitudes to the land and its use and management are still resulting in heavy annual losses of irreplaceable top-soil blown away by the wind or swept down by water. Even town-dwellers are becoming deeply disturbed at the reckless application of strong poisons, euphemistically described as herbicides and insecticides, without the least scientific evidence that they will not cumulatively build up permanent toxic hazards to animals, including man. Even the users are worried over the emergence of resistant strains of 'weeds' and 'pests' against which known methods may become ineffective. As lately as a quarter of a century ago most farmers were pretty satisfied with their state of knowledge, yet looking back on it in the light of modern practice and modern yields based on the application of a limited segment of science we can see now that their outlook and techniques were in many respects hopelessly inadequate and ineffective for getting the best out of their land and labour. It would be stupid to assume that this process has ended, and that other sciences, notably ecology, cannot contribute to further transformations in our knowledge and outlook.

An attitude of understanding and respect for conservation and the setting aside of areas for research and education could in some regions even now bring quicker and more substantial results than costly and much publicized development projects. Excessive or unwisely managed grazing, the abuse of forests, or the failure to use trees as allies in conservation of water and soil, underlie an immense amount of human poverty. This could be remedied by following out and demonstrating for different regions scientific principles already known, or becoming known, but not yet widely applied. For example, the sustained carrying capacity of many wild pastures may be much increased by identifying and bringing under scientific rotational use relatively small areas vital to livestock for trace elements essential to their health. Enormous losses of nitrogen, and thus of food-production, which are now taking place could probably be prevented by ecological techniques and by correcting wrong methods of effluent disposal. Unwise burning practices, and primitive attitudes to control of predators and pests are among other sources of chronic economic and social loss.

When particular problems of this kind are belatedly recognized the tendency often is to try to call in some technician as a smart 'fixer', who will remedy the symptoms, even if he cannot diagnose, let alone cure, the disease. The immediate and striking recent successes of agricultural chemistry have lent new encouragement to this age-old human foible. But this sort of quackery can work only in some cases and for a certain time; it is the patient who needs treating, and not only the disease.

There is no real substitute for a comprehensive policy of conservation founded on active understanding, deep knowledge and above all serious belief in its fundamental principles. It is no coincidence that a world which is complacently engineering the obliteration of many natural habitats, and the early extermination as wild species of many of its most outstanding animals and plants, is also suffering in physical and mental health, enjoyment, amenity and income from polluted air, rivers and beaches, poisoned and tasteless foods, soil erosion over vast areas, deterioration of pastures, deforestation with flooding and loss of pure water-supplies, growing congestion and lack of elbow-room due to lack of sense about land use and land management and about the right relation of people to this little, much-abused earth. In dumb protest and futile gestures of escape from these intolerable conditions millions of unconscious refugees calling themselves tourists pour out annually like lemmings from the main centres of the trouble, heading for national parks, shorelines, mountains, islands and other places in search of peace, quiet and refreshment. But this Holy Grail nearly always eludes them, for they have brought with them its antithesis, the present *Zeitgeist*, and they are destined to ruin and lose that which they seek blindfold. Yet they cannot give up the quest, since the craving which they cannot understand or explain is for an essential element in their nature which this civilization has filtered out of their lives, leaving them suffering from a kind of spiritual scurvy.

Out of this awareness, and of the ubiquity and conspicuousness of these evils, and the acute discomfort and inconvenience which they are causing to so many, the truth must soon dawn on people. An articulate demand will come for a more responsible, vigorous and scientific attitude towards the inherent human obligation of trusteeship for the future of the land and the sea and all that is on or in them. Such a demand will find scientists and others concerned ready with some of the answers and eager to get to work on the rest. But will it come too late? Unless conservation is promptly, fully and universally recognized as part of the duty of all men at all times while they are guests or tenants on this earth, the remedies found for particular evils will not add up to a whole worthy of mankind. The earth must in part be used as our home, in part be tended as our garden, in part be managed for our many needs in work and leisure, and in part be guarded against ourselves by a self-denying ordinance so that it may be handed down to posterity in a state of nature.

BIBLIOGRAPHY

Coyle, D. C. *Conservation: An American Story of Conflict and Accomplishment.* Rutgers University Press, 1957.

Haw, R. C. *The Conservation of Natural Resources.* London: Faber, 1959.

Heim, R. *Destruction et Protection de la Nature.* Paris: Collection Armand Colin, 1952.

Huth, H. *Nature and the American.* University of California Press, 1957.

International Union for the Protection of Nature:

Proceedings and Papers of the 2nd Technical Meeting. The Hague, September 20–22, 1951, published 1952.

Proceedings and Papers of the 4th Technical Meeting. Salzburg, September 15–19, 1953, published 1954.

Hydro-electricity and Nature Protection: Stating the Case, prepared by Lord Hurcomb. Brussels, 1955.

Proceedings and Papers of the 5th Technical Meeting. Copenhagen, August 25 to September 3, 1954, published 1956.

International Union for the Conservation of Nature:

Derniers Refuges. Atlas Commenté des Réserves Naturelles dans le Monde. Amsterdam: Elsevier, 1956.

Proceedings and Papers of the 6th Technical Meeting. Edinburgh, June 1956; London: Society for the Promotion of Nature Reserves, 1957.

Jacks, G. V. and Whyte, R. O. *Vanishing Lands.* New York: Doubleday, Doran & Company, 1939.

Nicholson, E. M. *Britain's Nature Reserves.* London: *Country Life,* 1957.

Osborn, F. *Our Plundered Planet.* Boston: Little, Brown, 1948.

Tansley, A. G. *Our Heritage of Wild Nature: A Plea for Organized Nature Conservation.* New York: Macmillan, 1945.

Thomas, W. L., ed. *Man's Role in Changing the Face of the Earth.* Chicago: University of Chicago Press, 1956.

Van Straelen, V. *Les Parcs Nationaux du Congo Belge.* Brussels: Et. Res. Nat. et Parcs Nat., 1937.

Vogt, W. *Road to Survival.* New York: Sloan, 1948.

H. J. MULLER

THE HUMAN FUTURE

H. J. MULLER, PH.D., D.SC.

Born 1890. Educated: Columbia University.
Professor of Zoology at Indiana University
since 1945; Distinguished Service Professor
since 1953. Nobel Laureate in Physiology
and Medicine, 1946. President of the Eighth
International Congress of Genetics, 1948.

Publications: *The Mechanism of Mendelian
Heredity* (co-author), 1919; *Out of the Night:
A Biologist's View of the Future*, 1935;
Genetics, Medicine and Man, 1947; and
about 200 articles on biological subjects.

THE HUMAN FUTURE

1. *The Shift in Our Outlook on Our Future*

Throughout past ages the great majority of people have looked upon the future as, by and large, a continuation of pretty much the same state of affairs as they were familiar with in their own day. Even when it was realized that men had advanced all the way from bestiality to civilization as a result of their own exertions, it was usually assumed that the process had almost reached its limit. In fact, it was widely suspected that retrogression or doomsday would soon follow the 'old age' into which, supposedly, civilization had already entered. As Bury has pointed out, before the nineteenth century only a scattered few bold thinkers, such as Seneca, Roger Bacon, Fontenelle, foresaw that knowledge would continue to increase, and still fewer, such as Francis Bacon and Condorcet, grasped its role in improving the lot of humanity.

It might have been expected that, in the nineteenth century, the demonstration of the awesome reaches of biological evolution would soon shake students of human affairs out of the complacency with which they regarded man's future. It is true that by that time technical and intellectual achievements and social ferment had entered upon too fast a growth to be disregarded any longer, and that 'progress' was coming to be taken for granted. The political parties of the Left made it one of the chief foundations of their platforms. However, it is doubtful that many either among the leaders or followers of these and other popular groups have, even yet, more than a vague glimmering of the inordinate immensity of that stream of 'progress' on which they have launched their bark. Most of them still seem to resemble the old-time fabricators of Utopias, in presuming that a nearly perfect State can presently be attained, one in which something like the old idea of a static Heaven will be actualized here below, and in which men can thenceforth live at ease, in the material equivalent of an opium dream.

Perhaps it should not surprise us that the human implications of the Darwinian revolution are still, a century after its promulgation, so feebly apprehended. Similarly, nearly a hundred years after Copernicus had published his great work, even such progressive thinkers as Bacon and Descartes were not yet convinced of it. In our time, to be sure, knowledge should diffuse much faster. But the destruction by the Copernican theory of the deeply rooted tenet of *geo*centrism, undermining though it was of the foundations of men's ancient faiths, required a far less thoroughgoing reorientation of men's outlook on the things nearest and dearest to their hearts than did the destruction by the Darwinian theory of the basis of their *anthropo*centrism. For, once the theory of evolution was accepted, only wishful thinking could avoid the logical conclusion, so aptly expressed by Shaw, that man has created God in his own image, rather than the reverse. An animal among millions of other species of animals, living and extinct, man was now confronted with the responsibility of justifying his own existence and of finding his own footing, or else of admitting his inadequacy. He found it far easier, however, to compartmentalize his mind and admit evolution on the one hand but, on the other hand, to proceed wishfully in other spheres of thought and living, as if the traditional types of human nature and society served as an unalterable framework within which the chief business was that of preparation for a happier 'after-life' on the part of the individual himself.

Yet the solidly established facts of evolution, though so commonly by-passed, did not give way but became ever more refined upon, better worked out, and more firmly grounded. Inevitably interactions between the new knowledge and the old dogmas did occur, in consequence of which the latter were subjected to increasing attrition, disintegration and transformation. But only those who have come to accept uncompromisingly the full meaning of evolution have won a vantage-point from which they can unequivocally face up to the world as it actually is, assess man's place in it, gauge the possibilities of the future, and plan realistically for their species. Those who undertake this task, when self-conscious about it, are likely to refer to themselves as Humanists.

At this point some objectors will rise up to ask: 'Is not your "Humanism" merely another term for "anthropocentrism" after all? If man is so insignificant a part of nature, why make him the centre of our ideals and efforts? Why not just drift and make merry while we can or, if we cannot fool ourselves to that extent, why not simply quit the game? By what authority *now* do we exalt man to this eminence?'

The answer is, by no authority this time but our own, and in obedience to no will other than our own. Our new, empirically gained knowledge of man's place in nature shows us humans to be greater, not lesser beings, relatively, than we had previously imagined. For we are now freed from our position of underlings to a supernatural dictator, and are seen nevertheless to stand, as a result of our very own efforts, at the front of the procession of living things on this earth. Moreover, we are seen to be far more significant, not less so, in the light of the open-ended nature of the march in which we find ourselves to be engaged. That is, in spite of and even because of our having gained this privileged place at the head of the list, there are grounds for the hope that the extent of our progress in the future will be as great, or possibly far greater, than what our long line of ancestors achieved on that fabulously extended trek which we now know them to have gone through in the course of earth's history. Moreover, if we only retain our faculties, there is no appreciable danger that any other terrestrial organism will defeat our purposes.

Here again some of our critics will interpolate, insisting that when we speak of progress, of ideals, and of standing at the head of the procession, we are defining these terms by purely anthropocentric criteria, since of course man, in consequence of the wishful thinking based on his egotism, regards himself as being at the head, and considers any steps in the direction of his own nature to be progressive. In answer to this, it is not rationalization to say that man is the latest and most dominant in the succession of dominant organisms. Man does clearly occupy the leading position by the objective criteria of adaptability. Included here are adjustment to and modification of the physical and biological environment in the organism's own interest, potentialities for indefinitely continued expansion, and the unique capability of consciously controlling evolution itself to some degree. If steps in these directions may be called progressive, then the line that led to man must be admitted to have been the most progressive of all. Moreover, these criteria themselves are far more broadly based than on a view centring *a priori* in man. They would be equally applicable, for example, on any planet harbouring life, for defining the directions to be taken by the forms that ultimately proved most successful.

'Ah, success is your criterion', our critic might then rejoin. 'So you believe that might makes right. Well, that is at least objective, but for my own part, I will have none of it.' Unfortunately this critic has here considered success and survival in too narrow and immediate a sense, and as opposed to values. As was already pointed out by Darwin in his *Descent of Man*, both the intellectual and the moral qualities of man by which we set such store were indispensable foundations for man's unparalleled success. Kropotkin in his *Mutual Aid in the Animal Kingdom*, Henry Drummond in his *Ascent of Man*, and others since their time have developed this thesis further. Thus man's values have arisen as an offshoot of his struggle for survival and the pursuit of them has been vital in his rise to objective ascendancy.

It is clear that the evolution of culture, that development almost peculiar to man which has raised him so immeasurably above other organisms in both his subjective and objective potentialities, has had its chief biological bases in man's superior intelligence and his exceptional propensities for co-operation: in other words, in his tendency to pursue, by rational means, the common good of his group. It should of course be disclaimed that a large proportion of man's thoughts and actions are thoroughly rational, or that his impulses are consistently social. But it has been through the leaven of those actions that were, in part at least, rational and social, that is, through behaviour of the sort that his considered judgment would define as *right*, that man and his culture have advanced so far. This is not to say, however, that the battle has yet been won all the way, or ever will be.

Thus, looking at these matters in a broader and more ultimate sense than that of our critic, and despite the myriad lesser triumphs of anti-social tendencies in nature, we are justified in turning his slogan around, and maintaining that, just as truly, it is right that has made might, in regard to things biological as well as social. This consideration has all-important bearings on our judgments and preparations concerned with man's future.

2. *The Laying of the Basis for Improving the Lot of Mankind*

With the development of science and technology, rationality and the potentialities of common action have advanced with ever greater acceleration and have been brought into play ever more effectively, so as to furnish the physical conditions for a richer life to human beings in general in considerable sections of the world. At the same time, the peoples everywhere have been brought into ever more intimate contact. As the geographical barriers between them have been broken down, the old boundaries of politics, economic systems, language, education, divergent mores and traditions, unequal conditions of living, and even racial distinctions are being increasingly worn away. Yet all this does not entail a flatter culture, for the specializations differentiating functional groups are increasing.

However, as most thinking people are aware, the present time of transition is a more critical one than ever before in history. For the world is not yet gravitating toward just one centre, politically or ideologically, but rather toward two at least. Each side is convinced that it has unique and indispensable values, the preservation of which would justify the greatest sacrifice short of such complete annihilation as would destroy those values themselves. However, a conflict once joined could all too readily grow beyond control, thereby unleashing the incomparable modern weapons that would bring utter catastrophe to both sides.

We must therefore hope and strive to attain a stage in which both sides recognize this situation and, led by this recognition and supported by an international organization, enter into mutual agreements that would strengthen their self-restraint. If they could in this way succeed in holding back from conflict for some decades, those seemingly important differences between them that are mainly semantic would tend to lose their edge, while those features of each side that are of real worth would tend to diffuse across, in somewhat altered guise, into the other side. The more vigorously the two sides can join in co-operative activities in the meantime, the sooner would this desirable consummation come to pass.

Even if a monolithic dictatorship, ruling from above through institutionalized dogma, deception and sycophancy, and through the fear engendered by an all-pervading secret police, should succeed without major war in grasping world power, it is difficult to believe that it would have a long-term stability of rule over a global population supplied with even today's technologies of communication, education and locomotion, permeated though all these functions would be by censorship and propaganda. For, as happened in Poland in the 1950s, the spectre of humanism (as it was sometimes called) would tend ultimately to break through and challenge the synthetic enthusiasms of the conformists. Although seeming to fail time and again, the forces of scepticism and of regeneration would work to wear away, from within, the sinews of the despotism. This process *might*, however, take as long as a rebuilding following catastrophic defeat, and the paroxysms entailed by it might be just as agonizing.

As yet, no reasonable person can feel sure that a holocaust bringing unprecedented calamity to both sides will be averted. If it should occur, the crippled survivors, crawling up pitifully from the ruins, will ultimately be confronted again with the same fundamental problem of organization as ours of today: how to achieve unification peacefully yet without enslavement. The monstrous potency of scientific agents of destruction, including not only nuclear explosives but also chemical, biological and radiological weapons, combined with the almost indestructible modern capabilities of delivering them, will continue to make such unification mandatory. At the same time, the effectiveness of scientific means of controlling thought and behaviour will make the avoidance of slavery in whatever form equally imperative. And the ferment will inevitably continue until sooner or later—we can only hope it will be sooner—all humanity has joined together in voluntary co-operation for the common good.

To engage in optimistic reflections concerning our future while ignoring our present unparalleled crisis would have been a species of wishful thinking amounting to criminal negligence. But even as gunpowder, spreading the means of ready death, spelled the end of feudal separatisms and in time helped to lay low the overlords, so our present incomparably deadlier tools are bound, after a period which *in retrospect* will appear short, to usher in the planet-wide community of man. The world community that endures will necessarily be based upon mutual agreement and trust. It will furnish all its members with the enhanced opportunities for enlightenment, self-development and rich experiences made possible by mankind's increased knowledge and improved techniques. It will accord them an ample range of choice in their work and in their leisure, the inspiriting realization that they are participants in activities valuable for the maintenance and progress of all humanity, and a share in the counsels whose judgments determine these matters.

This is no mere visionary fabrication. For a man of unusual mental flexibility and independence, plucked out of ancient Egypt or the Dark Ages of Europe and introduced into any one of several of our present-day Western societies, would be likely to consider that in it, despite the shocking absence of his True Religion, the above-described conditions had already been attained in a very high degree. As we of today know, however, there is still a world of room for further extending and enhancing them. Increasingly the economic forms must be fashioned so as to elicit men's best voluntary efforts, by utilizing their pride and aggressiveness, their workmanship, their desire for approval, and their spirit of service in the conscious accomplishment of such work as represents their most worthy contribution to the good of all. This means a 'mixed economy', one that continually experiments and remoulds itself in details and in the large as, on the one hand, material techniques and automation progress and allow the pursuit of ever greater objectives and as, on the other hand, increased understanding of human nature leads to the reconstruction of methods and conditions of work and to the improved education and motivation of those participating in it, for happier and more effective mutual adaptation. Similarly, the political forms will continue to be readapted to the changing types of association between men in their work and in their leisure, so as to allow them psychologically sounder as well as more effective and salutary means of taking part in community decisions. For this purpose, representation must be ever less grouped according to traditional geographical lines as the population becomes more mobile, and more along the functional lines that follow people's real associations, interests, and special knowledge, and that change as their ways of grouping change.

Of course work in today's sense of long routine toil for the provision of food, clothing, shelter and other necessities of living, not to speak of work for military purposes, will form a rapidly diminishing part of the efforts of men in the future. The place of such work will be increasingly taken by voluntary activities of two other types: on the one hand, those designed primarily to enrich the personal experiences and promote the fullness of development of the individual and his immediate associates and, on the other hand, those involving willingly given co-operation in the furtherance of the community's projects for advancement and expansion. It is evident that the most effective attainment of either of these two aims (which are of course overlapping) requires a balance between them that changes according to men's backgrounds, potentialities, and opportunities. But there is no ultimate antithesis, for beings whose nature is social, between the pursuit of individual and collective aims: instead, these two aspects of living are mutually reinforcing. Moreover, they can often be intimately combined, and it is this combination that can lead to the deepest sense of fulfilment.

The underlying principles sketched above do not help us much in fixing upon the specific forms of society, economic structure, or educational methods that will be used, for in these respects there is enormous latitude and indefinite room for readjustment and advancement. Ever longer-range, more deeply-based planning will help to direct these changes, as knowledge of men's minds and of how they interact with one another in society advances, and as more account is taken of the potential impacts of technological advances upon men's ways of life. Both in the formulation and the carrying out of the social changes to be desired, there will unavoidably, in all periods, be deep-seated differences of opinion, leading at times to bitter factionalism and dissension even though war has been outgrown. In such cases, where rigorous proof is lacking, the pluralistic procedure may often be employed, wherein trials of the different methods are carried out by their respective advocates, and the more general decisions are deferred until empirically obtained results can be compared.

This resort to objective evidence and to the test of experience would be but one manifestation of the more fundamental principle that man in the future world community will increasingly base his thoughts and actions on a view of nature, of himself, and of his works arising from the findings of science. Youths will be taught, with copious examples, the dire consequences of wishful, 'rationalized' thinking, of uncritical following of authority, and of allowing symbols to mask the realities that are supposed to be represented. They will be trained in the evaluation of evidence in varied fields, in the designing of tests, in the criticism of the methods and conclusions of their own and others, and, so far as it may be open to them, in creative thinking applied in diverse directions. At the same time they will be taught, both in its grand outlines and in the form of specific, vivid illustrations, what kind of a world they live in, how it operates, how it has come about and is still changing, man's nature and possibilities, and their own roles as active participants in the inspiring human enterprise. These teachings will be presented not as dogmas but with an appraisal of the grounds for them and for the evolutionary view of things in general. Moreover, the directions of the overall trends disclosed will be clearly brought out.

Science will thereby enter into the fabric of men's lives even more thoroughly than religion did in actuating the campaigns of the Moslems and the Crusaders. However, quite unlike the fanaticisms of old, the lodestars of science, when rigorously followed, lead men to ultimate agreement and to common effort instead of to mutual destruction. At the same time, men gain through the use of science ever more effective means for peacefully attaining their ends; they have ever richer experiences opened to them, and a longer-range, brighter vision of what is yet to come. All this, suffusing into their appreciation of nature and of the works of man, into their art, and into their daily acts of living, will immeasurably enhance the whole of their culture.

Only when the material benefits as well as the viewpoint, methods and spirit of science, science in the cause of humanity at large, have been spread equally throughout the world can the age-old bitternesses between peoples be replaced by wholehearted co-operation. Despite the resultant subsidence of those local peculiarities of culture, developed behind the shield of isolation, that so charm a sophisticated traveller today, the ever more catholic culture of the future, embodying contributions based on wider experiences, will afford, for any individual man or group, a far more diversified and felicitous ensemble. A much broader range of choice and opportunity for the sprouting of new shoots will thereby be provided than could be found in any of the more limited cultures of the separate nations of yesterday or today. At the same time, a better basis will have been laid for the individual's understanding and appreciation of these diversified developments, than would have been possible for persons brought up in the narrow confines that prevailed of old.

All these prospects of a more abundant, happier life for humanity can only be realized, however, if the scientific spirit develops throughout the world fast enough to lead men to exercise reasonable control over their procreation before overcrowding drains away their means of self-improvement. Here is another crisis, as menacing though not as spectacular as that of nuclear war, which must be resolved speedily if the potentialities of modern technology are to be applied to the enhancement of human life rather than to feeding the maximum number at the lowest standard of living. That this crisis *can* be resolved has been indicated by the example of Japan, but efforts in this direction in countries less developed economically will have to be pursued with as much vigour as those directed against disease before we can be reasonably sure that, barring war, our own age represents that of the great breakthrough from a stage of confusion to that of rational world-wide co-operation.

3. *Man's Future Conquests over Outer and Inner Nature*

When, sooner or later, man achieves this breakthrough to more rational and far-sighted vision, he will have removed himself from the danger that any other of the hundreds of thousands of species of organisms on this earth can ever challenge his supremacy. And he will find one horizon after another coming into view on his triumphant marches of conquest over the interminable reaches of external nature and the similarly inexhaustible immensities lying concealed within his very own being.

His conquest of external nature can include a mastery over energy, materials and mechanisms such as he has hardly dreamed of, especially if he succeeds in taming the energy of nuclear fusion and in storing up energy practicably in nuclear (its most concentrated) form. For abundant ready energy holds the key to all kinds of useful conversions of material on a mass scale. Among these are the wringing of pure from salt water and from hydrated minerals, the extraction of diverse elements from sea water and from other low-grade raw materials, and the support of endothermic reactions whereby nutritive substances, structural materials, fabrics and fuels are made. The still more massive uses of abundant energy, not merely in climate control but in wholesale engineering and earth-moving operations that will remould the planet for the benefit of man, must here receive inadequate mention.

Just as important as the making available of great supplies of energy is the devising of means for utilizing it more effectively and with a minimum of human guidance. Included here is the advance of automation to replace by far the greater part of the human labour that, even in the technically more advanced countries of today, is still expended in the production and distribution of the necessities of life. Included too are the development and use of automatic calculators and related apparatus for the rationalization and control of complex operations and systems of operation, and for the assembly, storage, collation, digestion, release and even application of the monstrously mounting masses of information of all sorts. Included is the radical remoulding of organisms of diverse types, plant, animal, microbial, in the service of man, and even, in time, the synthesis of some types *de novo*. As for the fabrication of inanimate materials, including the synthesis of food and of many other chemicals now manufactured by organisms or still unknown, it must be borne in mind that in these operations the availability of energy may be taken for granted and that the real difficulty arises in the working out of adroit techniques for effecting the desired transformations. Moreover, the complex molecules and polymers thereby gained can in their turn serve as the basis for higher supermolecular combinations of diverse kinds that will enormously enrich our future resources.

With such powers at their command, men's conquests over the now inhospitable reaches of the earth, such as jungle, desert, alpine and polar regions, must early become a part of the picture, and with it, the cultivation of the oceans. Already it is fashionable to say that we are at the beginning of the space age, and it is clear that, granted peace and a spread of rationality, man need no longer remain confined to his planet of origin. The subjugation for human use of some other planets and satellites of our solar system, even in a very limited way, would be a stupendous task, yet there are already grounds for inferring that it would not be beyond human accomplishment, and that the seed once planted could grow. As for the planets of other suns than ours, we face problems of a different order of magnitude, yet not qualitatively so different that we can deny eventual success to the efforts of generations of dedicated pioneers. Undoubtedly, one mode of human expansion that will present itself is that of migration outward. And, as once suggested by Bernal, even the reaches of empty space may present possibilities for colonization. We need not here speculate on whether the isolation of human colonies beyond our solar system would be so extreme as to lead to their drifting irrevocably away from us in cultural or biological respects. However, fundamentally the same human problems, and solutions of the same types, may be expected to be brought along by man to any remote outposts to which he may migrate.

Pari passu with men's progress in dealing with the world external to them will be their continued advance in understanding and control over their inner nature. We of today are only beginning to understand how to provide the types of social environment and the forms of activity most conducive to the development in the child of warmth of fellow-feeling, joy in co-operation and in accomplishment in general, curiosity and venturesomeness, the drive to solve problems, intellectual honesty along with the humility to criticize oneself and admit mistakes, moral courage and independence, persistence and self-discipline, keenness of appreciation and facility of expression in their varied forms. We have even less knowledge of how to modify suitably the methods used for these purposes, in adaptation to the great differences in the inherent nature of individual children. And despite much patter about Freud, we allow subconscious trends to grow up willy-nilly, so that they flower or, more usually, fester later in unexpected ways. Instead of using prophylaxis in this area we apply punishment or, at best, a patchwork palliative only after much damage has already been done. It is inconceivable that a higher civilization will not deal with these matters far more effectively, and thereby turn out adults better adjusted and equipped for the kind of world they have to live in.

As for intellectual education, we have already commented upon the central importance of conveying to the young an appreciation of the way science makes its findings and of the world view that has thereby been arrived at. A grasp of its role in the building of civilization is almost as essential. Along with this the child must be provided—up to the point of too greatly diminishing returns for that child—with the mental tools needed for grasping the concepts involved. Despite present dabbling with 'visual aids', the potentialities of recorded moving demonstrations of mathematical relations and of material processes, ranging from electron behaviour to evolutionary events, have hardly been touched. Neither have the means of elucidation and reinforcement been made use of that might be provided by playful manipulation and self-activity with materials and mechanisms illustrative of natural and artificial operations, and by games in which significant processes are dramatized.

It is not only through education that the road to the enhancement of individual capacities lies. Taking for granted the basic importance of conditions making for all-round good health and vigour and for increased longevity, we must in addition recognize the possibility of developing special physicochemical means of influencing the physiology and perhaps even the embryogeny of the individual in such wise as to promote the development and functioning of his intellect and of salutary features of his disposition and character. It is at present impossible to predict how far such methods, combined with advanced means of implanting early associations, could lift men above their present psychological level and open up for them a greater richness of life.

Whatever the lengths may be to which progress may go by all the above means, there is an additional mode of advance open, namely, that in the

genetic constitution of humanity. Unfortunately, however, the great
process of biological evolution, operating by means of the natural selection
of advantageous mutations, although so successful throughout the past
three billion years in having automatically raised life-forms from microbes
to men, can no longer be relied upon to carry us, by itself, still higher.
For with the advent of modern civilization we are so effectively saving the
lives and facilitating the reproduction of individuals afflicted with diverse
genetic impairments, arisen by mutation, that there is ground for inferring
the biological basis of man now to be actually deteriorating rather than
improving. These mutations are of the most diverse kinds, expressed in
physical, intellectual, moral or temperamental traits, as the case may be.
It is a serious question among geneticists whether this process, unless
checked by planned counter-measures, may not ultimately, carried on over
thousands of years, go so far as to result in the decay of civilization itself
(see Muller, 1960). However that may be, the ever higher complexities
and greater opportunities offered by our now rapidly advancing culture
would make an even higher level of the genetic basis of our native intelligence, our social proclivities, and our apperceptive capacities invaluable
for us, both personally and socially. Such betterment has as a prerequisite
the reorientation of human attitudes in regard to reproduction.

What is needed is an application of that same sense of social responsibility that we already employ in the education, training and nourishing
of the next generation to the provision for them, before procreation, of
the best genetic equipment that is available. This means a replacement of
our long-ingrained proprietary attitude that takes it for granted that the
children one brings up should carry one's own genetic material. A deeper
sense of fulfilment and at least as much affection, pride and feeling of
identification in regard to the children one brings up will be evoked when
one has chosen the germ-cells from which those children were derived
with as much solicitude and as careful consideration and wise counselling
as possible, from whatever available genetic sources one prefers or regards
as most ideal. As it becomes realized that techniques, involving germ-cell
banks and controlled implantation, are at hand for achieving this end, and
as pioneering efforts of this kind are seen to bring rewarding and enviable
results, the new mores of having children of choice rather than of 'fate'
will gradually become more prevalent.

The kind of choices that men make in this as in other realms of life—
what they consider best—depends of course on their sense of values, and
this will necessarily advance as the educational and social systems improve.
Here dictation would be abhorrent and self-defeating, but the average
individual would himself grant the desirability of a deeper intellect, a more

admirable character, finer perceptiveness, and more robust health. And in the pursuit of these objectives he would naturally avail himself of the aids provided by society. This change in reproductive practices will mark the genetic turning-point of civilized man from retrogression to renewed progression. And it will mark the turning-point of life in general from automatic to consciously guided biological evolution.

It should be understood that cultural evolution is capable of taking far more radical steps of innovation and of achieving an incomparably more rapid distribution of them, than can biological evolution, even when this is artificially guided. So, in any given period, the progress made will usually seem to have been based much more on cultural than on genetic advances. However, the two types of advance are reciprocally enhancing, once the culture is such as to allow conscious guidance in regard to matters of genetics. That is, the effect of a little rise in genetic respects is more marked if this happens at a cultural level that is already high, just as the effect of a little rise in culture is more marked when the genetic background is high. Thus the two processes are multiplicative rather than additive. Finally, it should be borne in mind that there is no sign of man having reached any limit in the possibilities of his biological evolution, especially if that be given the aid of ever more intelligent and far-seeing conscious guidance. Thus it seems a quite reasonable possibility that, once this corner leading to the path of rational control has been turned, our descendants may have before them a road of progress far outdistancing that which life on this earth has already travelled in its automatic course of trial and error.

Here our critic may return to put forward his old objection in a new guise, saying: 'If you believe in passing so far beyond that which we know as man, why do you claim to be "humanists"?' The answer is, the most unique distinction of man, and that which we value most, is his striving to attain a higher state for himself and his fellows through his rational efforts. This, the very substance of man, will not be relinquished but will be strengthened and exalted. Why lament if the adventitious wrappings should become replaced by worthier ones, so long as the inner essence is enhanced? And if the linguistic purist wishes to define as 'human' only that particular type of frame in which we find ourselves today, then the humanist will answer, 'Man will have better exploited his potentialities and will be truer to himself by transcending that frame and serving as the agent for the generation of a still nobler being than by deciding to stop short and stick forever where "Providence" happened to set that frame in the year 1960'. This illustrates the fact that modern Humanism must be evolutionary in its outlook. And in the enlightened world community that is to come there is little risk that people will be restrained from carrying ever farther any of the torches of progress, not even that of progress in genetic respects.

Thus we see the future for man as one of his own making, if only he will have it so. And it is deep in his nature to have it so if he can. The Prometheus who once stole common fire is now taming nuclear furies, probing the brain with electrodes, and taking apart and putting together the genes. Soon he will venture into the cosmos and his jobs of external creation will have begun in earnest. But his greatest job of creation will be that of a more sublime Prometheus. In exercising this self-appointed prerogative he will find his highest freedom.

BIBLIOGRAPHY

Bacon, Allan. *Man's Next Billion Years*. New York: Exposition Press, 1959.

Bernal, J. D. *The World, the Flesh and the Devil*. London: Kegan Paul, 1929.

Brewer, Herbert. 'Eutelegenesis', *Eugenics Review*, 27: 1935, pp. 121–6.

Brown, Harrison. *The Challenge of Man's Future*. New York: Viking, 1950; London: Secker & Warburg, 1954.

Bury, J. B. *The Idea of Progress* (revised edition). London and New York: Macmillan, 1932.

Hardin, Garrett. *Nature and Man's Fate*. New York: Rinehart, 1959.

Huxley, Julian S. *The Uniqueness of Man*. London: Chatto & Windus, 1941 (American title *Man Stands Alone*. New York: Harper, 1941).

Huxley, Julian S. *Evolution, the Modern Synthesis*. London: Allen & Unwin, 1942; New York: Harper, 1942.

Huxley, Julian S. *Religion without Revelation* (revised edition). London: Max Parrish; New York: Harper, 1957.

Huxley, Julian S. 'The Evolutionary Vision', *Evolution after Darwin*, Vol. 3, *Issues in Evolution*. Chicago University Press, 1961.

Huxley, T. H. and J. S. *Evolution and Ethics*. London: Pilot Press, 1947 (American title *Touchstone for Ethics*. New York: Harper, 1947).

Muller, H. J. *Out of the Night, A Biologist's View of the Future*. New York: Vanguard, 1935; London: Gollancz, 1936.

Muller, H. J. 'Life', *Science*, 121: 1955, pp. 1–9.

Muller, H. J. 'Human Values in Relation to Evolution', *Science*, 127: 1958, pp. 625–9.

Muller, H. J. '100 Years Without Darwinism are Enough', *School Science and Mathematics*, 1959, pp. 304–16.

Muller, H. J. 'The Prospects of Genetic Change', *American Scientist*, 47: 1959, pp. 551–61.

Muller, H. J. 'The Guidance of Human Evolution', *Evolution after Darwin*, Vol. 2. *Evolution of Man*. Chicago University Press, 1960.

Muller, H. J. 'The Integrational Role of the Evolutionary Approach throughout Education', *Educational Theory*, 10. 1960, pp. 274–279.

Rostand, Jean. *Can Man be Modified?* New York: Basic Books, 1959.

Simpson, G. Gaylord. *The Meaning of Evolution*. Yale University Press, 1949; Oxford University Press, 1950.

Symposium. *The Next Hundred Years*. New York: Seagram, 1957; London: Muller, 1959.

Symposium. *The Future of Man*. New York: Seagram, 1959.

Wilcox, Howard A. 'Our Future Civilization', *Science Digest* 47: 1960, pp. 30–5.

ALDOUS HUXLEY

HUMAN POTENTIALITIES

ALDOUS HUXLEY

Born 1894. Educated: Eton; Balliol College, Oxford.

Publications: *The Burning Wheel*, 1916; *Limbo*, 1920; *Chrome Yellow*, 1921; *Along the Road*, 1925; *Proper Studies*, 1927; *Point Counter Point*, 1928; *Brave New World*, 1932; *Beyond the Mexique Bay*, 1934; *Eyeless in Gaza*, 1936; *Ends and Means*, 1937; *After Many a Summer*, 1939; *Grey Eminence*, 1941; *The Perennial Philosophy*, 1945; *The Doors of Perception*, 1954; *Adonis and the Alphabet*, 1956; *Brave New World Revisited*, 1958, etc.

HUMAN POTENTIALITIES

Anatomically and physiologically, man has changed very little during the last twenty or thirty thousand years. The native or genetic capacities of today's bright city child are no better than the native capacities of a bright child born into a family of Upper Palaeolithic cave-dwellers. But whereas the contemporary bright baby may grow up to become almost anything—a Presbyterian engineer, for example, a piano-playing Marxist, a professor of biochemistry who is a mystical agnostic and likes to paint in water-colours—the palaeolithic baby could not possibly have grown into anything except a hunter or food-gatherer, using the crudest of stone tools and thinking about his narrow world of trees and swamps in terms of some hazy system of magic. Ancient and modern, the two babies are indistinguishable. Each of them contains all the potentialities of the particular breed of human being to which he or she happens to belong. But the adults into whom the babies will grow are profoundly dissimilar; and they are dissimilar because in one of them very few, and in the other a good many, of the baby's inborn potentialities have been actualized.

In the not too distant future it may be that the native abilities of large groups of human beings will be improved by deliberate selection. But until that time comes, we must be content with what we have. And what we have is so rich and so various that to make the best of it, to make actual the native potentialities of all the many breeds of men and women, will keep us busy for centuries to come.

The palaeolithic baby was as richly endowed with human potentialities as is the baby of today. How, in the course of history, were so many of those potentialities actualized? And what should be done now and in the immediate future to actualize the many and great potentialities which in most individuals still remain latent?

Let us begin by considering the conditions which make it possible for the inborn potentialities of developing human beings to be realized. Man's needs arrange themselves in a natural hierarchy. At the lower end of the scale are the basic physical needs—the need for food, the need for bodily safety. A stage higher we find the basic psychological needs—the need for love, received and given; the need for belongingness, for acceptance within a community; the need for respect and status. And finally, at the upper end of the scale, there are the least urgent but most specifically human of our needs—the need to satisfy curiosity and acquire knowledge; the need for meaning, order and comprehensibility in terms of a symbol-system; the need for self-expression through the manipulation of symbols; the need for self-transcending development (in other words, the felt urge to actualize more potentialities). The more specifically human needs at the higher end of the scale cannot be satisfied—indeed, they cannot even be felt—until the basic physical and psychological needs have received their proper satisfaction. Thus, love casts out fear—but only where circumstances are favourable. Hunger and stress, if sufficiently prolonged, cast out the very possibility of love. And along with the possibility of love they cast out the possibility of experiencing, and a fortiori of satisfying, any of the intellectual or emotional needs at the higher end of the scale. For certain individuals it may be possible to feel and satisfy certain of the more specifically human needs and to actualize some of their potentialities as symbol-manipulators, in a state of more or less complete lovelessness and isolation. But for most people and in most circumstances the actualization of their specifically human potentialities can be achieved only when the basic physical and psychological needs have been satisfied, only when they have enough food, enough safety, enough sense of belongingness, enough respect and enough love. Nature and nurture are always synergic. Unfavourable surroundings make it impossible for even the most highly gifted individuals to actualize their potentialities. Bad nurture will starve or smother, will mask or distort, the best of natures. Conversely a poorly endowed individual cannot be made by even the best environment to actualize potentialities which he does not possess. To achieve success, the eugenist must be a social reformer, the social reformer a eugenist.

We see, then, that it is only in a favourable environment that the inborn potentialities of the individual can be actualized. Today most of the members of the world's most civilized societies are brought up in the uneasy bosom of a small exclusive family group, within an overcrowded, highly organized, urban-industrial community, geared either to mass consumption or to national aggrandisement and the consolidation of the rule of a power élite, or to both simultaneously. This is most certainly not the perfect, or even a very good environment. But it is the best we have. And we can improve it—but only if we begin by diminishing the threat of war and solving the population problem. Meanwhile let us see what might be done, here and now, to help children to actualize more of their native potentialities.

Every adult human being is a multiple amphibian, the inhabitant, simultaneously or by turns, of several worlds. The most basic of these worlds is the electro-chemical world of our bodies in relation to their continuously changing environment. We can be conscious of the movement of our fingers as we play a Chopin mazurka. We can never be conscious of the innumerable and inconceivably complex electro-chemical events taking place in our eyes, our brains, our nerve-fibres and our muscles as we look at the symbols inscribed on the page before us and translate them into controlled and co-ordinated finger movements on the keys of the piano. It is only inferentially, through scientific research guided by an explanatory hypothesis, that we know how what we feel is related to what is happening on the electro-chemical level.

Above the electro-chemical world lies the world of first-order subjective experiences. We have internal experiences of visceral function or malfunction, of hunger, thirst and satiety, of fatigue or zest, of vivid rememberings and imaginings, of hunches, dreams, archetypal symbols, oceanic feelings, of muscular tensions and relaxations, of obviously caused or seemingly causeless joy and gloom, confidence and anxiety. And from the outside we have experiences of weight, heat, cold, colour, texture, form and all the rest.

Our brains, among other things, are instruments for automatically converting the bewildering profusion of first-order experiences into manageable symbols. These symbols are organized into systems, of which the most important is language. In the beginning, not of the universe, but most certainly of civilization, was the word. Language makes it possible for us to give meaning to first-order experiences, to classify and relate them, to explain to our own satisfaction what has happened and why, and to predict what is likely to happen in the future. Literature, science technology, philosophy, religion, ethical ideals, codes of law, social organizations—all the constituents of civilization are the products of activities directed by language on the higher levels of abstraction. But, alas, literature is more often tedious or vulgar than excellent. Religions, even the highest of them, consist at most times and in most places of one part of spirituality to nine of superstition, magic, priestcraft and bad science. The nature of our philosophy of life and of our legal and social institutions is such that we find ourselves under a compulsion to use our science and technology either foolishly, as in mass consumption and mass entertainment, or destructively, as in war and nationalistic rivalry. Over against the ethical ideals formulated by Gautama, Jesus and Lao-tze must be set the ethical ideals of a Jenghiz Khan, of the Puritans, of Hitler and Lenin. Language is like those Indian deities who are at once creators and destroyers. It makes us capable of acting with an almost god-like intelligence, but also with a kind of sub-simian stupidity. Through its formulation of rules, ideals and principles, it gives us the power to persevere in courses of angelic virtue, and also in courses of truly diabolic wickedness.

How can the human amphibians who inhabit these three worlds—of electro-chemical events, of first-order experiences, and of language on every level of abstraction—be helped to actualize more of their inborn potentialities? In its main lines, the answer is clear enough. The infant, who lives only in the two worlds of electro-chemical events and vague incipient first-order experiences, becomes progressively more human and progressively more himself as he is led farther and farther into the world of language. Precisely how human he will ultimately become and how fully himself depends in part upon the nature, propitious or otherwise, of his surroundings; in part on the structure and content of the local language and on the degree to which the prevailing philosophy of life encourages realistic thinking and appropriate feeling. Every child is educated in a particular language and (formulated in terms of that language's syntax and vocabulary) in a set of basic notions about the world, himself and other people. And along with the basic notions goes assorted information on a great variety of subjects. In civilized societies of the Western type, this verbal and notional education is systematic and intensive. All boys and girls are subjected to ten or twelve years of schooling, and some, the specialists, to as many as sixteen or eighteen years.

The results of all his compulsory, universal and gratuitous education hardly seems commensurate with the time, energy, money and devotion expended. Many suggestions for improving the present system have been offered, and in all countries new curricula, new methods of instruction are constantly being tried. I am not competent to evaluate these educational theories and practical experiments. All I shall do in the present context is to touch on the two gravest weaknesses, as it seems to me, in the current systems of formal education—the failure to give children an understanding of the nature and limitations of language, and the failure to take account of the all-important fact of human variability.

The analysis of language and the other symbol-systems has been one of the major intellectual achievements of the twentieth century. But in general education the results of this achievement have as yet hardly made themselves felt. There are, of course, compelling reasons for not telling children too much about the symbolic medium in which they live and move and have about 66 per cent of their being. Mass consumption depends on advertising, and religious, ideological and nationalistic zeal is kept simmering by the kind of propaganda that, to be effective, must be 'confined to a few bare necessities and then be expressed in a few stereotyped formulas'. (The words are those of the greatest propaganda virtuoso of modern times, Adolf Hitler.) Commercial, nationalistic, ideological—all propaganda depends, for its persuasive power, on the misuse of language (misuse, of course, from the rational Humanist's point of view). Any attempt to give all children an understanding of the nature of language would almost certainly meet with determined resistance on the part of enormous vested interests, commercial, religious, military and political. Meanwhile, let us have some educational experiments, sufficiently prolonged and on a scale large enough to permit us to assess the consequences of a thorough training, from childhood onwards, in semantics. To what extent would it help boys and girls to actualize potentialities which, if they had not received this kind of training, would have been buried under unexamined preconceptions and traditional notions or smothered by uncritically accepted propaganda?

And there is another question to be asked and answered. In very many persons, old and young, religious or political propaganda produces a zeal whose intensity depends, not on the rationality of what is said or the goodness of the cause that is being advocated, but solely on the propagandist's skill in misusing words in an exciting way. Zeal, especially aggressive zeal directed against some person or group, is a powerful psychosomatic pick-me-up. 'Damn braces, bless relaxes', as Blake wrote. How, then, shall the life of reason and kindliness be made as thrilling as the life of crusading unreason? This is a very serious problem to which we shall return.

From formal education's failure to give children an understanding of the nature of language let us now turn to its failure to take sufficient account of human variability. In no other species are the differences between individuals so great as in the human race. Turn the pages of Sheldon's monumental *Atlas of Men*. Those 1,175 photographs of naked Caucasians reveal creatures almost as unlike one another, at the extremes of viable variation, as hippos, antelopes and gorillas. And these structural dissimilarities are correlated, as we all know by everyday observation, and as Sheldon and his precursors have demonstrated by systematically studying large numbers of individuals, with temperamental dissimilarities no less striking. And this, of course, is not all. On top of the temperamental and anatomical differences (how correlated with them we do not yet know) are differences in biochemical make-up and differences in

general ability and special gifts—differences so great that they can almost
be regarded as differences, not in degree, but in kind. To herd all these
dissimilar creatures into one classroom and to subject them all to the same
kind of intellectual, emotional and ethical training seems, on the face of it,
absurd. At the present time, unfortunately, it is very difficult, for practical
reasons, to adopt any other course. But perhaps in the future, when the
problems created by rapid population-growth have been solved, and when
men of goodwill are free to think in terms, not of brute quantity, but of
quality, more realistic methods of differential education may be developed.
The beneficiaries of such methods will actualize their potentialities more
fully and effectively than the victims of the present system can hope to do.
The Sabbath was made for man; but, by conviction or economic necessity,
the dispensers of mass education think and act as though man were made
for the Sabbath. Departures from a statistical average of accomplishment
are adjusted to the system's Procrustean bed by stretching or chopping.
Those whose physique and temperament cause them to deviate from an
arbitrarily chosen norm of right-mindedness and good behaviour (or even
from the mere average) are bribed or dragooned into a semblance of conformity. (At the present time the exigencies of mass consumption, the
pressures of nationalistic rivalry and the pronouncements of such
prophets as Freud and John Dewey have combined to consecrate, as
humanity's ideal type, the extraverted good mixer, who combines back-
slapping geniality with aggressive drive. The almost perfect incarnation
of this ideal is Mr Krushchev.) The fate of those who, in a given society,
are condemned by their inherited anatomy, biochemistry and temperament to be heretics, is not an enviable one. For the sake of the community
(for no community can afford to waste its most precious asset, the gifts,
the fully actualized potentialities, of all its members), no less than of the
individual victims of an unrealistic ideal that happens at the moment to
be fashionable, the enormous spread of human diversity should be
recognized, respected and systematically made the most of.

We see then that, to be fully effective, training on the verbal level must
begin by taking into account the idiosyncrasies of individual physique
and temperament. In an age whose thinking is dominated by the notions
of environmental determinism in its Freudian, Marxian or Behaviourist
forms, this return to common sense and the immemorially obvious, this
advance into genetic realism, will be hard. We have grown accustomed
to books on the science of behaviour, in which no reference is made to the
behaver's hereditary make-up; we are all too familiar with psychoanalytic case-histories in which there is never the smallest indication of
what sort of creature, biologically speaking, the patient was. Did Mrs X

weigh two hundred pounds or ninety? Was Mr Y a daddy-longlegs or a jelly-fish, a bull or a marmoset? The disciples of the man who never mentioned any part of the human anatomy except the mouth, the anus and the urethra, leave these questions unanswered. But things are beginning to change, and in time, no doubt, the Freudians will discover somato-psychic medicine, Watsonism will come to be tempered by Sheldonism. Let us hope for the best.

In most societies (and this is especially true of Western societies) very little effort has been made to educate children and adults systematically on the non-verbal level of first-order psychophysical experience. Generally speaking, non-verbal training has been given only when advancing technology (the fruit of language-directed thought, experiment and organization) has made it necessary for some or all of the members of a society to use their mind-bodies in new ways. For example, the mass-production of automobiles has made it necessary for millions of men and women to learn the art of driving at high speed. In the process a number of hitherto latent potentialities were actualized in the trainees. Who, a bare sixty years ago, seeing Queen Victoria in her pony-drawn bath-chair could possibly have imagined that within a single life-time ladies of comparable age and dignity would be stepping on the gas along the Pennsylvania Turnpike or cornering at fifty miles an hour on the Corniche? Similar examples could be multiplied almost indefinitely. Thanks to the application of verbalized thinking to practical problems, new tools and processes are devised. To make use of these new tools and processes, new psychophysical skills must be learned, with the result that new first-order experiences present themselves to the learner's consciousness and unsuspected potentialities are actualized. This sort of thing has been happening, generation after generation, for the last several thousand years, and it is all to the good. But as a course of education on the non-verbal level, this sort of thing is too spotty and haphazard to be satisfactory. What is needed, if more of the potentialities of more people are to be actualized, is a training on the non-verbal levels of our whole being as systematic as the training now given to children and adults on the verbal level. 'Make the body capable of doing many things,' wrote Spinoza: 'this will help you to perfect the mind and so come to the intellectual love of God.' Spinoza's advice seems especially apposite at this time when so many of the old psychophysical skills have been rendered unnecessary by foolproof machinery. In the nature of things machinery that is foolproof is also inspiration-proof, spontaneity-proof and virtuosity-proof. With the advance of automation we can rely less and less upon the educative force of technology. This makes it all the more urgent to give what Spinoza calls 'the body', but what it would be more accurate to describe as the mind-body on its non-verbal levels, a systematic training specifically designed to actualize the greatest possible number of humanly valuable potentialities.

It is in this kind of training that we shall find the remedy for the excessive specialization, about which so many educators are now so deeply concerned. By most of these educators the problem is wrongly stated. Basically it is not a question of too much science and too little of the humanities, and the cure for specialization is not the Hundred Great Books or a course in Plato. Everybody, of course, should know something about the *Republic* and other great books. But a course in Plato can do nothing to educate the organism on its non-verbal levels. Like courses in physics and chemistry, it imparts a highly specialized training to the symbol-using mind, leaving the whole realm of first-order psycho-physical experience to take care of itself. The humanities are just another kind of specialization, and the cure for specialization is a course in the field of non-verbal learning.

Perceiving is at the root of all our thinking, feeling, willing and acting. It is therefore with perception that any systematic training on the non-verbal level must begin. 'Make the mind-body capable of doing many things.' Make it capable, first of all, of perceiving much, perceiving accurately, perceiving discriminatingly, perceiving with the fewest possible notional preconceptions. This perceptual awareness will 'help you to perfect the mind'—that is to say, the symbol-using, symbol-conditioned side of the thinking, feeling and willing organism. And this is not all; it will also help you 'to come to the intellectual love of God'—in other words, it will help you to go beyond discursive reasoning in terms of symbols and come to what the Buddhists call 'the wisdom of the other shore', to the unitive knowledge, obscure but self-evident, wordless and therefore profound, of the oneness in diversity, of

> . . . a World in a Grain of Sand,
> And a Heaven in a Wild Flower.

The value of systematic training in perception as a true yoga, a preparation for enlightenment here and now in the everyday world, was stressed many centuries ago by certain of the Tantric philosopher-psychologists of India. 'What is this life beyond form pervading forms?' the goddess enquires of her consort, Shiva. 'How may we enter into it fully, above space and time, beyond names and descriptions?' Shiva answers her in the most practical and scientific way, with a list of 112 exercises in awareness —awareness of first-order experiences, visual and auditory, tactile and visceral, imaginative and imageless. 'Radiant one, this consciousness may dawn between two breaths. After breath comes in and just before it goes out—*the beneficence.*' 'See as if for the first time a beauteous person or some ordinary object.' 'Intone a sound audibly, then less and less audibly, as feeling deepens into *this silent harmony.*' 'When eating or drinking, become the taste of the food or drink and *be filled.*' 'While being caressed, sweet princess, enter the caressing *as everlasting life.*' 'Wherever your attention alights, at that very point *experience.*'

This kind of Tantric training in pure receptivity, in being aware simply of the events going on within the mind-body or outside it, was used therapeutically in the early years of the present century by the Swiss psychiatrist, Dr Vittoz. Vittoz treated neurosis, not by dredging up the memory of traumatic experiences from the unconscious, but by training the patient to live here and now in the world of first-order experiences instead of in the world of emotionally charged symbols relevant only to events that took place long ago. The same Tantric approach to mental health is advocated in the *Gestalt Therapy* of Perls, Hefferline and Goodman, who prescribe a course of exercises in the awareness of first-order experiences almost as comprehensive as Shiva's. Like Vittoz, these authors have found that mental health can be greatly improved by teaching people to break out of their prison of symbols and memories— to escape by becoming aware, in a state of pure receptivity, of their first-order experiences. Combined with a sound education in the nature and proper use of language, such a training in awareness on the non-verbal level would undoubtedly help the developing child to actualize potentialities of intelligence, of sensibility and of enjoyment which, in all too many cases, our current systems of education fail, more or less completely, to bring to the surface.

And here let me stress the importance of that enhanced enjoyment which becomes available to persons whose perceptual awareness has been trained to the highest pitch of acuity and discrimination. 'If the doors of perception were cleansed', Blake writes in *The Marriage of Heaven and Hell*, 'everything would appear to man as it is, infinite'. The dirt which has to be wiped from the doors of perception is symbolic grime—a muddy residue of notions about what things 'really' (and in this context 'really' in fact means 'merely') are. But when we understand that words stand only for the similarities between first-order experience, each one of which is unique, when we learn to pass at will from the stale 'oldness of the letter' (the world of symbols) to the fresh 'newness of the spirit' (the world of first-order experiences), then and only then will our potentialities for enjoyment be actualized. Meister Eckhart has described the difference between the outer world as it is seen through the refracting glasses of symbols and notions (religious symbols, in this case, and theological notions) and the outside world perceived in first-order experiences, simultaneously sensuous and mystical. 'My inner man (the reflective, symbol-using mind of the theologian) relishes things not as creatures but as the gift of God. But to my innermost man (the enjoyer of mystico-sensuous first-order experiences) they savour not of God's gift, but of ever and aye.' And how eloquently Traherne speaks of the ever-and-aye landscapes of his first-order experiences as a child, and later, having 'unlearned the dirty devices of the world', as a mystic with cleansed perceptions. 'Your enjoyment of the world is never right till every morning you awake in Heaven.' ('Nature', in the jargon of the old theology, is the world conceptualized, the world as seen through the distorting medium of words and notions. 'The supernatural'—'Heaven', in Traherne's phrase—is the world, within and without, as it is apprehended in a first-order, mystico-sensuous experience.) Traherne was 'covetous and earnest to persuade others to enjoy the world' as he himself did, and he 'perfectly hated the abominable corruption of men in despising it'. They despise it so heartily and find it (their doors of perception being darkened by thick layers of conventional notions about what's what) so extremely boring, that they have to become television addicts, gamblers, revivalists, alcoholics, political agitators—anything so long as it will relieve the *taedium vitae* and 'give them a kick'. It is useless to preach the life of reason to people who find that life is flat, stale and unprofitable. But if the life of reason could be combined with the life of cleansed perceptions and a capacity for mystico-sensuous enjoyment, rationality could make a wider, stronger appeal, and the idiocies and delinquencies to which, in our boredom, we now resort would seem less alluring.

Let us now consider very briefly some of the other ways in which the non-verbal side of the organism might be trained with a view to actualizing more of the individual's desirable potentialities. It is an observable fact that good psychophysical functioning is dependent to some extent upon the maintenance, at rest and in action, of a certain specific relationship between neck and trunk. As they grow up, most children born into civilized societies develop bad postural habits, and these bad habits result in impaired functioning of the mind-body. Because the bad habits come in time to feel right and natural, it is difficult to become aware of their badness and still more difficult to replace them by good habits. A method of doing precisely this—a method of 'creative conscious control'—was developed by the late F. M. Alexander. In the opinion of John Dewey, who wrote introductions to several of Alexander's books and who had personally studied with their author, this method is to education what education is to life in general. For Dewey, ordinary education was merely training on the verbal level, combined with inadequate or downright bad training on the non-verbal level. By giving children a training in correct posture and the 'proper use of the self', Alexander's method would improve all-round functioning and permit the individual to exercise a measure of voluntary control over his unconscious processes. Dewey's advocacy of this kind of training has had no effect. On the non-verbal level most people's 'use of the self' is as bad as ever it was. In this respect schoolteachers and university professors are just as badly educated as their pupils. Indeed, being older and so having had more time to contract bad habits, many teachers have miseducated themselves to an extent that no mere child or adolescent can match. *Quis custodiet custodes?* For the would-be reformer, that is always the question.

'Be good, or else. . . .' This is the leitmotiv of traditional morality. Commandments are thundered down from Sinai, Categorical Imperatives are formulated in Königsberg, laws are promulgated and correct behaviour is everywhere prescribed. As children, as adolescents, as adults, we are constantly enjoined, exhorted and implored to do what gods and governments and the experts in etiquette command. If we obey, we shall be rewarded, or at least we shall escape punishment. If we fail to obey, we shall catch it, here and hereafter. Be good, in a word, or else. . . .

But, oddly enough, nobody ever tells us *how* to be good. None of the child's pastors and masters ever offers to teach him a practical way of implementing his New Year's resolutions, of actualizing his potential virtues. 'For the good that I would I do not; but the evil which I would not, that I do.' St Paul's problem is everybody's problem. How is it to be solved? Experience shows that bribes and threats, that punishments and rewards, that good intentions and efforts of will are, all of them, only moderately effective. Prisons are full of recidivists and 'the strongest oaths are straw to the fire i' the blood'. Even systematic conditioning has failed, up till now, to produce the results expected of it. The Jesuits boasted that by their educational methods they could condition any child into life-long obedience to the Church. But Voltaire was one of their star pupils, and the moral level of those who have received a religious education is not conspicuously higher than those whose education has been in secular schools. Modern dictators have borrowed freely from the Jesuits, have improved their methods and have engendered in their subjects a greater degree of orthodoxy than was achieved even in the palmiest days of the Counter-Reformation. But imposed orthodoxy offers no solution to our ethical problem. How can I get myself to do what I really want to do, and how refrain from doing what I really don't want to do? The only kind of universal conditioning that might be an unqualified blessing to all concerned is that which Arapesh mothers give their infants. While suckling and fondling the child, the mother brings it into physical contact with other members of the family, with visiting friends and with the domestic animals of the household and, as she does so, repeats the word 'Good, good, good. . . .' The blissful experience of being held, caressed, and nursed comes to be associated in the child's mind with affectionate contacts between itself and other human or sub-human creatures. This association is then associated with the sound of the word 'good'—a sound to which, in due course, the child will learn to attach a meaning, so that a first-order experience will come to be interpreted in terms of a positive value-judgment.

That we shall perish unless we learn to love more warmly and widely than we do at present is only too obvious. All the higher religions have stressed the supreme value of love. Christianity enjoins us to love our human neighbours and to regard as neighbours even our enemies. More realistically, Hinduism and Buddhism extend the field of love into the non-human world. We must love, the Indian prophets tell us, not only our fellow-men, but also our fellow-animals. The twentieth-century ecologist would add that we ought to love the whole planet and treat it as though it were a vulnerable living organism, refraining scrupulously from all those outrages against nature which have turned so much of the once fertile earth into treeless and eroded deserts, have befouled so much of what was once beautiful with excrement, industrial wastes and slums. Love is as necessary for human survival and growth as are bread on the physical and knowledge on the symbolic level. Buddhism, Christianity and modern science are in full agreement on this point. But how curious and how ironical that the only people to devise a method for conditioning children to love more warmly and widely should be a tiny group of savages in the wilds of New Guinea.

A general conditioning of young children to feel more affectionately towards more of their fellow-beings would doubtless improve the moral and emotional atmosphere of the societies in which it was practised. But it would still leave many of the problems of ethical method unsolved. Be good—but how? For a fairly large percentage of the population a fairly satisfactory answer to this question is provided by auto-suggestion. Professor Hornell Hart has described a number of auto-suggestive techniques for implementing good intentions and preventing oneself from doing what one doesn't want to do, in a very sensible and practical book.

And methods which are almost identical, except that the language in which the auto-suggestions are given has a vaguely theological cast, are used by members of the numerous sects and churches which have crystallized out of 'New Thought'. Individuals vary greatly in the degree of their suggestibility. But for the 60 or 70 per cent of people who, some with the greatest of ease, some with a good deal of difficulty, can make statements or give commands on the verbal level and have these statements attended to and these commands carried out on the non-verbal levels of the autonomic nervous system and the subliminal mind, the methods of auto-suggestion, in or out of hypnotic trance, are of great value, both ethically and therapeutically. These methods make possible the actualization of desirable potentialities which, if they were not used, would remain latent.

On its deepest, most unspeakable and ineffable level, the non-verbal side of our nature is a sequence of countless electro-chemical events. Illness is a disturbance of the order of these events, an upsetting of their balanced relationships. When the balance is restored, we become capable once more of actualizing the potentialities which, during our illness, had been forced, so to speak, below the surface, leaving us for the time being less fully human than we were in health. Most diseases, fortunately, are self-terminating; but it is possible in many cases to accelerate the restoration of our upset electro-chemical balance by means of drugs. If pharmacological methods work in illness, might they not also work in health? Might it not be possible, by means of suitable pills and shots, to establish a new and more favourable electro-chemical balance in the healthy organism and in this way cause hitherto latent potentialities to be actualized?

Human beings have been trying to do precisely this ever since Noah first planted a vineyard, made wine and got gloriously drunk. Unfortunately most of the classical stimulants, sedatives, and hallucinogens do their mind-changing work at a ruinous cost to the organism's electro-chemical basis. Recently, however, there has been a change. Pharmacologists still produce plenty of ambivalent miracle drugs, whose unpleasant side-effects are almost as remarkable as their healing powers. They still contribute to the ever-lengthening list of those 'iatrogenic diseases', which are caused by medical treatment. But they are now learning to synthesize drugs which powerfully affect the mind on the levels of first-order experience and of symbol-manipulation, without doing any harm, or more than a very little harm, to the electro-chemical substratum through which they work upon the mind. In certain cases of depression, for example, a few doses of one of the psychic energizers can totally abolish a deeply rooted conviction of sin, and can do so without changing the blood picture and without upsetting the heart, liver or kidneys. Within a few years it will probably be possible to lift the electro-chemical balance within many healthy individuals to a new position of equilibrium, at which organic functioning will be better, first-order experiences more enlightening, and symbol-manipulating easier and more effective. And all this at little or no physiological cost. It will also, of course, be possible, probably at an equally low cost to the body, to maintain a chronic ataraxia, to induce contentment with their lot even in slaves, to make people feel happy though sub-human, happy in spite of the fact that the conditions under which they live are stultifying and degrading.

That discoveries in the field of pharmacology might be used by future dictators for nefarious purposes is only too obvious. Knowledge is power and power is ethically neutral—at the service of anyone, malevolent or well-intentioned, stupid or intelligent, who can get his hands on it. How the fruits of science are to be used is decided not by scientists but by citizens—and at any given moment the leading citizen may be called Hitler or Stalin.

The likelihood of our leading citizens being called Hitler or Stalin will be greatest, it is obvious, in a world where nationalism is an axiom, where war is systematically prepared for, and where the biological reasons for dictatorship and organized violence are irresistibly compelling. At the present time we are running two races at once—the armament race and the population race. The armament race consumes about half of the energy and resources of the most highly civilized societies. What remains is enough, for the moment, to support those societies in comfort. It is not enough, however, to permit them to make headway in the race against world-wide population-increase. We have to choose, not between guns and butter for the rich, but between guns and bread for the have-nots, guns and the possibility of a more human life for the nearly 2,000 millions of us now condemned to a sub-human existence. Nationalism and the preparation for war prevent us from doing what must be done if a bad biological situation is to be prevented from becoming worse; and a worsening biological situation exacerbates nationalism and makes war more probable.

Our first and most urgent task is to break out of this vicious circle. This can be done, it seems to me, only if we deliberately shift our attention from the insoluble problems of national power to the difficult but soluble problems of demography and individual development. The glamour of the old nationalistic idolatry may prove to be irresistible: in that case we are in for trouble—worse trouble for more people than at any previous period. But if we can start thinking of the world in terms, not of national power, but of basic human needs and the human potentialities which may be actualized when (and only when) those needs are satisfied, we may look forward to the future with a certain sober optimism. We have enough knowledge even now to be able to save ourselves from being overrun by our own numbers, and to actualize those desirable potentialities which, up till now and in the overwhelming majority of men and women, have never emerged from a state of latency. The knowledge, I repeat, is there; but knowledge, by itself, cannot originate action; its function is to direct the action that is initiated and maintained by feeling and will. Feeling and will are moved, in their turn, by a philosophy of life and also, to some extent, by the detailed knowledge of what might be expected to happen if a certain course of action were adopted. Knowing the good things we might do, and knowing also the disastrous things that are happening and will happen if we continue to act as we are acting now, we may perhaps be moved to will the consummation which our philosophy assures us to be desirable—the realization of our full humanity.

Notes

Our first-order experiences are not, of course, experiences of things in themselves; they are experiences on the lowest level of abstraction to which access is possible to us. There are occasions, I believe, when we find ourselves below the verbal level in the world as abstracted from total reality by our nervous systems. More often a first-order experience is an experience on the lowest level of verbal abstraction, where it is not so fully conceptualized as to seem stale, familiar, all too human.

In regard to the actualization of artistic potentialities see *Education Through Art*, by Sir Herbert Read; *The Creative Process*, edited by Brewster Ghiselin; *Neurotic Distortion of the Creative Process*, by Lawrence S. Kubie, M D; and *Zen and the Art of Archery*, by Eugen Herrifel.

On the bad habit of using *normal* to mean *average* and its unfortunate results, see Joseph Wood Krutch, *Human Nature and the Human Condition*.

BIBLIOGRAPHY

Alexander, F. M. *The Universal Constant in Living*. New York: Dutton, 1941.
Bois, Samuel. *Explorations in Awareness*. New York: Harper & Brothers, 1957.
Hart, Hornell. *Autoconditioning*. New York: Prentice-Hall, 1956.
Kline, Nathan S. 'Clinical Experiments with Iproniazid', *Quarterly Review of Psychiatry and Neurology*. New York, June 1958.
Korzybski, A. *Science and Sanity*. New York: Inst. of Gen. Semantics, 1941.

Maslow, A. H. *Motivation and Personality*. New York: Harper & Brothers, 1954.

Pareto, Vilfredo. *The Mind and Society*. New York: Harcourt, Brace & Co., 1935.

Perls, Hefferline and Goodman. *Gestalt Therapy*. New York: Julian Press, 1951.

Read, Herbert. *Education through Art*. New York: Pantheon, 1945.

Reps. Paul. *Zen Flesh, Zen Bones*. Vermont: Tuttle, 1957.

Sheldon, W. H. *Varieties of Human Physique*. New York: Harper & Brothers, 1940.

Sheldon, W. H. *Varieties of Human Temperament*. New York: Harper & Brothers, 1942.

Sherman, Hoyt. *Drawing through Seeing*. New York: Hinds, 1947.

Suzuki, D. T., Erich Fromm and Richard De Martino. *Zen Buddhism and Psychoanalysis*. New York: Harper & Brothers, 1960.

Vittoz, Roger. *Traitement des Psycho-Névroses par la ré-éducation du contrôle cérébral*, Paris: J. Baillère, 1954.

Williams, Roger. *Free and Unequal*. Austin: University of Texas Press, 1953.

Williams, Roger. *Biochemical Individuality*. New York: Wiley, 1956.

Williams, Roger. *Alcoholism, the Nutritional Approach*. Austin: University of Texas Press, 1959.

THE END

DATE DUE

JAN 1 0 '64			
APR 1 5 '65			
GAYLORD			PRINTED IN U.S.A.